W9-BOM-999

UNDERSTANDING WOOD FINISHING

How to Select and Apply the Right Finish

BOB FLEXNER

Rodale Press
Emmaus, Pennsylvania

Our Mission
We publish books that empower people's lives.

RODALE PRESS

Published 1994 by Rodale Press, Inc.

Printed in the United States of America on acid-free ∞, recycled ♻ paper

Editor: Rick Mastelli
Designer: Deborah Fillion
Interior Photographer: Rick Mastelli
Illustrator: Lee Hov
Produced by Image & Word, Montpelier, Vermont

Rodale Press Staff:
Executive Editor: Margaret Lydic Balitas
Managing Editor: Jeff Day
Editor: David Schiff
Copy Editor: Barbara Webb
Copy Manager: Dolores Plikaitis
Cover Designer: Pete Chiarelli
Front Cover Photographer: Mitch Mandel
Art Director: Anita Patterson
Administrative Assistant: Susan Nickol
Office Manager: Karen Earl-Braymer

If you have any questions or comments concerning this book, please write to:
Rodale Press
Book Readers' Service
33 East Minor Street
Emmaus, PA 18098

Library of Congress Cataloging-in-Publication Data

Flexner, Bob.
Understanding wood finishing : how to select and apply the right finish / Bob Flexner ; [photographer, Rick Mastelli ; illustrator, Lee Hov].
p. cm.
Includes index.
ISBN 0-87596-566-0 hardcover
ISBN 0-87596-734-5 paperback
1. Wood finishing. I. Title.
TT325.F53 1994
684'.084—dc20 93-3433
CIP

Distributed in the book trade by St. Martin's Press

8 10 9 7 hardcover
2 4 6 8 10 9 7 5 3 1 paperback

To my loving wife, Birthe,
and our sons, Erik and Søren,
without whose patience and support
I could not have written this book.

Acknowledgments

A book of this sort can't be written by just one person. It takes the collaboration of many. My name appears alone on the cover, but many people deserve credit.

Most important I want to thank Rick Mastelli and Deborah Fillion who have supported me for many years and have done the editing, photography, design, and layout. If you find this book accessible and attractive, it is because of their work.

I also want to thank Jeff Day at Rodale Press, who believed in this book and campaigned for it. Jeff, along with David Schiff, also at Rodale, helped in the shaping and editing of the book.

Bob Stevenson read the entire manuscript and made many valuable suggestions. David Jackson read parts of the manuscript for chemical accuracy. The book is better for their efforts, though I assume responsibility for any mistakes it may still contain.

David Sloan at *American Woodworker,* Ian Bowen and Tom Clark at *Woodshop News,* Jeff Greef, Terrie Noll, and Graham Blackburn at *Woodwork,* and Bob Hoffman and Larry Okrend at *Workbench* have allowed me to explore in their magazines many of the topics included in this book.

Jim Biggs helped me see how to learn about finishes so that I could explain them to others.

I am fortunate to have many friends, both woodworkers and finishers, who have willingly shared their knowledge and experience with me and given me continued support. There's not space enough to name them all, but the following have contributed too much to be left out: Bobby Barnett, Randy Cain, Joe Goike, Matthew Hill, Bob Houston, Bill Hull, Alan Lacer, Art Mendel, Keith Morris, Ron Quinton, Bryan Slocomb, and Bob Welsh.

Contents

Introduction

Finishing is both easier and more difficult than you may think. It's easy because its requirements are not extensive. The tools are nothing more than brushes, rags, and spray guns. Only three basic substances make up most finishing materials—binder, pigment, and solvent. And, in contrast to woodworking, almost no hand/eye coordination is required.

Finishing is difficult because there are so many variables, so many things that can go wrong. And there is so little good information available about what to do when something does go wrong. One of the purposes of this book is to provide this information.

OVERCOMING THE FEAR OF FINISHING

Many woodworkers are afraid to attempt a finish any more complicated than brushing on a few coats of polyurethane or wiping on and wiping off some oil. They don't understand finishes, and they're afraid of ruining their woodworking. To remedy the situation, they look for techniques (tricks). What they really need is an understanding of the materials.

To feel comfortable with finishing, you need to understand the materials available to choose from, how these materials work, and what degree of protection and decorative effects they produce. Without this knowledge, you're forced to go through all the agony and frustration of reinventing the craft—discovering everything anew, as if no one had finished wood before you. You'll eventually achieve some competence, but you'll pay a steep price in failures and rework. With knowledge, finishing becomes fun. You can make intelligent choices to achieve the degree of protection you want. You can add another dimension of artistic expression to your work. You can avoid potential problems. And you can correct mistakes when they do occur.

In this sense, finishing is not much different than woodworking. Woodworking is a struggle until you learn the capabilities of your tools and the various ways to shape and join wood. Woodworking then becomes enjoyable because you can make choices—you have some control over the medium.

Because finishes are more difficult to understand than they are to apply, this book is devoted more to explaining how stains, sealers, finishes, and furniture polishes work than it is to putting these materials on the wood. This may be a bit confusing at first, especially if you are accustomed to finishing books that emphasize techniques. But you'll quickly see the greater value in learning about materials. And then the techniques will make sense, too.

FINISHES ARE SCIENCE

Information about finishing is riddled with myth, half-truth, and hyperbole. This situation creates countless problems because it diverts you from the information you need to understand finishing. Some of the myths imply that the old finishes, and the old ways of applying finishes, are somehow better than what we have and what we do today. Other myths suggest that finishes are a sort of alchemy, consisting of secret formulations that are held in confidence by those who, somehow, already know them. To make matters worse, many writers and editors don't have enough experience doing finishing or enough knowledge of the chemistry of finishes to distinguish between correct and incorrect information. So they convince themselves that everyone's opinion is equal and repeat or publish whatever comes along.

Old Finishes Are Not Better

The idea that the old finishes and the old ways of finishing are better than what we have and what we do today is a common misconception. Eighteenth- and nineteenth-century craftsmen had a very limited choice of finishes and methods for applying finishes. Claims you so often read and hear, that linseed oil is a wonderful finish, that natural stains made from colored earth, berries or exotic chemicals are better than our aniline dyes or synthetic pigments, or that French polish is more beautiful than any of our current finishes, are nonsense. Suggestions that turpentine is a better solvent than mineral spirits or that beeswax is better than other waxes because these were our ancestors' choices don't take into account either a scientific understanding of these materials or historic context.

Our ancestors used linseed oil, berries, turpentine, and beeswax because those were what they had. Aniline dyes were not developed and manufactured until late in the nineteenth century. Synthetic pigments were even more recently developed. Nitrocellulose lacquer, and alkyd, phenolic, and polyurethane resins, all of which are far more durable than linseed oil, were not developed until the twentieth century. Solvents distilled from petroleum didn't become available until the twentieth century. Neither did alternative waxes. The technique of French polishing was used to apply a high-gloss finish in the nineteenth century because that was the best way finishers at that time could produce a high gloss. Superior rubbing compounds and power buffers did not exist.

Not only were the finishing materials limited, so were the available application methods. One tool our ancestors did not have was the spray gun. The introduction of that tool in the late nineteenth century revolutionized the application of finishes.

The mistaken idea that old ways of finishing were better than our modern ways may be the result of our tendency to associate finishing with woodworking. Eighteenth- and nineteenth-century woodworkers were very highly skilled, the result of long apprenticeships available to few modern-day woodworkers. But eighteenth- and nineteenth-century finishing was primitive by our standards. The last thing we should do is hold up the finishing skills of our woodworking ancestors as our standard. Finishing is a craft that has improved vastly during the twentieth century.

There Are No Secrets

Even more crippling to the development of the craft of finishing is the persistent view that finish composition is shrouded in secrecy. At one time this may have been true. Individual craftsmen made up their own finishes from primitive raw materials, just as they made their own tools. But finish formulation has become a sophisticated science in the twentieth century. In fact, modern chemistry began with the development of dyes and coatings in the late nineteenth and early twentieth century.

Despite the changes, so-called secret formulas continue to circulate, seasoned with the notion that they have been passed down through many generations. In addition, most manufacturers do not list ingredients on their containers, and some even claim to have developed their products in someone's basement. This is to make us, the consumers, think that they know something the other manufacturers don't, that finishing is not a science conducted in the laboratories of companies like Dow, DuPont, and Union Carbide, but still an alchemy based on secret brews concocted by an inner circle of sorcerers.

There are no essential secrets in finishes—especially in the formulation of those finishes that are sold to the general public. Finishes are science. Contrary to the impression you may receive from the large number of product brands on paint-store shelves, and the advertising hype that often accompanies these products, the essential chemistry of almost all finishing products has been thoroughly understood for decades. There is very little that is new in finishes sold to small shops and the general public. And what is new has almost always been developed by the large chemical companies that produce the raw materials. These companies make their new information available to anyone who wants it, especially to the finish manufacturers who want to buy raw materials from them. So all of the manufacturers of stains and finishes (as well as you and I) have access to the same information. In addition, every large finish manufacturer has access to equipment that will analyze the content of their competitors' products. So everyone can find out what everyone else is selling. One of the pioneers of modern finishes, William Krumbhaar, once said, "The real reason for secrecy is the necessity of concealing the fact that there is nothing to conceal."

Misinformation Persists

Possibly most damaging to the development of the finishing craft is the incorrect information repeated over and over in books, articles, and pamphlets on finishing. Most of the people responsible for this information are not finishers, but professional writers who make their living writing rather than finishing. Even if they have done some finishing, they don't understand finish chemistry. They don't know the questions to ask or the problems to expect. Nor do they recognize when they are repeating nonsense that some other writer has written or when they are being misled by a manufacturer intent on increasing sales. These writers usually submit their work to publishers of woodworking magazines and books. The editors of these publications often know a lot about woodworking but seldom enough about finishing to critically evaluate the material they receive. Few, if any, understand that finish performance is a well-established science. There are right and wrong answers: A given finish will react in a predictable way for known reasons. There isn't a lot of room for opinion.

As a result, you continue to see the same incorrect information repeated. You may see it repeated so often that you begin to question your own experience. For example, how many times have you read or heard that rubbing an oil finish makes it penetrate deeper? Or that applying a second coat of stain will make the wood darker? Or that you can avoid bubbles in varnish simply by not stirring it? Or that wood contains oil that should be replaced with a good furniture polish?

These (and many other) commonly repeated claims are either misleading or ridiculous. In an attempt to end these myths, I highlight them throughout the book.

I am convinced that the understanding of finishing would be far less a chore (and this book much smaller) if there weren't so much misinformation to debunk. You may well find that it will take more effort to unlearn what is wrong than to learn what is right.

MY BACKGROUND

So, you're probably asking yourself, how does Flexner know what he's talking about?

I learned finishing the old-fashioned way—by experience. I worked for some time in a cabinet shop in Denmark, where the finishing methods were standard for the industry. When I returned to the United States I started my own shop and continued learning while doing finishing. I developed some competence, but, like most finishers, I never felt entirely comfortable with my understanding of what was happening. About six years ago I had an eye-opening conversation with a friend. I had called Jim about another matter, but on an impulse, I asked him if he could explain why alcohol would separate a furniture joint that had been glued together with animal hide glue. Jim has an extensive background in chemistry, but he had never heard of hide glue. "What's hide glue?" he asked. "It's glue that's made from animal skins," I explained. "Oh, protein!" he exclaimed. And he proceeded to tell me all about hide glue—all the information I had been unable to find in any of the woodworking books I'd searched through—how it worked, how and why it deteriorated, why it stuck without clamps, why alcohol would crystallize it and steam would dissolve it, et cetera. I was absolutely dumbfounded. For years I had been looking in vain for accurate information on the hide glue I used for restoring antique furniture. And Jim had known it all along, because he understood the chemistry of protein.

That conversation ended with Jim offering to take me over to the local university engineering library to see what we could dig up. We spent about two hours there, and I walked out with an armload of books dealing with hide glue.

Nearby the books on glues were several shelves of books on finishes, including books on the chemistry and technology of stains, dyes, solvents, oil, and wax. Several weeks later I went back and checked out a few of these books. I don't have a background in chemistry or engineering, so I found them difficult to understand at first. To further my education, I became a member of the Federation of Societies for Coatings Technology (FSCT), which is the national association of paint and finish chemists, and attended some seminars and conventions. I spent countless hours talking to the chemists who actually develop the products we use in finishing. I found these chemists to be much like the majority of woodworkers I've met: They love to share what they know with anyone who is interested.

After a few years of talking to chemists and reading the literature, I began to understand finishes better. I found it remarkable how this understanding helped me solve everyday problems in my shop. I also found it deplorable that no one had taken this information and put it in a form that would be useful to woodworkers and finishers. No one had tried to bridge the chasm that divides finish chemists, who understand quite well what's true and not true about finishes, from those of us who use finishes. So I decided to do it myself. I've spent the last 6 years studying the chemistry of finishes and applying what I've learned in my shop. This book is, therefore, the coupling of my experience finishing wood for the last 20 years with the knowledge I've gained about how finishes work.

My hope is that the effort I've put into this book will lead others to continue the exploration. The more we know about how finishes work, the better finishers we will be. Above all, I hope manufacturers will begin to help us learn about their products. They can start by listing the ingredients on their labels. There is no way for the craft of finishing to advance if we don't know what it is we're using.

HOW TO USE THIS BOOK

Books on finishing are difficult to read straight through because those parts you have no experience with are often difficult to follow. The information in this book is arranged linearly, in the order you actually apply a finish. But you needn't read the early parts to understand the later. A craft is not learned linearly. It's learned gradually, the conceptual understandings periodically buttressed by hands-on experience.

Turn to the sections of the book you're interested in. Try some of the finishes on scrap wood before you use them on a completed project. (You wouldn't attempt to cut your first dovetail joint on the actual drawer!) As your skills improve, your interests will change, and you can tackle other sections. You'll find that all the materials and techniques used in finishing are interrelated. The more you learn about one subject, the better you'll be able to understand another. As you gain experience, the entire book will become accessible to you.

Finishing is a complex subject. With so many variables, it's frustrating and often humbling. No matter how long you do it, you will continue to have problems. But that's what makes finishing fun. If it were straightforward, there wouldn't be a challenge. Everyone would be able to do it, and there wouldn't be any satisfaction when you accomplished something. In this way, it's just like woodworking. ■

Safety

Throughout the book I point out safety precautions you should take when using various finishing materials. Here is an overview:

Most of the materials used in finishing are bad for you. Solvents such as mineral spirits, naphtha, and lacquer thinner can cause dermatitis, dizziness, headaches, and nausea. Chemicals such as lye, oxalic acid, and chlorine bleach can cause respiratory and skin problems. Even the so-called "safe" strippers and water-based finishes contain solvents that are bad for your health if you breathe too much of them.

You should always protect yourself by arranging cross ventilation in your work area to provide a constant source of clean air. When you can't ensure a flow of clean air, wear a NIOSH-approved, organic-vapor, respirator mask. (NIOSH is the National Institute for Occupational Safety and Health. It is a federal agency that does research on matters concerning workers' health, and tests and certifies respiratory protection.) In addition, you should wear gloves to protect your hands when they come in contact with the finishing materials.

But, in spite of these warnings, don't be afraid of using finishing materials any more than you are afraid of using woodworking tools. This is an important point, because it's becoming more and more common to read dire warnings about the hazards of using certain finishing products. Some of the warnings come from manufacturers of competing products. Some come from writers repeating the most extreme warnings they've heard without researching their validity. In some cases, if you didn't know better, you could expect almost certain death from products you can buy at any paint store.

Rely on common sense when using finishing materials, just as you should when using woodworking tools. Pay attention to your body. If you start to feel light-headed or begin coughing, or if your hands become dry and chapped, protect yourself better. Since the risk of health problems caused by solvents and chemicals used in finishing increases with exposure (your body becomes sensitized), take greater precautions if you work with these products on a regular basis. ■

Don't be afraid of using finishing materials any more than you are afraid of using woodworking tools.

CHAPTER 1

Why Finish Wood, Anyway?

Why do we finish wood? It's an extra step, or steps, that most woodworkers don't find at all enjoyable. It's smelly and messy, and all sorts of things can go wrong. In addition, most woods look pretty good unfinished. Why bother? There are three good reasons for finishing wood: to help keep it clean, to help stabilize it, and to decorate it.

SANITATION

Wood is a porous material. It contains countless holes of various sizes. These holes can accumulate dirt and grime from handling, atmospheric contaminants, and food. Grimy wood is unattractive, and it can be a health hazard, providing a breeding place for bacteria. A finish seals the porous surface, making it less susceptible to soiling and easier to clean.

STABILIZATION

Besides being porous, wood is hygroscopic: It absorbs and releases moisture. Moisture within wood is called *moisture content;* moisture in the environment is either liquid water or water vapor (humidity). Wood responds to changes in the level of moisture around it. If you put very dry wood in water or in an area of high humidity, the wood will absorb moisture and swell. If you put wood that has a high moisture content in a relatively dry climate, the wood will release moisture and shrink.

NOTE

No amount of finish or paint totally stops water-vapor exchange. For example, finished or painted wooden windows and doors shrink and let in cold air in the winter but swell tight in the spring and summer. A good finish reduces the extremes of variation that would otherwise occur during seasonal humidity changes, but it doesn't stop these variations.

These dimensional changes, commonly called *wood movement,* do not occur consistently throughout a piece of wood. The surface of wood, for instance, responds more readily than the core. Wood swells and shrinks mainly across the grain; that is, in the width and thickness of boards, not appreciably in the length. And wood swells and shrinks more around the annular rings than it does perpendicular to the rings. The result of these different responses is that wood movement generates great stresses in wood and on the joints that hold pieces of wood together. The stresses cause splitting, checking, warping, and weakening of the joints. A finish slows moisture exchange, thus reducing the stresses and stabilizing the wood.

As a general rule, the thicker the coating of finish, the better it limits moisture exchange. This is the reason you should coat all sides of a piece of furniture—top and bottom, inside and out—equally. Another important understanding is that moisture exchange in wood does not have to be in the form of liquid water. It can be, and usually is, water vapor. Water-vapor exchange causes much damage to otherwise sheltered wood furniture and woodwork. It just does this more slowly than in wood subjected to liquid-water exchange.

Figure 1-1: When dry wood is exposed to moisture, the cell walls swell. If the wood can't expand, the cells compress.

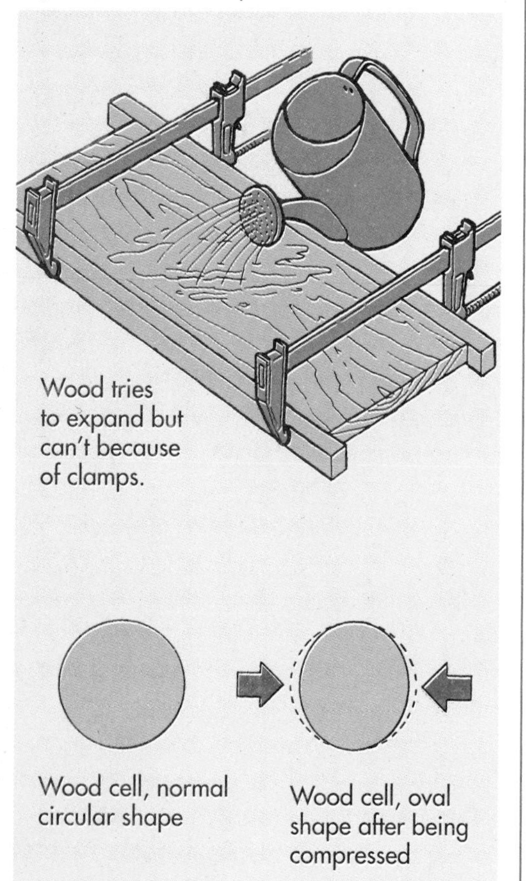

Splits, Checks, and Warps

To better understand how moisture exchange causes splits, checks, and warps, look at Figure 1-1. A solid piece of kiln-dried wood is clamped securely so that it can't expand in width. Then it is saturated with water. The cell walls swell and try to expand but are constrained by the clamps. So the cell walls compress, changing from cylindrical to oval in shape.

If the board is released from the clamps, the cells don't return to their cylindrical shape: They remain flattened. When the water evaporates and the cell walls shrink to their previous thickness, the board shrinks, becoming narrower than it was originally. The amount of shrinkage is as usual, but the starting point is now the clamped width rather than the width the board would have swollen to without the clamps. If the board is reclamped and made wet and dry again, it will shrink further. This phenomenon is called *compression shrinkage* (also *compression set*). It explains why nails and screws work loose in wood, and why the wooden handles of hammers and hatchets loosen over time, after becoming repeatedly wet and then dry.

Compression shrinkage also accounts for splits developing in the ends of a board, checks in the middle of a board, and cupping (a type of warp) on the side of a board that is exposed to the most moisture (Photos 1-1 through 1-3). In each case part of the board tries to expand more than the rest of the board will

Photo 1-1: When wood absorbs moisture, more is absorbed on the end than in the middle because there is more surface area and because the end grain is more porous than the other surfaces. The end of the board tries to swell more than the middle of the board allows it to. The middle of the board acts like a clamp on the end, causing compression shrinkage. After a number of cycles, the end of the board becomes narrower than the middle, and it splits to relieve the stresses. You see this type of compression shrinkage on the ends of any boards exposed to excessive moisture exchange.

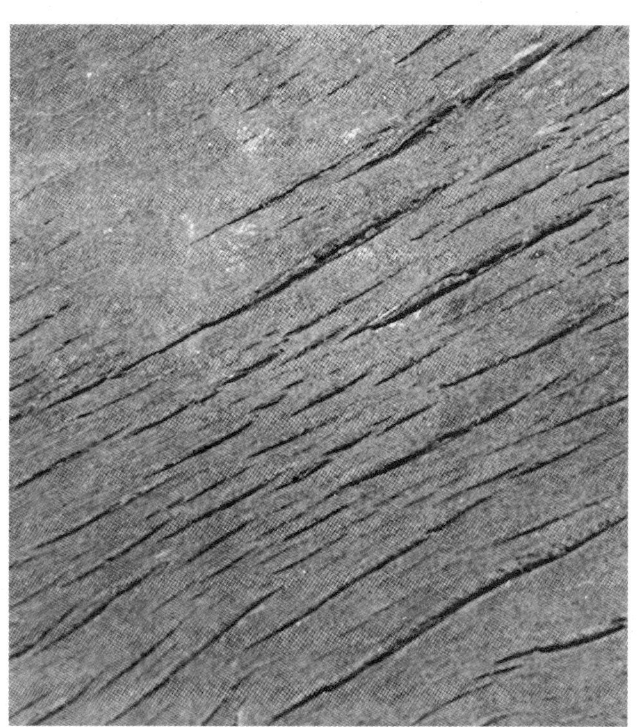

Photo 1-2: When moisture comes in contact with just a part of a board, that part tries to expand. But the surrounding wood acts like a clamp and prevents it. This causes compression shrinkage and the resulting checks. You see this type of compression shrinkage on exposed decks and tabletops subjected to high moisture, as from a leaking potted plant.

Photo 1-3: When wood is exposed to more moisture on one side than the other, the imbalance causes cupping. The side exposed to the most moisture is restricted from swelling by the other side. You see this type of compression shrinkage on decks and tabletops, where the cupping is always on the top side of boards, even though the direction of the rings would often indicate the opposite should happen, and even though the top may have been finished better than the bottom. Keep in mind it is the top of a table that gets wiped off with a damp cloth after meals.

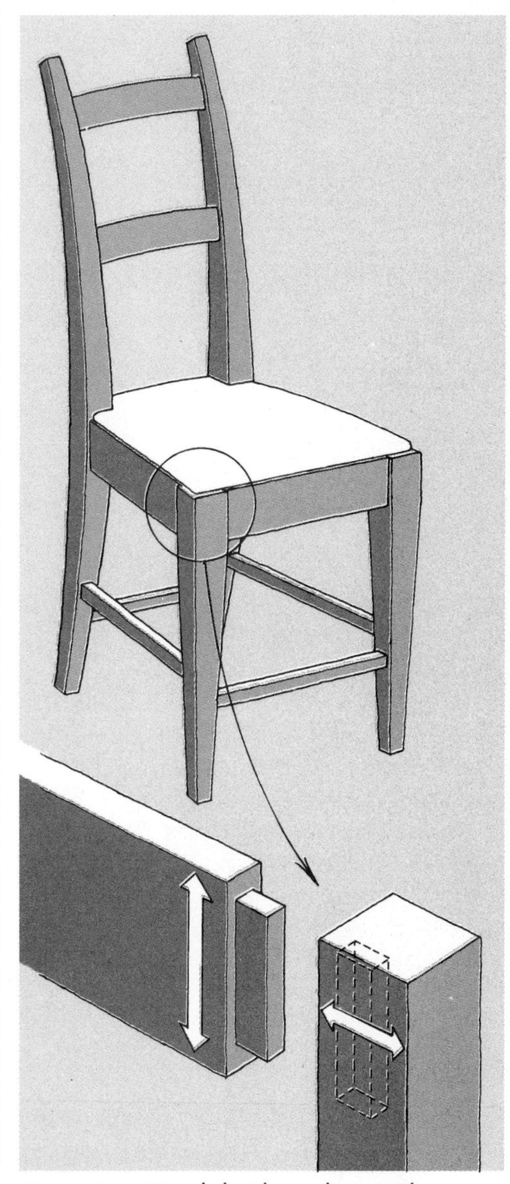

Figure 1-2: Wood shrinks and expands across the grain, not along the grain. When boards are joined with the grain running perpendicularly, the contrary shrinkage and expansion eventually causes joint failure.

allow it to. After a number of cycles of restricted expansion followed by full contraction, that part of the board changes shape or splits.

Joint Failure

Joint failure also is accelerated by excessive moisture exchange. The cells in wood are like soda straws running lengthwise in boards. The cell walls swell and shrink, changing the width and thickness of boards, but not the length. When boards are joined with the grain running perpendicularly, as they inevitably are in wood structures, the swelling and shrinking in different directions put great stress on the joints. As the glue ages and loses its flexibility, the contrary movement in any cross-grain construction causes joint failure. This is why glued furniture comes apart in time (Figure 1-2).

The speed at which moisture exchange damages wood or breaks the glue bond in joints varies depending on the environmental conditions. Wood or furniture left outside in the weather develops splits, checks, warps, and joint failure much sooner than wood or furniture stored under cover. Wood or furniture stored under cover develops problems much faster than wood or furniture stored in a controlled environment (such as inside your house). The best environment for storing wood or wooden objects is an environment of constant temperature and humidity. This is the type of environment museums try to maintain.

A finish slows moisture exchange no matter what temperature or humidity conditions surround the wood. A finish makes the wood, or the object made of wood, last longer (Figure 1-3).

DECORATION

In addition to stabilizing wood and protecting it from dirt and grime, finishing wood is decorative. Even if you apply nothing more than a simple oil or wax finish, you are making a decorative choice. There are an infinite number of ways you can decorate wood, but finish decoration divides into three categories: color, texture, and sheen.

Color

There are three ways you can apply color to wood. In a broad sense all three are a type of staining. The term *staining* commonly means applying color directly to wood. But you can also apply color in between coats of finish. This is called *glazing*. Or you can add color to the finish itself and apply it to the wood. This is called *shading* or *toning* if you can still see the wood through the colored finish, and *painting* if you can't. Each of these methods produces a different decorative effect:

- Stain applied to bare wood amplifies the figure and grain of the wood. Stain also highlights problems in the wood, such as scratches, gouges, machine marks, and uneven density.
- Glaze, applied thinly, changes the tone of the wood's color and adds the appearance of depth and age by highlighting pores and recesses. Applied thick, glaze can be manipulated to imitate wood grain, marble, or leather. These are called *faux* (false) *finishes*.
- Shading, toning, and painting change the tone of the wood's color without highlighting pores and recesses. Shading and toning allow you to see the figure and grain of the wood. Painting totally obscures the wood's features. Shading changes the color tone only in the areas you want. Toning changes the color tone evenly over the entire surface.

Texture

All woods have a natural texture dependent upon the size and distribution of the pores. You can preserve this texture by keeping your finish very thin. This thin-finish look is very popular. It's often called a *natural wood* look, and it is what you get when you finish with oil or wax. You can get the same look with film finishes, such as varnish, shellac, lacquer, or water base, as long as you keep them thin.

By filling, or partially filling, the pores, you can completely change the texture of the wood. You can fill the pores with paste-wood filler or with many coats of finish that you sand or scrape back. The most refined finishes (for example, those commonly used on very expensive dining table tops) have filled pores.

Sheen

Sheen is the amount of gloss the finish has. There are two ways to control sheen. The first is by choosing a finish that has the sheen you want built into it: high-gloss, satin, or flat. The second is by rubbing and polishing the cured finish to the sheen you want.

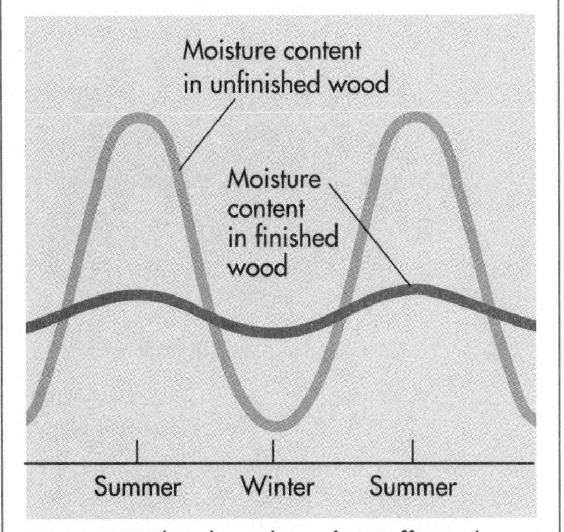

Figure 1-3: This chart shows how effectively a finish stabilizes the moisture content of wood through seasonal changes in humidity. Inhibiting moisture exchange effectively minimizes the stresses in wood that can be caused by wide swings in humidity.

Chapter 2

Preparing the Wood Surface

A quality finish is impossible to obtain if you don't prepare the wood properly. You probably know this already. I'm sure you've at least heard it. Most woodworkers dread the preparation steps, skip through them, and get a poor finish as a result. Others spend more time and effort than they need to—scraping, sanding, patching, sanding, steaming out dents, sanding, and more sanding. Both extremes are probably caused by a lack of understanding of what needs to be achieved.

The most glaring examples of how poor understanding leads to lower-quality work occur when the woodworker and the finisher are different people, and the communication between them is poor. This is common in house construction, where cabinetmakers and trim carpenters often pay scant attention to the little things they can do to make the finisher's job easier and of better quality. "Oh, the finishers will take care of that," they'll tell you.

The usual cause for over-preparation is the belief that sanding to 400 grit or finer produces better results. The wood looks better when sanded to 400 grit, after all. Why shouldn't the finish?

When you have control of a project from beginning to end, you'll find that it pays to begin thinking of the finish from the start. In fact, the old wisdom holds that a good finish begins with the selection of the lumber itself.

Photos 2-1 and 2-2: The single greatest advantage you have over factories is in the attention you can devote to wood selection and arrangement. The boards above are arranged poorly for making a round tabletop. The grain configurations do not align at the joints. It will be very difficult for a finish to make this arrangement cohere visually. The same boards are arranged much better at right.

There are four stages in preparing wood for finishing:

- *Selecting, cutting out, and shaping the lumber.* Many potential finish problems can be avoided by proper attention here.
- *Sanding or smoothing the surface.* This is the most unpleasant operation for most woodworkers, so knowledge of the tools and some thought about what you're trying to achieve can go a long way toward reducing the drudgery and improving results.
- *Dealing with glue that gets on the surface of the wood.* Glue will show up as light splotches through the stain and finish.
- *Correcting surface imperfections in the wood,* such as dents, gouges, and checks, and filling gaps in the joints left by a less-than-successful glue-up. This step could be called "the woodworker's eternal quest for a wood putty that takes stain."

PREPARING THE LUMBER

Wood varies greatly in color and figure—even wood of the same species and boards from the same tree. You need to pay attention to how boards look when you're putting them next to one another in a project. Otherwise, you may end up with color and figure differences that will detract from the appearance and be difficult to disguise with a finish.

Whether you're choosing boards at a lumberyard or from your own inventory, look through the supply and imagine how different grain and figure patterns would look if placed in various parts of your project (Photos 2-1 and 2-2). Be conscious of knots, splits, checks, and other defects, and determine how you would either use them to advantage or work around them. If you're using veneered plywood or plan to veneer the wood yourself, think of how the figure in the veneer can be used to best advantage. Above all, pay attention to color variations, unless you intend to paint the piece you're making.

For a table or chest top, lay the boards out in different groupings, flipping and turning them, until you find the best arrangement. Then mark the boards so you won't mix them up as you prepare them (Figure 2-1). If you're making the top from veneered plywood, decide what part of the 4 x 8 sheet you can use most advantageously. On a chest-of-drawers, give the same attention to picking the drawer fronts. When people look at what you've built, they won't see the wonderful joints you've spent so much time and effort making. They'll see the design, which includes your choice of boards and their positioning, and they'll see the finish. You won't regret the time you spent selecting and arranging your wood.

Before you begin working your lumber, make sure your tools are sharp and your machines are adjusted properly. Dull planer, jointer, or shaper knives and worn-out router bits will leave pronounced washboardlike mill marks in your wood that will require extra effort to remove (Photo 2-3). Chipped knives will leave unsightly ridges. And if the cutters on your machine tools are dull

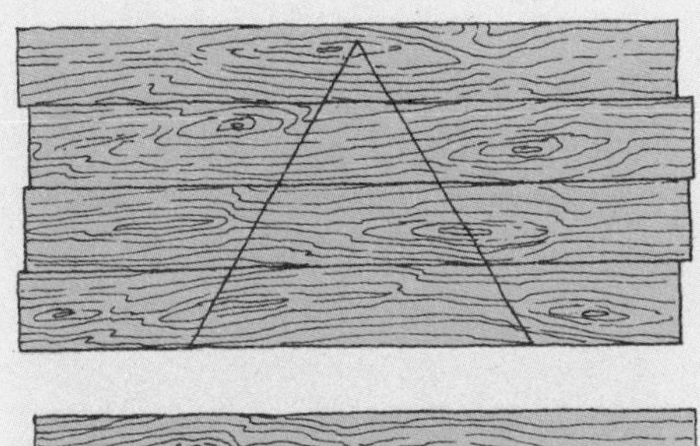

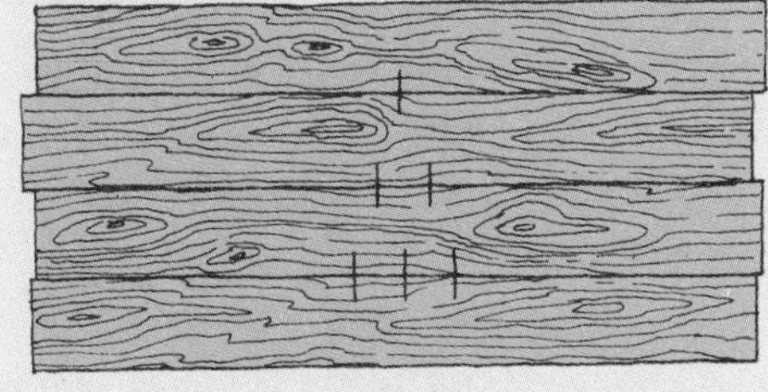

Figure 2-1: Marking the boards you have laid out for a table or chest top ensures that you won't get the boards mixed up as you joint them. Here are two ways to do it.

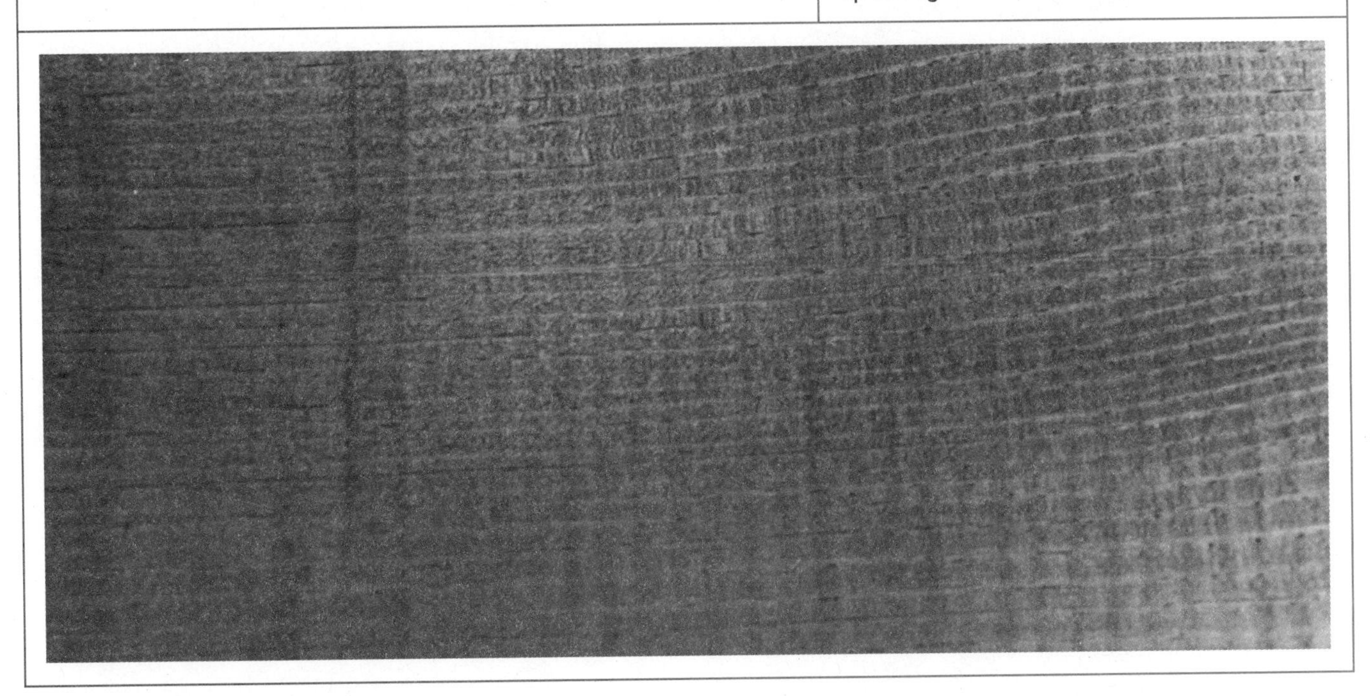

Photo 2-3: Dull or poorly adjusted machine tools leave much more obvious marks than sharp, well-adjusted tools. These marks show up through a stain and finish.

enough to burn or glaze the wood, they could ruin your project altogether. Poorly adjusted machinery can snipe the ends of boards and also cause glazing or burning. Always work toward the smoothest surface possible.

If you're joining a number of boards together to make a tabletop, you may want to use splines, dowels, or biscuits to line up the boards so the surface is as flat and even as possible. If, after glue-up, uneven alignment is more than you want to try flattening by hand and you don't have power equipment large enough to handle the job, look for a local millwork shop that will run the top through its wide-belt sander for you. The price and the trip are often worth it. If the top is too wide for any of the sanders in your area, plan to make the top in several sections; flatten each section separately; and then join them together with splines, dowels, or biscuits to line them up.

SANDING AND SMOOTHING

Of all the steps involved in making and finishing something of wood, sanding is the most universally detested. At the same time, curiously, it's the step that consumes the most wasted effort. There seems to be some mystique that the more you sand, the better the end product will be. But as an old finisher I knew used to say, "When you're in the bathtub and you're clean, get out!" Once the wood is smooth and the mill marks and other defects are gone, there's no reason to continue sanding. You're finished. Your goal should be to reach that end with as little work as possible.

There seems to be some mystique that the more you sand, the better the end product will be. But as an old finisher I knew used to say, "When you're in the bathtub and you're clean, get out!"

It will help to remember that just about the only reason you need to sand at all is to remove the washboardlike mill marks left in the wood by planers, jointers, shapers, and to a lesser degree, routers. Before the invention of these machine tools, there was seldom any reason to sand; indeed, there was no sandpaper.

The tools used to smooth and finish off furniture parts before the introduction of machines were hand tools—bench planes, molding planes, and scrapers of several sorts. These tools are still available, of course, and can often be used very effectively to remove mill marks. In fact, for some woodworking projects, a finely planed surface can be regarded as a final surface. In some applications, the evidence of hand-plane work—ridges from the edge of the plane iron or hollows from a scrub plane—add character to a surface. And for any woodworker who can't afford or is uninterested in large power sanding equipment, a simple tool like a scraper can be a godsend.

Before discussing the pros and cons of the various smoothing tools, however, I want to point out that whichever tools you use, you'll usually get a better job if you prepare all of the parts before assembling. You'll be able to secure each part to your workbench, where you can see what you're doing clearly in good light. And you'll be able to do your preparation in a comfortable position with any tool you choose. You'll also avoid the difficulty of trying to sand or scrape already-assembled, right-angle joints, such as stiles and rails, or legs and rails, without putting cross-grain scratches in the perpendicular pieces.

Turned and carved pieces shouldn't need any additional preparation. Turnings should be sanded while still on the lathe. Carvings shouldn't be sanded at all, as sanding inevitably softens the crisp lines left by the carving tools.

Table and chest tops, sides, panels, rails, door and drawer fronts, and most moldings, however, will contain mill marks that should be removed. The two most efficient tools you have, besides hand planes, to accomplish this task are sandpaper and scrapers.

TIP

Mill marks and other minor flaws are hard to see before stain highlights them. Then it is too late. The best way to spot these flaws before staining is to view the wood in a raking light. Hold the wood up to a light, or position a single-point light just above the plane of the wood. If you've never tried this, you'll be surprised at how much you can see.

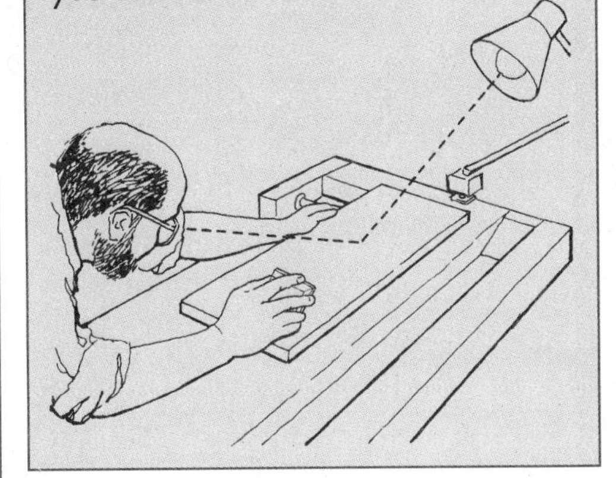

Sanding Basics

There are several types of sandpaper, but for almost all woodworking tasks, you will get the best performance from *garnet* paper, which is orange-to-red in color, or from *aluminum-oxide* paper, which is tan-to-brown.

Sandpaper comes in a series of numbered grits, from coarse to fine. The sequence is 60, 80, 100, 120, 150, 180, 220, 240, 280, 320, 360, 400, 500, 600, 1000, 1200, 1500, 2000. I usually start with 80 or 100 grit and rarely sand past 220 grit.

For finishes, *silicon carbide* is usually the better choice, and 280 grit is about as coarse as you'll ever need. There are two types of silicon carbide sandpaper: stearated, which is usually gray in color, and wet/dry, which is black.

Stearated silicon carbide sandpaper contains metallic soap (the stearate) to lubricate the sandpaper so it doesn't clog up as easily as unstearated sandpaper. Stearated sandpaper is also called *no-load* and *self-lubricating* sandpaper.

Wet/dry silicon carbide sandpaper is made with waterproof glue which continues to hold the grit to the paper backing even when the paper gets wet.

You can do your sanding with the aid of a machine, or you can sand by hand. Whichever way you choose, the process is basically the same. There are two steps:

- Remove the blemishes using the coarsest grit sandpaper necessary to do the job efficiently.
- Remove the scratches left by the sandpaper, using increasingly finer grits. Sand with any given grit until you can see no more improvement. Then move to a finer grit.

TRY THIS

To determine if you've removed all of the blemishes or coarser-grit scratches before moving to the next step, wet the wood with mineral spirits and look at the wood in a raking light. The mineral spirits will clean the sanding dust out of the blemishes and scratches, making them easier to see. Mineral spirits won't raise the grain of the wood and will evaporate rapidly.

MYTH

You get better results if you sand to 400 or finer grit.

FACT

Before you apply the finish, wood sanded to 400 grit will have a higher gloss than wood sanded to, say, 180 grit, because 400 grit polishes more than 180 grit. But after you apply the finish, you will have difficulty seeing any difference. Try it! You may save yourself countless hours of sanding in the future.

If you switch to a finer grit before you've totally removed the blemishes or before you've removed all the scratches of the previous grit, it will take you much longer. It's like trying to smooth over the hoed rows in a garden with a fine-toothed rake: If you use a coarse cultivator first, then a fine rake, it will go much faster and you'll get more consistent results. The most common error made in sanding is skipping to finer grits before you've made the sanding scratches of the prior grit uniform.

When you're sanding by hand, don't skip any grits. When you're sanding by machine, you can usually skip one or two grits, even with coarse papers. The greater speed of the machine makes up the difference. Always clean off the sanding dust before moving to the next finer grit. The dust will contain some of the grit from the coarser sandpaper, and this coarser grit will keep you from getting a uniform scratch pattern with the finer grit.

The second most common error in sanding is continuing to use sandpaper after it has become dull. Pay attention to what's happening. The cutting efficiency of sandpaper deteriorates fairly rapidly. You'll cut your sanding time significantly by changing sandpaper more often.

To what grit should you sand? Probably no question in woodworking elicits as much passionate controversy as this one. Most of the passion is based on how good the wood looks before the finish is applied. The finer the grit sandpaper you use, the more polished the wood will appear. But highly polished wood won't look more polished after you apply the finish. In fact, from about 120 grit up, it's difficult to see the difference once the finish is applied. For perspective, consider that furniture factories seldom sand above 150 grit.

My own preference is to sand to 180 grit when I'm applying a film (shellac, lacquer, varnish, conversion, or water-based) finish, and to 220 grit when I'm applying a thin oil finish. (The higher grit for oil finishes makes the wood feel smoother; it doesn't improve the appearance.) Sanding to 220 grit and above will polish the surface and hinder pigment-stain penetration.

No matter how fine the final grit you use, you won't remove all of the tiny wood fibers that swell and make the wood rough to the touch if water is applied. If you intend to use a stain or finish that contains water, you should sponge the wood after your normal sanding. Wet the wood and resand it smooth after the water dries out. (See "Sponging" on the facing page.)

Sanding Machines

There are three common hand-held sanding machines: belt sander, orbital pad sander, and random-orbit sander. The way each works determines the surface it produces (Figure 2-2).

Belt sanders will remove a lot of wood very fast. This can be an advantage when wood removal is the goal. But when you're trying to achieve flatness and smoothness, a belt sander is a dangerous tool to use. You must keep the sander flat on the surface, moving at all times, and avoid even the slightest rocking motion—side-to-side or front-to-back—or the sander will dig into the wood, leaving hollows or ridges. Make one mistake with this tool on solid wood, and you may find yourself spending hours correcting it, especially if, as is often the case, you don't notice the problem until you apply the finish. Veneer should never be belt-sanded. Except for those instances where I really do want to remove a lot of wood quickly, I don't find using a belt sander worth the risk, so I seldom use mine.

On the other hand, I have friends who use belt sanders and are pleased with the results they get. They tell me they damaged a lot of wood in the beginning but finally mastered the "touch" needed to avoid gouging.

Orbital pad sanders are much tamer than belt sanders, but they're also much less effective. Because this sander works with an orbital motion, it inevitably leaves small orbital scratches on

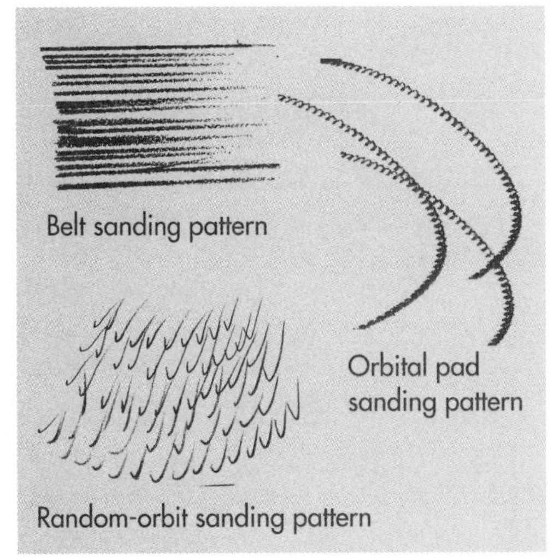

Figure 2-2: Each of the three sanding machines has its own distinctive sanding movement.

SPONGING

WHENEVER WATER COMES IN contact with wood, the wood fibers swell, causing the wood to feel rough to the touch after it has dried. The swollen fibers are often referred to as *raised grain.* All stains and finishes that contain water raise the grain of the wood. Raised grain telegraphs through the stain or finish, causing the surface to feel rough. It also reduces the wood's depth and clarity.

Raised grain will happen no matter how smoothly you sand the wood before you wet it. Since you can't prevent raised grain, you need to make the fibers swell and *then* sand them before staining. Once removed, the raised grain won't reoccur. This step is called *sponging, whiskering, dewhiskering,* or *raising the grain.*

After sanding the wood to about 180 or 220 grit, wet it with a sponge or cloth to the same extent as you will with the stain or finish. Just short of puddling is about right.

Let the wood dry overnight. Then sand off the raised grain with sandpaper that is at least as fine as the last grit you used on the wood. I usually use at least one number grit higher. Dull (used) sandpaper is best because it is less likely to remove more than just the raised grain.

Sand lightly. You want to sand just enough to make the wood feel smooth again. If you sand any deeper, you'll go below the wood fibers that have been swollen, and you'll raise the grain again when you apply water. (In practice, you'll always have some additional grain raising, but it will be minimal.) Always sand in the direction of the grain.

Don't use steel wool to remove raised grain when you intend to apply a water-based stain or finish. Small pieces of steel wool will break off and lodge in the pores. These pieces will then rust and spot the wood when you apply the water-based stain or finish. ■

TIP

If you don't have any used sandpaper lying around, you can make some quickly by rubbing two pieces of sandpaper together.

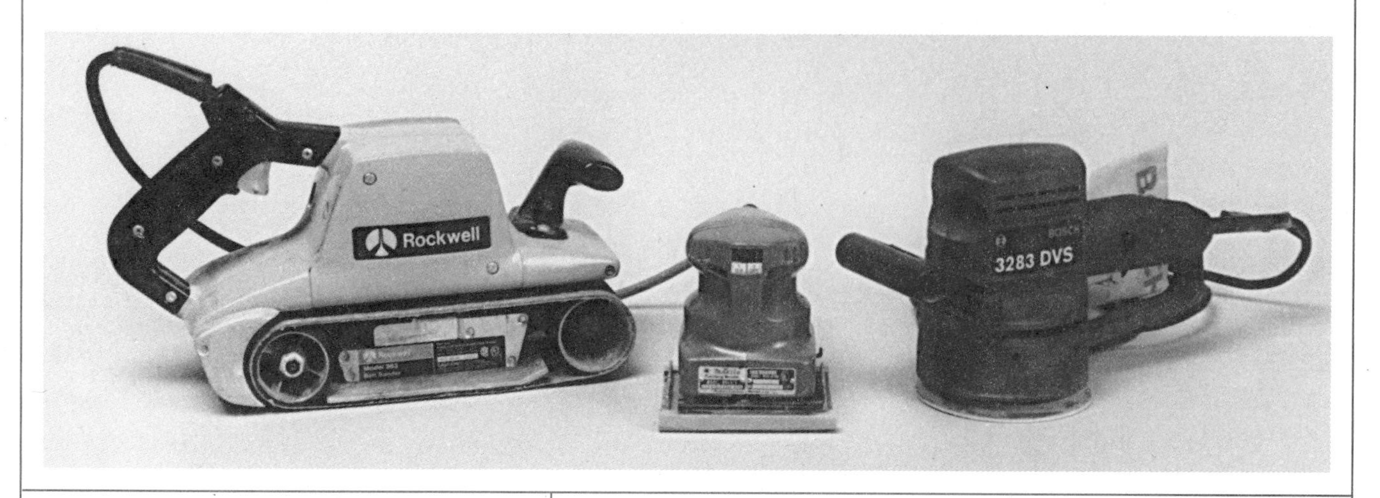

Photo 2-4: Three types of sander, from left to right: belt sander, orbital pad sander, and random-orbit sander.

the wood surface. These scratches are almost invisible until you put on a stain and finish. Then they scream at you. To reduce the scratching, don't set the sander down on the wood until it's running at full speed, and don't slow the sander down by pressing on it. Sand to what would normally be your finest grit if you were hand sanding. Move the sander back and forth slowly in the direction of the grain, and check often to make sure no splinter or other foreign object has become lodged between the sandpaper and the wood, as this will leave deeper orbital scratches. It's almost always wise to finish off by hand with fine sandpaper and a sanding block, sanding in the direction of the grain.

Personally, I find the orbital pad sander too slow, and I don't use mine very often. But pad sanders are very popular with many woodworkers.

Random-orbit sanders, which incorporate an orbital as well as a revolving movement, fall between belt sanders and pad sanders for their ability to remove wood. They are not as aggressive as

Photo 2-5: This board shows how ridges caused by a belt sander and swirls caused by a pad sander are darkened and therefore made more prominent by stain. These defects must be scraped or sanded out before finishing.

belt sanders and are far more effective than pad sanders. Random-orbit sanders are also far less likely than belt sanders to gouge the wood and somewhat less likely than pad sanders to leave scratches in the wood. For most sanding operations a random-orbit sander is the best machine choice.

Random-orbit sanders are so efficient because of their speed and the randomness of their scratch pattern. These two factors increase the cutting effectiveness while minimizing scratching.

For best results, start the sander while it is on the wood. (This is opposite of the way you start a pad sander. If you wait until the random-orbit sander is running at full speed to set it on the wood, the sander tends to gouge.) Use a light touch, and move the sander at an even speed in regular patterns, aiming to keep the surface as flat as possible.

Contrary to the publicity you hear about random-orbit sanders, they do leave scratches in the wood. It's best to finish off by hand sanding, the same as you should with pad sanders.

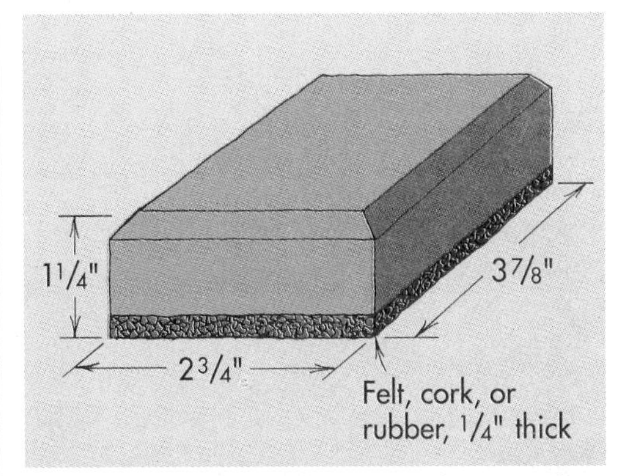

Figure 2-3: The ideal dimensions for a sanding block depend upon the size of your hand. The dimensions above are about average. If your block is made from wood, glue on a 1/4-inch-thick piece of felt, cork, or rubber to reduce sandpaper clogging.

Hand Sanding

Sanding by hand is almost a lost art, but I've always enjoyed it and found it a very effective way to sand wood. You can hold the sandpaper directly in your hand, or you can wrap the sandpaper around a block made of cork, felt, rubber, or wood. If you use a wood block, glue a piece of 1/4-inch cork, felt, or rubber onto the bottom to provide a cushion behind the sandpaper to reduce clogging. A chalkboard eraser or a material like ceiling tile can also be used to back your sandpaper.

It's almost always better, when sanding flat surfaces, to back up sandpaper with a sanding block (Figure 2-3) rather than your hand. Your hand will tend to dig out the softer grain in the wood, resulting in a dimpled or ridged effect that's noticeable after you apply the finish. On moldings and other curved surfaces you can't use a flat block. But if you have a large number of pieces to sand, you may find it advantageous to make a negative of the molding from wood, Styrofoam, or other firm material to give good backing to the sandpaper. (A dowel rod of the proper diameter can aid in sanding coves, for instance.) Otherwise, you can hold the sandpaper in your hand. The dimples you create won't show as badly on moldings or curved surfaces as they would on flat surfaces.

When I sand by hand, I tear the 9 x 11-inch sheets in thirds across the width (Figure 2-4). If I'm using a sanding block, I fold one of the thirds in half and wrap it around the sides of the block, holding it in place with my thumb and fingers. When one side is well used, I flip the sandpaper. When that is used, I unfold the sandpaper and wrap it all around the block so that the crease is under the block. This way, there is no waste.

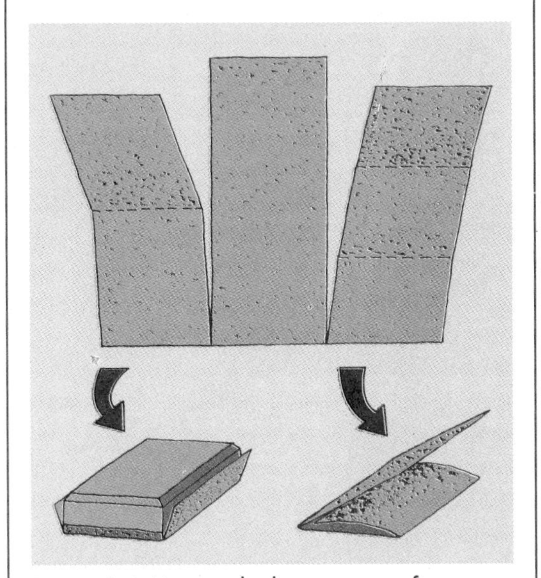

Figure 2-4: You get the best use out of sandpaper by tearing the 9 x 11-inch sheet in thirds across the width, then folding each of the thirds in half (for use with a sanding block) or in thirds again (for use with no block).

If I'm using my hand to back the sandpaper, I fold one of the thirds into thirds again and overlap them. This gives me three fresh surfaces that stay in place as I sand, and it reduces waste.

Whether you're sanding with your hand or with a block, you should always sand in the direction of the grain, or you will surely produce cross-grain scratches that will show through the finish. It's also wiser to move the sandpaper with the folded edge facing the direction of travel. An open edge of sandpaper is more likely to catch under a sliver of wood and lift it, which will, at the least, tear the sandpaper and could jam painfully into your hand.

As your final step, run the sandpaper lightly over every right-angled edge of the wood to remove sharp corners that can easily dent, can feel unfriendly to the hand, and might be too sharp to hold the finish. This is sometimes called *breaking the edges*.

Photo 2-6: For removing mill marks, the hand scraper works faster, cleaner, and more effectively than sandpaper.

Scrapers

The fastest, cleanest, safest, and most enjoyable tool to use for removing mill marks and other defects in wood is the scraper. There are two kinds: the hand scraper, which you hold directly in your hand, and the cabinet scraper, which is held in a cast-iron body that has a flat sole and two handles. (There is also the common paint scraper; however, this tool has limited use in woodworking.) Both scrapers are misnamed because they don't scrape the wood at all but rather slice very thin shavings.

These scrapers fit a category of hand tools that almost totally disappeared from use in the United States as a result of our love affair with power machinery. Recently, scrapers have begun returning to favor. I first encountered scrapers in the mid-1970s, when I was working in Denmark. Every cabinetmaker there had several handscrapers in his tool kit. I was employed as the shop finisher at the time and was taught to use the hand scraper to remove cured runs and sags in my finishes and to cut back and level a finish rapidly in order to create a mirror-flat surface. The hand scraper cuts off ribbons of finish far faster than sandpaper can scratch the finish off. It doesn't gum up the way sandpaper does, and it's more economical.

A scraper is to sandpaper what a word processor is to a typewriter. I've never known a woodworker who learned to use a scraper, or a writer a word processor, who wanted to go back. Scrapers and word processors both increase efficiency many times over. True woodworkers would rather make shavings than sawdust anyway!

To use the hand scraper, hold it between the thumbs and forefingers of both hands at an angle of about 50 to 70 degrees above the wood surface or until you feel the burr on the scraper edge

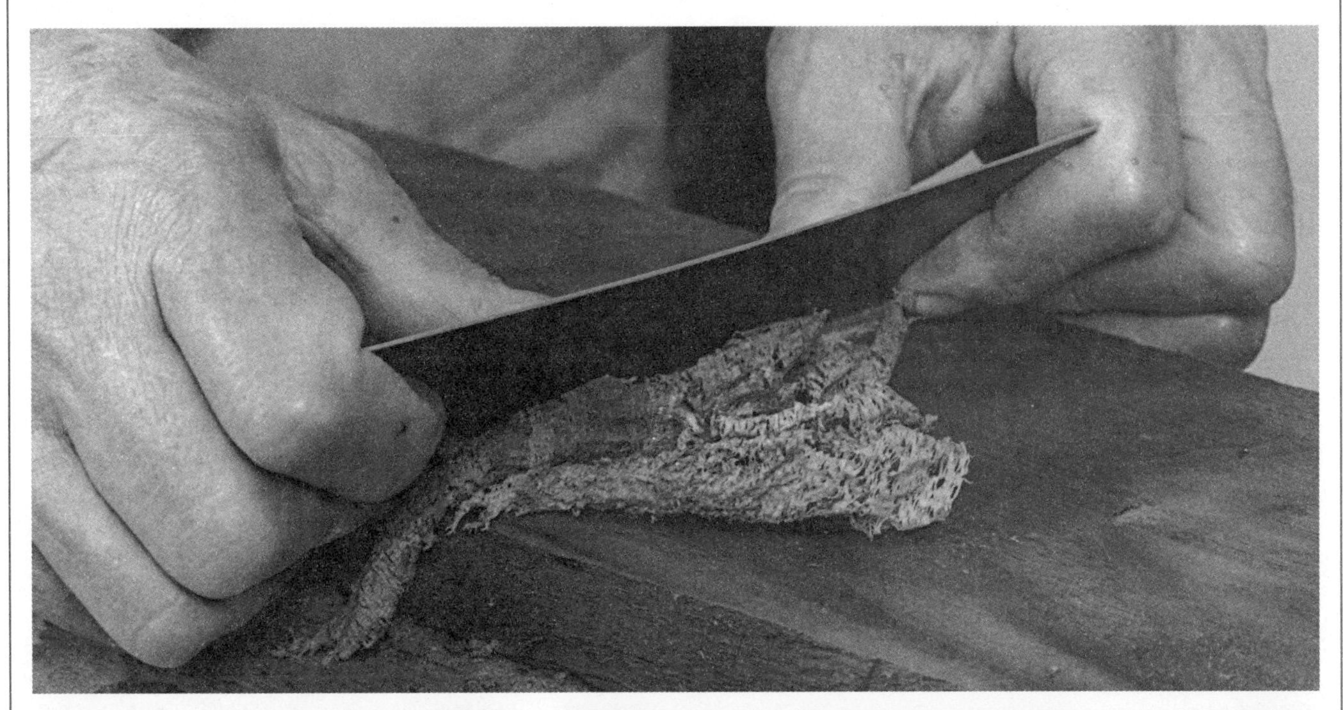

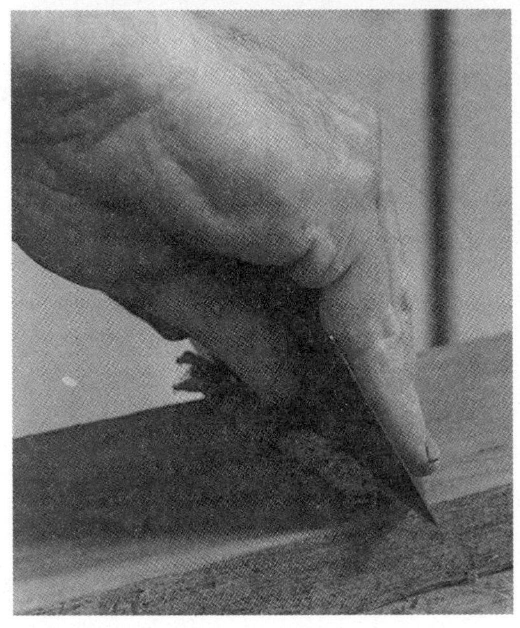

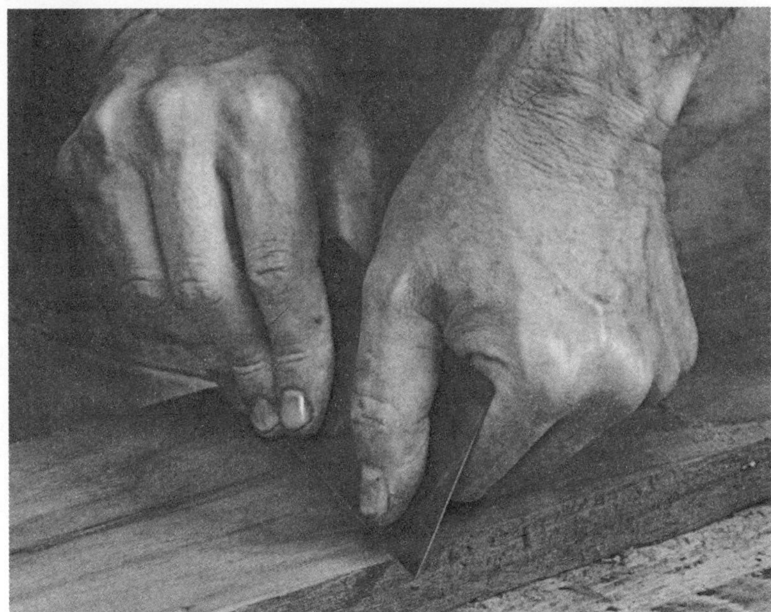

catch. Then push it away from you or pull it toward you, cutting a ribbonlike shaving as you go (Photos 2-7 and 2-8). You can also shift one hand to the reverse position and scrape sideways, perpendicular to your body (Photo 2-9). If dust is your only product, the scraper is not sharp. (See "Sharpening a Hand Scraper" on page 21 and "Sharpening a Cabinet Scraper" on page 24.)

When you push the scraper, it will tend to bow out slightly in the middle from the pressure of your thumbs. This will create a slightly convex edge and almost imperceptible hollows in the sur-

Photos 2-7, 2-8, and 2-9: There are three ways to use a scraper. At top: Hold it between the thumbs and forefingers at an angle of about 50 to 70 degrees or until you feel the burr on the scraper edge catch, and push it away from you. Above, left: Use a similar grip, but pull the scraper toward you. Above, right: Shift one hand to the reverse position and scrape sideways, perpendicular to your body.

Photo 2-10: Like the hand scraper, the cabinet scraper is misnamed: Both slice very thin shavings of wood. If your scraper is producing powder, it's dull.

face you're scraping. This unevenness could show up under a finish. You should sand out these hollows or scrape them flat using one of the other two hand positions, scraping toward you or sideways. But pushing the scraper is the most effective way to remove the most wood. To keep the scraper from heating up, turn it often to another edge. If the scraper gets too hot to hold, set it aside and let it cool for a moment.

When you're using a hand scraper to remove mill marks, hold it at a slight angle to the washboardlike rows, so you cut off the ridges rather than dip in and out of the hollows, accentuating the defect. Change your angle of cut with each pass.

Hand scrapers can also be used to smooth contoured surfaces: A straight hand scraper will follow a convex curve, and a French-curved scraper will get into concave contours.

The cabinet scraper cuts the same way as the hand scraper. However, the cabinet scraper has a flat sole, which makes it easier to maintain a level surface (Photo 2-10). I find it particularly useful when I want to even the raised edges of glued-up boards that didn't come together flat. I begin by scraping off the greater part of the raised edge (this could also be done with a belt sander). Next I scrape diagonally across the grain, alternating from a left diagonal to a right diagonal, until the top is flat. Then I scrape a few passes with the grain. A light sanding, and the panel is ready to finish.

Either scraper is more forgiving than a hand plane. Because of the high cutting angle, a scraper tends not to tear the grain; you don't have to worry as much about grain direction, swirls, or knots. You can scrape with, against, or across the grain.

(continued on page 26)

SHARPENING A HAND SCRAPER

BECOMING PROFICIENT AT sharpening any tool involves learning a few basics as well as a good deal of practice and experience. When you first try to sharpen a tool, it seems infinitely difficult. Later, when you've mastered the touch, it's so easy you can't understand why you had so much trouble earlier.

There are almost as many ways to sharpen a hand scraper as there are woodworkers using one. But all the methods follow the same principles. You want to make the two long edges of the scraper perfectly flat and perpendicular to the sides. Then you want to roll a very fine burr on each of the four junctures about 5 degrees off the perpendicular (Figure 2-5). This burr is what cuts the shavings when you push or pull the scraper along the wood or finish.

Begin by clamping the scraper vertically into a wood-jawed vise (metal jaws will mar the scraper and, eventually, the edge), leaving 3/4 to 1 inch of the long edge showing above the vise. Using a common 8-inch or 10-inch mill file, round the corners slightly at the ends of the long edge. This will reduce the likelihood of

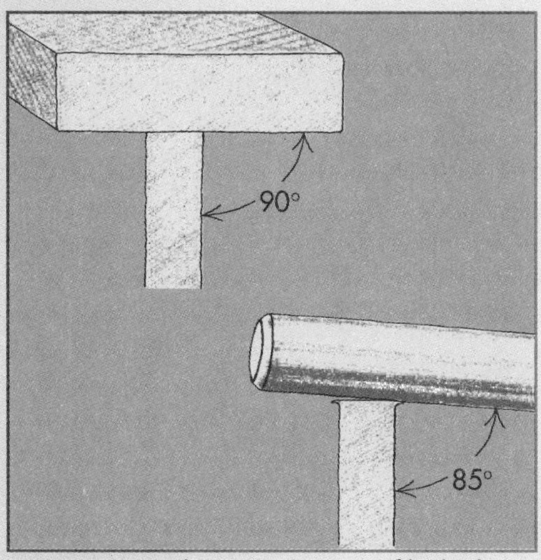

Figure 2-5: To sharpen a scraper, file the long edge perfectly flat, then turn the edges to make a burr about 5 degrees off the perpendicular.

Photo 2-11: Using a standard 8- or 10-inch mill file, file the edge of the scraper until the sheen is even. Hold the file in line with the scraper to avoid hollowing it.

Photo 2-12: The trick to whetting the edge of a scraper without rounding it is to bow the scraper slightly as you move it over the stone. Avoid cutting a groove in the stone by holding the scraper at an angle to your direction of travel.

(continued)

SHARPENING A HAND SCRAPER—continued

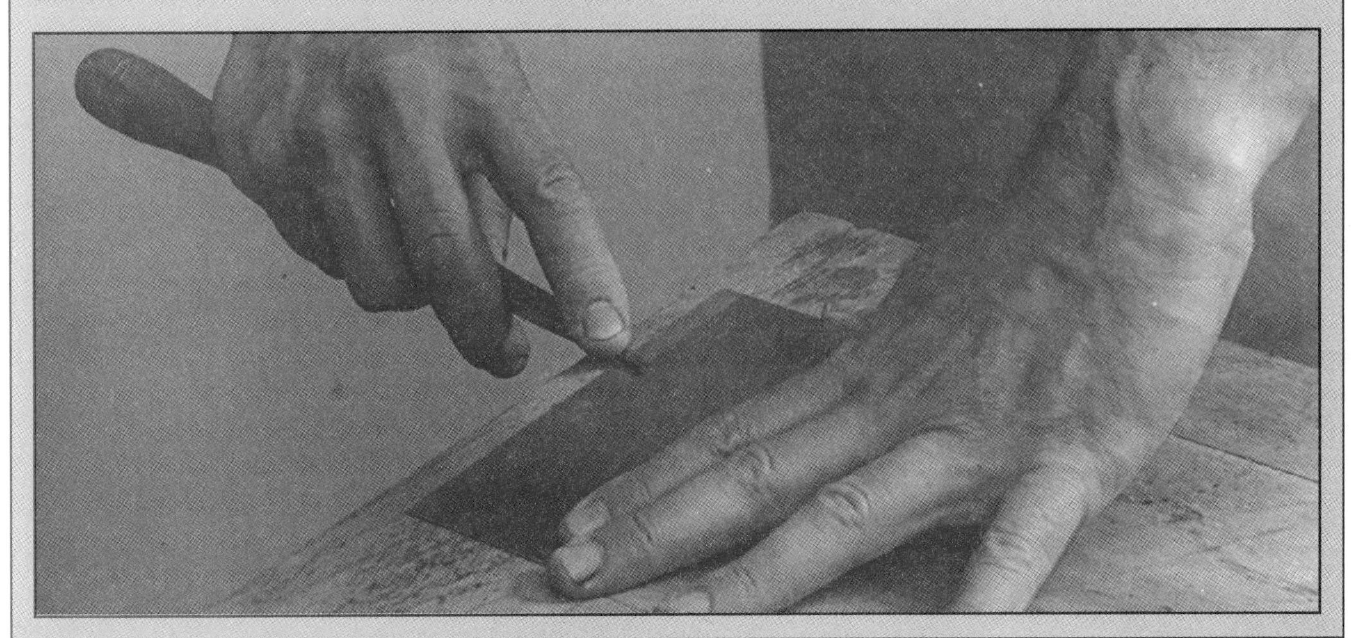

Photo 2-13: To raise a burr, run a burnishing tool back and forth along each edge at an angle just below the horizontal. Use moderate to heavy pressure.

cutting ridges in the wood when you scrape. Then file the long edge flat and square to the sides. File in line with the edge so the file is always in contact with the entire length of the scraper (Photo 2-11 on page 21). Holding the file perpendicular to the edge usually hollows or crowns the edge. You'll know that you've filed enough when the reflected shine of the edge is perfectly even. When you have one edge flat, flip the scraper in your vise and follow the same procedure on the other edge.

Filing the edge leaves small, sharp pieces of metal protruding from the 90-degree junctures. I like to remove these with a fine India stone (almost any stone will do) while the scraper is still in the vise. Make a couple of passes on each side, holding the stone flat against the scraper. No lubricating oil or water is needed. You simply want to remove the overhanging shreds of metal.

Your scraper will still have scratches left by the file. These scratches will transfer to the wood. Some woodworkers whet their scrapers on a soft Arkansas or fine Japanese stone to remove the scratches. But I find it easier and less time-consuming to remove the scratches from the wood by sanding it lightly with 180- or 220-grit sandpaper. I whet my scraper only if I'll be scraping finish, not wood.

If you do whet your scraper, you must not round the 90-degree corners even slightly (Photo 2-12 on page 21), or you won't be able to achieve a sharp rolled burr. This step of whetting the scraper causes so many failures for beginners that I recommend against it while you're learning.

The next step is to roll the burr. This can be done with any tool of steel harder than the relatively soft scraper, as long as the edge of that tool is smooth and slightly rounded; otherwise, it will tear the burr. An automobile valve stem, for instance, will work fine. Special tools for rolling the burr, called burnishing tools, are available. Shapes of burnishing tools vary from triangular (with rounded edges) to oval to round.

There are two steps to making the burr. The first is raising it, and the second is turning it. (Some woodworkers skip the first step.) To raise the burr, lay the scraper flat near the edge of a tabletop or your workbench. Run the burnishing tool back and forth six to ten times along each 90-degree juncture, holding the tool at an angle several degrees below the horizontal and pushing down firmly on it (Photo 2-13). You should hear a ticking sound as the burnisher slides off each end of the scraper and hits your worktable. (The burnisher has been called a "ticketer.") This will raise a burr that you should be able to feel on the edge of the scraper. It's most efficient to raise the burr on all four corners before turning each burr.

To turn the burr, you can hold the scraper and the burnishing tool in a number of different orientations. Probably the easiest is to lay the scraper flat on a tabletop, this time with its edge overhanging the edge of the table. Hold the scraper down with one hand (your left if you're right-handed), and hold the burnishing tool in the other. Position the tool upright with your hand below the scraper. You may have to get down on one knee to do this. Angle the burnisher at about 85 degrees to the plane of the scraper and point it slightly forward. Press the tool against the scraper and push upward and forward as you slide the tool along the edge at this angle (Photo 2-14). Use light to medium pressure. You can make one pass or several. I usually make just one. Then flip the scraper to roll the other three burrs. You should now be able to feel the burr when you run your thumb across the side and over the edge of the scraper.

The scraper and burnisher can be held in any position as long as you maintain the approximate 85-degree angle to the side of the scraper. You can usually reroll the burr several times before having to refile again. Go through both steps of raising and turning the burr each time.

Sharpen curve-edged scrapers in the same way as straight-edged scrapers. Just follow the curve with your file and your burnishing tool. To file the inside edge of a curved scraper, you'll have to use a round or needle-nose file.

The scraper is a relatively easy tool to sharpen. Even so, many woodworkers never quite master the technique, and they give up on the tool. If you have had or are having trouble, I suggest you do what I did when I first learned the technique. Get a couple of scrapers and a piece of wood at least 5 inches wide by a couple of feet in length. Clamp the wood to your workbench, and then alternately sharpen and scrape over and over for an hour or so, until you have the idea of what a sharp scraper feels like and how to make it so.

If you're not successful right away, try varying your burnishing angle and the amount of pressure you're using. Too little pressure and you won't roll the burr. Too much pressure and you'll break it off—a very small wire edge will fall away from the juncture, and you'll have to refile to create your sharp 90-degree angle again. Scrapers are inexpensive, and you can refile them dozens of times before they're too small to use.

Once you've mastered the simple sharpening procedure, which shouldn't take more than a minute or so if you skip the whetting step, you'll wonder how you ever did woodworking without this wonderful tool. ■

Photo 2-14: To turn the burr, push the burnishing tool simultaneously along and up one edge of the scraper. Maintain an 85-degree angle to the side of the scraper and tilt the burnishing tool slightly forward. Use light to moderate pressure.

SHARPENING A CABINET SCRAPER

THE CABINET SCRAPER WORKS on the same principle as the hand scraper. A burr on the long edge of the scraper blade cuts a very thin shaving when the blade is pushed or pulled along the wood. But a cabinet-scraper blade has a 45-degree bevel, and is much easier to sharpen than the hand scraper (Figure 2-6).

A new blade should have a bevel already ground into it. If your blade doesn't have a bevel, begin by clamping the scraper blade in a vise, with the cutting edge protruding about 1 inch above the vise. Then file a bevel of about 45 degrees using a common 8- or 10-inch mill file (Photo 2-15). File so you keep the long edge of the scraper blade and the bevel straight and flat. When the reflected edge of the bevel has an even sheen, remove the blade from the vise and whet both the bevel and the flat side of the blade on a fine sharpening stone—much as you would sharpen a chisel or plane iron (Photo 2-16). Though you can skip this whetting, it is not at all difficult or time-consuming (in contrast to whetting a hand scraper), and the better cutting edge is worth the effort. You don't need to make this edge nearly as perfect as the edge on a plane iron or chisel.

Roll the burr on the cabinet-scraper edge much as you do on a hand scraper.

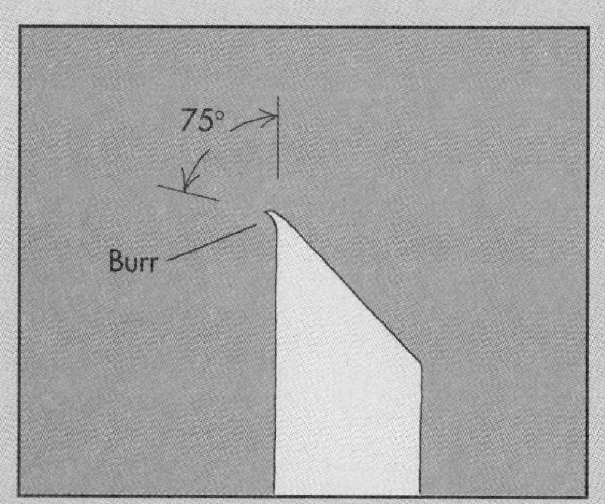

Figure 2-6: Cross section of a sharpened cabinet scraper blade.

Photo 2-15: Clamp the cabinet scraper blade in a vise and file a 45-degree bevel on one edge.

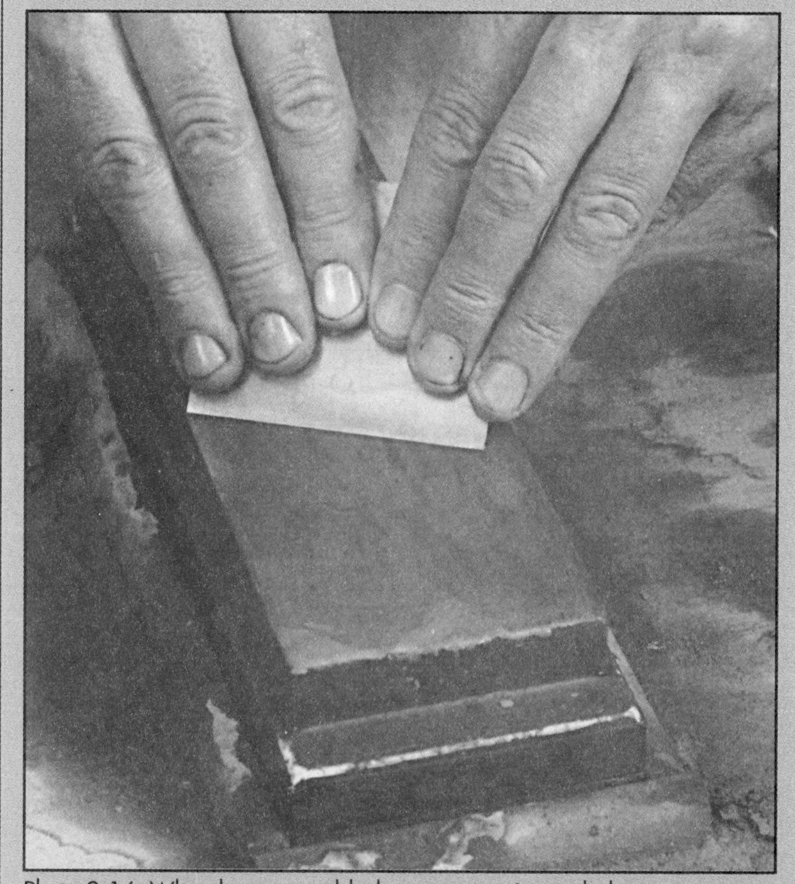

Photo 2-16: Whet the scraper blade on a stone in much the same way you would whet a chisel or plane iron.

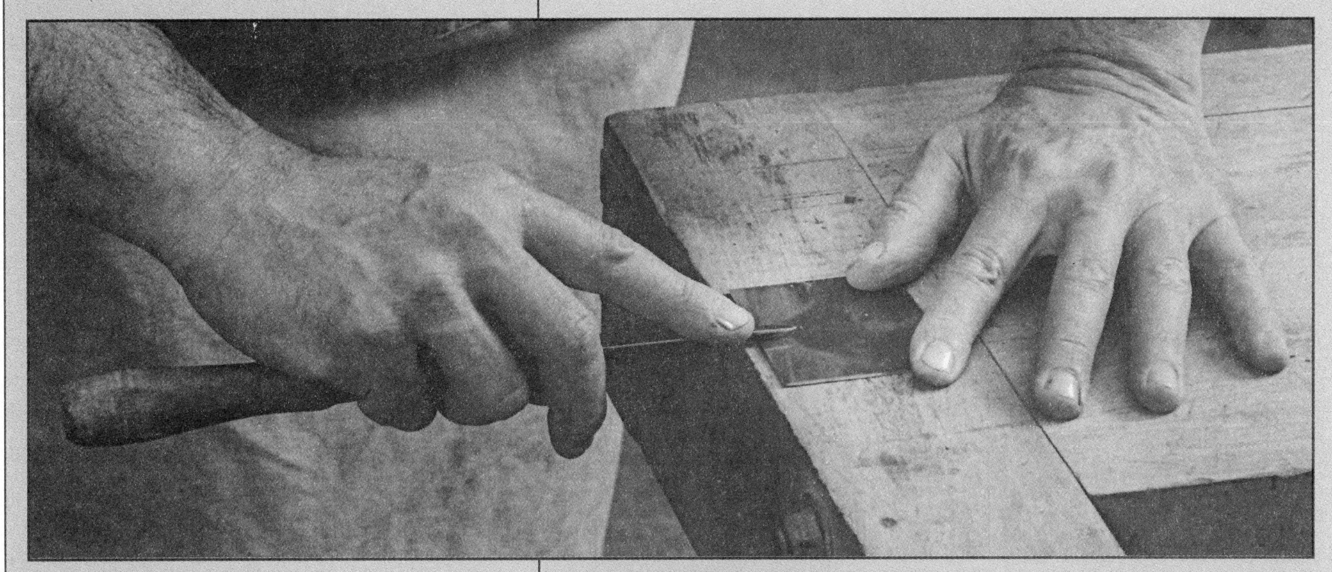

First, raise a burr by burnishing the back (non-beveled) side of the scraper. Lay the scraper blade flat near the edge of a table and run the burnishing tool back and forth six to ten times at an angle just below the horizontal (Photo 2-17). Use moderate to heavy pressure. Then clamp the blade in a vise and turn the burr from the bevel side. Hold the burnishing tool at about a 75-degree angle to the side, angle the tool forward just a little, and push it along the edge (Photo 2-18). You will turn a pronounced burr that should be obvious to both eye and hand.

You can eliminate the first burnishing step on the back side of the blade if you want. And you can turn the burr with several strokes instead of one: in a series of increasing angles, from 45 to 75 degrees. There is no right or wrong way. Different woodworkers do it different ways.

When you replace the blade in the cast-iron body of the cabinet scraper, insert it from the bottom side so as not to damage the burr. The bevel side should face the adjusting thumbscrew. Position the blade so it is exactly even with the flat sole of the body. Then tighten the clamp screws to hold the blade in place. You control the depth of cut by tightening the thumbscrew, which bends the blade to protrude below the sole. ■

Photos 2-17 and 2-18: Raise the burr by burnishing the back of the blade (top), then roll the burr with the burnishing tool held at a 75-degree angle (above). Tilt the tool slightly forward and push it the length of the beveled edge.

(text continued from page 20)

Unless the scraper has been sharpened perfectly, it will leave tiny ridges on the surface of the wood, finer than those left by a planer or jointer that has nicks in its knives. These ridges can be removed easily by a light sanding with 180-grit or finer sandpaper.

Cleaning Off the Dust

Whenever the last step involves using sandpaper, you will leave dust on the wood. This dust must be cleaned off before applying a finish. There are four ways to remove the dust:

- Brush it off.
- Wipe it off with a tack cloth (a cloth made sticky by the application of a very thin, varnishlike material that leaves a gummy residue).
- Vacuum it off.
- Blow it off with compressed air.

Brushing is usually the easiest and most convenient, but probably the least efficient, way of removing dust. Some very fine dust will always be left on the surface and in the pores. Nevertheless, brushing is usually adequate.

A tack cloth can be used after brushing to remove the rest of the surface dust. But a tack cloth still won't pull much of the dust out of the pores of porous woods like oak. Tack cloths are more

SOLVENTS FOR REMOVING CURED GLUES

GLUE	SOLVENT	COMMENT
Animal hide glue	Water	Hot water works much faster.
White glue and yellow glue	Water, acetone (contained in lacquer thinner), glycol ether (contained in water-based stains and finishes), toluene, and xylene.	Scrub with a stiff bristle or brass-wire brush to get the glue out of the pores.
Contact cement	Acetone, lacquer thinner	
Epoxy	None	The impossibility of redissolving this glue is good reason for using it sparingly in woodworking.
Plastic resin glue (urea glue; urea-formaldehyde glue)	None	The impossibility of redissolving this glue is good reason for using it sparingly in woodworking.
Cyanoacrylate glue ("Super Glue"; "Hot Stuff")	Acetone	
Hot-melt glue	Acetone, lacquer thinner, toluene, xylene	Acetone works best.

effective when used between coats of finish. (You shouldn't use a tack cloth when you're using water-based stain or finish. The varnishlike substance will hinder good flow-out and bonding.)

A vacuum is the most efficient way to remove dust if kicking dust into the air might create a problem in your finishing room. Otherwise, compressed air is the most efficient way. Use compressed air outdoors or in a well-ventilated space, where the airborne dust will be evacuated.

Though it seems logical that a better finish will be achieved if absolutely all of the dust is removed from the pores, don't be compulsive about it. You won't be able to see the difference anyway.

GLUE SPLOTCHES

No matter how hard you try to avoid it, it's likely that now and then you will get glue on the surface of the wood during glue-up (Photo 2-19). Either the glue will squeeze out of the joints as you clamp the pieces together, or you will transfer glue to the wood with your fingers.

Here are some tips to help you avoid getting glue on the wood:

- Don't put excessive amounts of glue in the joints. Only when gluing up boards edge to edge should you apply glue liberally. In this case you will want squeeze-out to indicate that you've applied enough glue and tightened the clamps adequately.
- Cut your mortises or dowel holes a little deeper to allow excess glue to collect at the bottom instead of being squeezed out.
- Cut a chamfer around the edge of your mortises and a countersink in your dowel holes to hold excess glue and to keep it from squeezing out (Photo 2-20). You can cut the chamfer with a chisel or rasp and the countersink with a needle-nose rasp, a countersink bit, or an oversized drill bit, used carefully so it doesn't cut too deeply.
- Have both a damp and a dry cloth nearby so you can remove any glue you might get on your hands. Wipe your hands with the damp cloth, then quickly dry them so you won't wet the wood.

Removing Glue from the Wood

There are two ways to remove glue from the wood:

- Redissolve it and wash it off.
- Scrape or sand it off.

If the glue is still wet, it will be easier to wash it off. If the glue has cured, it's usually easier to scrape it off. But it's also possible to wash off cured glue as long as you can dissolve it with water or a solvent. (See "Solvents for Removing Cured Glues" on the facing page.)

Photo 2-19: If any glue remains on the surface of the wood, it will prevent stain and finish penetration and will show up as a lighter splotch.

Photo 2-20: You can reduce glue squeeze-out by cutting chamfers around mortises (and countersinks around dowel holes) to hold excess glue.

If you choose to wash the glue off with water (hot water will work more quickly), you'll have to follow this by sanding the washed area, once it has dried. Or you'll have to wash the entire project. All areas have to be treated alike because any part of the wood that has become wet will show up darker when stained. The problem is worse on soft woods, such as pine, poplar, and soft maple.

To avoid swelling the grain, substitute acetone or lacquer thinner (which contains acetone) for the water. Acetone, toluene, and xylene break down (in effect, strip) white and yellow glue. Taking glue out of the pores with one of these solvents is much like taking paint out of the pores with stripper. You need to scrub the wet surface with a stiff bristle or brass-wire brush. Scrub with the grain so the scratching will be less visible. You'll have to resand the area you've scrubbed to match the surrounding areas.

Instead of dissolving the glue out of the wood, you can always scrape or sand the glue off. The disadvantage of removing glue splotches this way is that it's hard to tell when you've gone deep enough to get all of the glue out of the pores. The glue will still show up lighter under a stain. The advantage is that you don't damage the wood with water. Neither washing nor scraping is necessarily better. I've used both methods, and the one I choose depends on the situation, including whether a rag or a scraper is handy at the moment.

If you are prone to getting a lot of glue on the surface of your work, I suggest you do most of your sanding after you've assembled the piece. I also suggest that you sponge your work after you've finished sanding it. Sponging will highlight deposits of glue in the wood (they'll show up lighter than the surrounding wood) so you can be sure to remove them.

TIP

If you're using a water-based pigment stain over glue splotches caused by white or yellow glue, let the stain dissolve the glue. The solvent in these stains (glycol ether), together with the water, will break down the glue so it can be rubbed off with a cloth or scrubbed off with a bristle brush (a toothbrush works well). Simply leave the stain on top of the glue splotch for a minute or so, and then begin rubbing it with the cloth or scrubbing with the brush. Keep the area wet with stain. You should see the stain begin to "take" in less than a minute. (This trick won't work with any other type of stain.)

Removing Glue Splotches after Staining

Despite your best efforts, you may still have glue splotches after staining. Then what do you do?

It's usually best to scrape or sand the splotches to below the depth of the glue. Then restain. You can use a hand scraper, a paint scraper, or the sharp edge of a chisel used as a scraper. Whether you scrape or sand, you'll have to sand the area back to the same grit you've sanded everywhere else. Then reapply the stain. If there is any color difference between the repaired and unrepaired parts, apply more stain and sand the entire section with the same grit sandpaper while the stain is still wet. (If you are using water-based stain, you will have to use wet/dry sandpaper.) Then wipe off the excess stain. This wet sanding almost always blends the parts.

If you still have a color difference that you can't live with, you may have to strip the entire piece, resand (it's not necessary to get all of the color out of the wood), and start all over with staining.

DENTS, GOUGES, AND HOLES

No matter how careful you are, you will probably dent or gouge your wood somewhere in the preparation or assembly steps, and you may also have small holes, like finish-nail holes, that you'd like to cover up.

Steaming Dents

Dents are compressed wood. They often can be steamed flush, as long as the fibers have not been broken. Steaming swells the wood fibers, filling out the depression. Dents are easiest to steam flush if the surface is horizontal. Put a drop or two of water in the dent with an eyedropper or syringe. Let the water soak in a little. Add some more water, if needed to form a bead over the dent, and then touch the water with a very hot object to turn it into steam (Photo 2-21). You can use a soldering gun, the tip of an iron, or simply a pointed metal object that has been heated over a flame (wipe off any deposited soot before touching the metal to the water).

Steaming out dents is not 100 percent effective or predictable. But it's nearly so. If you'll let the raised grain dry thoroughly before sanding it smooth, you'll usually get away with a mark so slight you can barely see it.

TRY THIS

For especially stubborn dents, cover the water-soaked dent with thin shirt cardboard. Then put a hot iron on top. This traps the steam in the dent, forcing it down into the wood.

CAUTION:
It's often suggested that you lay a damp cloth over the dent and then put a hot iron on top of the cloth to create the steam. This method introduces steam to a much larger area than necessary and may result in a large area of moisture damage that will show through the finish.

Photo 2-21: To remove a dent, swell the wood flush by steaming. Wet the dent with water, enough to form a bead, then touch the water (not the wood) with a soldering gun, the tip of an iron, or any pointed metal object that has been heated over a flame (wipe the metal clean of soot before touching the metal to the water).

Photo 2-22: Patch large gouges and splits with wood of the same species and similar grain pattern. These patches are permanent and easier to disguise than solid-colored wood-putty patches. (The split and gouge in the above walnut board have been patched with pieces of maple for better visibility.)

When the grain has been severed, however, it's seldom possible to raise it flush again. Severed grain should be treated as a gouge. The wood will have to be either cut out and patched with another piece of wood or filled with a foreign material.

Wood Patches

If the gouge is large, a wood patch is best because it will be easier to disguise, and it will be permanent (Photo 2-22). A wood patch is also best for filling splits in the wood and gaps left by poorly fitted joints. A wood patch, its grain aligned with that of the surrounding wood, will shrink and expand with the surrounding wood and be less likely to crack and come out at a later date. Foreign materials, such as wood putty, are not flexible and are seldom permanent when used to fill large gouges, splits, or gaps.

The principle for patching a gouge with wood is the same as for plugging a screw hole. The patch will be less visible, however, if it is diamond shaped, or at least elongated, instead of round or square. Determine the shape you want to use and cut it out of another piece of wood that has a color and grain pattern close to the wood you are replacing. Trace the pattern onto the surface you're repairing, and cut out the necessary wood with a chisel. If the damaged area is large, you can use a router together with a jig to control the cut more exactly. (Alternatively, you can cut out the shape in your damaged surface first, and then transfer the shape to the patch with tracing paper.) It's best to make the patch a little thicker than necessary so it protrudes above the surface of the wood. Trim it flush with a chisel, plane, or hand scraper after the glue has dried.

Patching splits in wood or gaps in joints is easy. Simply cut some thin slivers out of the same type of wood, or use already-cut veneer, and insert the correct thickness into the opening. It's sometimes helpful to taper the sliver a bit so it will slide in easily and fill the gap. After the glue dries, trim the insert flush. This type of repair is usually easy to disguise and is almost as permanent as the surrounding wood.

Wood Putty

It's much less work to use wood putty to fill a gouge, split, or gap than it is to insert a wood patch. Wood putty can be quite effective for filling small defects.

Wood putty is simply a binder such as finish, glue, or gypsum (plaster of paris), and some solid material such as sawdust, whiting (calcium carbonate), or wood flour (very fine sawdust). The binder cures and holds the solid particles together to make the patch. You may not have thought of it before, but most of the wood putties available commercially are the same as the finishes you use, only with some wood flour or whiting added to provide bulk. This explains why wood putties don't take stain easily. Neither do finishes once they have cured.

There are three common types of commercial wood putties—those based on nitrocellulose lacquer, those based on water-based acrylic finish, and those based on gypsum. (See "Wood Putties," below.) You can tell which kind you have by the instructions on the container:

- Nitrocellulose-based wood putties can be thinned or cleaned up with acetone or lacquer thinner (which contains acetone).
- Water-based acrylic wood putties can be cleaned up with water until they harden.
- Gypsum-based wood putties come in powder form. You mix them with water.

Homemade wood putties are usually made from glue and sawdust. Take some fine sawdust, preferably from the same wood

WOOD PUTTIES

TYPE: Nitrocellulose-based

WORKING PROPERTIES:

Cures very fast. Thins and cleans up with acetone or lacquer thinner (which contains acetone).

TYPE: Acrylic-based

WORKING PROPERTIES:

Cleans up with water until it has cured. Then cleans up with acetone, toluene, or xylene. Difficult to thin effectively. Often sold in tubes.

TYPE: Gypsum-based

WORKING PROPERTIES:

Sold as a powder you mix with water. Does not redissolve once it has cured.

TIP

If the depression is deep, it's best to apply several coats of putty to build it level with the surface. One thick layer will take a long time to cure throughout and will probably crack from uneven curing. Let each application cure hard before applying the next.

NOTE

Ready-made colored putties, usually identified by the names of the woods they are designed to imitate, are not meant to look like the wood after it's stained. These putties can often be used successfully if you don't intend to stain.

you are going to patch, and mix it with any type of glue. Epoxy, white glue, and yellow glue are preferred. Use a minimum amount of glue with a maximum amount of sawdust. If you use too much glue, the patch will be much darker than the surrounding wood.

Whichever wood putty you use, apply it the same way. Take a little putty on a putty knife (or dull screwdriver if the hole is small), and push it down in the hole or gouge. If the depression is not very deep, smooth off the top by pulling the knife across the surface toward you. You want the putty to form a very slight mound so that when it shrinks as it dries, it won't leave a hollow. It's best not to manipulate the putty any more than necessary, since it becomes increasingly unworkable the longer it's exposed to air. Don't be sloppy. The binder in the putty is finish, glue, or plaster, so it will bond to any part of the wood it comes in contact with, preventing stain penetration and leaving a splotch.

Once the putty is thoroughly cured, sand it level with the surrounding wood. If you're working on a flat surface, back the sandpaper with a flat block.

To match the surrounding area, wood putty patches can be colored in one of two ways:

- Color the putty while it's still in paste form.
- Color the patch after it has cured.

To color the putty itself, you can use universal tinting colors, available at most paint or art-supply stores. Universal tinting colors will work with the three commercial types of wood putty as well as with homemade glue-and-sawdust mix. The color you want to match is the color the wood will be after it is stained and finished. It may take some experimentation to arrive at that color. You can practice on some scrap wood. The trick is to judge the colors while they are still damp. At that stage, the colors will be close to what you'll get when the finish is applied. The color of the dry stain or putty will not be accurate.

It's usually easier to color the putty before applying it, but you can get better results by coloring the patch after it is dry and has been sanded smooth. This is because wood is seldom uniform in color. It almost always has subtle differences as a result of grain and figure variations.

To color a putty patch, you should apply your stain (if you're using one) and your first coat of finish (the sealer coat) to the entire surface, in order to see the correct colors you want to imitate. (See "Sealers and Sanding Sealers" on page 133.) Once this sealer coat is dry, you need to paint in the grain and figure and the background color. The background color is the lightest color visible in the surrounding wood. You may also want to scratch pores into the patch with the point of a knife in order to imitate

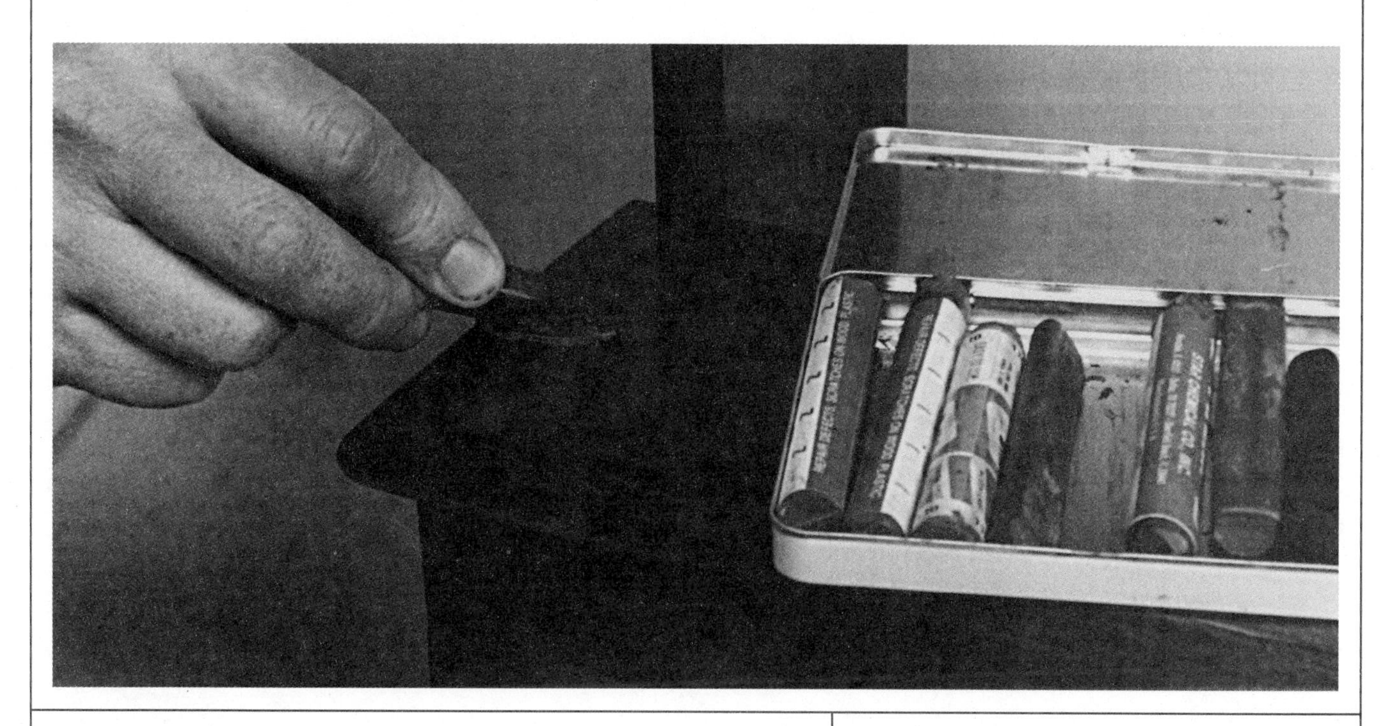

Photo 2-23: It's usually easiest to repair very small defects such as nail holes using a wax crayon after you have applied the finish.

deep-porous woods such as oak, mahogany, or walnut. (For instructions on graining a solid-colored patch to look like wood, see Chapter 16: "Repairing Finishes.")

No matter what you use to patch gouges, and no matter how well you color the patch, it will probably show after a few years. The surrounding wood will darken or lighten differently than the patch, causing the patch to stand out. The only way to avoid this problem entirely is not to patch. The closest you can come to keeping the colors the same is to make the patch from wood taken from scraps of the board it is set into.

Wax Crayons

It's seldom worth trying to fill small nail holes with wood putty. You'll make a mess around the hole because the putty will stick wherever it touches the wood. It's usually easier to wait until you complete the finishing. Then rub over the hole with a wax crayon of a close color. Wax crayons in wood tones are available at most paint stores and home centers. As long as the hole is small, you won't see the patch unless you look for it.

Chapter 3

Tools for Applying Finishes

There are only four tools for applying finishes: rags, brushes, rubbing pads, and spray guns. This minimal tool kit is a main difference between finishing and woodworking. In woodworking there are countless tools, with new ones coming on the market all the time. If you're a woodworker, you spend a good deal of time learning about the different tools, how they work, and the tricks they're capable of.

Finishing is very different. There aren't many tricks you can do with the four tools. The sole purpose of using one of these finishing tools, other than to keep your hands clean, is to apply the finish so it's smooth and level. You could, after all, pour a finish onto the wood and spread it around with your hand. After the finish cured hard, you could sand it level, rub it with rubbing compounds, and achieve presentable results. But it would be much easier if you applied the finish smoothly enough in the first place for you not to have to sand at all, or at least very little, to make the surface level.

You use the four finishing tools to apply smooth, level coats of finish. Here's what you need to know about these tools.

RAGS

The rags you use in finishing should be made of cotton. Polyester and other synthetic fabrics don't work well because they aren't absorbant enough. You can often substitute cheap paper towels for cloth rags if you don't have a supply of used rags—especially

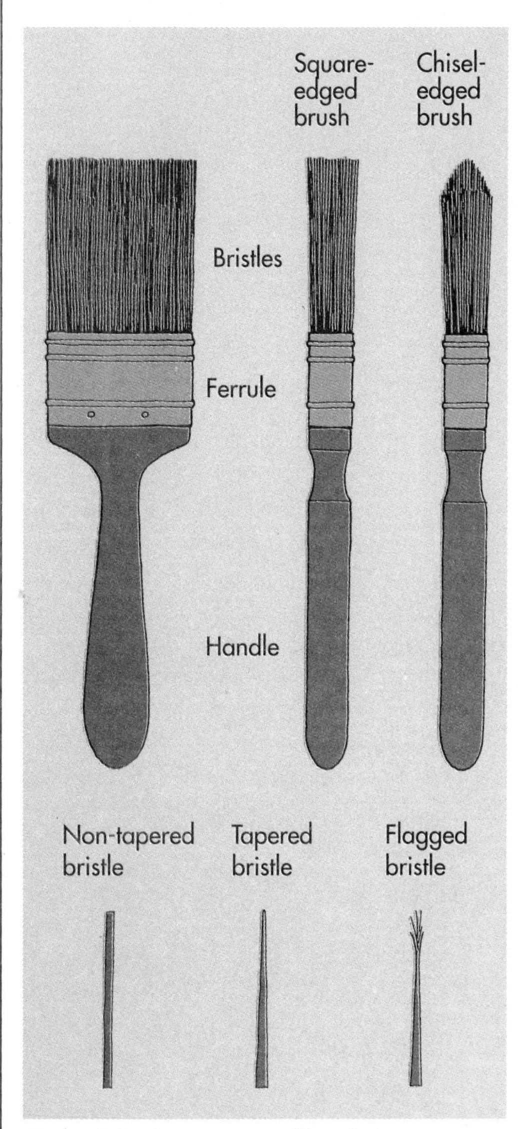

Figure 3-1: An anatomy of brushes.

when working with products that don't contain water. When working with products that do contain water, you can substitute Scott Rags, which are a paper product available at many home centers and discount stores. These rags won't fall apart when they get wet.

BRUSHES

Brushes are among the earliest finishing tools. Though the increasing popularity of spray equipment is making brushes less important, it's rare that a finisher doesn't own at least a few brushes.

Choosing a Brush

A good-quality brush is important if you expect good results. Good-quality brushes hold more finishing material (so you don't have to replenish the brush as often), and they spread the material more smoothly than poor-quality brushes.

There are three types of brushes: natural bristle, synthetic bristle, and sponge. There are also pad applicators, which may be regarded as a type of brush, since they are used in the same manner.

Natural- and synthetic-bristle brushes are made of bristles glued together at the top with epoxy and held to a wooden or plastic handle by a metal wrapping called a *ferrule*. The quality of the handle, glue, and ferrule varies and usually corresponds to the quality of the bristles. You can almost always judge the quality of a brush by its bristles (Figure 3-1).

There are three good qualities to look for in bristles:

- The bristles are arranged to form a chisel shape; the brush is not cut off square.
- Each bristle is tapered—thinner at the tip than at the ferrule.
- The tip of each bristle is *flagged*—that is, split into several strands.

Chisel-edged brushes (the center bristles are longer than the bristles on each flat side) do a much better job of putting on a smooth coat of finish than square-edged brushes. Square-edged brushes are cheaper and are useful for applying stripper or bleach, where smoothness is not important.

Tapered bristles perform better than non-tapered bristles. The thickness of the bristles near the ferrule provides strength. The thinness at the tip allows more bristles to come in contact with the surface. More bristles means the brush will hold more finish and spread it more smoothly.

Flagging doubles or triples the number of bristle fibers that

Photo 3-1: (Left to right) chisel-edged, square-edged, and foam brushes and a pad applicator.

contact the surface. As a result, flagged bristles carry more finish and apply it more smoothly than bristles that are not flagged.

The difference between natural and synthetic bristles is the difference between hair and plastic. Hair softens and becomes uncontrollable in water; plastic doesn't. Therefore, natural-bristle brushes do not perform well in water-based stains or finishes; synthetic-bristle brushes do. Both types perform well with all solvent-based stains and finishes, though most painters and finishers prefer the results they get from natural bristles.

Natural-bristle brushes are made from animal hair. The best brushes for applying solvent-based finishes are made from the hair of Chinese hogs. Synthetic-bristle brushes are made from polyester or nylon or both. For most people the best size brush for applying a finish is 2 to 3 inches wide with bristles 2 to 3 inches long.

Foam brushes are popular because they don't leave brush marks. But they do tend to leave distinct ridges at the edge of each brush stroke, where more finish is deposited. Foam brushes are cheap and, therefore, especially useful when you want to throw the brush away after using it rather than clean it. Foam brushes will dissolve in lacquer thinner and, depending on the type of foam used, possibly in alcohol. This means you shouldn't use these tools with lacquer or shellac.

Pad applicators have thousands of short filaments attached to a foam backing. They perform much like foam brushes, except that they're mounted in a flat plastic or metal holder, so they are useful only on flat surfaces. Because they hold a lot of finish, and they come in large sizes, they are popular with floor finishers.

MYTH

Some finishes are meant to be brushed, some are meant to be wiped, and some are meant to be sprayed.

FACT

All finishes can be brushed, wiped, or sprayed. (The wood can even be dipped into the finish.) Brushes, rags, and spray guns are simply tools for transferring the liquid finish from the can to the wood.

MYTH

You should brush first across the grain and then with the grain.

FACT

You can do this if you want to with slow-curing finishes, such as varnish and polyurethane, but you don't gain anything by it.

Pad applicators, like foam brushes, should not be used with lacquer or shellac.

Using Brushes

Here are the essentials for brushing a finish. Remember, your goal is to get the finish as smooth and level as you can.

- If your brush is new, hit the ferrule against your hand to shake out any loose bristles.
- Pour enough finish for the job at hand into another container, such as a coffee can or wide-mouthed jar. This way you won't contaminate your entire supply if your brush picks up some dirt.
- Hold the brush by the metal ferrule with the handle resting between your thumb and first finger. Dip the brush into the finish so about one-third to one-half of the bristle length is submerged in the liquid. Raise the brush and tap it against the side of the container to remove enough of the excess liquid so the brush won't drip.
- On large, flat surfaces, don't begin brushing with a fully loaded brush right at the edge of the panel, or else your finish material will run over the edge. Begin brushing about 2 inches from the edges. Brush toward the edges and then away from them, gradually covering the whole panel. You can begin brushing at either the front or back edge of a horizontal surface. Just be sure to position your container of finish so you won't be passing your finish-laden brush over just-coated wood.
- With each new brushload of finish, begin brushing a few inches ahead of your last stroke, and work back to it and then away from it.
- Brush with the grain of the wood so the ridges left by your brush will be less noticeable.
- On turnings, carvings, moldings, and other irregular surfaces, reduce the amount of liquid in your brush so you don't cause runs or puddles in recesses. It's easier to brush around rather than along the length of turnings.

Cleaning and Storing Brushes

You must clean and store your brushes properly after use, or they can become ruined and you may have to throw them out. Shellac and lacquer are the only finishes that allow you to fully reclaim a brush after the finish has cured.

If you are planning to use the brush with the same finish later that day or the next day, you can store the brush in the appropriate solvent or thinner (mineral spirits for oil, varnish, or polyurethane; alcohol for shellac; lacquer thinner for lacquer; and water for water base). Or you can wrap the brush in plastic wrap to shield it from air. If you store the brush in solvent or thinner, run a dowel rod or string through the hole in the handle (or drill one closer to the ferrule) and suspend the bristles in the solvent or thinner so the bristles aren't bent under the weight of the brush (Photo 3-2). You can reduce solvent or thinner evaporation from the container by covering it with a plastic coffee-can lid. Cut a hole in the middle of the lid for the brush handle to pass through.

If the finish you're using is water base, you can clean your brush by washing it in a bucket of water. After removing most of the finish with water alone, wash the brush again in soap and water. If you're using any other type of finish, follow these steps:

1. Wash the brush in the proper solvent or thinner. Sometimes you can wash the brush successfully by squeezing it against the bottom of a container that has an inch or two of solvent or thinner in it. But you may have to swish the solvent or thinner through the bristles with your fingers to get the finish loose near the ferrule. Wear gloves when doing this.
2. Repeat Step 1 in clean solvent or thinner until the brush is almost clean.
3. Wash again, this time in lacquer thinner. Lacquer thinner will remove the oiliness left by mineral spirits thinner, and it will remove any remaining finish.
4. After each cleaning, remove the excess solvent or thinner by shaking the brush or holding it between the palms of both hands and twirling it inside an empty finish can.
5. Wash the brush in soap and water, running your fingers through the bristles to be sure there isn't any remaining finish stuck to them. (This step is optional. Many finishers don't like to put water on their brushes. Personally, I don't see that it does any harm, and it does clean the brush better.)
6. If the bristles aren't straight, comb them out with a brush comb, available at paint stores. (A fork will also work.)
7. If you use the brush solely for oil or varnish finishes, rub a couple of drops of a light oil, such as mineral oil, onto the bristles. The oil will help keep the bristles soft, but it will interfere with all other finishes, so don't apply oil to general-purpose brushes.
8. Wrap the brush in heavy, absorbent paper such as construction paper, a brown paper bag, or heavy paper towels. Hold the paper in place with a rubber band or masking tape (Photo 3-3). This step is very important for keeping the bristles straight and clean as they dry out.
9. Store the brush flat in a drawer or hang it from a hook.

Keeping brushes in good shape is more mental than physical (it takes only 5 or 10 minutes). Make cleaning your brush a part of your routine. You will feel so much better the next time you use

Photo 3-2: You can store a brush temporarily without cleaning it by hanging it in a container of the appropriate thinner or solvent or by wrapping it in plastic wrap.

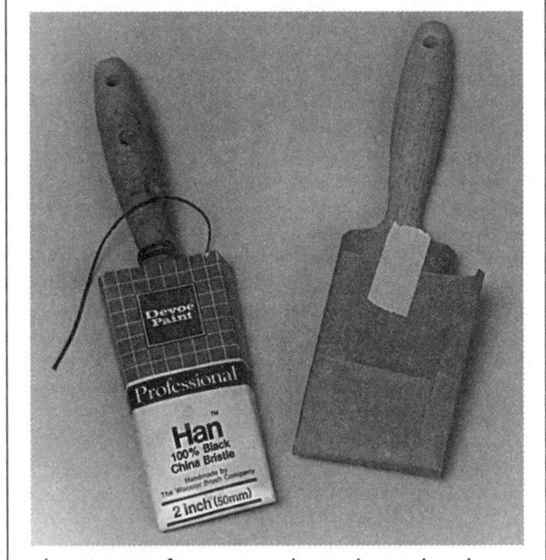

Photo 3-3: After you've cleaned your brush, wrap it in its original holder or in heavy absorbant paper to keep the bristles straight and clean.

TIP

If the finish does dry hard on your brush, there are several ways to reclaim the brush:

- For shellac and lacquer, soak the brush in the appropriate solvent (alcohol for shellac; lacquer thinner for lacquer) or wash the brush in a strong solution of trisodium phosphate (TSP), available at paint and hardware stores.
- For water base, soak the brush in paint-and-varnish remover, acetone, toluene, or xylene, and then wash with TSP.
- For oil, varnish, and polyurethane, try soaking the brush in paint-and-varnish remover, and then washing with TSP. It will be difficult to break all the finish away from the bristles.

MYTH

The outer cloth of a rubbing pad serves to control the discharge of finish from the inner cloth.

FACT

The outer cloth is used to pull the pad tight and remove wrinkles. It has no effect on the discharge of finish. When both cloths are wrapped tightly together, the wetness of the finish penetrates as if they were one cloth.

the brush if it is soft and springy instead of stiff and difficult to work. If you keep a brush clean and the bristles straight, it will provide good service for years. Only when the flagged bristles wear off will you have to buy a new brush. Use your worn brushes for less exacting tasks, such as applying stripper.

RUBBING PADS

Rubbing pads are very useful tools for French polishing and padding, and for rubbing out finishes. Make your own rubbing pad with two pieces of cloth—an outer cloth that doesn't stretch and an inner cloth that will absorb and hold liquid. Tightly woven cheesecloth, cotton, or linen is best for the outer cloth. Loosely woven cheesecloth, T-shirt cotton, or sweater wool is best for the inner cloth. (Polyester and other synthetics don't work well for either the outer or inner cloth.) Wrap the outer cloth tightly around a wad of the inner cloth to make the pad, as shown in Photos 3-4, 3-5, and 3-6. Draw the outer cloth tight during use to remove wrinkles from the bottom of the pad.

SPRAY GUNS AND EQUIPMENT

A spray gun is the most efficient of the four tools for applying finishes. You can lay down an almost perfectly smooth and level coat of finish on a large surface in a short time. Spray guns shoot a stream of fluid that is broken up into a mist of tiny droplets by two jets of air coming out of the horns on the air nozzle. The droplets hit the wood and flow together to make a smooth film. The breaking up of the finish into droplets is called *atomization.* It's important that the atomization be thorough, or the droplets won't flow together well.

The trick to achieving proper atomization is getting the right amount of air striking the fluid as it comes out of the tip of the gun. If you have too little air, the atomization won't be great enough, and the finish won't flow together. It will cure looking like the surface of an orange; the effect is called *orange peel.* If you have too much air, the finish will dry before it hits the wood, producing a dusty look. This is called *dry spray.* (See "Common Spraying Problems" on page 42.)

The two air jets that direct the atomizing air have an additional function. Because they are placed 180 degrees apart, in the horns of the air nozzle, they force the atomized air into an oval-shaped pattern called a *fan.* The fan is perpendicular to the line of the horns. By increasing the air flow through these jets, you widen the fan, so you can coat a wider area with each pass. By decreasing the airflow, you shrink the fan to a very small circular

Photo 3-4: Take a 6 x 6-inch piece of well-washed, tightly woven cotton or linen cloth, such as a bed sheet, a handkerchief, or cheesecloth, and put a wad of soft cotton or wool in the middle. If you are using cloth, fold it so it doesn't have wrinkles. If you are working on a large surface, use a large wad to make a large pad. Use a small wad for small surfaces.

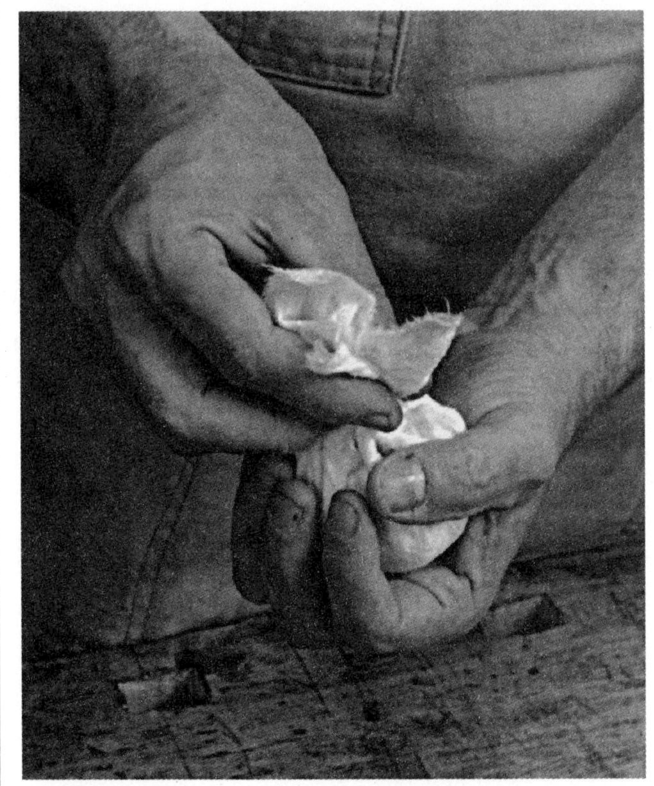

Photo 3-5: Lift the four corners of the outer cloth to a point and twist them.

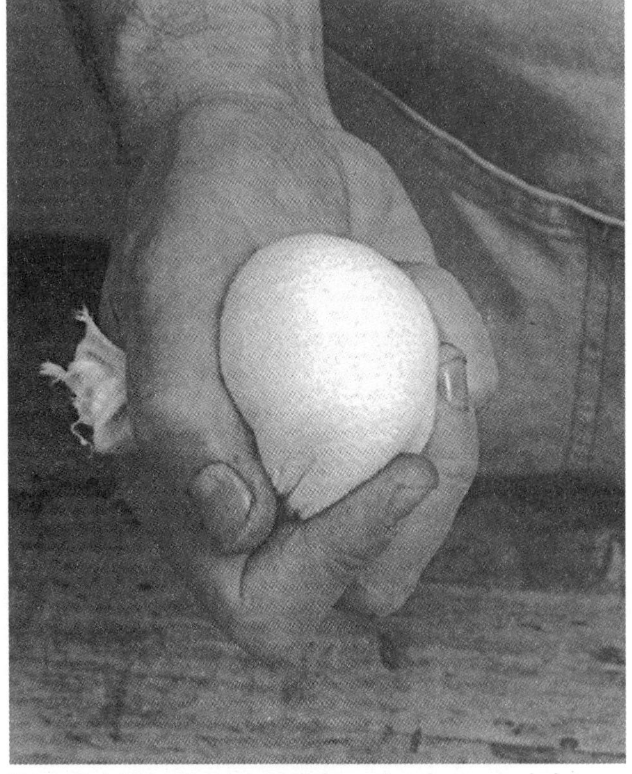

Photo 3-6: Twist the corners tight so that the outer cloth is drawn taut around the inner cloth. The bottom of the pad should feel smooth and be free of wrinkles.

COMMON SPRAYING PROBLEMS

PROBLEMS AND POSSIBLE CAUSES

Orange peel
- Inadequate atomization
- Insufficient solvent or thinner
- Gun held too close to the surface or moved too slowly, causing the finish to ripple

Dry spray
- Excessive atomization
- Overspray falling on already-sprayed surface
- Gun held too far from the surface or moved too rapidly

Runs or sags
- Finish applied too heavily
- Gun held too close to the surface or moved too slowly
- Finishing material thinned too much
- Trigger not released at the end of each stroke when the stroke doesn't go beyond the object
- Gun not held perpendicular to the surface

Gun sputters
- Clogged air vent in cup lid
- Finishing material is too thick
- Insufficient material in the cup or tipping the cup at an acute angle
- Leaky connection at fluid nozzle or needle-valve packing nut

Finish leaks from fluid nozzle of spray gun
- Needle-valve packing nut too tight
- Needle-valve packing itself in need of oil
- Damaged fluid-nozzle tip or needle-valve stem
- Wrong size needle-valve stem
- Worn or broken needle-valve stem spring

Finish leaks from cup
- Worn-out gasket

Orange peel.

Dry spray.

Runs or sags.

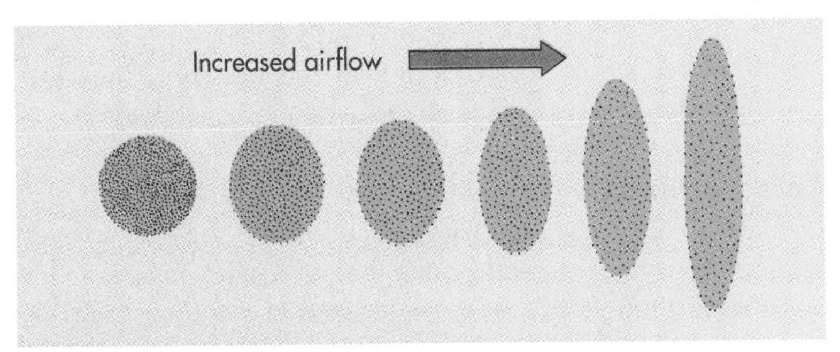

Figure 3-2: You can change the spray pattern by increasing or decreasing the airflow through the horns of the air nozzle. Increasing the airflow enlarges the fan. Decreasing the airflow shrinks the fan until it becomes a small circular pattern.

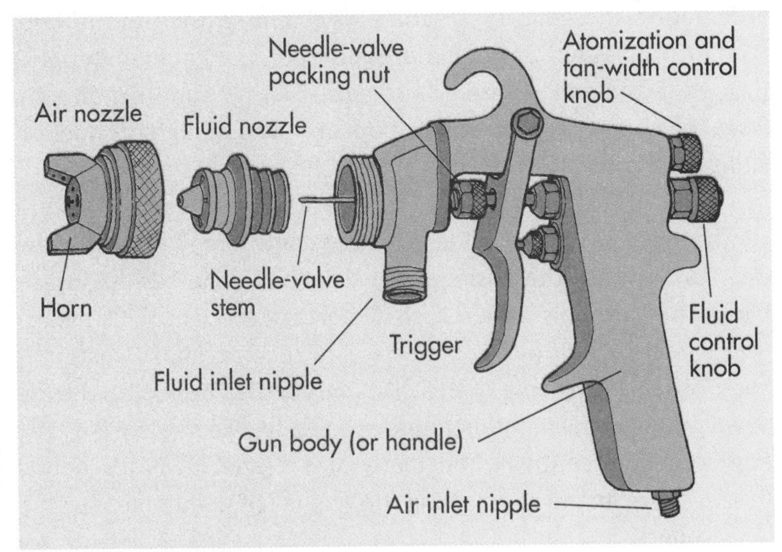

Figure 3-3: Anatomy of a spray gun.

pattern, which you can use to fill in small defects (Figure 3-2). By rotating the air nozzle, you can change the angle of the fan relative to the gun.

Most spray guns have two control knobs on the back side of the gun (Figure 3-3). The lower knob sets the amount you can depress the trigger, and therefore how much finish will be discharged. The upper knob controls the amount of air discharged, and therefore the amount of atomization and the width of the fan. Some spray guns have only the knob that controls the trigger and finish discharge. The airflow is constant. These spray guns usually let you control the fan pattern by turning the air nozzle.

There are two common types of spray guns used in finishing, and two common sources of air to the guns:

- Conventional (low volume/high pressure) spray guns work with compressed air and blast the finish onto the wood at 25 to 80 psi (pounds per square inch).

TRY THIS

To see how the adjusting screw knobs affect the fan pattern and atomization, close both knobs all the way. Then open the air-adjustment knob about one-quarter. Hold your gun about 6 to 8 inches away from a surface and begin spraying. Continue spraying while you open the lower, fluid-adjustment knob until you get a wet coat as you move the gun across the surface at about the speed of brushing. Change back to the upper, air-adjustment knob, opening it further as you continue to spray. You'll see the finish thin out until it doesn't wet the surface anymore; it just dusts it with already-dry finish. When the air-adjustment knob is fully open, begin opening the fluid-adjustment knob further. The finish will begin to wet the surface again. The optimal balance depends on how much pressure you spray with, how thin your material is, and how large a fan pattern you want to spray. You'll know the balance is right when the finish flows together well on the surface.

MYTH

HVLP spray guns are for water-based finishes only.

FACT

HVLP is simply a method of transferring liquid from a container to the wood. You can spray any liquid through it. Both conventional and HVLP spray guns can be used to apply any stain or finish.

Photo 3-7: Conventional spray gun with a cup and air compressor.

- HVLP (high volume/low pressure) spray guns work with either compressed air or turbine air and lay the finish onto the wood softly at 4 to10 psi. These guns create much less overspray.

Conventional Spray Guns and Compressors

Conventional spray guns and compressors were developed around the turn of the century, and their design has changed little since then (Photo 3-7). Air is compressed in a holding tank and then fed through a hose, either directly to the spray gun or simultaneously to the spray gun and to a separate pressure pot that holds the finish or paint. When the air is fed directly to the gun, the air siphons the finishing material out of a cup, which is attached to the gun, by creating a vacuum in the fluid nozzle. When the air is fed through a pressure pot, the liquid material is pushed to the gun, where it is atomized by air supplied directly from the compressor. Pressure pots are used in high-production situations; cups are used for low production.

Conventional spray guns have proven their value during a century of use. They provide excellent control of the liquid material that reaches the surface. But they have one serious drawback: They are only about 20 to 30 percent efficient. This means that well over half of the material you're spraying is wasted: It goes into the air. (Some of this *overspray* settles back onto the finished surface, making it feel dusty or sandy.) This waste was tolerated until recently, when many states and localities began passing laws aimed at reducing the release of pollutants into the atmosphere.

HVLP

HVLP spray guns were developed more than 30 years ago but are only recently becoming popular. HVLP guns can work with either compressed air or continuous air supplied by a turbine. Either way, the result is a low-pressure spray that creates very little overspray. HVLP guns are 65 to 90 percent efficient, which means that most of the material you're spraying ends up on the wood.

There are two advantages to using a turbine over a compressor with an HVLP spray gun:

- A turbine passes a high volume of air directly to the gun at about 4 psi. A compressor generates much higher pressure at lower volume. In order to raise the volume enough to operate the HVLP gun, the high-pressure air must be sent through a regulator. This transforms the high pressure to high volume and low pressure. It takes a large, expensive 3- to 5-horsepower compressor to adequately supply an HVLP gun, compared to a small, inexpensive turbine.
- Turbines warm and dry the air, which speeds curing and helps

reduce blushing (a moisture-related, off-white color that appears as some finishes cure).

There are also two advantages to using a compressor over a turbine:

- A compressor that is large enough (5-horsepower or larger) can generate more pressure at the gun than do commonly available turbines—up to 10 psi. This translates into more finish material being deposited onto the wood surface at a faster rate. The increase allows you to coat an object in less time. Turbine-supplied HVLP spray guns don't put out as much material as compressor-supplied HVLP guns or, for that matter, compressor-supplied conventional guns.
- A compressor can be used for other shop tasks, such as powering compressed-air woodworking tools and blowing dust off your work. Turbines are ineffective at these tasks.

Generally, amateurs and low-production shops use turbine-supplied air to run their HVLP spray guns (Photo 3-8). Often, large shops that have compressed air for other purposes will use it to run their guns.

Photo 3-8: HVLP gun powered by a turbine.

Comparing Conventional and HVLP Spray Systems

Conventional spray guns continue to be used because the investment has already been made, and many people like to stick with tools they're used to. But HVLP guns and turbines are gaining favor, especially for low-production situations. If you are just starting out and don't already have a large compressor, I suggest you get an HVLP spray gun and run it with a turbine.

Whichever type spray gun or spray system you choose, deciding which specific one to buy is much like deciding on a woodworking machine tool. Generally, the more you pay the greater your possibilities for fine adjustment.

Using Spray Guns

There are three tricks for using a spray gun successfully.

- Use the fluid nozzle, air nozzle, and needle-valve stem sizes recommended by the manufacturer for the type of finish you're applying.
- Get optimum atomization of the finishing material.
- Use proper techniques for applying the finish to the wood.

Various sizes of fluid nozzles, air nozzles, and needle-valve stems are offered by most spray-gun manufacturers. Generally, the standard parts that come with your gun are appropriate for all types of clear finish. But you may need different sizes for paint or colored lacquers. Check with your supplier or the manufacturer.

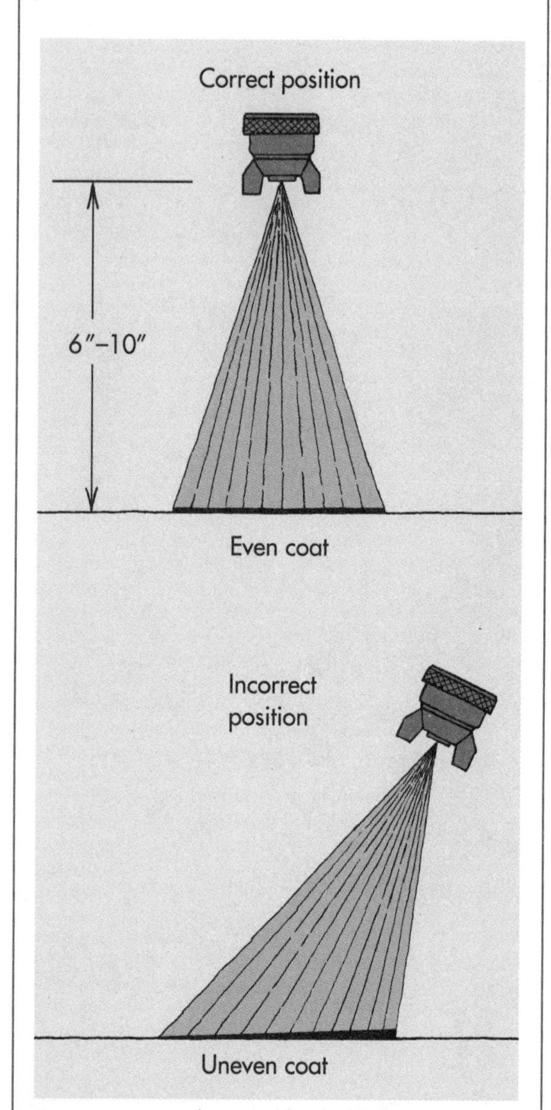

Figure 3-4: For best results, hold the spray gun perpendicular to the surface you're spraying, and move it in a straight line over the wood.

Optimum atomization can be attained, as I've described on page 43, by manipulating the discharge ratio of finishing material to airflow. It can also be attained by using thinners. The thinner the fluid, the less air pressure it takes to atomize it.

Manufacturers of finishes often recommend the optimum viscosity for spraying their finishes. You can follow those recommendations for thinning the finish, or you can use the following rule of thumb: Thin the finish until the stream of liquid that runs off a stirring stick breaks cleanly into drops, and there's no longer any stringiness in the liquid. This viscosity will give you good results.

Proper spraying techniques are very logical. They take a little practice, but they're not hard to learn. Here are the basic principles for quality spraying:

- Plan a systematic spraying routine that will reduce waste and overspray. On a chair, for example, spray the insides of the legs and stretchers first, then work around the outside. Follow by spraying the back of the chair back, the arms and chair seat (if there are any), and then the front of the chair back. Always work from less visible to more visible areas.
- Arrange a light source above and in front of you so you can see what's happening by looking at the reflection in the surface.
- Keep the spray gun pointed perpendicular to the surface of the wood. Don't rock the gun from side to side, or you will get an uneven build (Figure 3-4).
- Set your gun to a fan pattern that covers the surface with the fewest passes and the least overspray. Use a small fan pattern on edges, rails, turnings, and other narrow surfaces. Use a wide fan pattern on large, wide surfaces.
- Begin spraying 6 inches to the side of the wood, and move the spray onto the wood. Keep moving at a uniform speed—about what you would use if you were brushing.
- Keep the gun a uniform distance from the surface of the wood—between 6 and 10 inches. If you move it too close, you will make runs; move it too far away, and you will have dry spray. You usually have to hold an HVLP gun several inches closer to the wood than you do a conventional gun.
- Finish your stroke several inches past the edge of the wood. Make it a habit to release the trigger of the gun at the end of each stroke. Otherwise, you may deposit excessive amounts of finish in situations where the stroke doesn't go off the wood, such as where a stretcher joins a leg.
- Overlap each previous stroke by half. This will give an even thickness overall. This is especially critical when you're applying colored material. Uneven thickness will result in streaking.

- Spray the edges of tabletops or flat panels before you spray the top.
- Don't spray directly into inside corners. Spray each side of the corner instead.
- Don't be intimidated by stories you may hear about how hard it is to do good spraying. It's not. Learning to use a spray gun is no harder than learning to use a table saw or router. The first time you pull the trigger, you won't feel much control. Within an hour or so, you'll get comfortable.

Cleaning and Storing Spray Guns

Cleaning your spray gun thoroughly is very important. If you leave finish to harden in the gun, the gun will become unusable, and it may be very difficult to get it clean again. Follow these steps:

1. Spray solvent through the gun after each day of use, or anytime you won't be using the gun for several hours. This is especially critical with water base and varnish, which are difficult to remove once cured. The best solvent to use for all finishes is lacquer thinner.
2. Remove the air nozzle and needle-valve stem after each day of use. Store them in lacquer thinner solvent, or clean them and put them back in the gun.
3. Some finishers also like to remove the fluid nozzle and clean it. This step is especially important when you finish a project and won't be using your gun for a while.
4. If you're using a cup with the spray gun, clean the cup thoroughly, including the gasket. Be sure to keep the air inlet hole at the top of the cup clean and open at all times. The spray gun will sputter if this hole gets clogged with finish. If you're spraying finish through a pressure pot, clean it and the hose thoroughly.

Where to Spray

You can spray in a garage with the doors open, or outdoors, preferably in the shade when there's a very slight breeze. Or you can spray indoors with an exhaust system to remove the fumes and overspray. The best setup for indoors is a spray booth, which exhausts the air through a filter that catches all the solid finish particles. Don't use a fan in a window unless it is an explosion-proof fan, which has a shielded motor. Otherwise, sparks from the motor might ignite lacquer and varnish fumes; also, the solid particles from your overspray will build up on the fan's electrical components, increasing the fire hazard.

> **TIP**
>
> Many finishes, both clear and colored, are available in aerosol cans. For small jobs, you may find it easier to use an aerosol can instead of a spray gun.

Photo 3-9: The best setup for spraying indoors is a spray booth equipped with an explosion-proof fan.

Chapter 4

Oil Finishes

In the last few decades, oil finishes have become among the most popular finishes used by woodworkers. This is partly due to the pleasing, close-to-the-wood look that oil finishes produce. But it is primarily due to how easy they are to apply. In most cases all you have to do is wipe on and then wipe off a couple of coats. (See "Applying 'Oil' Finishes" on page 51.)

In spite of the ease of application (or maybe because of it) there is a great deal of confusion about oil finishes. Here are some of the most commonly asked questions about oil finishes:

- Does oil protect as well from inside the wood as other finishes do on the surface of the wood?
- Is it better to rub the oil into the wood?
- Do more coats produce more gloss?
- Is boiled linseed oil made by boiling raw linseed oil? Can you make your own?
- Is tung oil better than linseed oil?
- What is Danish oil or teak oil? Moreover, what is antique oil or Val-Oil?
- What is the best way to maintain an oil finish?

To answer these questions—to know what to expect from oil finishes and how to choose between them—you need to overcome three prevalent myths. These myths are perpetuated in books, articles, and manufacturers' advertising. Even if you are new to woodworking and are not familiar with these myths, you will no doubt encounter them. They need to be debunked.

MYTH #1: Oil finishes were the favored wood finish used by our eighteenth- and nineteenth-century predecessors.
FACT: There's no evidence at all that oil was a well-regarded finish until the rapid growth of the consumer market beginning in the 1960s.

MYTH #2: Oil finishes penetrate into the wood and protect the wood from the inside.
FACT: The penetrating qualities of oil finishes are of very little significance in protecting wood.

MYTH #3: All finishes sold as "oil" are some type of oil.
FACT: There are four significantly different types of finish that are sold as "oil." Not all are oil.

OUR ANCESTORS AND LINSEED OIL

In the eighteenth and nineteenth centuries, only minimal attention was given to finishing wood. Finishing is a twentieth-century craft.

One of the primary rationalizations for using oil as a finish is that eighteenth- and nineteenth-century craftspeople used and valued oil for finishing—specifically, linseed oil. If you've done much woodworking, you've surely developed a profound respect for our ancestors' woodworking skills. It's not a big jump to assume that if these craftspeople were so good at woodworking, they must also have been good finishers. And if they used linseed oil, they must have chosen to do so because linseed oil made a great finish.

The idea that our forebears were skilled finishers pops up now and then in woodworking books and articles. It's often bolstered by the suggestion that if you follow their practice of rubbing coats of linseed oil into the wood once a day for a week, once a week for a month, once a month for a year, and then once every year thereafter, you will produce one of the most beautiful and durable finishes possible—maybe even better than anything that has been invented since.

This is all myth:

- It's myth that our ancestors thought linseed oil was a great finish. They used linseed oil, of course. It was cheap, compared to other finishes, and it was available. But there is no evidence from surviving records, such as cabinetmakers' account books, that linseed oil was well thought of as a finish. On the contrary, most of the finer, eighteenth-century, city-made furniture, and almost all nineteenth-century, factory-made furniture, was finished with shellac or varnish.
- It's myth that our predecessors expended much effort applying linseed oil when they did use it. Rubbing linseed oil into the wood does absolutely no good. There is some mention in cabinetmakers' account books of rubbing linseed oil, in combina-

APPLYING "OIL" FINISHES

"OIL" FINISHES ARE very easy to apply. In most cases, you just wipe them on the wood and then wipe off the excess. Here's a little more detail.

1. *Prepare the wood.* On new wood remove the machine marks and sand smooth to 180 or 220 grit. For tabletops it's a good idea to "sponge" the wood so water spills that work their way through the finish when the table is in use won't raise the grain of the wood. Sponging also reduces grain raising that often occurs after several years of humidity changes and causes the initially smooth surface to feel rough. (See "Sponging" on page 15.)
2. *Clean the wood.* Remove as much of the sanding dust as possible with a brush, tack cloth, vacuum, or compressed air.
3. *Choose the finish.* Choose which type of "oil" finish you want—straight oil, polymerized oil, wiping varnish, or oil/varnish blend (see "Types of 'Oil'" on page 55). If you've never used one of these finishes before, I recommend you begin with a wiping varnish (for a glossy appearance) or an oil/varnish blend (for a satin look).
4. *Apply the first coat.* Flood the wood with the finish. You can use a cloth, brush, or spray gun, or you can dip the wood into the finish. Let the finish remain wet on the wood for about five minutes. If any dry spots appear, apply more finish. Before it becomes tacky, wipe off all the excess finish. Polymerized oil and wiping varnish become tacky much faster than straight oil or oil/varnish blends, especially in hot weather; so you may have to remove the excess before five minutes has passed.
5. *Remove "bleeding" before it cures.* Any "oil" finish can bleed back out of the pores. Little puddles will form soon after you have removed the excess finish. Continue to wipe these puddles dry until they stop forming. If you allow them to cure into scabs, you'll have to abrade or strip them off the wood. (See "Bleeding Oil Finishes" on page 62.)
6. *Apply additional coats.* Allow the first coat to cure overnight. Smooth any roughness that remains by sanding with 280-grit or finer sandpaper. (Sandpaper is far more effective than steel wool for smoothing the first coat.) Clean off the dust and apply the next coat. You can combine the two steps by sanding the wood with wet/dry paper while the wood is wet with the second coat of finish. Wipe the wood dry. You can then apply as many coats as you want, allowing at least one day's drying time between each coat. But there's no

MYTH

Applying more coats of "oil" increases the gloss.

FACT

This is true about any finish for the first two, and sometimes three, coats. The first one or two coats penetrate into the wood and seal it. Until the wood is sealed, the finish will appear fairly flat. It's only after sealing that you begin to get a build on top of the wood, and with it a certain sheen. But this sheen cannot be raised by then applying more coats. To increase the gloss, you'll need to rub the cured finish with very fine rubbing compounds, apply paste wax, or both.

(continued)

APPLYING "OIL" FINISHES—continued

point in applying more than three or four coats unless you're using wiping varnish or polymerized oil and trying to build a thicker film.

7. *Build the finish, if you wish.* If you're using wiping varnish or polymerized oil, you may want to build the finish to a thicker film to give the wood better protection or increase the appearance of depth. To do this, leave each coat wet on the wood's surface; don't wipe off all the excess. Use a brush, spray gun, or lint-free cloth to apply the finish. (You can leave wiping varnish as thick as you want, but you can't leave polymerized oil thick, or it will develop small cracks in the film.) You'll need to take extra care that the space you're working in is relatively dust-free. If dust settles on and sticks to the finish, sand it lightly between coats with 320- or 400-grit sandpaper to remove the dust nibs. Use stearated (gray) sandpaper dry, or wet/dry (black) sandpaper with mineral spirits as a lubricant. Be very careful sanding the first two coats–don't sand through the thin finish.

8. *Finishing the finish.* No matter which finish you're using, you can make the final coat smoother to the touch, remove dust nibs, and raise or lower the sheen:

- To smooth the last coat of an oil or oil/varnish blend, wet-sand it with more of the same finish and 400-grit or finer wet/dry sandpaper. I use 600 grit. Then wipe off the excess.
- To smooth the last coat of wiping varnish or polymerized oil, sand after the final coat has cured with 600-grit or finer wet/dry sandpaper, using mineral spirits as a lubricant.
- To smooth *and raise* the sheen of any "oil" finish, rub the last coat very hard with a cloth (turners often rub while the piece is spinning on the lathe), or rub the cured finish with a commercial rubbing compound.
- To smooth *and lower* the sheen of any "oil" finish, rub the last cured coat with #0000 steel wool. You can lubricate the steel wool with mineral spirits, a non-curing oil, or paste wax to reduce scratching. (See Chapter 14: "Finishing the Finish.") ■

MYTH

You can get a mirror finish by filling the pores with oil and sawdust.

FACT

This notion is based on the idea that sanding the wood while it's wet with oil makes a paste of oil and sawdust which fills the pores. In reality you can't avoid wiping most of the oil-laden sawdust back out of the pores when you remove the excess oil from the wood. So this is a very inefficient way of filling the pores, if that is your intention. Using paste-wood filler would be a better method. But the real beauty of an "oil" finish is its sharp delineation of the pores. This is lost when you fill, or even partially fill, the pores. If you want a filled look, you should use a film finish, such as shellac, lacquer, varnish, or water base, which will give you much better protection as well.

tion with brick dust or pumice, to fill the pores of wood. But you have to get into the twentieth century before you find written reference to anyone in the eighteenth century rubbing oil alone into wood. (How could the writers have known?)

- It's myth that linseed oil applied in any manner is a durable finish. A linseed oil finish is too thin and soft to protect well against heat, stains, or wear. And linseed oil, no matter how you apply it, or how many coats you apply, is quickly and easily penetrated by water and water vapor.
- It's even myth that eighteenth- and nineteenth-century woodworkers were skilled finishers by today's standards. Surviving cabinetmakers' account books indicate that only minimal attention was given to finishing wood. Finishing is a twentieth-century craft.

So the fact that our predecessors used oil now and then as a finish is no reason for us to use oil—especially linseed oil. They used linseed oil when they had nothing better. We have an entire array of finishes that are better in almost every way.

OIL FINISHES AND PENETRATION

Oil finishes are penetrating finishes, and they are sometimes marketed as protecting the wood from the inside. They are contrasted with film finishes, such as shellac, lacquer, varnish, and water base, which protect the wood by building a film on the surface of the wood. To assess the accuracy of the claim that penetrating finishes protect from the inside, you need to understand how penetration occurs and what value it has (or does not have) in protecting the wood.

Liquids penetrate wood by means of capillary action. It's the same way that water and nutrients rise in the live tree. It doesn't matter whether the liquid is on top, on the side, or on the bottom of the wood. If it is in contact with the wood, the liquid will work its way through the wood channels.

The trick to achieving deep penetration is to keep the surface of the wood wet for a while. You can put a straight-grained piece of wood into a jar containing about an inch of oil finish, and the finish will work its way up through the wood and come out the top. Only if the finish cures hard in the wood, preventing further penetration, or if it hardens in the jar, will penetration stop (Photo 4-1).

But what good does penetration do? Very little. You can totally fill a piece of wood with a linseed oil finish, and it will do nothing to protect the surface of the wood from damage. Coarse objects will scratch the wood, stains will stain the wood, and water will smudge the wood almost as easily as if there were no

MYTH

Rubbing an oil finish into the wood increases penetration.

FACT

Rubbing warms the finish. The warmer the finish the faster it cures. The faster the finish cures, the quicker the pores are capped off (sealed), which prevents further penetration. Rubbing a finish actually decreases penetration.

Photo 4-1: Penetration occurs by capillary action. The linseed oil in the jar has risen through the oak and is coming out the top. Deep penetration is achieved by keeping the surface of the wood wet for an extended period of time.

HOW OIL AND OIL/VARNISH FINISHES PROTECT

OIL AND OIL/VARNISH FINISHES shouldn't be built up on the surface of the wood because they cure too soft. Therefore, they can't protect by forming a thick film, as other finishes do, between the wood and the surrounding environment. Any protection oil and oil/varnish finishes provide has to be either in the wood or very thin on the surface of the wood. In fact, it's a little of each, and both are necessary to achieve maximum protection.

Oil and oil/varnish finishes don't provide much protection against water-vapor exchange. But what little protection they do provide comes from the finish that penetrates the wood. A barrier forms just below the surface, which slows the exchange of water vapor and thus reduces swelling and shrinking. The finish that remains on the surface of the wood (some finish does remain on the surface, no matter how hard you try to wipe it all off) provides limited protection against stains, water damage (smudges), and abrasion.

Straight oil soaks into the wood much more deeply than oil/varnish blends because straight oil takes much longer to cure. But oil/varnish blends usually form a better surface barrier because of the added varnish. Neither finish provides very much protection against abrasion or water damage, because they are so soft and thin. It is therefore important that you maintain the integrity of this surface film by recoating it anytime it becomes scratched, worn, or dull.

To achieve the best protection with an oil or oil/varnish blend, you have to create a continuous film, one with no voids. The best way to do this is to apply the first couple of coats very wet and let them soak in for at least five minutes before wiping them off. If any dry spots appear (caused by all the finish soaking into the wood), apply more finish until the soaking-in stops. The heavy, wet coat will allow the finish time to penetrate and form an internal barrier against water-vapor exchange. It will also stop up the larger pores so a continuous film can form over them (Figure 4-1).

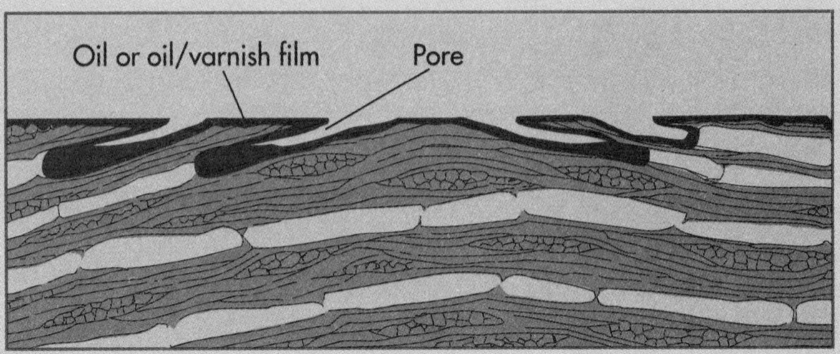

Figure 4-1: When using a straight oil or oil/varnish blend, it's important that you apply the finish wet and allow it time to penetrate into the pores. The finish will span the pores, forming a continuous film.

Large-pored woods, such as oak, require more coats than small-pored woods, such as maple. Apply three or four coats to oak, two or three coats to maple. You can tell you have a continuous film when the sheen no longer improves with additional coats.

With film finishes, such as shellac, lacquer, varnish, and water base, you don't have to fill the pores to achieve a continuous film. They build a film thick enough on top of the wood to bridge the pores. ■

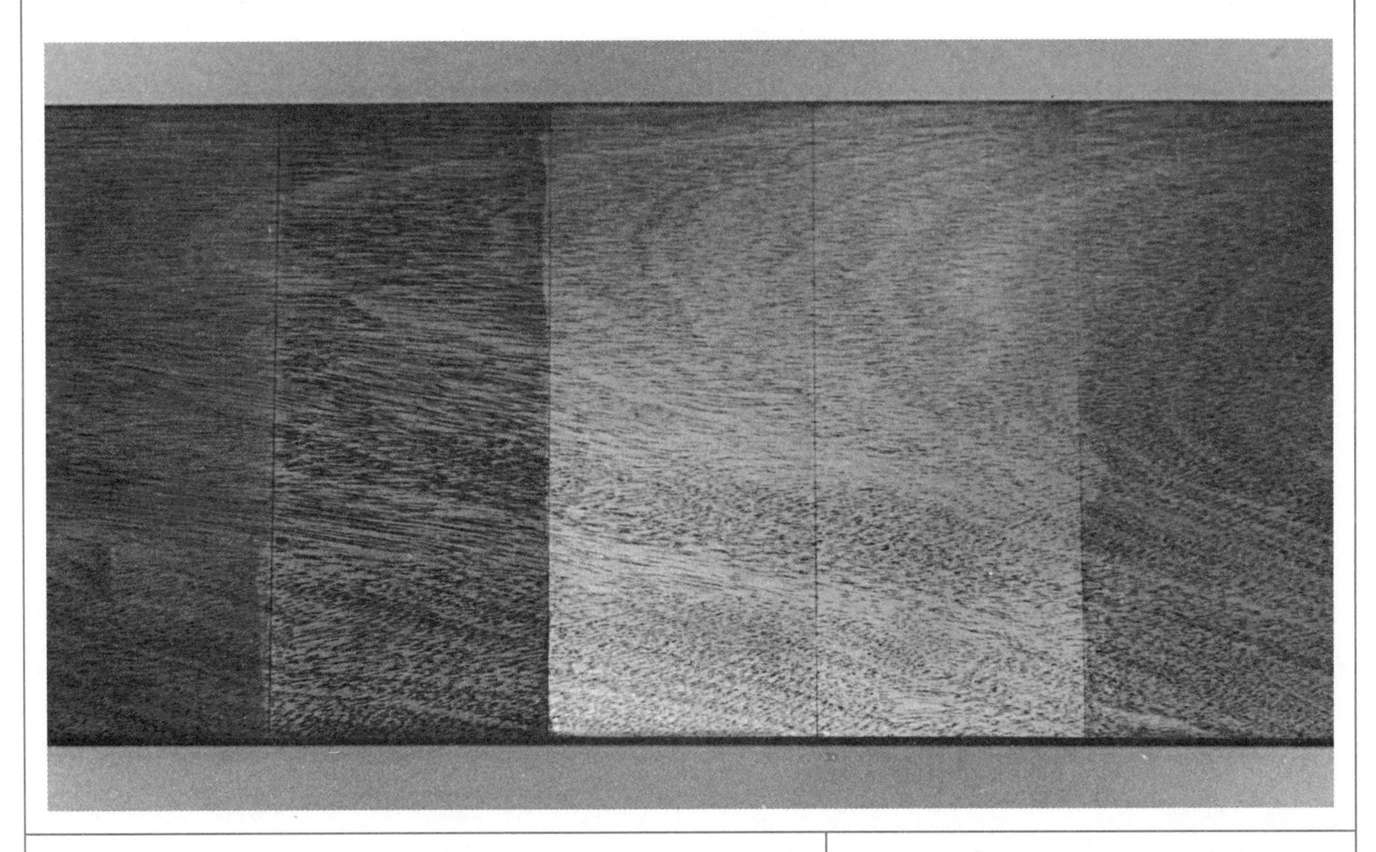

Photo 4-2: Each section of the panel above is finished with three coats of a different "oil" finish (left to right): linseed oil, tung oil, polymerized oil, wiping varnish, and oil/varnish blend. They produce quite different sheens.

finish in the wood. The only possible advantage gained by filling the wood with finish is to stabilize the wood from shrinkage and swelling caused by water-vapor exchange. You plasticize the wood by filling all the cavities with cured finish. But if you are looking for a finish to provide protection to the surface, the amount that a finish penetrates is of no significance. (See "How Oil and Oil/Varnish Finishes Protect" on the facing page.)

TYPES OF "OIL"

Much of the confusion about oil is generated by the marketplace, which offers four significantly different finishes, all called oil:

- *Straight oil,* of which there are two principal kinds–tung oil and linseed oil. Tung oil is usually sold as "pure" or "100 percent" tung oil or "China wood oil." Linseed oil comes in two forms, raw and boiled.
- *Polymerized oil,* of which there are two principal kinds–polymerized tung oil and polymerized linseed oil. Polymerized oils perform more like varnish than like straight oil. They are expensive and not widely available.
- *Regular varnish* (including polyurethane) that has been thinned with two to three parts mineral spirits to one part varnish. This finish is often sold as oil but is actually a wiping varnish.

MYTH

Boiled linseed oil is made by boiling raw linseed oil.

FACT

Boiled linseed oil is made by adding metallic driers to raw linseed oil—not by boiling. Raw linseed oil used to be heated (not boiled) to help incorporate the driers. Now, liquid driers are available that don't require heating. But the product is still labeled "boiled linseed oil."

- *A blend of straight oil and varnish* (including polyurethane). This oil/varnish mixture is often sold as Danish oil.

These "oil" finishes look different: They range from glossy to flat, and from very thin on the wood to quite thick. They perform differently: Some are very effective barriers against scratches, stains, water, and water-vapor exchange, while others aren't. And they can be applied differently: Some can be left wet on the wood, others have to be wiped almost dry. (See Photo 4-2 on page 55 and "Guide to 'Oil' Finishes" on page 70.)

Straight Oil

Oil is a natural substance that is extracted from plants, nuts, fish, and petroleum. Some oils, such as linseed oil and tung oil, cure—they change from a liquid to a solid by absorbing oxygen from the air. Linseed oil absorbs so much oxygen when it cures that its weight increases as much as 12 percent. Oils that cure can be used as finishes. Other oils, such as mineral oil, olive oil, and motor oil, don't absorb oxygen and therefore don't cure. Because they don't solidify, they are ineffective as finishes. Still other oils, such as walnut oil, soybean oil, and safflower oil, are semi-curing: They cure very slowly and never very hard. They are only marginally effective as finishes. (See "Safety and Oil Finishes" on the facing page.)

Straight oils used as finishes have certain characteristics in common. They cure slowly compared to every other finish, and they cure to a satin (not glossy) sheen after you apply several coats. They also cure soft. This makes them impractical for use as finishes unless you wipe off the excess after each application. Straight-oil finishes are true penetrating finishes. You can't build a thick, hard, protective film on the surface of the wood the way you can with film finishes. If you have some cured overspill around the top of a can of linseed oil or tung oil, push your fingernail into it and notice how soft it is compared to other finishes.

Linseed oil is extracted from seeds of the flax plant. This oil, in its raw state, is an inefficient finish because it takes many days to cure. So, to make it more effective, metallic driers are added. These driers are usually salts of cobalt, manganese, or zinc. They act as catalysts to speed the curing. (Lead was once used as a drier but is no longer, because it is a health hazard.) With driers added, linseed oil cures in about a day and is called "boiled" linseed oil. Unless you want an oil that cures very slowly, there's no reason to use raw linseed oil.

Of all finishes except wax, linseed oil is the least protective. (See "Using Wax as a Finish" on page 59.) It's a soft, thin finish, so it provides no significant barrier against scratching. It's also easily penetrated by water and water vapor. Liquid water will work

SAFETY AND OIL FINISHES

THERE ARE TWO AREAS of safety to consider when using oil finishes:

- safety to you while applying the finish
- safety of the finished object, particularly if it might come in contact with food or someone's mouth

Safety during Application

Any finish that contains a solvent or oil is a fire hazard. There are two rules you should always follow when working with oil finishes:

- Never heat the finish over an open flame or electric burner. If you want to warm the finish, always do so by putting the finish container in a pot of hot water and placing the pot over a fire or burner.
- Never leave oily rags bunched together in piles. The absorption of oxygen, which brings about curing, generates heat as a by-product. When oil- or varnish-soaked rags are piled up, enough heat can be generated to cause spontaneous combustion. Always dispose of your used rags by placing them in an approved oily-waste container. Or hang them over a branch or fence so they're totally exposed to air and can dissipate the heat. Once the finish has cured on the rags (they will become stiff), you can safely toss them in the trash.

Safety for Food or Mouth Contact

The safety of "oil" finishes for food or mouth contact is unclear. The Food and Drug Administration (FDA) lists all the common oils, resins, and driers used in these finishes as safe if the finishes are properly formulated. Proper formulation is necessary to ensure that potentially harmful ingredients won't leach out once the finish has cured. Some manufacturers market their finishes as food-safe, calling them "salad bowl finishes." Others don't. (*None* have FDA approval). Yet within each of the four types of "oil," the ingredients used and the formulation methods employed are almost identical.

It's most likely that *all* commonly available "oil" finishes are safe to eat off of, or to bring in contact with your mouth, once the solvents have evaporated and the finish has cured. (You can tell that the solvents have evaporated when the smell is gone.) Neither the chemistry nor long experience using these finishes suggests a problem. Nevertheless, if you are concerned, stick with one of the brands that claims to be safe for food contact. That way, you have the assurance that the manufacturer stands legally behind the product's safety.

Alternatively, you can use walnut oil or mineral oil, which are edible. Note, however, that walnut oil cures extremely slowly and mineral oil doesn't cure at all. (Don't use vegetable oils; they often turn rancid.) Both of these oils will leave the wood with a very low sheen. After a couple of washings, as might occur on wooden bowls and utensils, the oil will be gone. But you can reapply more oil whenever the wood is dried out. As long as there is oil in the pores of the wood, the wood will have a richer color and water penetration will be slowed. ■

TIP

It's a good habit to hang oily rags over the edge of a worktable if you don't have time to take them outdoors immediately. That way, you are safe from the threat of fire if you should happen to forget.

Photo 4-3: No matter how many coats of linseed oil you apply to the wood, or how you apply the coats, water will penetrate through the finish and smudge the wood in less than 10 seconds, as shown in the center of the board, above. If an old finish doesn't water-smudge, then it's not linseed oil.

through a linseed oil finish and cause a smudge within 5 to 10 seconds (Photo 4-3). Water vapor will pass through a linseed oil finish almost as if it weren't there.

You may find it interesting that old paints based on linseed oil performed well precisely because water vapor could pass through so easily. These paints allowed moisture to escape through the walls of houses without blistering the paint film. Modern alkyd-based paints blister easily because they form a much better barrier to water-vapor exchange. This is why water-based, latex paint is recommended for use on the outsides of houses. Like linseed oil–based paint, latex paint "breathes."

Tung oil is extracted from nuts of the tung tree, which is native to China. Tung oil has been used for centuries in China, but it was not introduced into the West until the very end of the nineteenth century. It is now cultivated in South America. Though tung oil is more expensive than linseed oil, tung oil has established a firm position in the paint and coatings industry because it is one of the most water-resistant oils. Many high-quality varnishes are made with tung oil. But, contrary to what you might think, tung oil is seldom used as a finish in its own right.

Tung oil can be made fairly water-resistant after five or six coats. But it is too soft and thin to resist scratching or water-vapor exchange, and it is difficult to make the finish look nice. The first three or four coats appear flat and splotchy on the wood and feel rough to the touch. Only after five or six coats, sanding between each coat, can you get an even, satin sheen. But the finish is still not as smooth to the touch as linseed oil.

In addition, tung oil cures very slowly, and it turns white if left to cure in any thickness. The curing is faster than raw linseed oil but slower than boiled linseed oil, so you need to wait several days between coats. This makes tung oil an inefficient finish to use. The white color can cause problems in large pores and cracks in the wood. There is no way to remove the white color if it occurs, short of stripping the wood and starting all over.

About the only advantage tung oil has over linseed oil, other than better water resistance after five or six coats, is that tung oil yellows less than linseed oil. This can be important on blonde woods that you don't want to darken too much.

Polymerized Oil

Any curing or semi-curing oil can be heated in an oxygen-free environment to around 500 degrees Fahrenheit to increase its gloss and hardness and reduce its curing time. Oil processed in this manner is called *polymerized* or *heat-bodied* oil. Polymerized oil is commmonly used in ink and outdoor paint.

USING WAX AS A FINISH

IN SOME WAYS wax is like oil and oil/varnish finishes: It is easy to apply, produces a satin sheen, and cures soft. But a wax finish is even less protective than linseed oil. In fact, wax is the least protective of all finishes. It is the closest thing to having no finish at all on the wood.

Wax provides no significant barrier against heat, water, water-vapor exchange, or solvents. The melting point of wax, around 140 degrees Fahrenheit, is too low to protect against hot objects. Wax is soft, which necessitates wiping off all the excess, so a wax finish is not thick enough to be an effective barrier against water or water-vapor exchange. (However, a thick wax coating, as is sometimes applied to the ends of newly sawed boards, is a good barrier.) All common solvents, including those in liquid furniture polishes, dissolve wax on contact.

The only protection a wax finish provides is to reduce abrasive damage, such as scuffs and scrapes. Wax makes the surface of the wood slicker, so glancing blows tend to slide off rather than dig in. But reducing scuffs and scrapes is not a good reason to use wax as a primary finish. Wood that receives the sort of use that requires scuff resistance will quickly become dirty if wax is the only finish. The dirt gets worked into the soft wax, and a dirty wax finish can't be repaired. It has to be stripped, and often the wood has to be sanded to get it clean.

The only reason to use wax as the sole finish is to keep the color of the wood as close as possible to its natural color while giving the wood some sheen. Wax doesn't darken the wood as much as other finishes do. A wax finish may be very effective on a decorative, carved, or turned object that won't receive much handling. As the artist who created the object, you might choose wax for aesthetic reasons. A wax finish is better than no finish at all, but only because dusting is easier (with a feather duster, not furniture polish).

You may have seen instructions for wax finishes that suggest applying several coats of shellac, oil, or some other finish underneath the wax. This is an excellent practice for making a more durable finish than wax alone. But a finish that uses another finish to seal the wood underneath the wax isn't a wax finish. It's the other finish. The wax is being used as a polish on top of that finish. Wax is an excellent polish used on any other finish. (See Chapter 15: "Caring for the Finish.")

Applying Wax

For those cases where wax provides the look you want, the application is quite easy. Begin with any commercial or homemade paste wax. Put a lump of it in the center of a 6 x 6-inch piece of cotton cloth, gather the corners of the cloth together, and twist the cloth around the ball of wax. Now, holding the enclosed lump of wax between your fingers, rub it

MYTH

Beeswax must be a great finish because woodworkers of yesteryear used it.

FACT

Our woodworking forebears used beeswax as a finish for the same reason they used linseed oil: Beeswax was available and relatively cheap. Beeswax, or any other wax, is not a good finish.

(continued)

USING WAX AS A FINISH—continued

onto the surface of the wood. (If the wax is too hard, knead it between your fingers to warm and soften it.) The wax will seep from the cloth, controlling the amount you're applying. (For the same technique used to apply wax as a polish, see Photo 15-4 on page 231.) Don't cake it on; too much will make removal difficult. Allow the solvent to evaporate (the sheen will become flat). Then rub off the excess wax with a clean, soft cloth. You'll probably need several applications at least several hours apart to get the maximum sheen because the wax will be absorbed by the wood. But if you like the sheen after one coat, you can stop there. You can raise the sheen by buffing with a cloth or an electric buffer and a lamb's-wool pad.

On carved or turned objects with cavities that are difficult to get into, you can use a soft polishing brush, like a shoe brush, to buff the shine. You can also apply the wax with a brush.

Softer woods are more difficult than hard, dense woods to finish with wax. Softer woods absorb so much wax that it's difficult to develop a sheen. You can keep applying coats until the pores are filled, or you can apply the wax with the help of heat to melt it into the pores. This will speed up the process. A hair dryer, heat gun, or similar heat source that will raise the temperature of the wax above 140 degrees Fahrenheit will work. But don't get the wood so hot that it scorches.

Compatibility with Other Finishes

You'll come across formulas that suggest mixing wax with other finishes such as linseed oil or a mixture of linseed oil and varnish. Though it is possible to mix wax with these finishes, it is generally not a good idea. The resulting finish will be even softer than without the wax. In many cases the finish will be so soft that you will smudge it every time you touch it.

You can apply wax over any finish, but you can't apply every finish over wax. Only straight oil, oil/varnish blend, and shellac can be applied over wax. Oil and oil/varnish blend will dissolve the wax, making a mixture like the ones described above. Shellac contains some wax naturally, so it will combine with the wax and establish a bond with the wood or finish below. Too much wax, however, will soften the shellac. Water-based finish will wrinkle when applied over wax. Lacquer, varnish, and polyurethane will cure softer and more slowly. In all cases the wax will prevent a good bond with the wood or finish below.

How to Make Your Own Paste Wax

Commercial paste waxes are as good as anything you can make yourself (see Chapter 15: "Caring for the Finish"). But you may want to make your own just for fun. Here's how:

1. Shred some beeswax into a container.
2. Add mineral spirits or turpentine in the ratio of 1/2 pint of solvent to 1 pound of wax.
3. Put the container in a pot of hot water, and let the wax and solvent melt together. You can keep the pot of water hot by placing it on a heat source, but never put the container of wax itself directly over a flame or burner; it can catch fire.
4. When the wax has cooled, it will be the consistency of butter in summertime. If you want it thicker, add more wax and reheat. If you want it thinner, add more solvent and reheat.
5. You can add rottenstone or stain (oil-based pigment or dye) to the dissolved wax to create different antique and scratch-covering features. Add enough colorant to make the wax a uniform color. ■

Polymerized oil is sometimes used as a finish by itself. It cures very fast and very hard and resists water and water-vapor penetration. Many gun owners like the results they get when they rub this oil (usually sold by other names, such as Tru-Oil) onto their gun stocks. Because the oil is hard when cured, its possible to build a film from many thin coats.

There are two problems with using polymerized oil as a finish on large surfaces such as furniture: It's expensive, and it cures too fast to be applied and wiped off unless it has been thinned a lot with mineral spirits. (You can't apply polymerized oil in thick layers as you can varnish, or tiny cracks will develop in the cured film.) Besides, there's no evidence that polymerized oil protects significantly better than varnish. For these reasons polymerized oil is not widely used as a furniture finish.

Wiping Varnish

Most of the "oil" finishes you see on store shelves are varnishes that have been thinned enough so you can wipe them on the wood. Many of these wiping varnishes have names that lead you to believe they are oil. They're not oil, they're varnish. There's a big difference between oil and varnish.

I've described oil above. *Varnish* is made by cooking one or more oils with natural or synthetic resins. The heat causes the oil and resin to combine chemically, forming an entirely new substance. Manufacturers use linseed oil and tung oil, or semi-curing oils such as soybean oil and safflower oil. They once used natural resins (fossilized sap of pine trees) that were imported from Africa and New Zealand. Now, most varnishes are made from synthetic resins such as alkyd, phenolic, and polyurethane. (For more on these resins, see Chapter 10: "Varnish.")

Varnish cures much faster than oil. It also cures glossy (unless the manufacturer adds flatting agents to give a satin or flat sheen). And it is hard when cured (again, check the overspill around the caps of your cans of varnish or wiping varnish).

The most important difference is the hardness. This permits you to build up varnish in relatively thick coats to a significant film on the surface of the wood. When varnish is built up, it protects the wood from all but the most severe scratches, and it forms an excellent barrier against stains, water, and water-vapor exchange. Though it might be easier to wipe on a thinned varnish than it is to brush on an unthinned varnish, it will take many more coats to achieve the same thickness and therefore the same amount of protection.

Wiping varnishes vary in hardness and water resistance, depending on the types and ratios of resins and oils used to make the varnish. But no wiping varnish I know of lists these variables

Most "oil" finishes are really varnishes that have been thinned enough so you can wipe them on the wood.

$$\text{Resin} + \text{Oil} \xrightarrow{\text{Heat}} \text{Varnish}$$

CAUTION:
Don't try making your own varnish. It's very dangerous because of the possibility of fire.

TIP

You can easily thin regular varnish to make your own wiping varnish by thinning a can of varnish with mineral spirits until it is easy to spread with a cloth. The result will be less expensive but no less effective than a manufacturer-mixed wiping varnish.

on the container. For wipe-on/wipe-off applications, it probably doesn't matter what quality the varnish is—the film is too thin. But it does matter if you intend to build the varnish to a thicker film on the surface of the wood. You don't want a soft varnish film on a heavily used surface such as a tabletop, for example. So, in some cases, you may be wise to buy the type and quality of varnish you want and thin it yourself. (For an explanation of the differences, see Chapter 10: "Varnish.")

The amount of thinner used varies. But most brands of common wiping varnishes contain at least 2 parts mineral spirits to 1 part varnish.

BLEEDING OIL FINISHES

OIL FINISHES SOMETIMES bleed back out of the wood's pores and form tiny puddles around the pore openings (Photo 4-4). If you allow the finish to cure, glossy scabs form, which are difficult to remove. You will have to abrade or strip these scabs off, and you can't do either without also removing the surrounding finish. So allowing any bleeding to cure creates a serious problem.

There are two causes of bleeding:

- If the finish contains thinner, the thinner brings the finish back out of the pores as it evaporates.
- The finish expands back out of the pores when it is heated. Heating can occur when you rub the wood vigorously, or when you take recently finished wood from your cool shop or garage into your warm house or out into the sun.

Bleeding occurs more often in large-pored woods and in parts of wood where the cell structure allows deep penetration. The larger the retaining cavity, the more likely it is that the finish deposited there will bleed out. Bleeding no longer occurs after the pores are

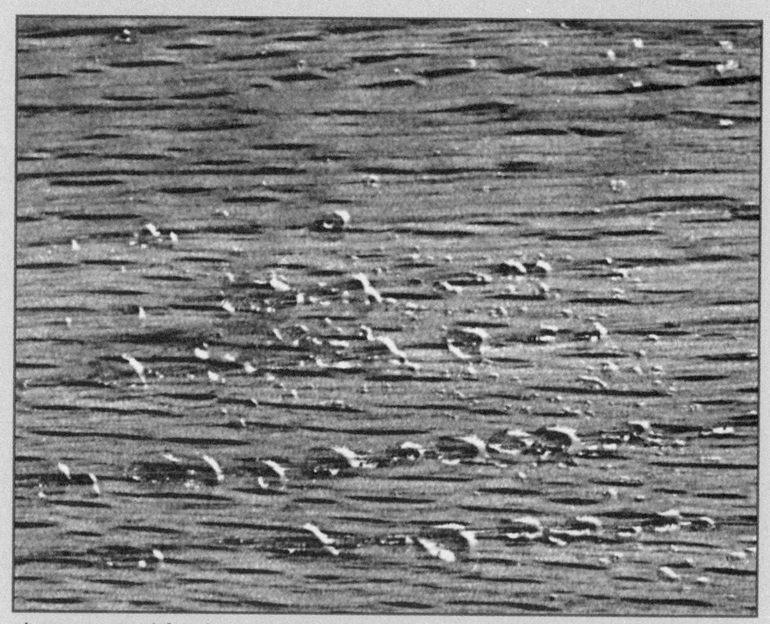

Photo 4-4: Oil finishes sometimes bleed back out of the pores, cure, and form scabs on the surface of the wood. You should wipe off any bleeding before it cures, or you will have to abrade the scabs off or strip and refinish.

Oil/Varnish Blends

Oil and varnish (including polyurethane) are compatible, so they can be mixed. The resulting finish performs with some of the characteristics of each. The oil part of the blend reduces the gloss and makes the finish cure slowly. Application is therefore easy because you have plenty of time. But the oil also makes the finish cure soft (again, test the overspill around the container spout of your oil/varnish blend). This means you can't build oil/varnish blends to a more protective thickness. The varnish part of the blend gives the finish more body and more gloss. As a result, you can achieve an even satin sheen with only two coats instead of the three to six it usually takes with straight oil. The varnish also makes the oil/varnish blend more protective than

Oil + Varnish —No heat→ Oil/Varnish Blend

sealed—usually after the first or second coat has cured.

Oil/varnish blends bleed the most, probably because of the added thinner and because they are naturally slow-curing. Bleeding is worse on hot days because the thinner evaporates much faster. Since straight oil doesn't contain thinner, it seldom bleeds unless you warm the wood. Wiping varnish and polymerized oil don't easily bleed because they begin to cure so quickly.

To keep scabs from forming, wipe the bleeding off before it cures. Go back over the wood once every hour or so with a dry cloth until the bleeding stops. I usually apply the first coat of finish fairly early in the day, so there is plenty of time to get all the bleeding wiped off before quitting time.

There are two ways to remove cured scabs:

- Abrade the scabs off with fine steel wool or synthetic steel wool (Scotch-Brite). This often works well on medium- and small-pored woods, such as walnut and maple. But on large-pored woods, such as oak, it is almost impossible to remove all the gloss from the pores. If you are satisfied with the results you get from abrading the scabs off, apply another coat of finish to replace the finish you've rubbed off. (You can combine the two steps by rubbing with steel wool after you've wet the surface with more finish.) As long as the pores are sealed, you won't have any more bleeding.
- Strip off the scabs with paint-and-varnish remover. This will mean that you have to begin your finishing all over again. ■

MYTH

You can remove cured scabs by wiping with mineral spirits, lacquer thinner, or refinisher (which is lacquer thinner).

FACT

Neither mineral spirits nor lacquer thinner dissolve cured "oil" finishes. If you want to remove scabs with a solvent, use a paint-and-varnish remover.

straight oil, because varnish is harder when cured and more water- and water-vapor-resistant than oil.

As you would expect, not all mixtures of oil and varnish give the same protection. Some combinations are better than others, though the differences are often too subtle to detect. Since store-bought blends seldom tell you the types or ratios of oil and varnish used, many woodworkers have chosen to make their own. There are many variables, but the following generalizations should help you decide on a formula:

- The higher the varnish-to-oil ratio, the better the scratch, water, water-vapor, and stain resistance. But if you get the percentage of varnish too high, you will lose some ease of application. A ratio of 90 percent varnish to 10 percent oil, for instance, will perform very much like varnish alone. Begin by mixing half-and-half, and vary the formulation from there.
- Using tung oil rather than linseed oil in the mixture will make the finish significantly more water-resistant. But the higher the percentage of tung oil you use, the more coats it will take to achieve an even, satin sheen.
- Though there are significant differences in the protective qualities of the various varnishes you might use, the differences are difficult to detect when the film is thin. Your choice of varnish is not as significant as your choice of oil.

Photo 4-5: Sometimes you can tell if a finish is a wiping varnish or an oil/varnish blend from the overspill around the cap of the container. But if there is no overspill, pour some of the finish onto a piece of glass and let it cure overnight. If it cures wrinkled or soft enough to dig your fingernail into, it is an oil/varnish blend (left). If it cures smooth and hard, it is a wiping varnish (right).

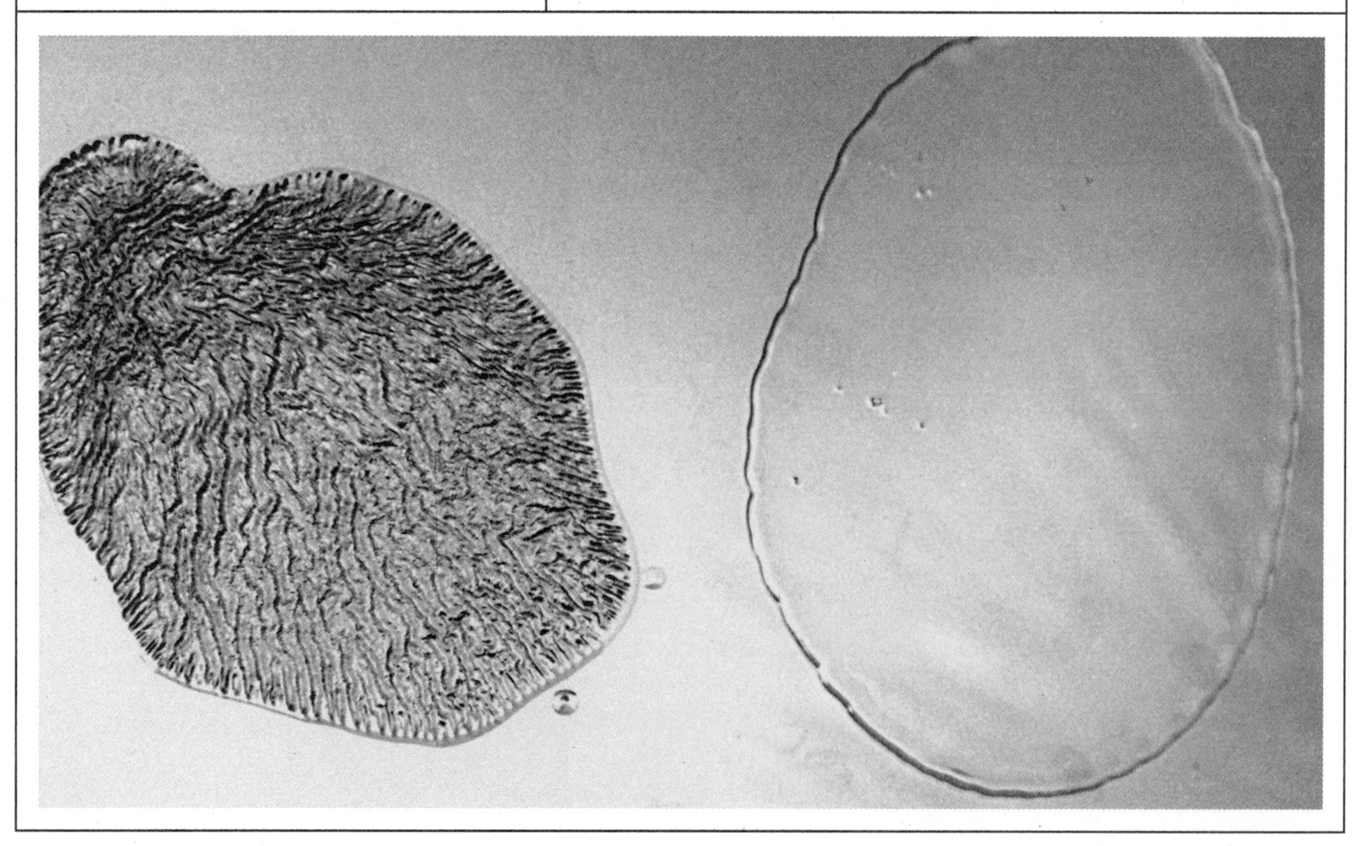

- You can thin any blend with mineral spirits. This will make the oil/varnish mixture easier to spread over large surfaces. But it will also thin the coating, so it won't stop up the pores as well on the first application. And it will increase the likelihood of bleeding. (See "Bleeding Oil Finishes" on page 62.)

WHICH ONE IS WHICH?

Manufacturers use the name "tung oil" on all four types of "oil" finish. They also use nondescript names such as Antique Oil, Val-Oil, Profin, and Seal-a-Cell. In most cases, when you buy an "oil" finish, you don't know what you're getting. You need to know how to tell which you have.

Straight oils—linseed oil and tung oil—have distinct smells. Once you've smelled one of these oils, you will always be able to recognize it. Both are nutty smells. Tung oil is sweeter-smelling than linseed oil, which is more pungent.

Most polymerized oils, wiping varnishes, and oil/varnish blends smell like mineral spirits, because they contain a significant percentage of mineral spirits. This means smell won't aid in distinguishing them. I don't know any way to tell if you have a polymerized oil unless the container tells you. (This is probably not a problem since there are so few on the market.) But there are three indicators you can look for to tell whether you have a wiping varnish or an oil/varnish blend:

- *How fast the finish cures.* Oil/varnish blends cure slowly. They can take up to an hour or more to become tacky, depending on the ratio of oil to varnish. Wiping varnish becomes tacky in 20 minutes or less. (Times will vary depending on temperature and humidity.)
- *Whether the finish is hard when cured.* Wiping varnish cures hard. Oil/varnish blends cure soft enough to dig your fingernail into, especially if the film is thick.
- *Whether the finish wrinkles severely when it cures thick.* Any finish containing oil (10 percent or more oil-to-varnish ratio) will wrinkle when it cures in a thick film. Varnish won't wrinkle unless the film is exceptionally thick (Photo 4-5). (See also "How to Tell Which 'Oil' You Have" on page 66.)

Additional Confusion

The confusion about oil finishes doesn't stop with the four types. Some manufacturers market different "oils" for different woods. I saw the most outrageous example of this marketing ploy in a furniture store in Denmark. The store had an entire cabinet full of 2-ounce bottles of teak oil, rosewood oil, walnut oil, oak oil, birch oil, ash oil—a special oil for every type of wood furniture the store

MYTH

The term "tung oil" in the name of a finish means that the finish contains tung oil somewhere in the formula.

FACT

This is not necessarily the case. "Tung oil" has come to mean any finish that you wipe on the wood. This causes great confusion. If someone tells you he or she used tung oil on a project, you have no idea what was really used. It could have been any of the four types of "oil."

NOTE

For many years the manufacturers of Watco Danish Oil Finish claimed their finish made the wood 25 percent harder. This idea that an oil/varnish blend can make the wood harder has become part of the lore of oil finishes. But the claim is silly. Any finish cured in the wood's pores will help the surface resist abrasions and thus make the wood seem to be harder. But of all finishes except wax and straight oil, oil/varnish blends have the least hardening effect. Varnish, shellac, lacquer, and water base all cure much harder than any oil-containing finish.

HOW TO TELL WHICH "OIL" YOU HAVE

Clues	Raw and Boiled Linseed Oil	Pure Tung Oil	Polymerized Linseed and Tung Oil	Thinned Varnish or Polyurethane	Oil/Varnish Mix
The label will almost always tell you correctly	Yes	Yes	No	No	No
The "oil" has a distinctive smell	Yes	Yes	No	No	No
A thin coat gets tacky quickly under a hair dryer	No	No	Yes	Yes	No
Excess remains smeary, even if heated with a hair dryer	Yes	Yes	No	No	Yes
Cures flat with excess wiped off, even after several coats	No	Yes	No	No	No
Cures satin ("rubbed") after several coats with excess wiped off after each coat	Yes	No	No	No	Yes
Cures glossy after several coats with excess wiped off after each coat	No	No	Yes	Yes	No
Cures wrinkled when puddled on glass	Yes	Yes	Yes*	No	Yes*
Cures smooth when puddled on glass	No	No	No	Yes	No

* Usually wrinkles less than raw or boiled linseed oil or pure tung oil.

carried. Customers were instructed to use only the proper oil on each of the woods in their house!

Teak oil creates the greatest confusion. There are at least three different types of finish that are sold in the United States as "teak oil." There is mineral oil, which doesn't cure. There is a mix of wax and mineral oil, which also doesn't cure. And there is a mix of linseed oil and varnish, which does cure. The teak oil that is sold by Watco, Behlen, and most Scandinavian furniture stores is this third kind. This "oil" is essentially the same as other oil/varnish blends. None have anything added to make them better suited for teak or other oily woods.

Oily woods, such as teak, rosewood, cocobolo, and ebony, present a problem in finishing because the wood's natural oil inhibits the curing of oil and varnish finishes. (The oil also prevents other finishes, such as lacquer and water base, from establishing a good bond with the wood.) Since no "oil" finish contains anything to counteract the problems caused by wood's oil, it's usually best to wipe the wood down with a fast-evaporating solvent, such as naphtha, acetone, or lacquer thinner, before applying the finish. The solvent temporarily removes the wood's oil from the surface of the wood. The finish then has time to bond well and cure thoroughly before more of the wood's oil seeps back to the surface.

Choosing an "Oil" Finish

With so many different types of oil, how do you choose which one to use? Of the four types of "oil," two can be eliminated from consideration: straight oil and polymerized oil. Neither of the two straight oils—linseed oil or tung oil—performs well, so it would be rare that you would want to use one of these. Polymerized oil performs well, but it is expensive, is not widely available, and offers no advantage over wiping varnish (with the possible exception of an unthinned variety used on small objects such as gun stocks because it cures so quickly).

That leaves oil/varnish blend and wiping varnish. Oil/varnish blend is the easier of the two to use, because you have plenty of time to apply it and get the excess wiped off. Oil/varnish blend also produces a pleasing satin sheen that is very popular. But it doesn't protect the wood very well against water, water-vapor exchange, or wear. Oil/varnish blend should be your choice when protection is not of primary importance and you want maximum ease of application and a satin ("rubbed") appearance. Oil/varnish blend is a poor choice for a tabletop, for example, but might be used on a rocking chair, bed, or decorative object.

Wiping varnish is more difficult to apply than oil/varnish

Of the two practical choices for an "oil" finish, oil/varnish is easier to apply; wiping varnish offers more protection and gloss.

MYTH

Oil finishes should be maintained with lemon oil.

FACT

Lemon oil, an oily mineral-spirits solvent with a lemon scent added, is a very short-lived maintenance product. It is a furniture polish that will help pick up dust, add temporary shine to a dull surface, and reduce scratching until it evaporates—which it will do within a few days. The fresh scent it imparts is a large part of its appeal.

blend because it cures much faster. You have less time before it begins to set up. Also, if you choose to build a thicker film on the wood by not wiping off all the excess, you will have problems with dust settling on and becoming embedded in the finish–just as with unthinned varnish. Wiping varnish produces a glossy sheen unless you use a brand that is made to cure to a satin sheen (in which case you should stir or shake the finish before using), or unless you buff out the gloss with fine steel wool or synthetic steel wool (Scotch-Brite) after the finish has cured. Wiping varnish should be your choice if you want a gloss sheen, or if you want to build a thicker film on the wood. (See "Guide to 'Oil' Finishes" on page 70.)

HOW TO MAINTAIN AND REPAIR "OIL" FINISHES

Maintaining a thin, wiped-on/wiped-off "oil" finish is usually more critical than maintaining any other finish except wax. Even slight wear will create voids in the film, leaving bare wood exposed to spills. The best way to maintain a thin "oil" finish is to recoat it now and then, anytime it begins to look a little dry or show wear. Recoating can be done with the same finish you used originally, or with any other "oil" finish.

"Oil" finishes can also be maintained with paste wax. Paste wax will raise the sheen of a dull surface and will reduce scratching significantly by making the surface slick. But once you've used wax, you should remove it with mineral spirits before applying another coat of finish. Otherwise, the finish will cure softer and smudge easier. (For more on using wax to maintain finishes, see Chapter 15: "Caring for the Finish.")

Woodworkers often cite the easy repairability of "oil" finishes as one of their primary advantages. Repairing a thin finish is often successful precisely because of its thinness. When you wipe another coat of finish over the surface, it penetrates and darkens all scratches. Unless the scratches are severe, the new coat often disguises them (Photo 4-6). But the scratches haven't disappeared: The finish has blended in the color. Any finish can be repaired equally well if it is thin enough.

The problems that are difficult to repair in "oil" finishes are water smudges and color differences. Water smudges usually raise the grain of the wood, creating a visually different texture than the surrounding wood. Applying a coat of finish to the smudge seldom removes it from view. It usually helps to rub the surface with steel wool or to sand it lightly with 400- or 600-grit sandpaper and then apply more finish. (You can also apply more finish and then rub or sand while the finish is still wet.) If this

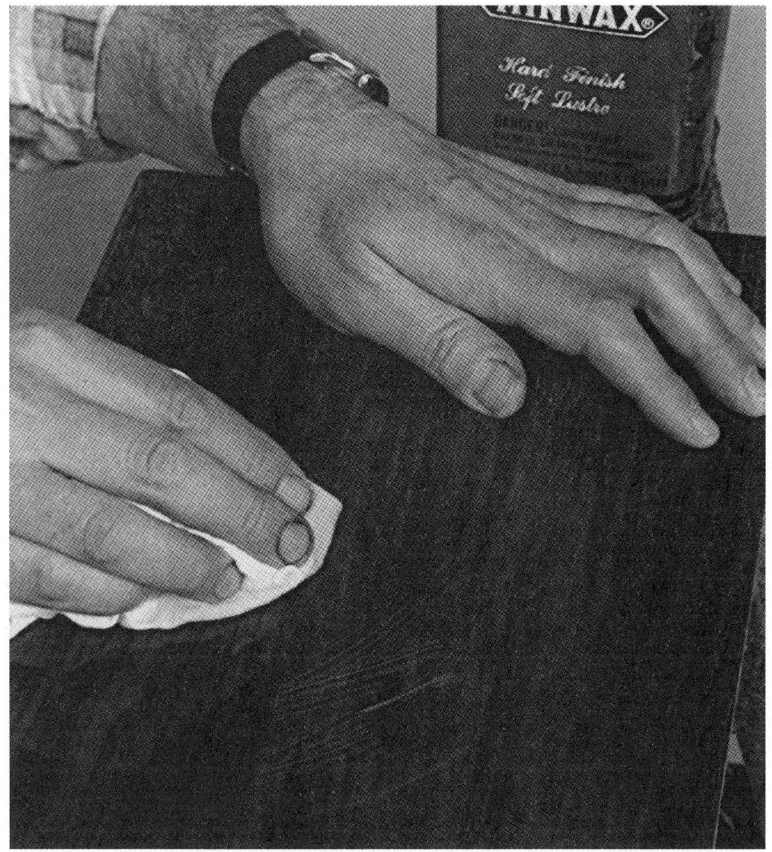

Photo 4-6: "Oil" finishes are appreciated for their repairability. When you wipe another coat of finish over scratches, the finish penetrates and darkens the scratches, making them seem to disappear. Any finish can be repaired equally well if it is thin enough.

doesn't remove the smudge, continue applying more coats of finish to the damaged area until the two sheens blend.

Color differences can be caused by heat or spills staining the wood, or by removal of patina (changing the color of the wood itself), or by eliminating the original stain. You can remove heat or burn stains only by sanding through the damage. You can sometimes bleach out spill stains with oxalic acid or household bleach (see "Bleaching Wood" on page 80). You can sometimes fake patina with stain or bleach. And you can sometimes replace the original stain successfully. All of these problems can be difficult to repair to perfection. (For more on repairing finishes, see Chapter 16: "Repairing Finishes.")

If you realize, after you've applied the finish, that one piece of wood or a part of a piece of wood is lighter than the rest, you can darken it with any dye stain that uses alcohol or lacquer thinner as a solvent. (See Chapter 5: "Staining Wood.") The solvent/dye solution will bite into the finish enough so that you won't remove the color when you wipe on and wipe off the next coat of finish.

TIP

If your oil or oil/varnish finish cures tacky because you didn't wipe it off well enough, scrub the finish with fine steel wool lubricated with mineral spirits, naphtha, or more of the same finish. Then apply some more finish, if necessary, and wipe off the excess.

GUIDE TO "OIL" FINISHES

Finish	Protection[1]	Sheen	Ease of Application	Cost	Color[2]	Penetration[3]
Raw linseed oil	Poor	Satin (rubbed)	Very easy	Low	Dark	Deep
Boiled linseed oil	Poor	Satin (rubbed)	Very easy	Low	Dark	Deep
Pure tung oil	Poor until five or more coats	Dull until five or more coats	Very Easy	High	Light	Deep
Polymerized linseed and polymerized tung oil	Potentially excellent if built up	Gloss	Easy on small surfaces	Very high	Light	Shallow
Wiping varnish	Potentially excellent if built up	Gloss	Easy	Medium	Light	Shallow
Oil/Varnish	Medium	Satin (rubbed)	Very easy	Medium	Medium	Medium

[1] Indicates protection against wear, dirt, water, and water-vapor exchange.
[2] Indicates the relative degree of color (darkness) the finish adds to the wood.
[3] Indicates how deep the finish will penetrate if the surface is kept wet.

Raw linseed oil.

Boiled linseed oil.

Working Properties

Cures soft and extremely slowly—many days. There's no reason to use raw linseed oil in finishing unless you have a specific need for a very slow-curing oil.

Cures soft about four to six times faster than raw linseed oil—in about a day. Produces a satin sheen after several coats. Shouldn't be built up, or it will be soft and gummy. Wipe off the excess between coats. Minimal protection. Darkens the wood more than other oils.

Cures faster and more water-resistant than raw linseed oil. Cures soft so shouldn't be built up on the wood. Doesn't darken as much as linseed oil. Produces a very dull sheen until five or more coats.

Thicker than linseed oil or tung oil unless thinned with mineral spirits, which it usually is. Cures very fast unless thinned. Cures hard and glossy. Develops cracks in the film if applied thick.

Cures fairly fast to a glossy sheen unless it has been made satin or flat by the addition of flatting agents. Can be built up to any thickness you want by leaving each coat wet on the surface.

Varies somewhat in curing time and gloss, depending on the oil-to-varnish ratio. Cures more slowly than varnish to a satin sheen. Shouldn't be built up because the oil in the finish causes the finish to cure too soft.

Pure tung oils.

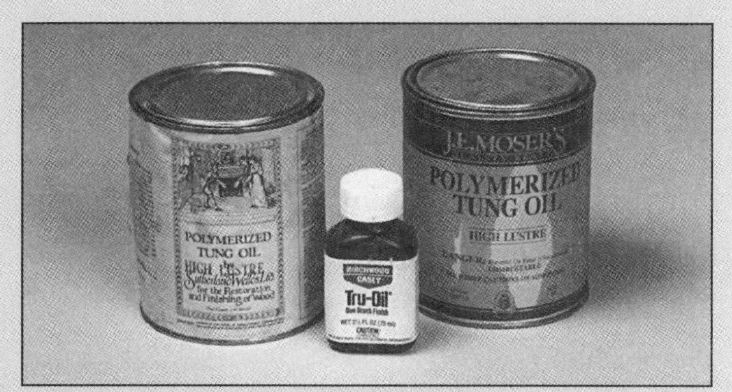

Polymerized linseed and polymerized tung oils.

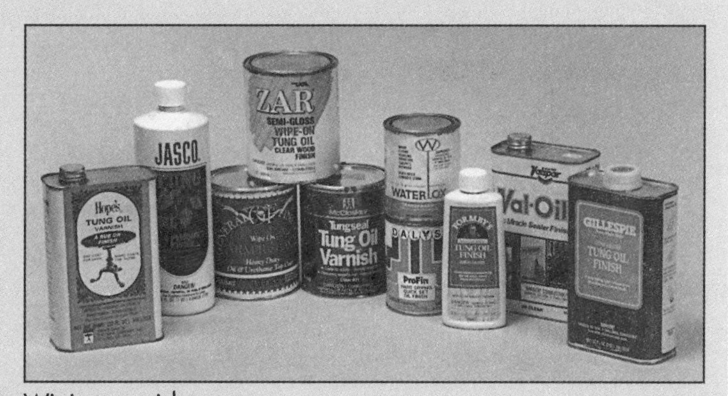

Wiping varnishes.

Oil/varnishes.

Chapter 5

Staining Wood

Of all the steps in finishing, staining causes the most problems. Because of such difficulties as splotching, streaking, color unevenness, and incompatibility between stain and finish, many woodworkers avoid the use of stains altogether. I'm convinced that the popularity of the "natural wood look" among woodworkers is at least partly because they think stains are difficult to use.

Used properly, though, stains beautify wood, and they solve problems rather than create them. Stains add richness, depth, and color to wood. They help disguise problem areas and smooth color variations between different boards, and between heartwood and sapwood in the same board. They even allow you to make cheap, uninteresting woods like poplar and soft maple resemble higher-quality woods like walnut and mahogany (Photo 5-1 on page 87).

You probably think of staining as simply applying a colored liquid to bare wood. Staining is this, but it is also much more. It includes glazing, toning, and shading, all ways of applying a colorant so that you can still see the wood through the color.

Unfortunately, most books treat glazing, toning, and shading as specialized techniques, not as part of staining. This obscures their real value for solving problems. Often, applying stain directly to wood just won't produce the look you want, while glazing, toning, or shading will. Therefore, I'm treating these operations in this chapter, so you will see how they complement staining.

Most staining problems are caused by using the wrong stain for the effect you're after or by peculiarities in the wood.

Most likely, you choose a stain for its color. You're probably not thinking about other important considerations, such as what the stain is made of, how fast it dries, or how it will behave on the wood. Manufacturers don't make it easy to find out what is in their stains, or what you can expect from them. Reading the can won't tell you what to expect—except, of course, "professional results."

This is unfortunate because ignoring the differences in stains can lead to results you don't want. Some stains, such as Watco and Minwax, penetrate deep into the wood; others, such as Wood-Kote and Bartley, very little. Some stains, such as Behlen 15 Minute, dry fast; others, such as Red Devil, slowly. Some stains, such as Carver Tripp Safe and Simple, raise the grain of the wood; others, such as Carver Tripp Wood Stain, don't. If you've done much staining, you've surely noticed some of these differences.

Woods also differ, and stains act differently on different woods. Some woods, such as mahogany, look nice with any stain. Other woods, such as pine, present problems no matter which stain you use. But no wood is consistent in color, porosity, or density; therefore different pieces of the same species and even different parts of the same board may stain differently. In addition, veneered plywood usually stains lighter than solid wood because the veneer is so thin, and the glue blocks deep penetration.

Most staining problems aren't caused by the way you apply

WHAT MAKES A STAIN

Stains vary according to colorant, binder (common finish), and thickness. Pigment can be used with any binder. Dyes don't require a binder but can be added to one, as in combination pigment/dye stains. Each dye and each binder has a corresponding solvent or thinner.

Colorant	Pigment				Dye		
Binder	Oil[1]	Varnish[1]	Lacquer	Water-base	—	—	—
Solvent or Thinner	Mineral Spirits	Mineral Spirits	Lacquer Thinner	Water, Glycol Ether	Water	Alcohol	Oil (Mineral Spirits or Lacquer Thinner)
Other Formulations	Gel[2]	Gel[2]	—	Gel[2]	NGR[3]	—	—

1 These can be mixed to make an oil/varnish binder.
2 Gel stains combine a colorant and binder with thixotropic agents that prevent the stain from flowing unless it is physically manipulated.
3 NGR (non-grain-raising) stain is water dye dissolved in a glycol ether solvent so it can be thinned with alcohol or lacquer thinner.

the stain. They're caused by choosing the wrong stain for the effect you're after or by peculiarities in the wood. If you are going to use stains successfully, you need to understand how various stains and woods interact (Photos 5-2, 5-3, and 5-4 on pages 88–89; see also "Common Staining Problems, Their Causes, and Solutions" on page 114).

UNDERSTANDING STAINS

There are a number of ways to classify stains. Understanding the ingredients, their properties, and how they interact helps in predicting how a stain will perform. (See "What Makes a Stain" on the facing page and "A Guide to Stains" on page 76.) Here are the things that make a difference:

- *Colorant*—is it a pigment or a dye?
- *Binder*—is it an oil-, varnish-, lacquer-, or water-based finish?
- *Thickness*—is it a liquid or a gel?

Pigment

Pigment is finely ground solid, colored particles that resemble colored earth. Until recently, all pigment actually *was* colored earth, mined in various parts of Europe and America. Now, most pigments are synthetic. Since pigment is opaque, it is used as the colorant in paint. When you pile enough pigment particles on top of each other, you can no longer see through to the wood. Because pigment is heavier than the liquid it is suspended in, pigment particles settle to the bottom of the container and have to be stirred back into suspension before use. Most manufactured stains are made with pigment.

Pigment colors wood by lodging in depressions, such as pores, scratches, and gouges. The larger the cavity, the greater the amount of pigment that will lodge there, and the darker and more opaque the cavity becomes. This is why pigment stains highlight large pores, gouges, and cross-grain sanding scratches (Photos 5-5 and 5-6 on pages 89–90). (Pigment lodged in sanding scratches running in the direction of the grain is usually difficult to distinguish from the grain itself.)

Pigment can also color wood by building to a thickness on the surface. Building occurs when you don't wipe off all the excess stain, and it is equivalent to painting the wood with a thinned paint. You can control how much you obscure the wood by how much pigment you leave on the surface. Some stains, such as Behlen 15 Minute, dry rapidly and are difficult to wipe off entirely. Not removing all the excess pigment stain can produce a more even color, like paint, but the wood doesn't show through.

MYTH

You can darken wood by leaving a pigment stain on the wood longer before wiping off the excess or by applying a second coat.

FACT

The first wet coat of pigment stain fills all depressions within seconds. Letting the stain remain longer on the wood won't darken the wood more because the depressions are already filled. The same is true for the second coat. Only if you didn't apply a good wet coat of stain the first time, or if you don't wipe off all the excess, will the second coat of stain darken the wood.

A GUIDE TO STAINS

Pigment in an oil-based binder

Most common and easiest to use. Allows the most time to remove excess. Let cure overnight before applying a finish.

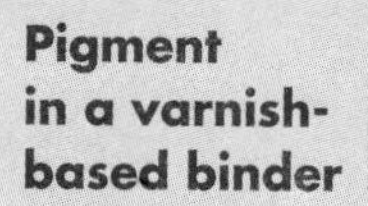

Pigment in a varnish-based binder

Gets tacky quickly. Allows little time to remove excess. Apply a finish after overnight curing.

Pigment in a lacquer or short-oil varnish binder

Cures very rapidly. Remove excess almost immediately after application. Spray, usually in combination with lacquer. Coat over in 15 minutes.

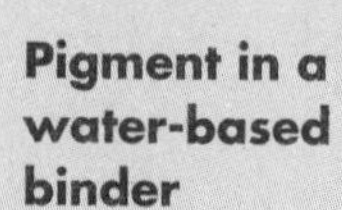

Pigment in a water-based binder

Cures fairly rapidly. Begin removing excess stain quickly. Apply a finish after two to four hours. All water-based stains raise the grain of the wood.

Pigment and dye in an oil-based binder

Colors wood more evenly than stain that contains only pigment. Dye penetrates better into dense areas between pores in woods such as oak and maple.

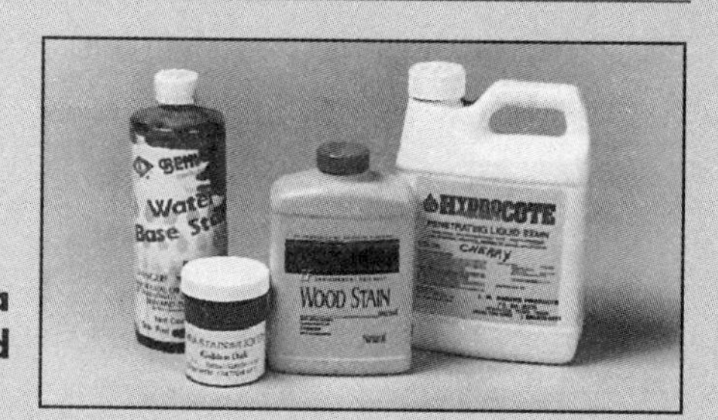

Pigment and dye in a water-based binder

Colors wood more evenly than stain that contains only pigment. Dye penetrates better into dense areas between pores in woods such as oak and maple.

Asphaltum in an oil/varnish binder

Acts very similar to dye stain. Colors wood more evenly than pigment stain.

Pigment or dye in a varnish- or acrylic-based gel

Different from all other stains, no matter what the colorant or binder. Gel stains don't flow, so they don't penetrate into the wood.

Dye

The coloring in coffee, tea, berries, and walnut husks is dye. These and other natural materials such as logwood, alkanet root, cochineal, and dragon's blood were once used to dye wood. (Chemicals are also used; see "Bleaching Wood" on page 80 and "Chemical Stains" on page 82.) Now, far superior, synthetic *aniline dyes* are available. Aniline dyes are made from aniline and related chemicals. Aniline is derived from petroleum. These dyes were developed in the late nineteenth century and quickly came to dominate the dye industry because of their greater range of colors, ease of use, and better resistance to fading *(lightfastness)*.

Dye is molecular. Each individual unit of dye is a molecule. In contrast to pigment, which colors wood by lodging in crevices, dye colors wood by saturating the wood fibers with color. Dye molecules, much tinier than pigment particles, penetrate into the very composition of the wood (Figure 5-1).

Unlike pigment particles, dye molecules adhere to the wood on their own. Dye does not require a separate binder to glue it to the wood as pigment does. All that is necessary is a solvent to put the dye into solution. Once dye is dissolved in the solvent, it

(text continues on page 80)

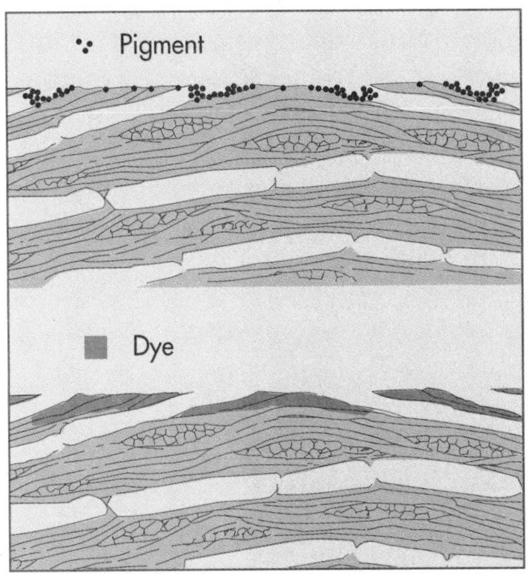

Figure 5-1: Pigment lodges in the pores, scratches, and defects in the wood, highlighting them. Dye saturates the wood fibers with color, usually producing a more even appearance.

USING ANILINE DYES

WATER-, ALCOHOL-, AND OIL-SOLUBLE dye stains are usually sold in powder form. You have to dissolve them in a solvent. Non-grain-raising (NGR) dye stains come already in solution.

Mixing Your Own Dye Stains

If you are mixing your own dye stain from powders, be sure to use the proper solvent specified by the manufacturer. Mix 1 ounce of powder to 1 quart of solvent for a standard stain. Use distilled water for water dye, denatured alcohol for alcohol dye, and mineral spirits or lacquer thinner (or both) for oil dye. Always use a glass or plastic container. Metal will react with the dye and could affect the color.

At first, having to mix the dye yourself may seem an inconvenience, but you will come to appreciate the greater control you have over the color. If you want it darker, add less solvent than the directions suggest. If you want it lighter, add more solvent. You can blend colors while they are still in powder form, but it is much easier and it eliminates the respiratory hazard to blend them after they have been dissolved. The color of the dye powders is not always the same as the color of the dye when it is dissolved. You can mix the dyes in any combination and between any brands, as long as they all dissolve in the same solvent. Measured amounts of one brand of dye and its solvent should produce the same color over and over, but to be safe, always mix more than enough dye to complete any given project. It's a good idea to strain the dissolved dye through tightly woven cheesecloth to remove impurities and any undissolved dye, which could cause spotting.

Water dye will dissolve quicker and

(continued)

USING ANILINE DYES—continued

more thoroughly in hot water than cold. But I've often used cold with no problems. The water dye can be applied to the wood hot or cold, the difference being that hot dye is thinner and more active and probably will penetrate deeper. So you want to be sure to use dye at about the same temperature over the entire surface.

Use distilled water for best results; tap water often contains mineral salts that can affect the color of the dye.

Some commercially available dyes are a combination of water- and alcohol-soluble dyes. You will need to blend in a little alcohol with your water to bring out the full color. Follow the manufacturer's instructions.

Applying Aniline Dyes

It's wise to test the color of the dye on a scrap piece of wood–ideally a cutoff of the same wood used to make the piece you're about to stain. As with any stain, the color of the dye while still damp on the wood will be very close to the color you will get after you apply the finish.

There are two ways to apply aniline dye: You can apply a wet coat and wipe off the excess before it dries, or you can brush or spray on thin coats and build the color to the darkness you want without wiping. Dyes are totally transparent, so you can continue to apply coats without obscuring the wood.

Removing the Excess Dye

Unless the object is very small, water dye is the only dye that allows enough time to apply and wipe off a coat before it dries. But water dye will raise the grain of the wood, so you should sponge the wood first to get the best results. (See "Sponging" on page 15.)

As with other stains, you don't have to worry about grain direction when you apply the water-dye stain, as long as you wipe off all the excess. Often, instructions tell you to apply the stain with a brush. This isn't necessary. In fact, using a brush is inefficient because it is so slow. The best way, other than using a spray gun, is with a well-soaked sponge or cloth.

Coat an entire section at a time. Work rapidly so you get everything coated before the dye dries. It's a good idea to work from the bottom up on vertical surfaces. This way if you drip some dye stain, the drips won't sit on the wood longer and penetrate deeper than the dye on the rest of the wood, resulting in spots.

Leaving the Excess Dye

You can apply any dye without wiping off the excess. Because dye is transparent, you won't obscure the wood. Each new coat of dye dissolves the already-existing dye, making a higher dye-to-solvent ratio. If you leave the newly applied dye to dry, the color will be darkened or changed depending on the dye you apply.

Because alcohol, oil, and NGR dyes dry so rapidly, they are rarely wiped off after application. Water-soluble dyes can be applied either way. The most common dye used by industry and large woodworking shops is NGR dye. It is sprayed on the wood, and the color is built up. The most common dye used by amateurs and small woodworking shops is water dye. It is usually wiped off because brushing and leaving the excess to dry requires more skill.

If you spray the dye onto the wood and don't wipe off the excess, it's best to spray highly thinned coats and gradually build the depth of color you want. That's the reason NGR dye stains are sold in a highly thinned solution. If you try to get the final color all at once, you may get it too dark, and then you have to go to the trouble of removing some of it.

The trick to brushing dye stain is achieving an even coverage. Brush out the dye in long strokes with the grain. Use a good-quality natural- or synthetic-bristle brush (you have less control with a sponge brush). Brush the dye out until the brush is too dry to continue. Keep a wet edge–that is, be sure each brush stroke overlaps dye that is still wet. Continue to brush out any wet parts without using more dye until the surface appears dull.

If the dye stain appears streaky when dry, wet a cloth with the appropriate solvent and wipe over the entire surface. You will remove much of the color and even out what is left. Then reapply the dye with a brush before the solvent evaporates. The wet wood will help evenly spread the dye the second time.

Techniques for Controlling Color

By building dye colors, you can reduce or eliminate color differences between heartwood and sapwood, and between different species. In woods with extremely dissimilar heartwood and sapwood, such as walnut and cherry, try brushing or spraying a coat of dye onto the sapwood. Use a dye that will bring the color of the sapwood close to that of the heartwood. When the surface wetness has disappeared, apply a dye to the entire surface. Alternatively, coat the entire surface first, then recoat the sapwood with a color dye that will bring it in line with the heartwood. Either way you are putting double the amount of color into the sapwood to balance it with the more colorful heartwood (Photo 5-7).

If you are staining the wood darker than the heartwood is anyway, you can often blend sapwood with heartwood by applying two coats of the same dye to the sapwood and one coat to the heartwood.

To blend end grain with side grain, apply some solvent to the end grain just before applying the dye. The solvent in the wood will dilute the dye so it colors the end grain less.

To color wood without highlighting the grain or potential problems and without obscuring the wood, spray on almost dry coats of dye stain (Photo 5-8 on page 90). Keep the coats of dye dry enough so they don't penetrate, and apply as many as necessary to get the color you want.

You have great control of color when you use dye. If you want the color lighter, wipe the wood with the dye's solvent. If you want the color darker, apply the same dye and don't wipe off all the excess, or mix the dye in a higher dye-to-solvent ratio and apply it. (You can't make the color much darker by applying the same dye and then wiping it all off.) If you want to change the color, apply a different-colored dye and either wipe off the excess or leave it. Even if you wipe off the excess, the new color will partially dissolve and blend with the original color to give you a color somewhere in between (Photo 5-9 on page 91). ■

Photo 5-7: You can color lighter sapwood to match darker heartwood. Simply apply a second coat of dye to the sapwood and don't wipe off the excess. (You may have to alter the color some to achieve a match.) You can color the sapwood to match the heartwood before staining overall, or you can stain overall and, while the stain is still damp (so you can see the color you're matching), apply the second coat to the sapwood.

doesn't settle out—even after years of sitting on the shelf.

Because dye is a soluble colorant, it can be redissolved by its solvent long after it has been applied to the wood. This can be an advantage, allowing you to lighten the color of the dye or change it to another color after you've applied it to the wood. Simply apply more solvent or another color dissolved in the same solvent and wipe off the excess. On the other hand, this characteristic can be a disadvantage. If your finish contains the solvent for the dye, the finish will redissolve the dye, causing it to smear or bleed into the finish. (See "Using Aniline Dyes" on page 77.)

There are literally thousands of dyes synthesized from ani-

BLEACHING WOOD

YOU CAN PUT COLOR *IN* WOOD with stain. You can take color *out* of wood with bleach. You can use bleach to lighten almost any wood to an off-white color. Then you can apply a finish to the wood as is, or you can stain the wood darker to match the color you want. Use bleach when you want to make the color of wood lighter than it is naturally. You can also use bleach to lighten two different-colored woods so you can stain them to a common color.

The procedure for bleaching wood is not at all difficult. The trick is to use the right bleach for the job. There are three types of bleach used in woodworking, and each serves a different purpose. *Two-part bleach* (sodium hydroxide and hydrogen peroxide) removes the natural color from wood. *Chlorine bleach* removes dye from wood (just as it removes dye from clothes). And *oxalic acid* removes rust and water stains from wood (Photo 5-10).

Use two-part bleach when you want to lighten the color of the wood itself. Use chlorine bleach and oxalic acid to remove dye stain or black water rings from old furniture (see "Using Oxalic Acid" on page 293).

All three types of bleach are often sold as "wood bleach." This makes it difficult to know which you're getting. The key is that two-part bleach always comes in two separate containers. Neither chlorine bleach nor oxalic acid is sold this way.

Bleaching wood with two-part bleach requires four steps:

1. Pour some chemical from the container labeled "A" or "1" into a glass or plastic container. Never use metal. Both parts of the bleach will react with metal. Apply a wet coat of the chemical to the wood using a synthetic bristle brush or a cloth. Work from the bottom up to avoid spots that might occur from drips onto uncoated parts. Be sure the coat is wet all over. Protect your eyes and your skin from contact with this chemical. It is usually sodium hydroxide (also called lye or caustic soda), which is extremely caustic and will burn you severely on contact. (Have some water nearby to wash it off your skin, just in case.) Sodium hydroxide will darken many woods. Don't let this bother you; the next step will change things.

2. Pour some "B" or "2" chemical, usually hydrogen peroxide, into a glass or plastic container. Before the first chemical dries, apply the second chemical on top of the first. (Sometimes manufacturers reverse the order, putting hydrogen peroxide in the "A"

line and related chemicals. Each of these dyes dissolves naturally in a solvent. Some dyes dissolve in water, some in alcohol, some in mineral spirits or lacquer thinner. (See “What Makes a Stain” on page 74.) The dyes are usually sold in powder form and are labeled according to their solvent: “water,” “alcohol,” or “oil.” (Those that dissolve in mineral spirits or lacquer thinner are called oil-soluble dyes.) Make your own stains by mixing the powder with the appropriate solvent or with a finish that is compatible with the dye solvent—water dye with water-based finish; alcohol dye with shellac; oil dye with oil, varnish, or lacquer.

Generally speaking, water-soluble dyes are the most lightfast

NOTE

Almost all modern dyes used in woodworking are derived from a family of chemicals called aromatic amines, the simplest of which is aniline. It is conventional in woodworking to call all of these dyes "aniline dyes."

container and sodium hydroxide in the “B” container. It doesn’t matter. It’s the reaction of the two chemicals together that does the bleaching.) Use a separate brush, or thoroughly wash out the brush you used for the first chemical before using it in the second. You should see a foaming as the two chemicals react, and the wood will turn lighter. Let it dry overnight.

3. Apply a mild acid, such as white vinegar, to the wood to neutralize the alkalinity of any remaining sodium hydroxide. Pour about 1 part vinegar into 3 or 4 parts water and wash the wood. Alternatively, if you are working outside, you can douse the wood with a hose, which will wash away any alkalinity. Let the wood dry overnight.
4. Sand the wood lightly with 280-grit or finer sandpaper to remove the raised grain. Don’t sand more than is needed to make the wood feel smooth, or you may sand through to unbleached wood.

You can combine two steps into one by mixing the two chemicals and applying them as one coat. If you do this, you must apply the mixture at once. The alkaline sodium hydroxide and the acidic hydrogen peroxide will begin neutralizing each other immediately upon contact (the reason they are packaged separately). The mixture quickly weakens.

One application of two-part bleach is usually enough. However, there are several ways you can try to lighten the wood further if necessary:

- Bleach the wood a second time.
- Do your bleaching in sunlight (a mild bleaching agent in its own right).
- Apply a second coat of hydrogen peroxide while the first coat is still wet.
- Apply a solution of oxalic acid to the still-wet sodium hydroxide/hydrogen peroxide application. ■

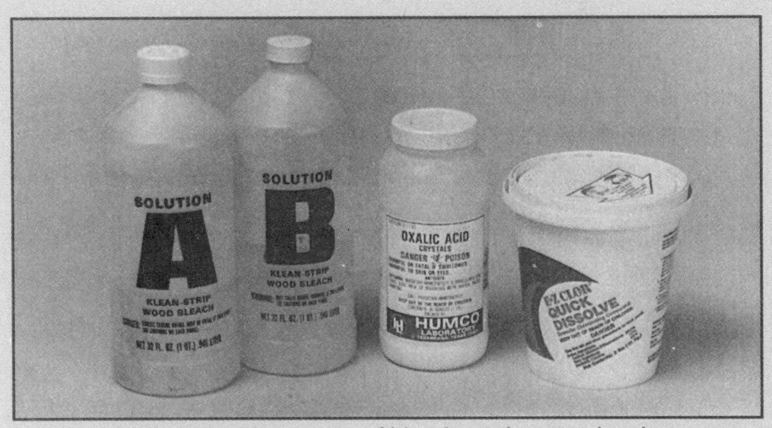

Photo 5-10: There are three types of bleach used in woodworking: two-part bleach (sodium hydroxide and hydrogen peroxide), oxalic acid, and chlorine bleach.

CHEMICAL STAINS

CAUTION

Potassium dichromate is toxic. Wear a dust mask when mixing the crystals and gloves when applying the stain.

SOME CHEMICALS REACT with certain woods to produce color in the wood. Before the development of aniline dyes, these chemicals were sometimes used as stains in place of natural dyes or earth pigments. Some of the chemicals used were lye, ammonia (the process of coloring with ammonia is called fuming), potassium dichromate, potassium permanganate, copper sulphate, ferrous sulfate, and nitric acid. If you've read much about finishing wood, you've probably seen some of these chemicals mentioned.

These chemicals pose two serious problems.

- They are dangerous to use. Most burn your skin on contact. They are generally bad for your health.
- They are difficult to control. If you get the wood too dark or the wrong color, it's often impossible to correct the problem by any method short of sanding all the color out and starting over.

Since aniline dye can imitate any color produced by chemical stains, there's no reason to take the risks using chemicals—with one exception. Potassium dichromate is very useful for coloring some woods in marquetry or mixed-wood designs without coloring others.

Potassium dichromate darkens all woods that naturally contain tannic acid. These woods include mahogany, walnut, oak, and cherry. Marquetry often uses these woods for the background and some of the darker pieces in the design. By applying a solution of potassium dichromate, you can darken the background and darker parts of the design without darkening the lighter woods such as holly, boxwood, and satinwood.

You can buy potassium dichromate crystals from specialty finish suppliers (see "Sources of Supply" on page 305) and chemical supply houses. Dissolve the crystals in water and apply just as you do aniline dyes. Experiment on scrap pieces of wood to determine the solution strength required to give you the darkness you want before you apply the stain to the marquetry itself. ■

MYTH

NGR (non-grain-raising) dyes are oil-soluble dyes.

FACT

NGR dyes are water-soluble dyes made thinnable with alcohol or lacquer thinner by being dissolved first in glycol ether.

of the three types. Lightfastness is an important quality, because it means the colors will remain true longer. As a result, alcohol- and oil-soluble dyes are not as popular. Also, water-soluble dyes are the slowest drying, so you have more time to remove the excess stain (but longer to wait before going on to your next step). The slow drying allows the dye to penetrate deeper, bringing out more richness and depth in the wood.

The use of water as the solvent in water-soluble dyes makes these dyes cheap, devoid of toxic fumes, non-flammable, and nonpolluting to the atmosphere. But water raises the grain of the wood. In order to get around this problem, chemists have come up with a way of dissolving these dyes without using water. They first dissolve the dye in a special solvent called glycol ether. (See "Glycol Ether" on page 187.) Then they thin the solution with alcohol and lacquer thinner. You buy these dyes as non-grain-raising (NGR) dyes. They almost always come in liquid form. You can thin them with more alcohol or lacquer thinner. You can also add them to water-based finish, shellac, or lacquer to make these finishes into colored stains or toners. (See "Shading Stains and Toners" on page 111.)

Dissolving water-soluble dyes in a solvent minimizes grain raising and preserves the dye's lightfastness, but it nullifies the advantages of cheapness and safety. (Dyes dissolved in lacquer thinner, mineral spirits, or alcohol also raise the grain minimally or not at all. But they aren't called non-grain-raising stains.)

You can buy aniline dyes in pure colors or wood tones. If you want a wood-tone color and you aren't experienced at mixing colors, I suggest you stay away from the pure colors. It is not easy to create the color of walnut from red, yellow, and black. (See "Matching Color" on page 84.)

Dyes versus Pigments

There are three significant differences between dye and pigment:

- Dye is transparent; pigment is opaque (Photo 5-11 on page 92; see also "Ebonizing Wood," below).
- Dye penetrates everywhere more or less equally. Pigment lodges only in places that are large enough to hold it (Photo 5-2 on page 88).

CAUTION

Certain aniline dyes, specifically those containing benzidine, have been linked to bladder cancer. To my knowledge none of the dyes available to the woodworking trade contain these possible carcinogens. Nevertheless, you should treat aniline dyes with care, because they can cause respiratory problems and allergic reactions in some people. Wear gloves and a particle mask when working with the dye powder, avoid making it airborne, and wear gloves when applying the dissolved dye stain.

EBONIZING WOOD

EBONIZING WOOD MEANS to make the color of wood black (Photo 5-12 on page 92). It used to be done with chemicals. The most common ebonizing chemical was iron (nails or steel wool) soaked for several days in vinegar. You still see this concoction recommended in books and articles as the best ebonizing material. But it was replaced a century ago by black aniline dye, which is far more effective and easy to use.

You can use any aniline dye—water, alcohol, oil, or NGR (non-grain-raising). The only problem you might have is with water dye. It doesn't effectively color the pores of oak. If you use water dye, you may have to apply a black pigment stain over the dye (after it has dried) to get the pores black. Use an oil/varnish-based pigment stain (water-based stain will lift the dye), and wipe off all the excess. Black pigment will remain in the pores.

Sometimes you can get the dye concentrated enough to color the wood sufficiently with one coat. But it usually takes several coats, which means you should brush or spray the coats and not wipe off the excess. Allow each coat to dry. Then brush or spray on another coat until you achieve the blackness you want.

The reason black dye works so well for ebonizing wood is that dye is transparent. You can make the wood totally black and still see the wood through the color. You could also use a pigmented stain or finish for ebonizing, but you will totally obscure the wood. ■

MATCHING COLOR

OF ALL THE STEPS in finishing, matching colors is the hardest. It's also the most difficult to describe. There are a few general rules, and I can provide some pointers. But experience is really the best teacher.

General Rules about Color

- Learning pure color theory is helpful only to a point. Pure colors– red, yellow, and blue–are seldom used on wood. Colors for wood are closer to earth colors–raw and burnt umber, raw and burnt sienna, yellow ocher, and Van Dyke brown. But in order to match colors you have to look for the pure colors within the earth colors.
- Green is the complementary color to red. If you want to eliminate some of the reddish color of a wood like mahogany, use a stain with a greenish tint. If you think a wood, or a stain, is too cool (that is, has a green or blue cast), add some red.
- Black reduces the intensity of any color.
- Black added to orange, which is a blend of red and yellow, makes brown.
- Brown is the most important color in wood finishing. You can begin with brown and add black, red, green, or yellow to get almost any of the common wood-stain colors.
- Light affects how a color appears. North light and daylight fluorescent bulbs bring out more of the green or blue (coolness) in a color. Incandescent (ordinary) light bulbs bring out more of the red (warmth) in a color. You can buy fluorescent bulbs that are fairly neutral, but they are usually quite expensive. They will have a color temperature of about 3500 degrees Kelvin (daylight bulbs are about 6300 degrees Kelvin; incandescent bulbs are about 2500 degrees Kelvin). You can also mix daylight fluorescent and the warmer incandescent bulbs to bring out both ends of the color spectrum, or you could mix daylight and cool white fluorescent bulbs. You should be aware that you can have a perfect color match under one light source and be noticeably off under another, because the different light sources pick up different aspects of the colorants. The best *natural* light to work under is north light, because it remains fairly constant throughout the day. But there is no agreement about which artificial light source is best.

Additional Practical Considerations

- Always take the color of the wood into account. The wood's color affects the way the stain will appear. If you can, test your stain on a scrap piece of the same wood you intend to stain.
- Colors in both the wood and the stain change over time–usually as a result of light bleaching or oxidation. Different pieces of wood and different pigments and dyes change in different ways and at different rates. Achieving a color match is therefore often temporary.
- When mixing colors for a match, begin with small amounts of color (very little red or black goes a long way), and keep adding until you get what you want.
- Since you are almost always mixing blends of colors (rather than pure colors), you will develop your skills quicker if you build an inventory of colorants and always work from these. You will get used to the way the colors combine. Just be sure you're always working in compatible systems–water/dye, oil/pigment, and so forth. ■

- Dye, dissolved in a solvent, is much easier than pigment stain to lighten, darken, or change to another color after it has been applied to the wood (Photo 5-9 on page 91).

Some stains contain both pigment and dye. These stains must include a binder to glue the pigment to the wood. Many woodworkers like this type of stain because the dye colors dense woods or dense parts of wood that the pigment doesn't (Photo 5-13 on page 93).

Manufacturers seldom tell you what type of colorant—pigment or dye—they use. You can tell a stain contains pigment if sediment settles to the bottom of the can. You can tell a stain contains dye if after all pigment (if any) has settled to the bottom, the liquid portion will color a light piece of wood.

Some manufacturers confuse the difference between pigment and dye stains when they market pigment stains as "penetrating" stains. Pigment doesn't actually penetrate into the wood fibers; it lodges in depressions such as pores and scratches. Dye is a true penetrating stain, because it saturates the wood fibers.

Binder

Binder is the glue that holds pigment particles to the wood (Figure 5-2). Without binder, the particles could be brushed or blown off the wood like dust once the solvent evaporated. All binders are one of the four common finishes: oil, varnish, lacquer, or water base.

You can make your own stain by mixing some pigment with the appropriate binder and thinning if necessary: Use ground-in-oil pigment with oil or varnish. Use artists' acrylic colors with water-based finishes. Use universal-tinting pigment with oil, varnish, lacquer, or water-based finishes.

The choice of binder doesn't affect the way the stain looks on the wood. The binder determines how much time you have to wipe off excess stain. Oil binder cures slowly. Varnish and water-based binders cure moderately quickly. Lacquer binder cures rapidly. (Some "lacquer" stains are actually based on a very short-oil varnish, which is explained in Chapter 10: "Varnish." Since these stains act just like lacquer stains and are usually referred to as lacquer stains in the finishing trade, it's easier to lump the two together.) Temperature and humidity affect the curing time of each of these stains. The higher the temperature and the lower the humidity, the faster the stain will cure. (For more on how these finishes cure, see the chapters on these specific finishes.)

Manufacturers seldom tell you which binder they are using, but they usually provide clues on the container:

- Stains using an oil or varnish binder list mineral spirits

WHAT'S IN WATCO?

The walnut coloring in Watco and Deft oil finishes is not technically dye. Nor is it pigment. It is asphaltum (also called bitumen or gilsonite), a heavy petroleum derivative. When thinned with mineral spirits and stored in a container or applied to wood, asphaltum acts more like dye than pigment. It doesn't settle easily, and it soaks into the fibers of dense woods, such as maple, and dense parts of woods, such as in oak.

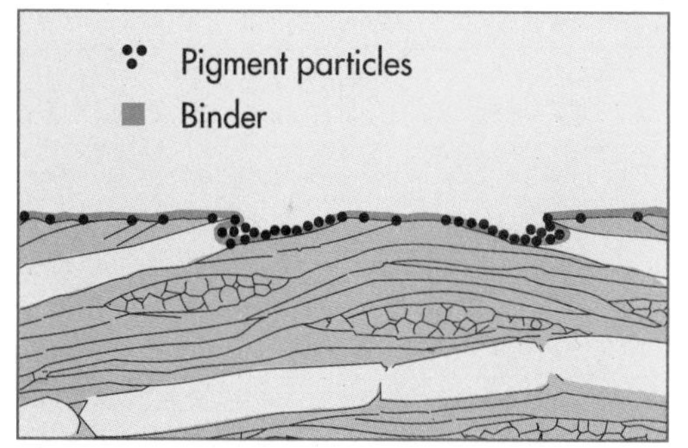

Figure 5-2: Binder glues the dustlike pigment particles to each other and to the wood. Without a binder, the pigment could be brushed or blown off the wood.

TIP

You can run into problems with a pigment stain that dries while you're trying to stain a large area. If the stain hardens before you've had a chance to remove the excess, you get streaks and splotches. The solution to the problem is to switch to a stain that cures more slowly. Stains based on an oil binder are, by far, the easiest to use if you intend to remove the excess from a large surface. Stains based on any of the other three binders may cure too rapidly to wipe the excess off. These stains are the better choice when you don't intend to remove the excess, or when you want to move rapidly to the next step.

(petroleum distillate) as a thinner or clean-up solvent.

- Stains using a lacquer (or short-oil varnish) binder list lacquer thinner (or xylene) as a thinner or clean-up solvent.
- Stains using water-based acrylic or emulsified oil list water as the thinner or clean-up solvent.

It doesn't matter whether the water-based binder is acrylic or emulsified oil. I can't tell any difference between them in drying time. But what is important is whether the binder is oil or varnish. Oil cures much more slowly than varnish. (Mixtures of oil and varnish cure slowly like oil, so I treat them as oil for the purpose of understanding stains.) It's rare that manufacturers give you enough information to determine whether the binder is oil or varnish. You can look for clues such as "Allow overnight for drying," which indicates oil, or "Can be coated over within several hours," which indicates varnish. The instructions also imply how much time you have to remove excess stain. If the manufacturer instructs you to wait overnight before applying a finish, you have more time to remove the excess than if the manufacturer requires only two hours before applying a finish. The less time the manufacturer suggests to wait before applying a finish, the more quickly you must remove the excess.

If there are no clues and you want to know which you have before using the stain, pour a puddle of stain onto a piece of glass; let the puddle cure overnight. If it cures soft and wrinkled, the binder is oil. If it cures hard and smooth, the binder is varnish. (For more information on the difference between the way oil and varnish cure, see Chapter 4: "Oil Finishes.")

Some stains contain a much higher ratio of binder to pigment. These stains often are sold as a combined stain and finish (for example, Minwax Polyshades). When using these stains, there is no reason to wipe off the excess because the point is to get a build on the wood. You should treat these stains as thinned paint, because that is what they are.

Solvents and Thinners

Solvents and thinners make it possible to apply dyes and pigment stains. Solvents are used in dye stains to put the powder dye into solution. Thinners are used in pigment stains to thin the binder so the stain is easy to apply to the wood. Each dye and each binder has a specific solvent or thinner that is appropriate for it. Other solvents or thinners won't work. You need to learn which goes with which. (See "Compatibility of Stains and Finishes" on page 104.) The term "vehicle," which sometimes appears on cans, indicates a binder and thinner combined. The vehicle is the entire liquid portion of the stain.

Since each solvent or thinner is tied to a particular dye or

(text continues on page 103)

A Sampler of Wood Stains

Stains add richness, depth, and color to wood. They help disguise problem areas and smooth color variations. And they allow you to make cheap, uninteresting woods resemble higher-quality species. This section of color photos illustrates some of the effects and characteristics of the various staining materials.

Photo 5-1: With stain, you can radically change the appearance of wood. Here, a water-soluble dye stain makes a birch panel a rich red-brown.

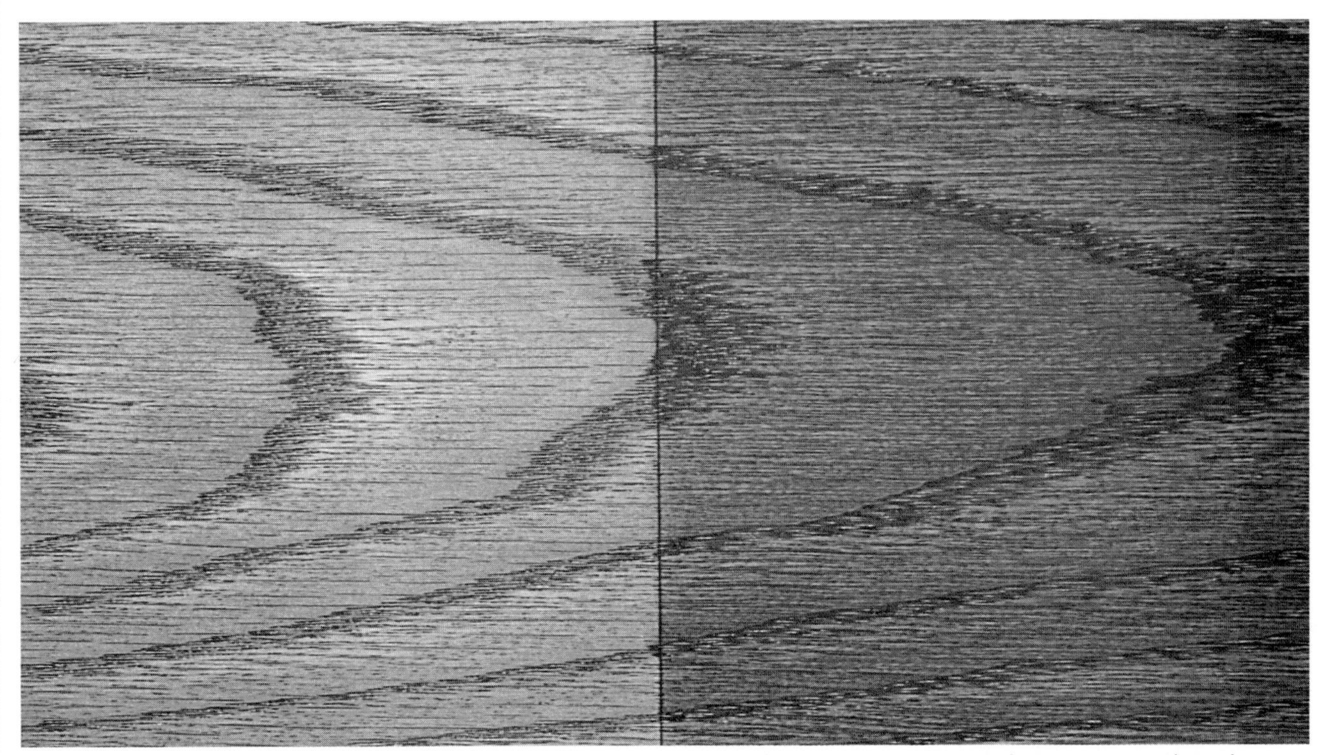

Photo 5-2: Pigment stain (left) highlights the contrast between porous and nonporous grain in oak. Dye stain (right) colors oak without exaggerating the contrast.

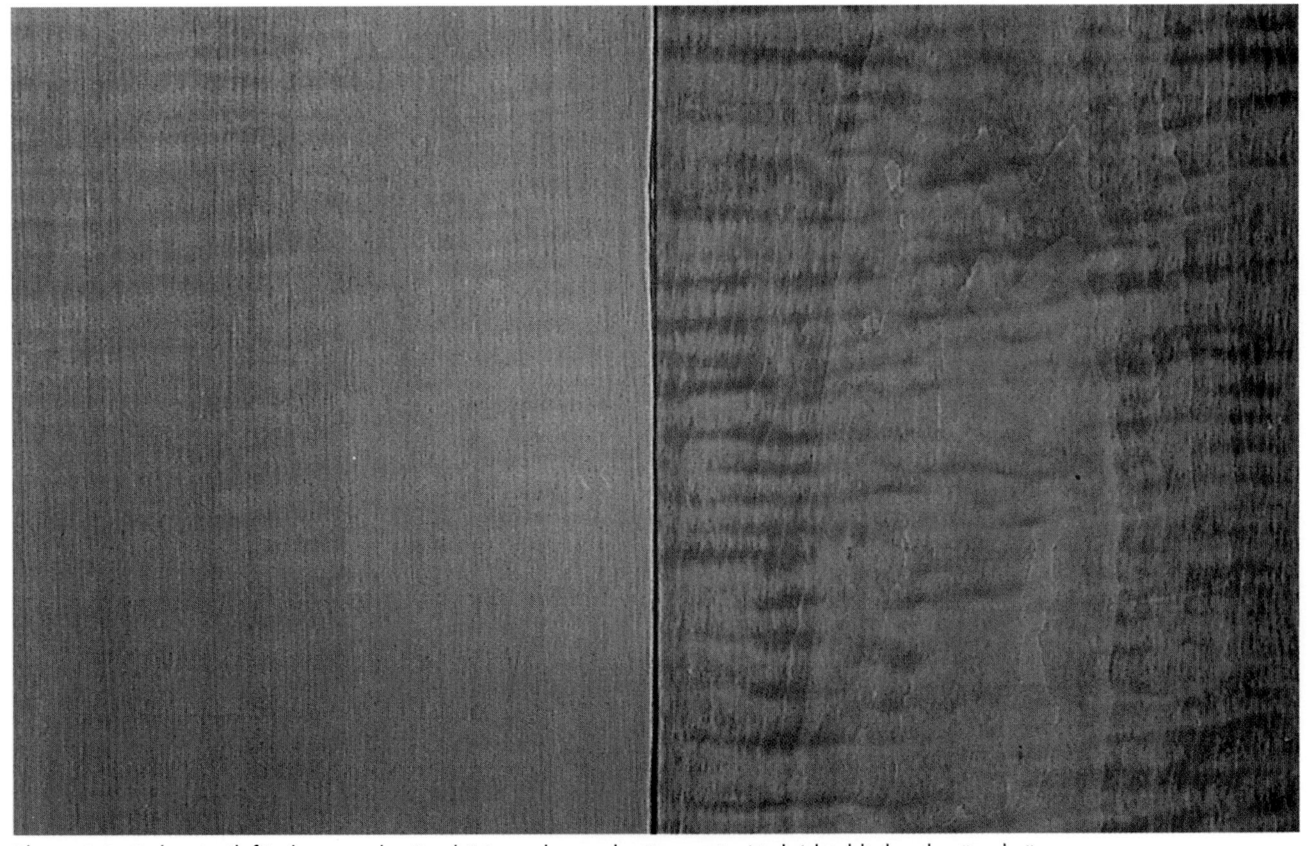

Photo 5-3: Gel stain (left) obscures the "curls" in curly maple. Dye stain (right) highlights the "curls."

Photo 5-4: Pigment stain (left) penetrates and amplifies contrasts in pine—including splotches. Gel stain (right) doesn't penetrate much, so it doesn't amplify the contrasts as much.

Photo 5-5: The pigment in pigment stains remains thick in all pores, gouges, and sanding scratches, making them appear much darker than the surrounding wood. Thus, pigment stains highlight wood pores and problems that you may not otherwise notice.

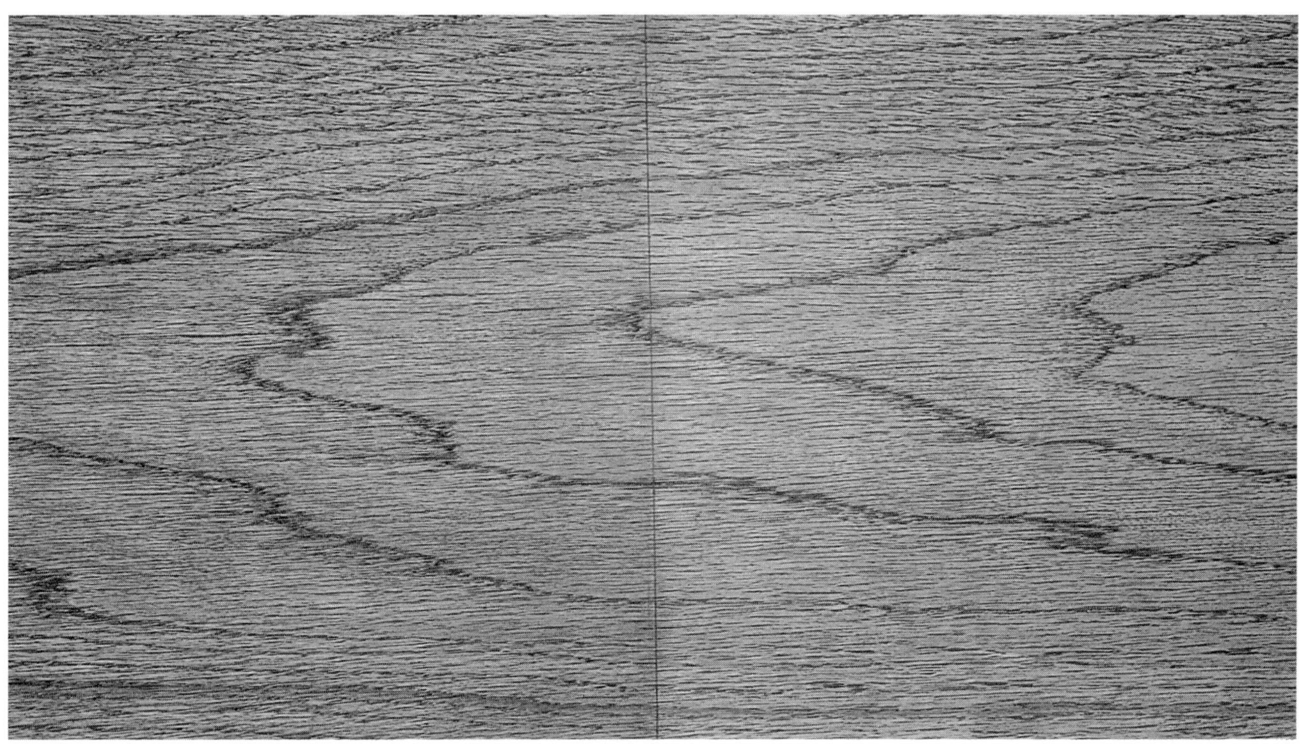

Photo 5-6: You can affect to some extent how dark your pigment stain appears on the wood by varying the final grit you sand with. Coarser grits (left) will leave a surface that accepts more pigment, making the wood appear darker. Finer grits (right) will make finer scratches that won't accept as much pigment, making the wood appear lighter.

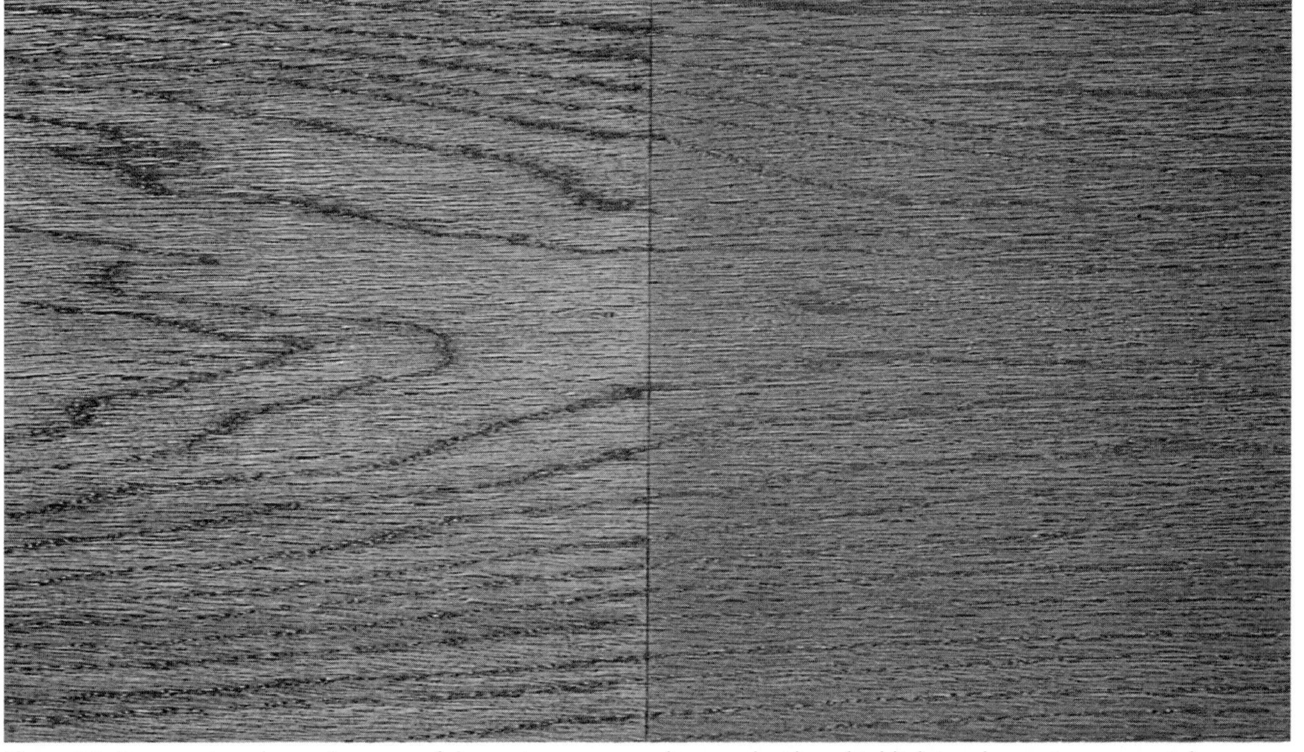

Photo 5-8: By spraying almost-dry coats of dye stain, you can color wood without highlighting the grain or potential problems in the wood and without obscuring the wood. On the left is oak with dye applied wet and wiped off. On the right, almost-dry coats of dye have been sprayed on.

Photo 5-9: Dye stains are much more versatile and forgiving than pigment stains made with a binder, making it possible to adjust both value and hue. The middle section of each of these two sample boards was colored with a single coat of dye stain. If you get the wood too dark, you can wipe it with a cloth wet with the appropriate solvent. You will redissolve some of the dye, allowing you to remove it and lighten the color (board at left, top). If the wood is too light, apply another coat and don't wipe it off. You will darken the color without obscuring the grain (board at left, bottom). If the wood is the wrong color, wipe it with a cloth containing a complementary color that will bring the original to the color you want (board at right, top and bottom). (Be sure to use dye dissolved in the same solvent.) The new color will blend with the original, producing a color somewhere in between.

Photo 5-11: The transparency of dye makes it possible to darken some parts of wood more than other parts, without obscuring the wood as pigment stain does. Dye has been applied to the left side of this panel and pigment to the right side. The bottom half of both sides has multiple coats, not wiped. Note that the dye retains transparency. This characteristic allows you to use dyes to blend color variations between different woods, between different boards of the same species, and between heartwood and sapwood—all without obscuring the wood.

Photo 5-12: The top half of this maple board was ebonized with a black dye stain. The entire board was then finished with lacquer.

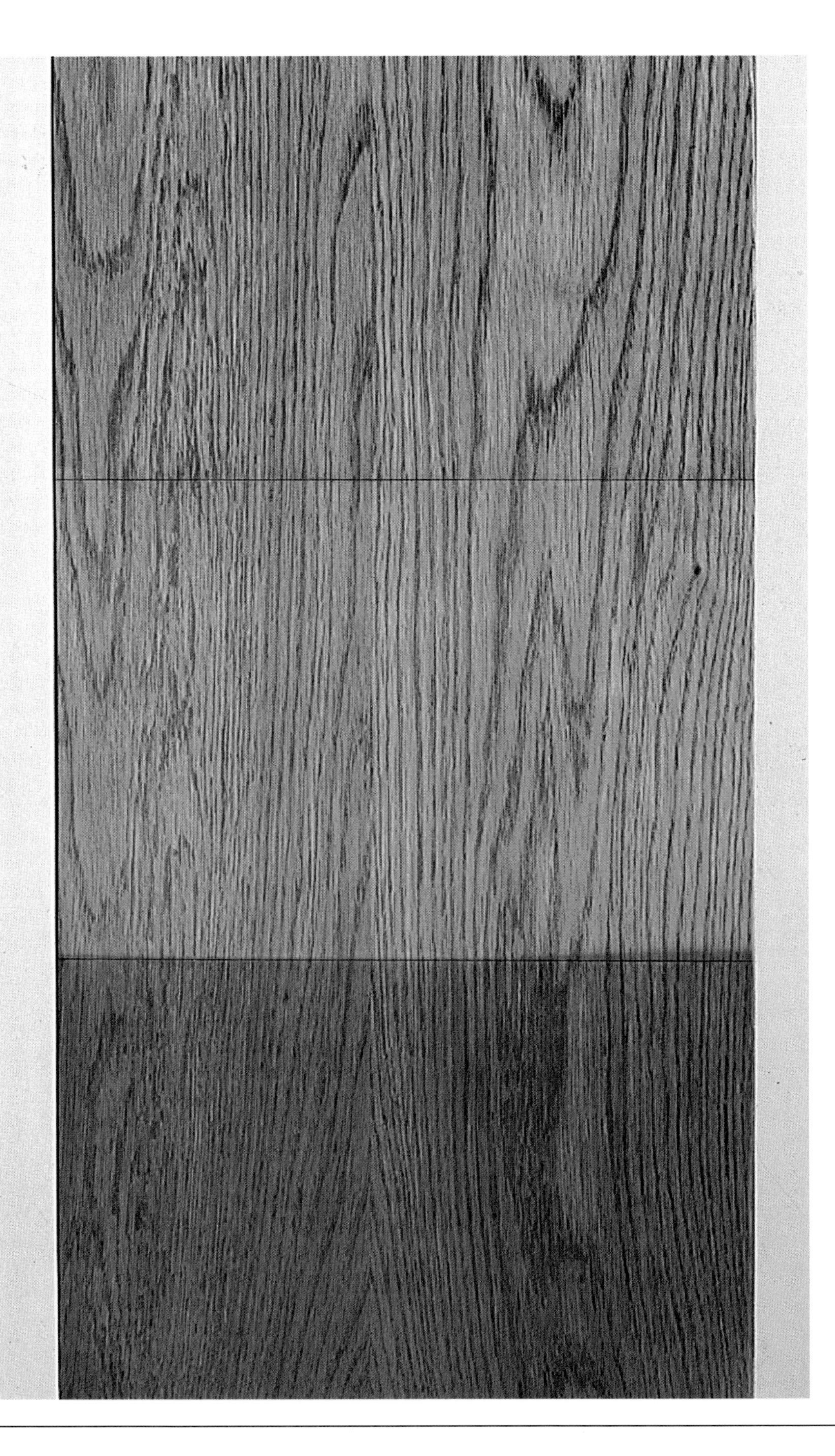

Photo 5-13: Pigment stain (top) lodges in the large earlywood pores of oak, highlighting them. But it doesn't add much color to the dense latewood. Pigment/dye combinations (center) also highlight the pores, but the overall coloring between earlywood and latewood is more even. Dye stains (bottom) color both earlywood and latewood the most evenly of any stain.

Photo 5-15: Gel stain is perfect for pine because it doesn't penetrate, and thus produces a smooth, even finish, like the one shown on the top left. A liquid stain, which penetrates, highlights pine's irregularities, as on the bottom left. On a figured wood, such as bird's-eye maple, a gel stain (top right) masks the grain. A liquid stain (bottom right) emphasizes the figure of the grain.

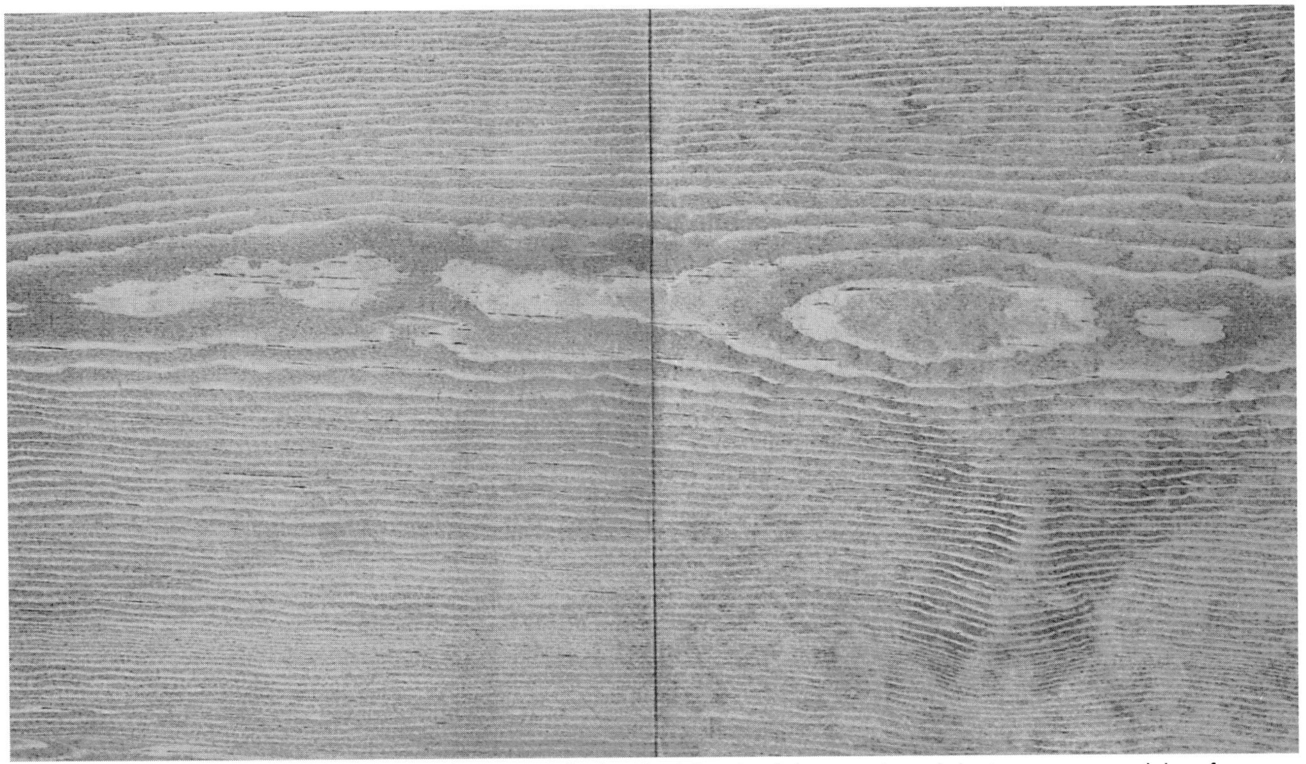

Photo 5-16: Thick gel stains, such as Wood-Kote, applied to the left side of this pine board don't penetrate and therefore don't splotch as much as thin gel stains, such as Minwax, applied to the right side.

Photo 5-19: Burled woods are valued because of their beauty, which is accentuated with stain (right). The beauty is due to the swirly grain, which stain penetrates unevenly.

Photo 5-20: The uneven density natural to pine makes it the most difficult wood of all to stain evenly. Cherry, birch, and maple can also present problems.

Photo 5-24: Washcoating (right) reduces splotching and uneven coloring by reducing stain penetration. But reduced stain penetration means the wood won't get as dark.

Photo 5-25: Glaze can be used to change the color of wood without significantly obscuring it. In the example above, unfinished mahogany (left panel) has been stained with dye (second panel from left), filled with paste-wood filler (third panel from left; see Chapter 6: "Filling the Pores") and then glazed (right panel) to change the color.

Photo 5-26: Glaze can be used to add depth to turnings, as is shown on the one at right.

Photo 5-27: The top half of this ash cabinet door was pickled using a white pickling stain. The entire door was then finished with a nonyellowing water-based finish.

Photo 5-28: Shading (top) means to spray a thinned coat of colored finish to a part of the wood—usually the borders. This has the effect of highlighting the rest. Toning (bottom) means to spray a thinned coat of colored finish evenly over the entire surface. This has the effect of changing the color tone of the wood.

Photo 5-29: Stain applied and wiped off on the top half of this ash cabinet door highlights the pores. Pigmented toner applied to the bottom half produces a fairly even color.

Photo 5-30: Pigment in a shading stain or toner (top) muddies this ribbon-stripe mahogany. Dye (bottom) is transparent, so it adds color without obscuring the wood.

Photo 5-31: Most of the methods discussed in this chapter can be combined as in the example at left. From top to bottom the ribbon-stripe mahogany is bare wood, stained with a yellow dye, sealed with a coat of lacquer, glazed with a brown glaze (wiped off) to highlight the pores, washcoated with thinned lacquer, toned with green NGR dye to reduce red, washcoated, toned with red NGR dye to reduce too much green, and topcoated with two coats of lacquer. Notice that each coat of toner not only changes the color tone but also darkens the color slightly.

Photo 5-32: Stain loses some of its intensity when it dries, but the intensity comes back when you apply a finish over it. In the above example, the dye stain without finish (left) becomes darker and more intense when the finish is applied (right).

(text continued from page 86)

binder, you have little control over which solvent or thinner to use once you've chosen the dye or binder (see "Solvents and Thinners for Dyes and Stains," below). Dyes that use water as a solvent, and water-based binders that use water as a thinner, present a problem in that the water raises the grain of the wood. To get a smooth finish with either of these types of stain, you usually have to sponge and sand the wood before applying the stain. (See "Sponging" on page 15.) If you apply the stain and then try to smooth the raised grain with sandpaper, you may cut through the stain and create light spots.

Thickness

The thickness of stains varies. Most stains are liquid, but some are thicker and usually are sold as gel or paste stains. *Gel stains* are a relatively recent innovation. Most gel stains are made with pigment in a varnish binder. Some gel stains use dye in a varnish or water-based binder. All gel stains are unique in that they don't flow. You can sometimes turn an open can of gel stain upside down, and the stain won't come out. Gel stain doesn't flow because it is made with a *thixotropic* agent that resists flow unless it is mechanically disturbed. Ketchup is an example of a thixotropic substance. You have to shake the bottle to get the ketchup out. When it hits your food, it remains as it landed until you spread it with your knife.

Marketers of gel stains usually tout them for their no-drip property. This property may appeal to you if you are worried about dripping stain on your workshop or garage floor. But it is not the main reason for choosing a gel stain over other stains.

MYTH

Some manufacturers claim their water-based stains don't raise the grain of the wood.

FACT

All stains (and finishes) that contain water raise the grain of the wood . . . period!

SOLVENTS AND THINNERS FOR DYES AND STAINS

A solvent puts a solid into solution. A thinner thins the solution. The same substance can be a solvent in one situation and a thinner in another.

	Mineral Spirits	Alcohol	Lacquer Thinner	Xylene	Glycol Ether	Water
Solvent for:	Oil-soluble dye stain	Alcohol-soluble dye stain	Oil-soluble dye stain		NGR dye stain; water-based pigment stain	Water-soluble dye stain
Thinner for:	Oil-based pigment stain; varnish-based pigment stain	NGR dye stain	Lacquer-based pigment stain; NGR dye stain	Short-oil varnish-based pigment stain (often referred to as "lacquer" stain)		Water-based pigment stain

The main reason to use (or not to use) a gel stain is that it penetrates the wood much less than liquid stains.

On problem woods such as pine, birch, and cherry, reduced stain penetration means reduced splotching (Photo 5-14). It also means you'll get less contrast between side grain and end grain on carvings, turnings, and other objects that feature the two grain orientations. And though it's a minor point, reduced stain penetration means greater coverage, because less stain is absorbed into the wood. This means you'll have less stain to buy for a given job.

On the other hand, when you're working with highly figured woods, such as burls, curly maple, or mottled mahogany, you usually want maximum stain penetration to emphasize depth and

COMPATIBILITY OF STAINS AND FINISHES

BEFORE YOU CHOOSE A STAIN, you need to consider what finish you will use—especially if you intend to wipe or brush the finish onto the wood. Some finishes will pick up and smear some stains.

The key to figuring out whether your stain and finish are compatible is knowing the solvent or thinner used in each.

- If the solvent or thinner is water, alcohol, or lacquer thinner in both stain and finish, you may have problems.
- If the thinner is mineral spirits (petroleum distillate) in either stain or finish, you won't have compatibility problems. (The only exception is if you coat over an oil-soluble dye with oil or varnish.)

The explanation is this:

- Dye, dissolved in a solvent, is redissolved by its solvent, and thus by a finish that includes its solvent. Water-based finishes redissolve water and non-grain-raising (NGR) dye. Shellac redissolves alcohol dye. And oil, varnish, and lacquer redissolve oil (mineral spirits or lacquer thinner) dye.
- The binder used in water-based stains can be redissolved by glycol ether or lacquer thinner. Water-based finish contains glycol ether. Lacquer contains lacquer thinner. Generally, if you spray either of these finishes over water-based stain, you won't have any problem. But if you wipe or brush water base or lacquer over water-based stain, you may dissolve the binder, and the cloth or brush will lift some of the pigment.
- The binder used in lacquer stains can be redissolved by lacquer thinner. So lacquer, which contains lacquer thinner, will dissolve and lift lacquer stains. Again, there is seldom a problem unless you brush or wipe the lacquer over the stain. The mechanical contact will lift and smear the stain. (The same will happen if you try to apply a second coat of lacquer-based stain over a first coat with a cloth or brush. You will almost instantly redissolve the first coat and smear the pigment.)

If you are wiping or brushing your finish, you will always be safest if either your stain or your finish, or both, uses mineral spirits as the thinner.

You will find a more complete explanation of why shellac, lacquer, and water-based binders and finishes redissolve, while oil and varnish binders and finishes don't, in Chapters 7–11, which cover those finishes. ■

Photo 5-14: Gel stains don't flow, so they don't penetrate into the wood. This can be an advantage on problem woods, such as pine (above).

contrasting figure. Gel stain is not a good choice in these situations (Photo 5-15 on page 94).

Gel stains are not all the same. Some are much thicker than others, and thus much less likely to penetrate into the wood. Wood-Kote is the thickest gel stain. Minwax is the thinnest (Photo 5-16 on page 95).

There is no one "best" stain. All stains have advantages in certain situations and disadvantages in others. With so many different possibilities, how do you choose the stain that is best for you or for the piece you're finishing? For my thoughts on this, see Chapter 17: "Finishing Different Woods."

HOW WOODS REACT TO STAINS

When you look at wood microscopically, you see the reasons wood can be decorated with stain and the causes of many staining problems. Wood is composed of countless, tightly packed channels that resemble soda straws. The fibrous walls of these channels are proportionately thicker than the walls of soda straws, and the cores are seldom totally empty as they are in soda straws, but the resemblance is there (Photo 5-17).

The wood's channels carry water and nutrients through the tree when it is alive. When the tree is sawed into boards, these channels are cut through, creating a porous surface. Compare the effects of staining wood with the effects of applying stain to a piece of glass, which has no pores. When you wipe the excess stain off of glass, all the stain comes off. There are no pores or fibrous channel walls in glass to retain any stain.

The same pores and fibers that make decoration possible cause many staining problems. You should be familiar with these

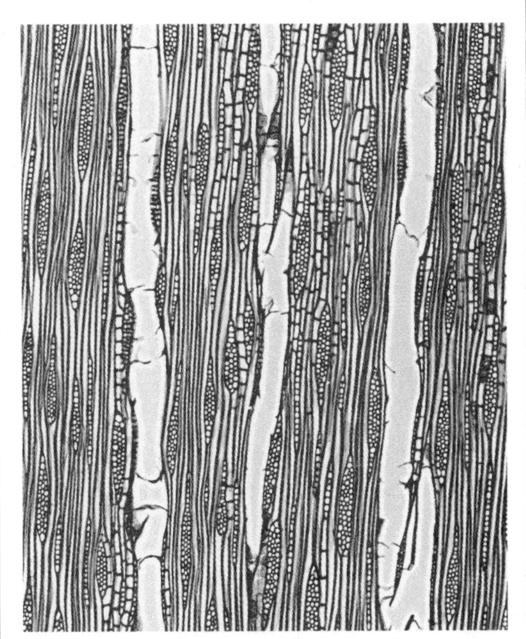

Photo 5-17: When you look at wood microscopically, you see the reasons wood can be decorated with stain and the causes of many staining problems. Wood is composed of countless, tightly packed channels that resemble soda straws. (Photo of a tangential section of black walnut, courtesy of USDA Forest Products Laboratory.)

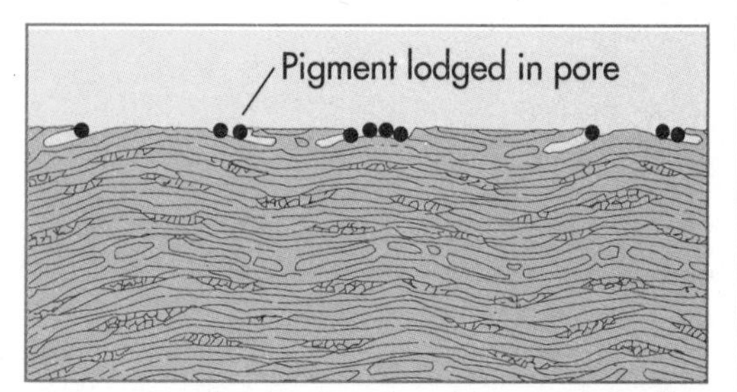

Figure 5-3: The pores in maple are too small to hold much pigment. As a result pigment stain is not very effective at coloring maple unless you build the stain on the surface of the wood like paint. Dye stain, which saturates the fibers of the wood, is much more effective.

Photo 5-18: The uneven distribution of large and small pores in oak (top) makes it difficult to color oak evenly with pigment stains. Dye stains work better. Because mahogany pores (bottom) are so consistent in size and distribution, pigment stains color mahogany evenly.

potential problems before you choose and apply a stain, because fixing the problems after the fact is often difficult. There are four areas to consider:

- the size of the pores
- the distribution of different-sized pores in a board
- the angle at which the pores are cut through
- irregular density in the walls of the pores

Pore Size

The size of the pores varies in different woods. The pores in some woods such as maple and birch are very small. As a result, it is difficult to color these woods with pigment stains. There is not much room in the pores for pigment to lodge (Figure 5-3). Dye stains usually are the better choice for these woods, because dye saturates the wood fibers with color.

Pore Distribution

The uneven distribution of different-sized pores makes it difficult to get good-looking results on woods such as pine and oak, and almost impossible to stain these woods to look like other woods, especially if you use a pigment stain. More pigment lodges in the large pores, making them much darker than the small pores. While dye also makes these large pores darker, it colors the dense areas in between the large pores much better than pigment does (Photo 5-18). With dye there is much less contrast between the different-sized pores.

Minwax, Benjamin Moore Penetrating Stain, Valspar Kleartone, Devoe Wonder Woodstain, Grayseal Designer Wood Stain, and the walnut colors of Watco and Deft stains also work well on uneven woods. In addition to pigment, they contain either dye or asphaltum, which colors dense parts of uneven woods such as oak. As a result, the overall color is more even than with stain containing only pigment.

Pore Angle

The angle at which pores are cut through is significant. You get the most extreme variations in light and dark where stained side-grain is next to stained end-grain. Side grain results from cutting pores lengthwise. End grain results from cutting pores crosswise. Just as there is much less depth in a soda straw cut lengthwise than crosswise, there is much less depth for stain to penetrate into side grain than into end grain (Figure 5-4). The uneven stain penetration occurs with both pigment and dye stains, but it is usually more evident with pigment stains. Dye stain's greater penetration into side grain makes the contrast less pronounced.

You don't have to encounter the extremes of side grain and

end grain to get variations in stain penetration, however. Trees don't grow in a straight line, boards aren't always cut from trees directly in line with the grain, and your tooling of the boards (especially in turnings and carvings) often cuts through pores at various angles. The greater the angle at which the pore is cut through, the darker the wood in that area will appear (Photo 5-19 on page 95).

Fiber Density

The irregular density of pore wall fibers is a primary cause of stain splotching. Pine is the worst offender. Other woods such as cherry, birch, and maple can also be a problem. It is impossible to get an even color on a wood that has areas of uneven density if the stain penetrates into the wood (Photo 5-20 on page 96).

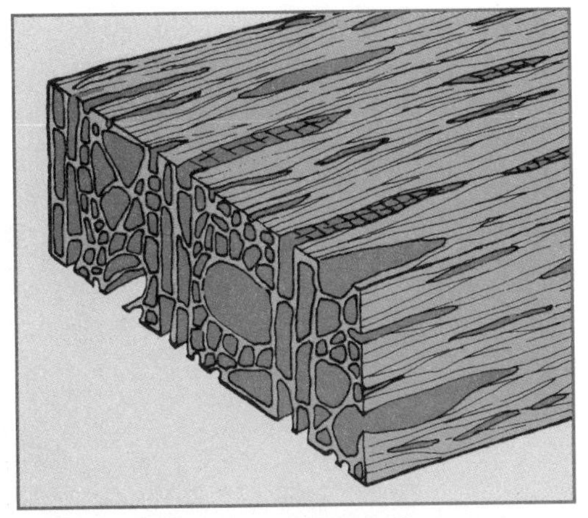

Figure 5-4: Stains penetrate much more into end grain than into side grain. This makes end grain darker. The contrast is greater with pigment stains than with dye stains because dye stains penetrate side grain more than pigment stains do.

APPLYING STAIN

There are two ways to stain wood. You can apply the colorant to bare wood, so that it soaks in. Or you can apply the colorant to sealed or partially sealed wood, so that the colorant remains on top of the wood or penetrates only very little.

Letting the colorant soak into the wood emphasizes the wood's grain. It also highlights any problems in the wood, such as uneven density, scratches, gouges, and mill marks. Put colorant into the wood when the wood has a natural beauty you want to amplify.

Applying a colorant on top of sealed or partially sealed wood adds color without highlighting the wood's figure or problems. You apply colorant this way when the wood has characteristics you don't want to call attention to. You can also apply colorant on top of sealed wood to highlight pores or recesses without changing the color of the wood itself, or to change its overall tone.

Applying Stain to Bare Wood

There is not much involved in applying stain to bare wood. You wipe, brush, or spray the stain onto the wood, or you dip the wood into the stain. Then you either wipe off all the excess stain before it dries, or leave it to dry as is (Photo 5-21 on page 108).

You can't darken the color by applying a second coat of stain and wiping off all the excess. Since the pores or wood fibers are already filled with the first coat, you will just remove all the second coat when you wipe. But you can darken the color if you don't remove the excess. If you're using a dye stain, not removing the excess is equivalent to increasing the strength of the dye that is already in the wood from the first coat. After all the solvent evaporates, it is as if you had used a stronger solution of dye in

MYTH

You should always apply and wipe stain off with the grain.

FACT

As long as you wipe off all the excess stain, it doesn't matter in what direction you apply the stain. (I usually wipe the stain rapidly onto the wood in all directions with a soaked cloth.) It also doesn't make any difference in what direction you wipe the stain off. It is important only that you make a final pass with the grain, so that any streaks you might unintentionally leave will be less noticeable.

Photo 5-21: Two ways to apply stains to bare wood. To get the effect at left, wipe off while the coat is wet. This is the easiest way to stain wood. To get the effect at right, apply thin coats and leave them. You get the best results by spraying. Brushing often leaves streaks, especially with pigment stains. (See Photo 5-11 on page 92.)

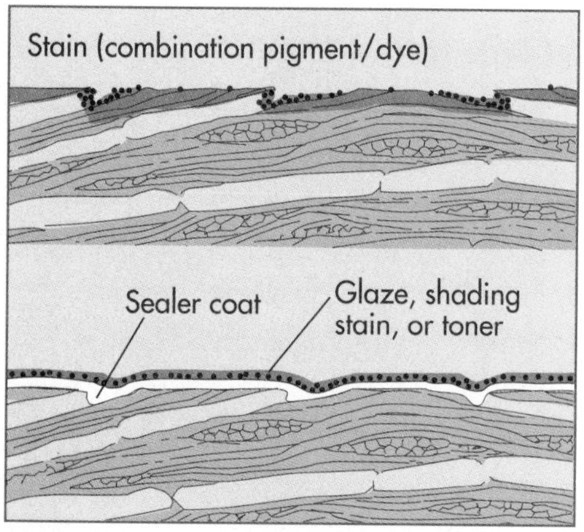

Stain (combination pigment/dye)

Sealer coat

Glaze, shading stain, or toner

Figure 5-5: Stain penetrates unsealed wood (top). Stain, referred to as glaze, shading stain, or toner (bottom), doesn't penetrate through the sealer into the wood.

the first place. If you're using a pigment stain, not removing the excess is equivalent to applying a thinned coat of paint on top of the wood. The stain will obscure the wood slightly.

Applying Stain to Sealed or Partially Sealed Wood

In coloring wood there are many reasons you may want to control the stain's penetration. These include the following:

- reduce or eliminate contrast between side grain and end grain
- reduce or eliminate splotching caused by irregularities in the wood's density
- mute the visual impact of the wood's color, figure, and grain
- highlight the wood's pores without changing the color of the wood itself
- make two or more different woods resemble each other
- fine-tune a color match
- mask splotching caused by uneven stain penetration

You can control stain penetration by partially sealing the wood before applying the stain, or you can eliminate stain penetration by completely sealing the wood before staining. Partially sealing the wood is called *washcoating.* If you completely seal the wood and then apply a colorant, the procedure is called *glazing* (applying colorant between coats of finish, Figure 5-5) or *shading* and *toning* (putting colorant into the coats of finish). These are forms of staining, though they are not generally referred to as staining.

Washcoating partially fills the pores of the wood (Figure 5-6). You washcoat wood when you want to reduce, but not totally eliminate, stain penetration. The most common reason to washcoat is to reduce splotching. The results you get by staining over a washcoat are very similar to what you get when using gel stain. In both cases the stain doesn't soak deeply into the wood.

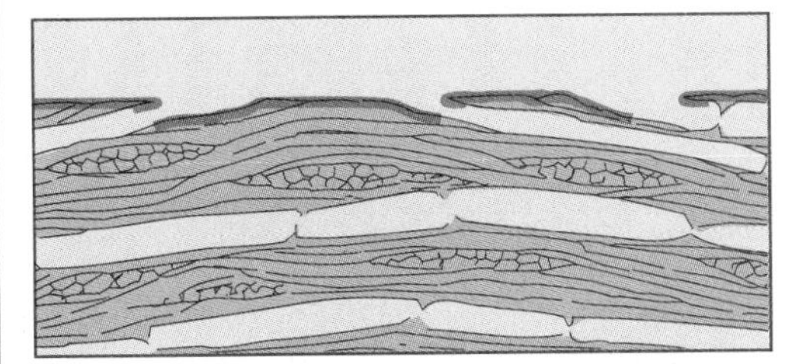

Figure 5-6: Washcoating controls penetration by partially stopping up large pores and low-density areas before staining. A washcoat can be a slow-evaporating solvent or a highly thinned coat of finish.

There are two methods for washcoating wood:

- You can use a slow-evaporating solvent that remains in the pores while you are staining. Any slow-evaporating solvent, such as mineral spirits, will do. You can also use a commercial washcoat that operates on the same principle (Photo 5-22). Flood the wood with the solvent. Allow the solvent to soak in. Wipe off the excess. Then apply the stain before the solvent evaporates out of the wood.
- You can use a highly thinned finish that only partially seals the wood. Any finish will work, and you can thin it to whatever degree you want. The traditional choice is $^1/_2$- to 1-pound-cut shellac. (See Chapter 8: "Shellac" for how to prepare shellac from solid flakes.) A shellac washcoat can be mixed from liquid shellac, as it's sold in cans at hardware stores (typically a 3-pound-cut), by diluting 1 part with 2 to 5 parts of alcohol. You can also use a commercial washcoat that operates on the same principle (Photo 5-23). Whatever you use for a washcoat, the more thinner you add, the less the finish will stop up (seal) the pores, and the more the stain you apply afterwards will penetrate. This type of washcoat is permanent in the wood. Once the washcoat has cured, you can apply the stain over it at any time.

Photo 5-22: Some commercial washcoats, such as those above, are based on slow-evaporating solvents. Apply the stain before the washcoat has had time to evaporate.

Photo 5-23: Some commercial washcoats, such as those above, are thinned finishes that must be allowed to cure before you apply the stain.

Both methods reduce the amount of colorant you can get into the wood. Both methods, therefore, prevent you from getting the wood as dark as you could if you applied the stain to bare wood. But neither method totally eliminates splotching, because neither method entirely eliminates stain penetration (Photo 5-24 on page 96).

(When washcoating with a thinned finish, sand the wood's surface lightly with 280-grit sandpaper before applying the stain. This will remove the washcoat from the surface of very dense areas, such as the latewood on pine, so more stain can penetrate there.)

Personally, I don't find washcoating wood to be as effective a method of achieving even stain penetration as using a gel stain. It's hard to know how much washcoat you should apply to be effective. If your washcoat is too heavy, you won't get any stain penetration at all. If your washcoat is too light, you'll get too much stain penetration, and you won't be able to correct the problem short of sanding out the color.

Glazing is applying a thin coat of colorant between coats of finish, and either brushing the colorant out evenly or wiping it off high spots (Figure 5-7). The glaze can be applied by spray gun, brush, or cloth. (See "Applying Glaze," below.) The colorant is almost always pigment. Glazes contain a binder to glue the pigment to the previous finish coat.

Most high-quality, factory furniture has one or more layers of glaze in the finish. Glaze offers many decorative possibilities:

APPLYING GLAZE

GLAZE IS LIKE THINNED PAINT or thick stain. You apply it over a sealer coat or between coats of finish. Here are the basic steps:

1. Apply a sealer coat (see "Sealers and Sanding Sealers" on page 133) to wood that you may or may not have stained (depending upon what you're trying to achieve).
2. Allow the sealer coat to cure thoroughly.
3. Sand the sealer coat lightly in the direction of the grain with 280-grit or finer sandpaper to make the surface smooth and also to etch it with fine scratches.
4. Apply glaze to the surface with a brush, cloth, or spray gun. Be sure to get it into all corners, moldings, beadings, and crevices.
5. If the glaze is thick in places, wipe off the excess with a cloth, leaving only a thin coating.
6. Brush out the glaze until you have a uniform film entirely free of brush marks and smudges. Wipe the brush off on a dry cloth or paper towel whenever the brush becomes too loaded with glaze.
7. Allow the glaze to cure thoroughly—at least overnight, longer if the weather is especially humid or cool. If you like, you can rub more of the cured glaze off with steel wool, Scotch-Brite, or sandpaper. This technique is especially effective if you want to imitate wear on rounded edges, corners, or high spots on carvings.
8. When the glaze has thoroughly cured, apply a coat of finish to protect it from being scratched off. The coat should be thin if you want to glaze again. Otherwise, continue with additional coats of finish.

Techniques to Try

- If you want to accentuate the shadows for more dramatic carvings, turnings, or moldings, apply a fairly thick coat of glaze, let the solvent evaporate until the glaze loses its sheen, then rub off the glaze from the high spots, leaving some of it in the recesses. If the glaze cures too hard to remove with a cloth, rub with steel wool.
- If you want to create a distressed spattered look, put some glaze on a toothbrush and pull your finger across the bristles, flicking little dots of color onto the sealed wood.
- If you're spraying lacquer over an oil- or varnish-based glaze, you don't have to wait overnight to allow the glaze to cure. You can apply the finish after only a few minutes—enough time for the thinner to evaporate. The lacquer will penetrate through the glaze layer and bond to the finish underneath. This will work only if the glaze layer is thin, and if you spray the lacquer coat before the binder in the glaze becomes tacky. ■

- As a corrective colorant, it can be used to darken wood, refine a color match, blend heartwood and sapwood, or blend differently colored woods. (See Photo 5-25 on page 97.)
- It can add the appearance of richness and depth to the wood. (See Photo 5-26 on page 97.)
- It can subdue the brightness of a stain to produce a mellowed or softened look.
- It can add decoration on top of a painted surface, such as making a solid-colored surface look like marble or wood grain.
- It can highlight pores.
- It can be used to imitate a worn, antique appearance.

Most glazes are pigment suspended in an oil-, varnish-, or water-based binder. Essentially, they are thinned paint or thick stain. You can use your own thinned paint or common stain if you want. However, commercially prepared glazes are formulated to flow out evenly and cure at just the right speed.

You can make your own glaze by thinning some japan color (pigment ground in a varnish binder) with mineral spirits or naphtha. If the glaze cures too fast, add a few drops of boiled linseed oil. (Japan color is available from stores and mail-order suppliers that sell to professional finishers.)

The most common color used for glazing is brown. But you can use whatever color gives you the effect you want.

Glazes made with an oil- or varnish-based binder have a couple of advantages compared with glazes based on a water-based binder:

- Oil- and varnish-based glazes are slower-curing, and so afford more time to manipulate.
- Oil- and varnish-based glazes don't bite into the underlying coat of finish, so you can completely remove them before they cure by wiping with mineral spirits. Water-based glazes won't entirely wash off with water.

The disadvantage of oil- or varnish-based glazes is that they contain much more solvent. If you're glazing a number of cabinets or a room filled with paneling, solvent evaporation can be a health and safety problem.

Glaze is the material used to do *marbling, graining,* and other types of *faux* (false) *finishes.* You manipulate coats of glaze to make one material resemble another. Glaze can also be used to *pickle* wood. Pickling means to apply a white stain (or thinned white paint) directly to the wood, or to a sealed or partially sealed surface. (See "Pickling" on page 112.)

Shading stains and toners represent another way to apply a colorant to the surface of the wood. These are finishes with a pigment or dye added. They can be used to achieve all the same

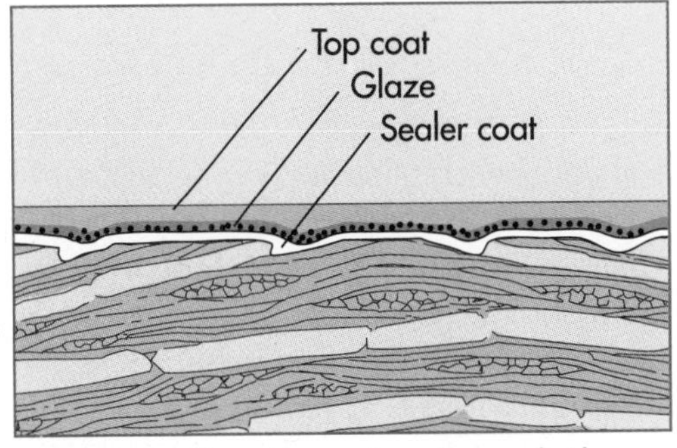

Figure 5-7: Glaze is a stain color applied between coats of finish. A glazing coat doesn't penetrate into the wood at all. You can brush the glaze out evenly or wipe it off areas where you don't want it.

PICKLING

THE INTENT OF PICKLING is to make wood look old. Early attempts using strong acids to "gray" the wood are no longer practiced. The modern idea of pickling probably originated when someone tried to remove the paint from old paneling. Since it's almost impossible to remove all the paint from the pores of wood, what was left was a thin, somewhat uneven color, through which wood was clearly visible. Though I'm sure these results were disappointing at the time, this look is now very fashionable, and you can recreate it without having to paint, and then strip, the wood.

Pickling, in it's simplest form, is nothing more than wiping either a heavily pigmented stain or a thinned paint over wood and then wiping off as much of the excess as necessary to give you the look you want. Usually the stain or paint is white or off-white in color (Photo 5-27 on page 98). But it can be any color, including a pastel. You must remove enough of the color so you can see the wood underneath, or you are painting rather than pickling.

Pickling can also mean applying a white or off-white glaze over a sealed surface. Allow the glaze to lose its gloss, and then wipe off as much of the excess as you want, but enough so you can see the wood underneath.

If you use a stain, it should be heavily pigmented, like glaze, so it's easy to leave a significant amount of color on the surface of the wood. If you use a paint, you should thin it with about 25 percent of the proper thinner (mineral spirits for oil-based paint, water for latex paint) so it will be easy to spread.

You can use an oil-based stain or paint, or you can use a water-based stain or paint (latex). Each has its advantages. Oil-based dries much slower so you have more time to spread it and remove just the right amount. Oil-based also doesn't raise the grain of the wood. Water-based doesn't have the solvent content of oil-based, so the air you breathe is much cleaner, especially when you're pickling large surfaces, such as paneling.

Pickling is usually done on pine, oak, ash, or elm. It's effective on pine because the underlying grain is very pronounced, so it shows through even a fairly heavy layer of color. It's effective on oak, ash, and elm because more of the color remains in the deep pores, accentuating the feel of wood underneath. In all these cases enough of the color remains on top of the wood to even the contrasts between earlywood and latewood.

When you are happy with the appearance, apply one or two coats of finish to protect the color. Otherwise, the color will be easily scratched off. In cases where the pickling has been done with white or off-white color, water-based finish is the best finish to use. Water base has no amber tint as other finishes do, and it doesn't yellow over time. Usually, you'll want to use a satin or flat finish, rather than a gloss, to better imitate the appearance of age. ■

decorative effects as a glaze, except for highlighting the pores. (You can wipe off excess glaze, leaving a little color in the pores. You can't do this with shading stains or toners.)

You can buy shading stains and toners from stores or catalogs that supply professional finishers. Or you can make your own. Just add a compatible colorant to lacquer or water-based finish. Add lacquer-based pigment stain, universal-pigment colorant, oil-soluble dye, or NGR dye to lacquer. Add water-based pigment stain, universal-pigment colorant, water-soluble dye, or NGR dye to water-based finish.

Shading stain and toner actually are the same material; the different terms refer to different uses. Shading stain is used to darken some parts of wood in order to highlight other parts or to color sapwood (or lighter boards) to match heartwood (or darker boards). Toner is used to change the color tone of the entire surface of the wood (Photos 5-28 and 5-29 on pages 99–100). Sometimes the terms *shading stain* and *toner* are used to distinguish whether the colorant is a pigment or a dye. This usage is incorrect and causes confusion.

Unlike glazes, shading stains and toners are always applied by spraying and are not wiped off or manipulated after spraying. When lacquer is used as the binder, the colorant is always a shading stain or a toner. This is because lacquer dissolves part of the previous coat and then cures very rapidly. As a result, you can't touch it or you'll make a mess. When oil, varnish, or water base is used as the binder, the colorant can be either a shading stain/toner or a glaze. It's rare that oil- or varnish-based stains are used as shading stains or toners, because they cure too slowly.

Whether you use pigment or dye in your toner or shading stain makes a big difference. Pigment, applied heavily, muddies the appearance of the wood's figure and grain. Pigmented toners and shading stains were used a lot on factory-made oak furniture in the 1920s and 1930s. Dye is transparent, so it adds color without obscuring the wood. Dye toners and shading stains are often used to adjust a color after a coat of finish has been applied (Photo 5-30 on page 101).

Apply shading stains and toners with a spray gun. Build the color slowly, that is, with many highly thinned coats. You can always add another coat to darken the color. But if you get the color too dark, you can't remove a coat; you'll have to strip everything and start all over. Once you have the color you want, apply several coats of finish over it to protect it (Photo 5-31 on page 102). Because the color is in the finish and not the wood, scratches are very difficult to repair. You can't simply apply a colored stain to the scratch. It will color the wood, giving a different effect than color in the finish.

TRY THIS

Make a pigmented toner that you can remove if you don't like it. Thin some japan color with naphtha and spray it on a sealed surface. If the color seems correct while it's still damp, wait until the solvent evaporates and spray your next coat of finish. If the color is wrong, wash it off with naphtha or mineral spirits and try it again.

NOTE

You can't glaze, tone, or shade successfully with straight oil or oil/varnish blend finishes. These finishes don't provide enough film build. It would also be very difficult to glaze, tone, or shade with wiping varnish for the same reason. You can glaze successfully with lacquer, shellac, water base, or varnish. The easiest finish with which to shade or tone is lacquer, followed by shellac and water base.

COMMON STAINING PROBLEMS, THEIR CAUSES, AND SOLUTIONS

PROBLEM	CAUSE	SOLUTION
The stain didn't give you the color implied by the name on the can.	The name of the color on the can is a manufacture's interpretation; actual colors will vary. You should test the color on scrap wood before applying it to your project.	Remove as much of the color as you can with the appropriate solvent. Then restain with a color that will give you the result you want.
The stain highlighted washboardlike mill marks and tear-outs that you had not noticed before.	The stain penetrates unevenly into these machine marks. Sand, scrape, or plane them out before you apply the stain.	Resand and restain. You don't have to remove all of the color before restaining.
The color came out different from that of the store sample.	1) The piece of wood used for the store sample is not from the same board, the same tree, and maybe not even the same species of tree as the wood you're staining. Different colors, textures, densities, and grain patterns in different boards, and even in various parts of the same board, affect the color and overall appearance of the stain.	Adjust the color of the stain so it produces the color you want (see below). It's best to test the stain on a scrap piece of wood first. You can adjust a color that's not right by adding compatible pigment or dye colors and by thinning with the proper solvent or thinner.
	2) You may be applying the stain differently than the person (or machine) that made up the store sample. A significant difference comes from how long dye stains are left on the wood before they are wiped off and from how thoroughly dye or pigment stains are wiped off. Your own staining may vary from part to part, or from your test piece to your project, for the same reasons.	To darken the color, reapply the stain and don't wipe off all of the excess. To lighten the color of a stain that contains a binder, wipe with the proper solvent, if the stain hasn't cured, or strip with paint-and-varnish remover. If the stain does not contain a binder, use the proper solvent. Then build the color back to the darkness you want, possibly by applying several thinned coats and not wiping off the excess.
The color came out unevenly on doors, drawers, and other parts of the same set of cabinets or piece of furniture.	The main reason stains appear different on different pieces of wood is that the pieces of wood themselves are a different color, texture, density, or grain pattern. Stains can also appear different on solid wood and veneer.	If the problem is different-colored pieces of wood, refer to the solution above. If the problem is different texture, density, or grain pattern, strip as much of the color out of the wood as possible and glaze, shade, or tone the wood to get the appearance even. In other words, build the color on top of the wood rather than in the wood. If the problem is uneven stain penetration between solid wood and veneer, build the stain on the lighter parts to match the darker parts. You could also apply a washcoat and then stain.

PROBLEM	CAUSE	SOLUTION
The end grain became too dark.	End grain absorbs much more stain than side grain, causing end grain to appear darker.	You can inhibit the penetration of stain into end grain by washcoating it before applying the stain.
The stain came out splotchy.	1) The wood grain is swirly, so stain penetrates more into some parts than others. These parts will appear darker.	You won't be able to get out all the splotchiness unless you sand to below where the stain penetrated. You can try masking the splotchiness by glazing, shading, or toning the wood.
	2) The wood varies in density, causing uneven stain penetration.	Same solution as above.
	3) Glue has gotten on the surface of the wood. Glue prevents even stain penetration. This shows up as light spots under the stain. Glue splotching occurs often around joints.	Scrape or sand off the glue. Restain. Blend any color variations by sanding the spot and the wood all around the spot while it is still wet with the stain.
	4) Some original finish remains on the stripped wood. The finish seals these areas, preventing even stain penetration. The sealed areas don't change color.	Restrip and restain. You don't have to remove all of the color before restaining.
	5) You didn't apply a sufficiently wet first coat of stain, or you didn't allow the first coat to penetrate thoroughly before wiping it off. This occurs most often with water-based pigment stains. The wood appears mottled—lighter and darker in areas not characterized by swirly grain.	Apply another coat and let it remain on the wood longer.
	6) You didn't wipe off all of the excess stain evenly. This usually occurs with pigment stains. The darker splotches will be somewhat opaque.	Apply another coat and wipe it off evenly. If the splotched stain is thoroughly cured pigmented stain, you may have to strip the wood and reapply the stain. If it's a dye stain, remove it with the appropriate solvent. You don't have to remove all of the color before reapplying the stain.
The second coat of pigment stain didn't darken the wood.	As long as the first coat of pigment stain filled pores, scratches, and gouges, a second coat of pigment stain won't darken the wood—not if you wipe off all the excess.	You have to apply more stain and not wipe off the excess. This will obscure the wood. Or you have to strip and restain with a darker stain (or switch to dye stain).
Drips from a dye stain showed up darker after you applied the stain to the entire area.	The drips of dye stain have penetrated farther into the wood than the rest of the stain because the drips were there longer.	Allow the dye stain to remain wet on the wood long enough to penetrate to an equal depth as the spots. The spots will no longer show.

(continued)

COMMON STAINING PROBLEMS, THEIR CAUSES, AND SOLUTIONS—continued

PROBLEM	CAUSE	SOLUTION
The stain dried before you could get all of the excess wiped off.	You're using a stain that dries too fast; you're trying to stain too large a surface at one time; or you're not applying and wiping off the stain fast enough.	Recoat and rewipe. Wipe as you recoat and dissolve the stain, or recoat the entire surface and wipe off more quickly.
The stain didn't dry.	1) Assuming you're refinishing, some wax from the stripper was left on the wood. Wax retards the curing of most finishes.	Restrip and then wash the wax off thoroughly with mineral spirits, naphtha, alcohol, or lacquer thinner.
	2) The wood is an oily wood such as teak, rosewood, or cocobolo. The wood's oils inhibit the curing of all oil- and varnish-based stains.	Strip and then remove the surface oil from the wood by wiping with mineral spirits, naphtha, acetone, or lacquer thinner. Then reapply the stain.
	3) You left an oil-based stain too thick on the wood. Oil takes a long time to cure, especially if it is thick.	Allow longer for the stain to cure; remove the excess stain by scrubbing with fine steel wool and mineral spirits; or remove the excess stain with paint-and-varnish remover. Then restain and wipe off the excess.
	4) The stain is too old. It no longer cures hard. (This is rare. It's caused by the evaporation of certain rarely used driers.)	Strip and restain with another stain.
The finish lifted some of the color and streaked it, or the stain bled into the finish, showing up as small spots of color over some of the pores.	The finish contains a solvent (usually lacquer thinner or water) that either dissolves the binder in the stain or puts the dye back into solution.	Strip off the finish and restain. Then either use a different, non-interfering finish or apply a barrier coat of shellac before applying your finish.
The wood feels rough or fuzzy after you applied the stain.	The stain contains water. (Alcohol- and NGR-dye stains will also raise the grain a little if the stain is applied wet.)	1) Lightly sand off the raised grain with used 320-grit or finer sandpaper. Avoid sanding through. If you do, reapply the stain over the entire surface and wipe off the excess.
		2) Apply a sanding sealer, which will lock the raised grain in place. Then sand it smooth.
The stain didn't get the wood dark enough.	The ratio of pigment to binder, dye to binder, or dye to solvent is not great enough. Or the wood is too dense to accept any more pigment.	Reapply the stain as evenly as possible and don't wipe off the excess. This may obscure the wood if you are using a pigment stain.

PROBLEM	CAUSE	SOLUTION
The stain shows streaks through the finish.	Either you didn't wipe off all of the excess stain, or you brushed on a finish that dissolved and streaked the stain.	Strip off the finish. This will also remove the streaked stain. Then restain, being careful not to leave streaks, and refinish.
The stain color intensified and got darker when you applied the finish.	When stain dries, the color loses much of its richness. The richness comes back when you apply the finish (Photo 5-32 on page 102).	If the color is too dark, you will have to strip off the finish and remove some of the stain. Stain that is still wet looks much like it will after the finish is applied. Once the stain is dry, you can approximate the look it will have when finished by wetting it with a noninterfering solvent, often mineral spirits or naphtha.
The stain or glaze turned an off-white when coated over with finish.	The stain or glaze wasn't fully cured. The problem shows up most often in the wood's pores, where the stain or glaze is thickest.	You can try spraying the wood with lacquer thinner. If this doesn't clear up the problem, you'll have to strip and start all over. Be sure to allow plenty of time for the stain or glaze to cure, especially on humid or cool days.
Dark scratches appeared when you applied the glaze.	The last coat of sealer or finish wasn't cured enough when you sanded it. Or you used sandpaper with too coarse a grit.	Before the glaze cures, wash it off with mineral spirits (for oil- or varnish-based glaze) or water (for water-based glaze). Let the undercoat cure thoroughly, resand with fine-grit sandpaper, and reapply the glaze.
The glaze penetrated into the wood, causing a splotchy appearance.	You didn't totally seal the pores of the wood. Or you sanded through the sealer in places.	Strip the wood and start all over.
You got the color too dark with toner or shading stain.	You probably tried to build the color too fast and overdid it.	Strip off the finish and start all over. Build the color slowly.

CHAPTER 6

Filling the Pores

All woods have a natural texture that results from the size and distribution of the wood's pores. Some woods, such as maple and cherry, have a smooth, even texture because their pores are small and uniformly distributed. Other woods, such as walnut and mahogany, have a coarse, even texture because their pores are fairly large and uniformly distributed. Still other woods, such as oak and ash, have an uneven (alternately smooth and coarse) texture because their pores vary in size, the spring-growth pores being much larger than the summer-growth pores.

The texture of the wood largely determines how the wood looks with a finish on it. The textures of maple and oak, for example, are so different that it is nearly impossible to make one of them look like the other—even if you get the color the same.

Though you often can't make one wood look like another, you can affect a wood's texture by the finish you choose and how you apply it. If you apply a very thin finish, the finished wood will have almost the same texture as the unfinished wood. If you fill or partially fill the wood's pores while you're applying the finish, you can significantly change the wood's appearance. A *mirror* finish results when you totally fill the pores, so that there is no evidence of pitting in reflected light. You will often see this elegant effect on the tops of high-priced tables, but it doesn't require expensive materials or equipment to achieve (Photos 6-1, 6-2, and 6-3 on page 120).

Photos 6-1, 6-2, and 6-3: You get very different effects on mahogany with its pores (as shown in the sample from left to right) unfilled, partially filled, and totally filled.

There are primarily two ways to fill or partially fill the pores of wood—with the finish and with paste-wood filler. Filling the pores with the finish is less problematic and, with small-pored woods, quicker. Also, it produces a surface that has more clarity. Filling pores with paste-wood filler is faster with large-pored woods, and the filler shrinks less in the pores. Also, paste-wood fillers offer a greater range of effects. (See "Filling the Pores: Finish versus Paste-Wood Filler" on the facing page.)

MYTH

You must fill the pores of large-pored woods like oak, ash, mahogany, and walnut.

FACT

You don't have to fill the pores of any wood. It's entirely an aesthetic decision. Earlier in this century certain popular styles called for filling the pores of these woods. Rules for finishing in these styles are often repeated as if they were rules for the woods themselves.

FILLING THE PORES WITH THE FINISH

To fill the pores of wood with finish, you apply a number of coats of finish and cut back the coats by sanding or scraping finish off the high areas between the pores. When the finish in the pores builds to the same level as the surrounding area, no more pitting will show. It's possible to do this with any finish except wax, oil, and oil/varnish blends. These finishes don't cure hard, so they shouldn't be built up to a thick film. Shellac, lacquer, varnish, and water base all can be used to fill the pores.

You can apply a number of coats and then cut them back all at once, or you can cut back each coat a little, until the surface is mirror smooth. Cutting back the coats all at once is more efficient, especially if your goal is to fill the pores entirely. But if you cut back the finish one coat at a time, you can simultaneously sand out dust and other flaws between coats. Either way, be careful not to cut through the finish and dig into the wood. This is especially important if the wood is stained. If you do, you will find

FILLING THE PORES: FINISH VERSUS PASTE-WOOD FILLER

Advantages of Finish	Advantages of Paste-Wood Filler
Fewer application problems.	Doesn't shrink as much in the pores as a finish does. Therefore, pitting is less likely to reappear after several months.
Faster to fill small-pored woods, such as maple and cherry.	Much faster to fill large-pored woods, such as oak and mahogany.
Gives more clarity. (Paste-wood filler muddies the wood somewhat.)	Can be used to create the appearance of greater depth in the wood. (Use a color slightly darker than the color of the wood itself, or of the stained wood.)
	Can be used to highlight the pores. (Use an entirely different color than the wood itself, or than the stained wood.)

it almost impossible to repair the damage without starting over. If you've never cut back a finish before, I recommend you practice on a test board before you tackle an important project.

There are two tools you can use to cut back the finish—sandpaper and a scraper.

Using Sandpaper to Cut Back the Finish

Most finishers use sandpaper to cut back the finish. It's slower than using a scraper, but it's safer. You're less likely to cut through to the wood. If you're sanding after every coat, use stearated sandpaper on the first couple of coats to reduce sandpaper clogging. If you're sanding after applying several coats, use wet/dry sandpaper and a lubricant to increase efficiency. Here are some suggestions for how to proceed:

- Begin with 220- to 320-grit sandpaper.
- To remove finish evenly on flat surfaces, back the sandpaper with a flat cork, felt, or rubber block.
- If you're using mineral spirits as a lubricant, you can add a little mineral oil to slow evaporation. Using a soap-and-water lubricant is risky because if you cut through the finish, the water will raise the grain of the wood. The damage will be difficult to repair.
- When you're satisfied with the amount of finish you've sanded off, sand with finer-grit sandpaper to remove the coarse-grit scratches. (See Chapter 14: "Finishing the Finish.")
- You can continue abrading with increasingly finer grit sandpaper (up to 600-grit or finer) followed by rubbing compounds

CAUTION

Some finishers like to fill the pores with sanding sealer instead of finish because sanding sealer is so much easier to sand. This is not a good idea, because it weakens the overall finish film significantly. (See "Sealers and Sanding Sealers" on page 133.)

(fine abrasive powders described under "Rubbing compounds" on page 214) until you get the sheen you want, or you can apply more finish. If you choose to apply more finish, wipe the surface first with naphtha to remove any oiliness remaining from the lubricant.

NOTE

Paste-wood fillers using an oil/varnish binder are commonly called "oil-based." But they are seldom if ever based on oil alone; oil cures too slowly. Varnish is almost always the main ingredient, with oil added to slow the curing. I call these paste-wood fillers "oil/varnish."

Using a Scraper to Cut Back the Finish

A scraper can greatly reduce the amount of sanding needed to cut back a finish. But with a scraper there's a greater chance of cutting through the finish.

You scrape a finish just as you do wood (see "Scrapers" on page 18). When the surface is level, sand the finish as described above to remove scratches left by the scraper.

FILLING THE PORES WITH PASTE-WOOD FILLER

Paste-wood filler is essentially a binder (finish) with *silica* (finely ground sand or quartz) added to provide bulk. A pigmented colorant is added, either at the factory or by you, to provide color. The silica fills the pores and is held in place by the binder, which is either a thinned oil/varnish blend or a water-based finish. The colorant colors the filler, but it also can be used to stain the wood. Paste-wood fillers do not look good under wax, oil, or oil/varnish blend, because these finishes are too thin.

Paste-wood filler is not the same as *wood putty,* which is used to fill nail holes and gouges and is sometimes called *wood filler.*

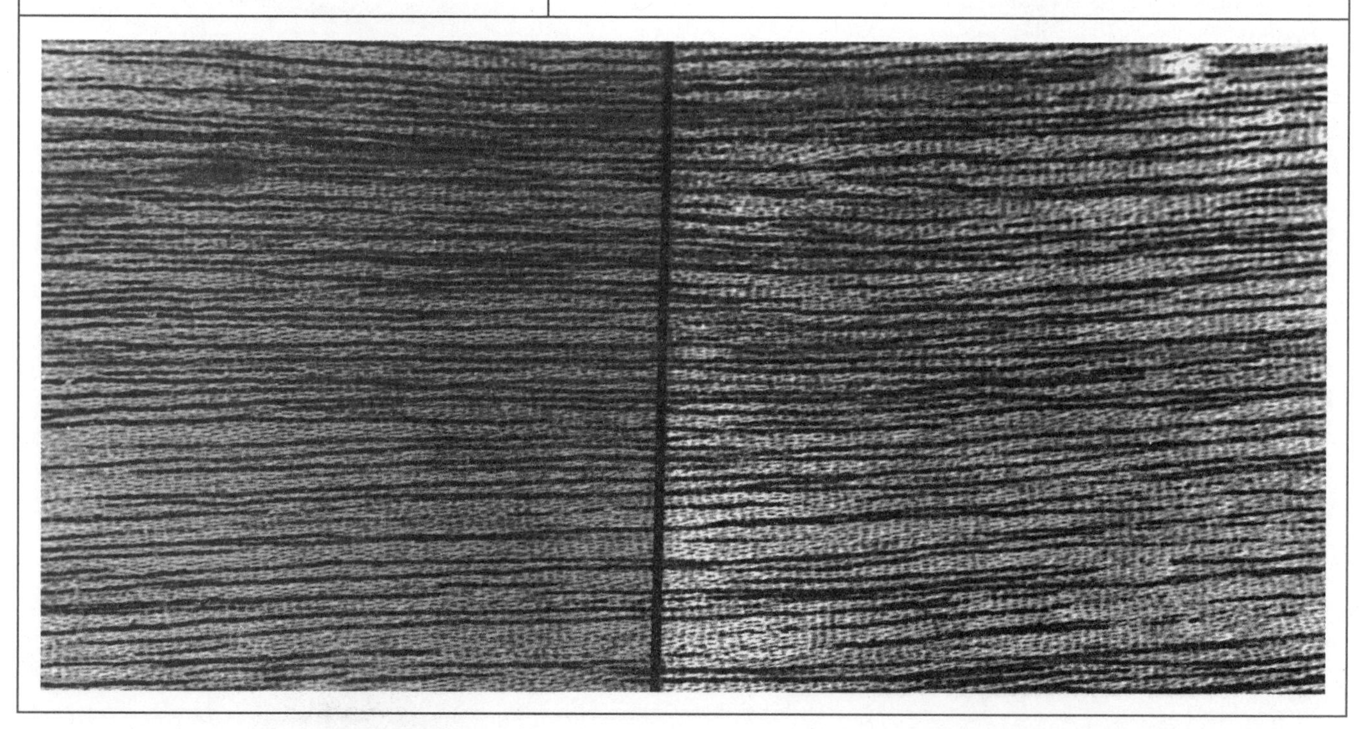

Photo 6-4: Deciding whether to seal the wood before applying paste-wood filler depends on whether you want to highlight the pores (coloring them differently than the surrounding wood) or play them down. Applying colored paste-wood filler directly to the wood (left) colors the wood and fills the pores. Applying paste-wood filler over sealed wood (right) puts filler and color only in the pores.

There are three differences between paste-wood filler and wood putty:

- Paste-wood filler is thinned much more than wood putty.
- Paste-wood filler uses silica instead of wood dust for the bulking agent.
- Most paste-wood fillers use oil and varnish for the binder, while wood putties use lacquer or water base. (Some paste-wood fillers use water-based binders.)

You can buy paste-wood filler in wood-tone colors, or you can buy it without colorant (called *neutral)* and color it yourself. Oil/varnish paste-wood filler won't take stain after it has cured, so you have to make it the color you want before applying it. Water-based paste-wood filler will take some stains, but you'll get better results if you color it before application. To color paste-wood filler, you can add a compatible stain: oil- or varnish-based stain to oil/varnish-based filler, or water-based stain to water-based filler. But it's usually better to add compatible pigment and thin the paste-wood filler with the appropriate thinner if needed. Different binders and thinners in the stain may alter the drying time of the paste-wood filler. Ground-in-oil and japan-color pigment are compatible with oil/varnish-based filler. Universal- and base-color pigment are compatible with water-based filler.

You can apply colored paste-wood filler directly to the wood, in which case it serves as both the stain and the filler. Or you can apply it over a thin first coat of finish (the *sealer* coat—see page 131), so the filler colors only the pores. The difference is one of aesthetics. If you want the pores and the wood to be the same color, apply the paste-wood filler to unsealed wood. If you want to highlight the pores, making them a different color than the rest of the wood (whether stained or not), seal the wood before applying the paste-wood filler (Photo 6-4).

(It's very difficult to stain wood successfully after you've filled it with oil/varnish paste-wood filler, because stain won't penetrate evenly through the binder that remains on the wood's surface. It is possible to stain wood after you've filled it with water-based paste-wood filler, but only with certain stains such as lacquer or water base, which penetrate through the binder. You can glaze, shade, or tone over either paste-wood filler, however. See Chapter 5: "Staining Wood.")

If you choose to seal the wood before applying paste-wood filler (the most common procedure), keep the sealer coat very thin. This way the edges at the tops of the pores will still be sharp. Rounded-over edges, caused by a thick coat of finish, make it likely you'll pull the filler back out of the pores when you remove the excess filler (Figure 6-1).

CAUTION

Most woods darken as they age. Therefore, if you use the colorant in your paste-wood filler as a stain for the wood (applying paste-wood filler directly to the wood), the filled pores are likely to appear lighter than the surrounding wood after a few years. The color of the pores will remain the same, but the stained wood surrounding the pores will darken.

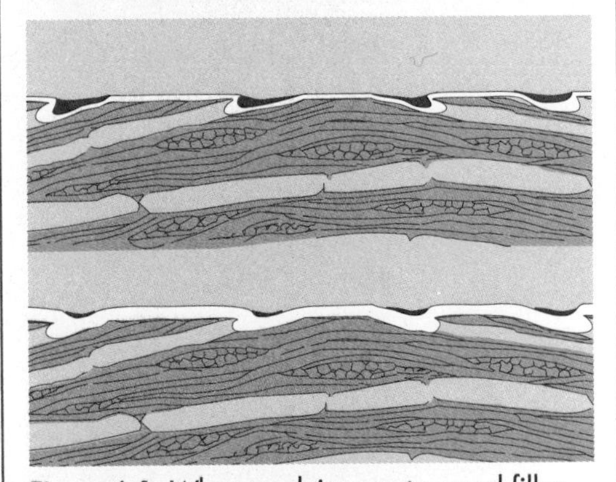

Figure 6-1: When applying paste-wood filler over a sealer coat, keep the sealer coat very thin so the edges at the tops of the pores remain sharp (top). You'll leave more filler in the pores when you remove the excess. If the pores are rounded over by a thick coat of finish (bottom), you'll pull much of the filler back out when you remove the excess.

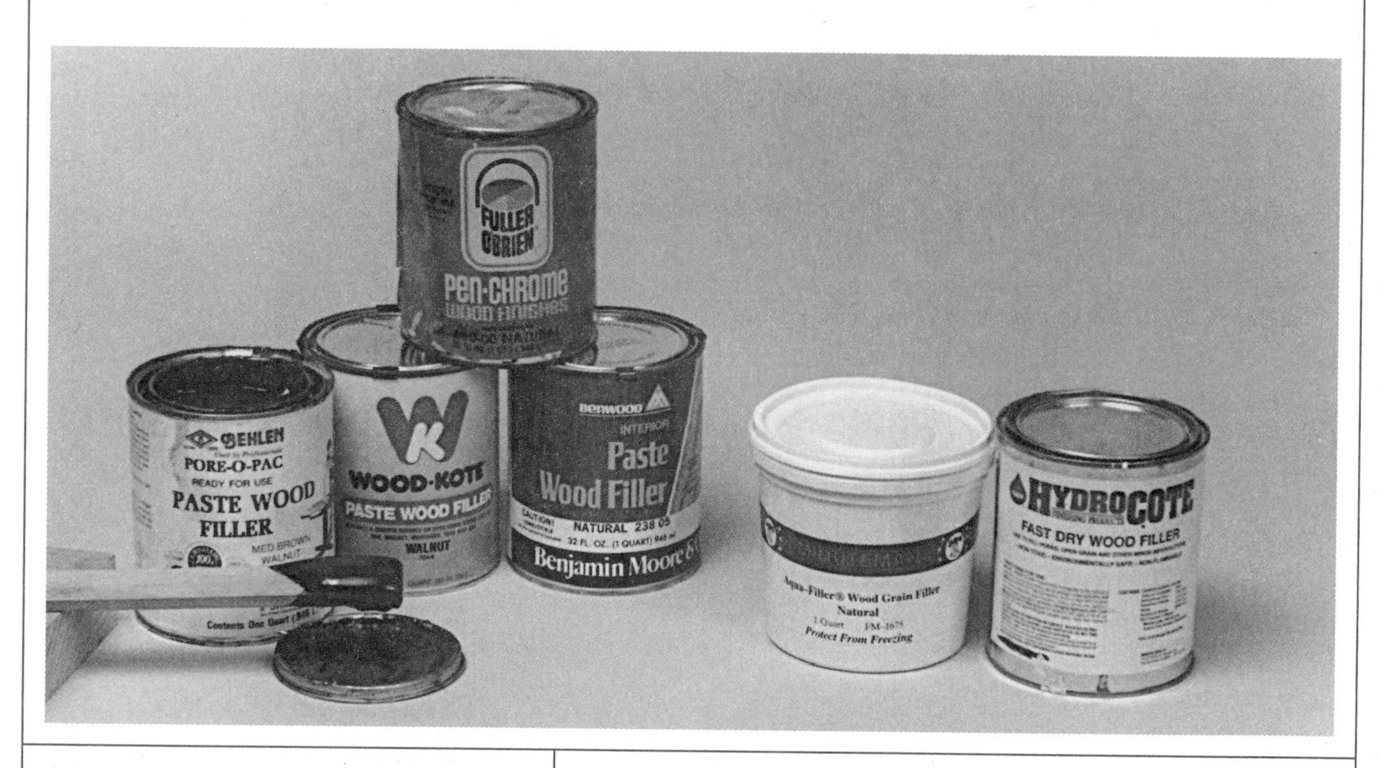

Photo 6-5: There are two types of paste-wood filler—those with an oil/varnish binder (left), which use mineral spirits for a thinner or clean-up solvent, and those with a water-based binder (right), which use water.

Types of Paste-Wood Filler

There are two basic types of paste-wood filler—those based on a linseed-oil-and-varnish binder and those based on a water-based binder (Photo 6-5).

Linseed-oil-and-varnish-based paste-wood fillers are by far the most common. (See "Using Oil/Varnish Paste-Wood Filler" on the facing page.) They vary in drying time, depending on the ratio of linseed oil to varnish used. The higher the percentage of linseed oil, the more time you have to remove the excess filler. Of course, more linseed oil also means you have to wait longer before you can apply the finish. (For more on the differences between oil and varnish, see Chapter 4: "Oil Finishes.")

The problem is that manufacturers seldom tell you the ratio of oil to varnish used, so you can't know in advance what the working properties of the paste-wood filler will be. You can learn only by trying different brands. If the paste-wood filler cures too fast, you can slow it by adding a very small amount of boiled linseed oil to the filler before applying it. Begin by adding no more than 1 teaspoon to 1 quart of filler. The linseed oil will keep the paste-wood filler soft and moist longer. If the paste-wood filler cures too slowly, you can shorten its curing time by adding japan drier. Begin by adding a few drops to a quart of filler, and work up from there. It's always best, however, to find a brand of filler that gives you the working characteristics you want. Tampering with manufacturers' formulations sometimes causes curing problems.

USING OIL/VARNISH PASTE-WOOD FILLER

ALTHOUGH OIL/VARNISH PASTE-WOOD filler is the most commonly used type of filler, some woodworkers and finishers avoid using it because of problems they've had with it or problems they've heard about it. Application is actually uncomplicated. Problems are usually caused by not removing all the cross-grain streaks or not allowing the filler to cure totally before applying the finish. Here are the basic steps for applying oil/varnish-based paste-wood filler:

1. Stir the filler, and keep it stirred while you're using it.
2. Thin the filler if the manufacturer suggests—and sometimes even if the manufacturer doesn't suggest. Filler should be the consistency of cream. Use mineral spirits when you want to lengthen the time before the paste-wood filler is ready to be wiped off. Use naphtha when you want to shorten the time. I almost always use naphtha except in very hot weather. (The choice of thinner has no effect on the ultimate curing time of the paste-wood filler.)
3. Apply a thick coat of paste-wood filler to the wood with a cloth or brush (use a cheap or old one that can be thrown away after use, since it will be difficult to clean). Apply the paste-wood filler in any direction you want, and don't worry about applying it evenly. You're going to wipe off the excess anyway.
4. Push the paste-wood filler into the pores with a wide plastic or metal spreader, or by rubbing in a circular pattern with a cloth (Photos 6-6 and 6-7). If you use a metal spreader (such as a wide putty knife), file off the sharp corners so you don't scratch the wood. You must pack the filler into the pores to reduce the possibility of pinholes popping through when you apply the finish.

Photo 6-6 and 6-7: Immediately after applying the paste-wood filler, push it into the pores with a plastic or metal spreader (above) or a cloth rubbed in a circular pattern (below).

(continued)

USING OIL/VARNISH PASTE-WOOD FILLER—continued

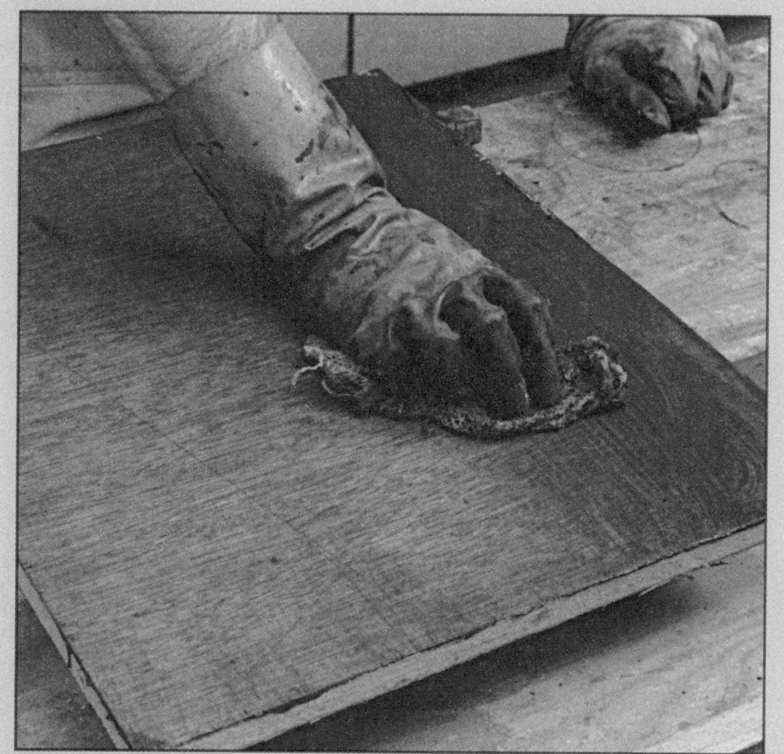

Photo 6-8: When enough of the thinner has evaporated for the paste-wood filler to have lost its shine, remove the excess by rubbing across the grain with a coarse cloth, such as burlap.

5. Let the thinner evaporate to the point that the paste-wood filler loses its shine. Temperature, air circulation, and type of thinner used will govern how long this will take, but it's usually not very long. A soft, moist residue should remain.
6. Remove the excess paste-wood filler by rubbing *across* the grain with a coarse cloth, such as burlap (Photo 6-8). Be sure the cloth is free of any dirt or hard objects that might scratch the wood. You rub across the grain to avoid pulling the filler back out of the pores.
7. On turnings, carvings, and inside corners, use a stiff brush or a sharpened dowel to remove the excess.
8. When the wood is clean, remove any remaining cross-streaks by wiping lightly in the direction of the grain using a soft, white, cotton cloth. Wipe until almost no color comes off on the cloth.
9. Let the paste-wood filler cure for three or more days before continuing. If the weather is cool or humid, let it cure at least a week.

Problems using oil/varnish-based paste-wood fillers are almost always caused by waiting too long to remove a fast-curing paste-wood filler, or by not giving a slow-curing paste-wood filler long enough to cure before applying the finish.

If you don't get all the excess paste-wood filler removed before it cures, you'll have cross-grain streaks that will be very difficult to remove later.

If the paste-wood filler isn't totally cured when you apply a finish, the following problems could occur:

- The finish and paste-wood filler won't bond to one another.
- The filler will turn gray in the pores.
- The paste-wood filler will swell, causing it to protrude from the pores.
- The finish will develop a pronounced orange-peel texture and will cure soft.

10. On large-pored woods, such as mahogany and oak, it's a good idea to *double fill:* Apply paste-wood filler a second time after the first coat has cured.

11. Sand the wood lightly in the direction of the grain to be sure there are no remaining streaks running across the grain. Avoid cutting through any stain. If you do cut through, apply more of the original stain to that area, wipe the stain off quickly, and let it cure before continuing.

12. If you are using lacquer over the paste-wood filler, follow one of two procedures to reduce the chance of the lacquer thinner swelling the paste-wood filler and causing it to push up out of the pores:
- Apply a washcoat of shellac before the first coat of lacquer. (A washcoat is a very thin coat, made from mixing 1 part liquid shellac with 2 to 5 parts alcohol; for more information see "Washcoating" on page 109 and "Shellac as Sealer, Washcoat, and Barrier Coat" on page 146.) Then apply several light coats of lacquer before applying heavy coats. The shellac will slow the penetration of the lacquer thinner into the paste-wood filler.
- Apply several light coats of lacquer before applying heavy coats. The light coats won't soak the paste-wood filler as much.

13. When you apply a finish on top of the filled wood, you will notice that there is still some pitting. This indicates that you wiped some of the filler out of the pores when you wiped off the excess. It can't be helped. To get a perfectly mirror-flat surface, you will have to use the finish to complete the filling. (See "Filling the Pores with the Finish" on page 120.)

CAUTION

Don't apply paste-wood filler to such a large area that the filler hardens before you can get it all wiped off. Wiping is hard work even when everything is going right. You don't want to make it harder. It's better to work in smaller sections and overlap, which won't cause any problems as long as you remove all the excess. If the filler does begin to harden, soften it by wiping it with a cloth dampened with mineral spirits.

The only correction for any of these problems is to strip the finish and the paste-wood filler and begin all over.

Water-based paste-wood fillers use water-based finish for the binder. Water-based finish cures very fast, so you don't have much time to remove the excess filler before it gets hard. Adding water won't slow the curing much, but adding glycol ether will. (See "Using Water-Based Paste-Wood Filler" on page 128.)

Water-based paste-wood filler is more difficult to use than oil/varnish-based, because the water-based filler cures so fast. But it's the better filler to use with water-based finish, since you are less likely to have bonding problems with it.

USING WATER-BASED PASTE-WOOD FILLER

THE DISTINGUISHING CHARACTERISTIC of water-based paste-wood filler is that it cures very quickly. If you apply the filler either straight from the can or thinned with water, you will have very little time to remove the excess. You can increase your working time by adding glycol ether to the filler. (See "Glycol Ether" on page 187.) Glycol ether is available from most manufacturers of the paste-wood filler. Here's how to apply the filler:

1. Stir the filler, and keep it stirred while you're using it.
2. Use the filler straight from the can, or thin it with water or glycol ether. If you use the filler unthinned or thinned with water, you will have very little working time: You will have to remove the excess filler almost while you apply it. If you use filler thinned with glycol ether, you will increase your working time, but you still won't have nearly as long as you do with oil/varnish paste-wood filler.
3. Apply the paste-wood filler with a cloth, brush, or plastic spreader. Apply it quickly in any direction you want. Work on a small section until you get a feel for how quickly the filler cures.
4. Using a plastic spreader (metal will rust), spread the filler quickly over the surface, pressing it into the pores and removing the excess into a can or onto a scrap board (Photo 6-9). Be sure to remove any filler that hardens on your spreader: It will scratch the wood.

Photo 6-9: Since water-based paste-wood filler cures very quickly, you have to remove it quickly. You can do this by using a plastic spreader to press the filler into the pores, removing the excess from the surface at the same time.

5. Remove as much of the surface filler as you can before it dries. If you've thinned the filler with glycol ether, you'll have more time to remove the excess. Wipe across the grain with a coarse cloth such as burlap. Unlike oil/varnish paste-wood filler, it is almost impossible to get all water-based paste-wood filler off the surface of the wood before it hardens; you'll have to sand it off.
6. Allow the filler that remains on the surface to harden for an hour or two. It may take longer if you've added glycol ether.
7. Using medium-grit (150- to 220-grit) stearated sandpaper and your hand to back the sandpaper, sand off the paste-wood filler that has hardened on the surface of the wood. The filler should powder like plaster. Sand in the direction of the grain if the filler is so thin that you are liable to scratch the wood.
8. Sand until you reach the wood or the sealer coat of finish. If you are sanding to unstained wood, it won't hurt if you sand a little into the wood. If you are sanding to a coat of finish, you will feel and hear the difference between sanding the filler and sanding the resistant finish. Also, your sandpaper may begin to clog up with finish. When you reach the finish, stop sanding—you've removed all the surface filler. If you've stained the wood, you should put a thin coat of finish between the stain and the filler to protect the stain from being removed when you sand the filler.
9. Clean off the dust and continue with your finish coats. If you've done a good job, you should have very little or no pitting that requires filling with finish.

TIP

You can stain water-based paste-wood filler after application with some stains if you apply the stain the same day as the filler (before the filler has totally cured). Stains that use glycol ether, alcohol, or lacquer thinner as a solvent will bite into the filler enough to color it. Dye stains are much easier to control and work better than pigment stains. Since the solvents in these stains also strip the filler, you should spray stain coats light enough so you don't have to wipe them off. Wiping or brushing will lift the softened filler out of the pores. The following types of stain will work:

- non-grain-raising (NGR)
- water-soluble dye dissolved in water and glycol ether
- alcohol-soluble dye dissolved in alcohol
- oil-soluble dye dissolved in lacquer thinner
- water-based pigment stains
- lacquer-based pigment stains

NOTE:
No oil- or varnish-based stain will work.

CHAPTER 7

Introduction to Film Finishes

Finishes can be divided into two groups: penetrating and film. Penetrating finishes contain straight oil and don't cure hard, so they shouldn't be built up on the surface of the wood. (See Chapter 4: "Oil Finishes.") Film finishes cure hard and can be built up to any thickness you want. There are five common film finishes used in woodworking (see "What's in a Name?" on page 133):

- shellac
- lacquer
- varnish (polyurethane is a type of varnish)
- water base
- conversion (conversion varnish and catalyzed lacquer)

Film finishes protect better than penetrating finishes because of their thickness on the surface of the wood. The thicker the finish, the better it protects the wood from scratches, water, and water-vapor (humidity) exchange. (There are practical limits to film thickness, however, because if the finish is too thick it may develop cracks as a result of expansion and contraction of the wood underneath.)

Film finishes also offer more possibilities for decoration than penetrating finishes. You build a finish film the way you make a sandwich—in layers. The first layer, or coat, of finish is called the *sealer* coat. It stops up, or *seals,* the pores of the wood. (See "Sealers and Sanding Sealers" on page 133.) Subsequent coats, called *topcoats,* increase the thickness of the film, add decorative color, and increase or reduce the sheen if you choose.

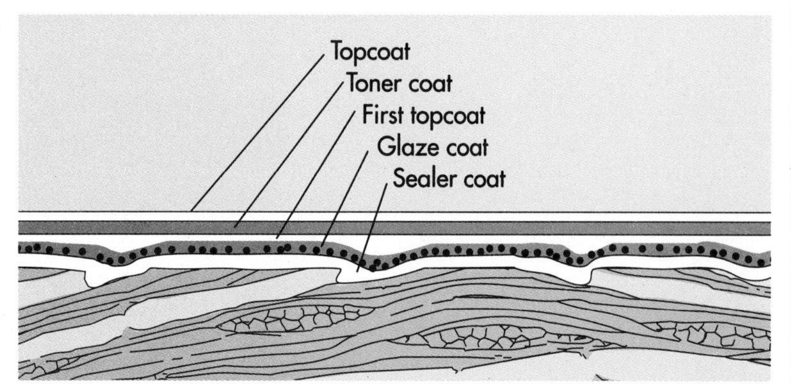

Figure 7-1: A film finish is built up in layers. The first layer is the sealer coat. This is followed by topcoats. You can add color in between layers of finish—called glazing. Or you can put color in the layers of finish—called toning if it covers the entire surface, and shading if you apply it to only part of the surface. A complex finish might include all of these layers.

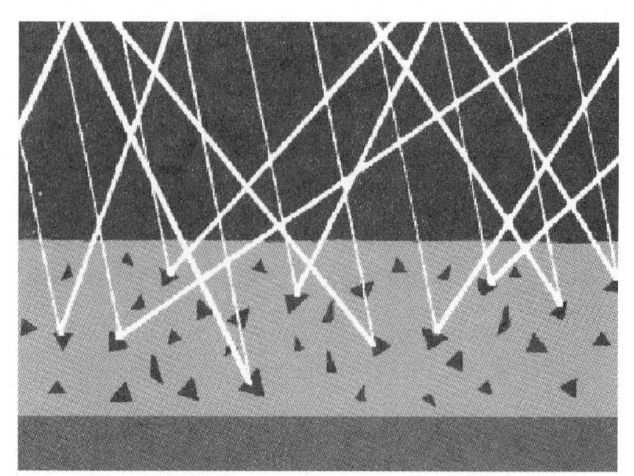

Figure 7-2: Flatting agent reduces gloss by scattering reflected light. The more flatting agent added, the duller the appearance and the greater the loss of film clarity.

You can incorporate decorative color in a film finish in several ways (Figure 7-1):

- You can add color by putting it in the finish–called *toning* if the coat covers the entire surface or *shading* if it covers only part of the surface.
- You can add color by putting it in between coats of finish–called *glazing*.

(For more detailed information, see Chapter 5: "Staining Wood.")

You can control the sheen of the finish by rubbing the last coat with abrasive compounds (see Chapter 14: "Finishing the Finish"), or by using a finish that has a *flatting agent* included (Figure 7-2). The most commonly used flatting agent is *silica* (finely ground sand or quartz). It reduces the gloss of the finish by partially absorbing and scattering reflected light. Scattering light also reduces transparency, so finishes with flatting agent aren't as clear as gloss finishes.

Lacquer, varnish, conversion, and water base can all be purchased with flatting agent added, or you can add flatting agent yourself. When the manufacturer adds the flatting agent, the finishes are sold as semi-gloss, satin (eggshell), flat, and dead flat, depending on how much has been added. Flatting agent settles, so be sure to stir these finishes thoroughly before using, in order to mix it in.

Flatting agent has a cumulative effect. Each additional coat with flatting agent decreases clarity. You don't have to put the same amount of flatting agent in every coat. For example, you can apply several coats of gloss followed by one or two coats with flatting agent in order to avoid accumulating too much of the flat-

TRY THIS

If you want to rub a tabletop to a satin sheen but don't want to spend the effort on the table legs or the chairs, apply a gloss finish to the tabletop (for better clarity) and a satin finish to everything else. Rub out the tabletop (see Chapter 14: "Finishing the Finish") and leave everything else as is. The two will blend for an even appearance.

WHAT'S IN A NAME?

SOME OF THE CONFUSION surrounding film finishes exists because of an imprecision in the names used for the finishes. Shellac, lacquer, and varnish are each identified by a number of different names:

- Shellac used to be called spirit-varnish (in contrast to oil-varnish), and it is sometimes still referred to by this name. Shellac is also identified as lacquer when referring to its "lac" bug origins or when the word "lacquer" is used to indicate any finish that cures by evaporation. For example, "padding lacquer" (see Chapter 16: "Repairing Finishes") is essentially shellac that has oil included so it can be used for French polishing.
- Lacquer is called varnish when the term "varnish" is used to indicate any finish that dries to a hard, glossy, transparent coating.
- Varnish is called lacquer when referring to Chinese or Japanese lacquer, which is actually a reactive-curing resin tapped from certain trees. Varnish is also called lacquer when it's baked hard and used as a coating in food cans.
- Water base is often called lacquer or varnish for marketing reasons. It makes an entirely new type of finish seem familiar. Water base is also called polyurethane for the same reasons when some polyurethane resin is blended with the usual acrylic resin.

This interchangeability of names adds to the confusion about film finishes. When you hear or read that someone varnished a table, it could mean he or she applied either of the evaporating finishes (shellac or lacquer), a reactive finish (varnish), or a coalescing finish (water base).

In this book I use the names most often associated with each of the finishes. In the case of water-based finishes, I avoid calling them lacquer, varnish, or polyurethane, as is so often done by marketers, because this leads to confusion and does nothing to distinguish one water-based finish from another. All water-based finishes have far more in common with each other than with any of the finishes that have traditionally been identified by those names. ■

SEALERS AND SANDING SEALERS

MANY PEOPLE THINK THEY have to use a special *sealer* to seal wood, because the finish won't do it. This is not correct. The first coat of any finish seals the wood. It penetrates, cures, and stops up the wood's pores (Figure 7-3). Liquids, including the next coat of finish, won't penetrate through the cured first coat. So *all finishes* are sealers.

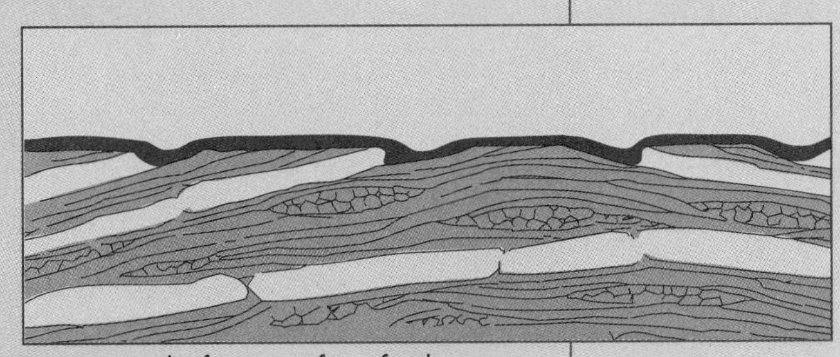

Figure 7-3: The first coat of any finish stops up the pores in wood, thus sealing them. You don't need a separate sealer to do this.

Separate sealers exist not to seal the wood but to make the first coat of finish easier to sand. They speed production time. Whatever finish you use, the first coat will lock some wood fibers in an upright position. These fibers make the

(continued)

SEALERS AND SANDING SEALERS—continued

NOTE

Polyurethane doesn't bond well to finishes that contain mineral soaps or to shellac that contains wax, so you shouldn't use a separate sanding sealer or wax-containing shellac under polyurethane.

surface feel rough. You need to sand off these fibers to create a smooth base for subsequent coats, or each additional coat of finish will feel rough. Some finishes are difficult to sand, however, so manufacturers make up special products to use as the first coat. These products are *sanding sealers.*

Sanding sealers are the regular finish with mineral soap (zinc stearate) added. Mineral soap is similar to hand soap. It acts as a lubricant to help keep the sandpaper from clogging up. Unfortunately, sanding sealers are often referred to as "sealers," and this leads to confusion. It makes you think you have to use a special sealer to seal the wood.

Varnish, water base, and most lacquers are difficult to sand. So sanding sealers exist for each of these finishes. Shellac, polyurethane, and some lacquers that have mineral soap included are not difficult to sand. So no separate sanding sealers exist for these finishes. Shellac, in fact, is often used as a sanding sealer under lacquer, because of its exceptional properties as a barrier coat. (See "Shellac as Sealer, Washcoat, and Barrier Coat" on page 146.)

MYTH

Sanding sealer provides a base for better finish adhesion.

FACT

The opposite is the case. The mineral soap in sanding sealer weakens adhesion to the finish. Perhaps this myth is rooted in the need to use a primer before applying paints. Paints have so much pigment that proportionally there's not enough binder to both glue the pigment particles together and create a good bond to bare wood. Primer is less pigmented, so it has a higher proportion of binder and therefore bonds better to the wood.

The problem with sanding sealers is that they are softer and much less water-resistant than the finish itself. This is just what you would expect from a finish that contains soap. So it's not a good idea to apply more sanding sealer to wood than is necessary for sanding the surface smooth. One coat is almost always enough. More coats will weaken the finish.

On some surfaces, such as tabletops, you may not want to weaken the finish. You may want to avoid the use of sanding sealer entirely and apply the finish directly to the wood, even though the finish is more difficult to sand. You can do this. Sanding sealer is not necessary; all clear finishes bond well to clean wood.

With some finishes, such as lacquer, there's another alternative. You can use *vinyl* sealer. Vinyl sealer is made by modifying lacquer with vinyl resin. Mineral soaps are usually not included. This makes vinyl sealer tougher and more water-resistant than sanding sealer, but also more difficult to sand. Nevertheless, it is easier to sand than the finish itself. And both vinyl sealer and the finish give better clarity and adhesion than sanding sealer.

If you do use a separate sealer, whether sanding or vinyl, you should always use one made for the finish you're applying—varnish sealer with varnish, lacquer sealer with lacquer, and water-based sealer with water-based finish. ■

ting effect. You can also blend cans with different sheens if you want, as long as they are the same finish. The inclusion of silica to reduce the gloss doesn't have any significant effect on the durability of the finish.

THE WAY FINISHES CURE

All finishes fall into one of three types—*evaporative, reactive,* and *coalescing.* Each type cures differently. (See "Finishing Materials: How They Cure," below.) The way a finish cures—that is, changes from a liquid to a solid on the wood—and the role of solvents and thinners in the curing tell you a lot about that finish. Among other things these tell you the following:

- how water-resistant or water-vapor-resistant the finish will be
- how well the finish will hold up to heat, wear, solvents, acids, and alkalis
- how easy the finish will be to rub to a pleasing sheen
- how easy the finish will be to repair or strip
- how compatible the finish will be with stains and other finishes (see "Stain and Finish Compatibility" on page 136)
- how to handle many of the problems you may have applying the finish

Shellac and lacquer are evaporative finishes. They cure by

FINISHING MATERIALS: HOW THEY CURE

Once you understand the three types of curing—evaporative, reactive, and coalescing—you gain much better control over almost all finishing products. Except for dyes and bleaches, all the products you use in finishing cure by one of these three methods. Generally it's easy to tell which type of curing you're dealing with from the solvents, thinners, and clean-up materials listed on the container.

EVAPORATIVE

(solvents are alcohol, acetone, and lacquer thinner)

- shellac
- lacquer
- pigment stains with lacquer binder
- wood putty with lacquer binder
- wax (solvent is mineral spirits or turpentine)

REACTIVE

(thinners are mineral spirits and naphtha, often listed as "petroleum distillates")

- linseed oil and tung oil
- oil/varnish blend
- wiping varnish
- varnish
- polyurethane
- pigment stains with oil or varnish binder
- all-in-one stain, seal, and finish using an oil or varnish binder
- paste-wood filler with oil or varnish binder
- glaze with oil or varnish binder

COALESCING

(solvent is glycol ether; thinner is water)

- water-based finishes
- pigment stains with water-based binder
- all-in-one stain, seal, and finish using a water-based binder
- wood putty with water-based binder
- paste-wood filler with water-based binder
- glaze with water-based binder

STAIN AND FINISH COMPATIBILITY

THE COMPATIBILITY OF different stains and finishes depends on two factors:

- the thickness of the two layers
- the effect that the solvent or thinner in the new stain or finish has on the existing stain or finish

Layer Thickness

Finishes shrink and expand at different rates. Anytime you put a thick layer of one finish on top of a thick layer of another finish, the layers are likely to crack or separate. The softer (more flexible) the underlying layer, the sooner the top layer will crack. No finishes are totally compatible over an extended period of time.

But it is possible to successfully put a layer of finish on top of a different finish if one of the layers is thin. For example, shellac and lacquer are often applied successfully over a stain, glaze, or paste-wood filler that uses oil or varnish as a binder. Lacquer, varnish, and water base are often applied successfully over a thin sealer coat of shellac. And oil/varnish blends are often used successfully as a touch-up coat on top of other finishes.

The Effect of Solvents and Thinners

The bigger issue is the effect that the solvent or thinner contained in the new finish has on the existing finish (or binder). The solvent or thinner can do one of three things to the existing stain or finish:

- dissolve it
- soften and maybe blister it
- nothing, which may compromise bonding

If you apply a finish that contains the solvent for the underlying stain or finish, you will dissolve that stain or finish. This is generally all right if you are spraying. But if you are brushing or wiping, you may dissolve and smear the underlying stain or finish. For example, if you apply a water-based finish over a water-soluble dye, you will redissolve the dye. If you're spraying, the dye will just dissolve into the finish and shouldn't cause any problem. But if you are brushing the finish, you'll smear the dye. (The same thing can happen when you brush water-based finish over water-based pigmented stain. You will lift some of the stain onto your brush, but it's usually not enough to cause an uneven appearance.)

If you apply a finish containing a solvent that softens and blisters the underlying stain or finish, it may partially strip that finish. This can occur no matter how you apply the finish—by brush or by spray. For example, if you apply lacquer over varnish or over a thick varnish-based glaze, it may blister the varnish or glaze, causing it to separate from the wood.

If you apply a finish containing a thinner that has no effect on the underlying stain or finish, you may not achieve a good bond. The softening of an existing layer by the solvent in a new layer makes a strong bond possible. The two layers mesh. If the solvent doesn't cause the two layers to mesh, you have to accomplish this artificially. Scuff the existing layer with sandpaper or steel wool to create enough tooth for a mechanical bond. This is not generally necessary over a stain, because a stain is not thick, and the wood pores provide the tooth. Scuffing the existing finish layer is generally necessary with varnish. Varnish doesn't bond well to itself or other finishes because its thinner is mineral spirits, which doesn't soften or dissolve any finish (except wax).

The solvent or thinner used will allow you to predict bonding characteristics of all finishing materials except sanding sealers containing stearates. Stearates cause their own bonding problems. Use sanding sealers only under the finishes for which they are made. (See "Sealers and Sanding Sealers" on page 133.) ■

CLASSIFIYING FINISHES

	FINISH	TYPE OF CURE
FILM	Shellac	Evaporative
	Lacquer	Evaporative
	Varnish (including polyurethane)	Reactive
	Water base	Coalescing
	Conversion (conversion varnish and catalized lacquer)	Reactive
PENETRATING	Oil and oil/varnish blend	Reactive

the *evaporation* of their solvents—alcohol for shellac, and lacquer thinner for lacquer.

Varnish, curing oil, and conversion finishes are reactive finishes. They cure by a chemical *reaction* that takes place within the finish after most of the thinner has evaporated. Varnish and oil cure by reacting with oxygen in the air. Conversion finish cures when a catalyst is added.

Water base is a coalescing finish. It is made up of already-cured droplets of finish emulsified in water. It cures into a film when the water evaporates and the droplets come together, or *coalesce*. (See "Classifying Finishes," above.)

Evaporative Finishes

Evaporative finishes are made of solids that have been dissolved in a solvent. The more solvent you put in, the thinner the solution; the less solvent, the thicker the solution. When all the solvent evaporates from the solution, only the solids are left. These solids are essentially the same as they were before they were dissolved. They've just changed shape from solid flakes or pellets to a film on the wood.

The molecules in evaporative finishes are long and stringy. You can picture them as microscopic strands of spaghetti. Just like spaghetti, the strands intertwine when they are softened. When they dry out, they harden, interlocking to form a continuous film. But nothing bonds the strands together. So when the solvent is reintroduced, the strands soften and separate. Evaporative finishes can change back and forth between liquid and solid by the introduction or evaporation of the solvent (Figure 7-4).

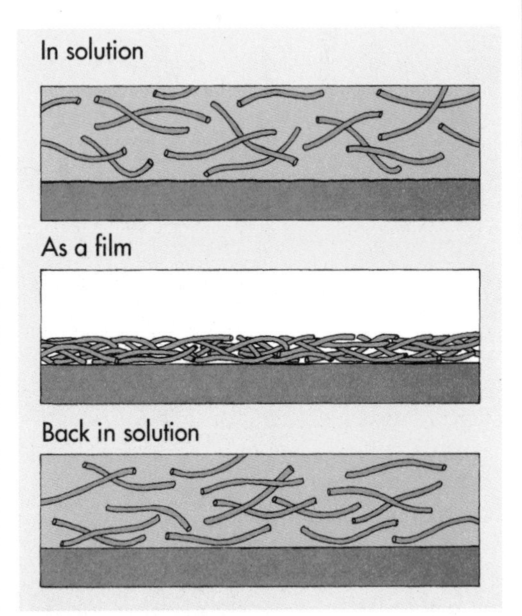

Figure 7-4: Evaporative finishes are made up of long, spaghetti-like molecules that pack together and interlock when the solvent evaporates. When the solvent is reintroduced, the molecules separate, and the finish returns to liquid form.

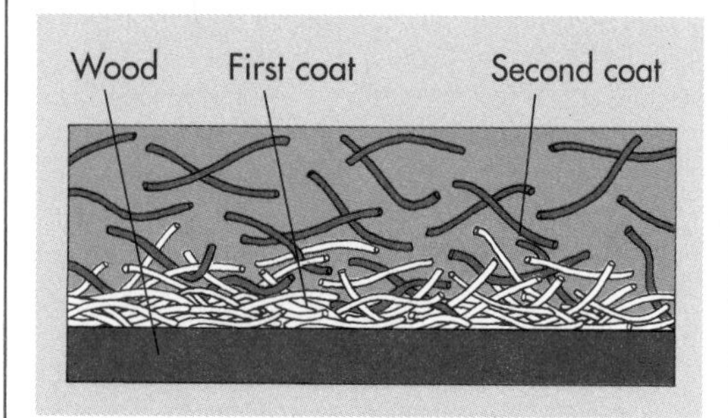

Figure 7-5: When you apply a coat of evaporative finish over an existing cured coat, the solvent in the new coat partially dissolves the underlying coat, and the molecules of each interlock, making one thicker layer.

In solution

Cured

With thinner reapplied

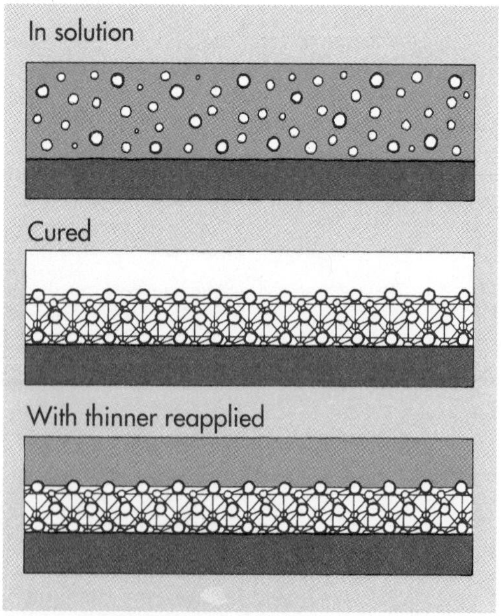

Figure 7-6: Reactive finishes crosslink when they cure. The molecules of resin bond together chemically, resembling a tinker-toy-like network on a molecular scale. Reintroduction of the thinner doesn't break these bonds apart.

Common evaporative finishes include shellac and lacquer. Wax is also technically an evaporative finish. It is dissolved by petroleum or pine-sap distillates. But wax is more of a polish than a finish, so I'm not including it in this discussion.

When you apply one coat of an evaporative finish on top of another, the solvent in the new coat partially dissolves the previous coat. (It also dissolves any finish dust left from sanding previous coats.) The solvent puts the spaghetti-like strands back into solution, so the coats interlock or *fuse,* making one thicker layer (Figure 7-5).

If you touch the finish while it is wet, you will make a depression through the top coat into the coats underneath. The finish may be softened all the way through. When you apply a new coat of evaporative finish, don't touch it for any reason (for example, trying to remove a speck of dust or a hair) while it is still wet. You will make the problem much worse. Wait until the finish has cured. Then sand out the problem.

Evaporative finishes cure from the bottom up. The solvent at the bottom of the coat has to work its way through the film layer to get out. As a result the top is the last part to cure. This is the reason evaporative finishes don't skin over in the can. You can apply coats of evaporative finish over coats that haven't totally cured. In fact, they can be still wet. It will just take longer for all the solvent to work its way out of the finish. When the top becomes hard, you can be sure the film is hard all the way through.

Reactive Finishes

Reactive finishes change chemically when they cure. As the thinner evaporates, the resin molecules come closer together. Then, a chemical reaction occurs: The molecules link together in a tinker-toy-like network that can't be broken by reapplying the thinner (Figure 7-6). This chemical reaction is often referred to as *crosslinking* or *polymerization.*

Reactive finishes fall into two categories: those that cure by reacting with oxygen and those that cure by reacting when a chemical catalyst is introduced, much like epoxy glue does. Varnish is an oxygen-curing finish. (Linseed oil and tung oil also cure by reacting with oxygen, but they are penetrating, not film finishes.) Catalyst-curing finishes, called *conversion finishes,* include conversion varnish and catalyzed lacquer. These finishes are not as well known or commonly available as other finishes, but they are often used by professional finishers.

Varnish differs from all evaporative finishes in that when you apply an additional coat of finish, the thinner in it (mineral spirits) does not soften the existing cured coat. The cured coat has crosslinked and can no longer be dissolved. So there is no bonding between coats. If you want to remove the new coat before it has cured, you can do so easily and without affecting the existing coat by wiping it off with a cloth soaked with mineral spirits or naphtha. (You may want to do this if the new coat is too thick and won't flow out, if it has dirt in it, or if the color of an oil/varnish-based glaze is not right.)

You can also remove dust specks or hairs, if you are brushing the finish, without fear of damaging the finish deeper than the coat you are applying. If you are brushing varnish, for example, you can smooth over the area you've just touched with another brush stroke.

Since a new coat of varnish won't fuse to the previous coat, you have to sand the previous coat to make fine scratches for the new coat to lock onto mechanically (Figure 7-7). You also have to remove all sanding dust, because it won't be redissolved into the new coat of finish.

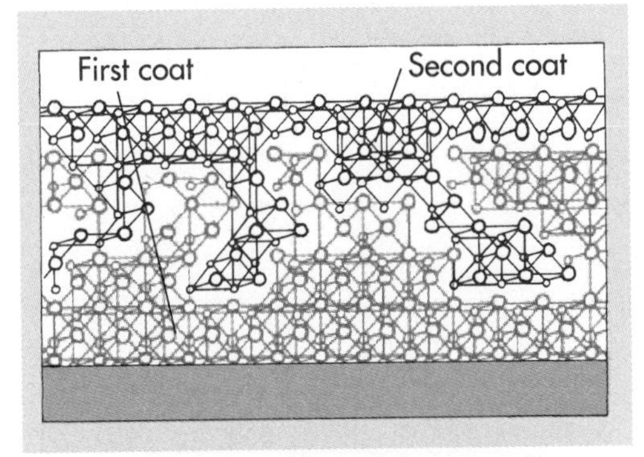

Figure 7-7: Reactive finishes don't bond chemically between coats once the underlying coat has cured. The molecules of the two coats don't interlock. To get the two coats to bond, you have to make scratches in the underlying coat with sandpaper or steel wool, so the new coat can interlock mechanically.

Conversion finishes differ from varnish in that there is a window of time specified by the manufacturer during which they bond like evaporative finishes. You can apply another coat of finish, and it will fuse with the previous coat. You don't have to sand to get a mechanical bond. But once the window has passed, the rules are basically the same as with varnish over varnish: You must scuff the surface with sandpaper or steel wool to create a mechanical bond.

You can apply varnish over other finishes, but it's necessary to sand the other finish first so a mechanical bond can be achieved. If you apply a conversion finish over other finishes, the solvents may damage the underlying finish. (See "Solvents and Thinners for Various Finishes" on page 142.)

Another difference between varnish and conversion finishes is how the film cures. Since varnish cures by reacting with oxygen in the air, it cures from the top down. Oxygen makes contact with the top of the finish coat first, and has to work its way through to cure the bottom of the coat. Once the top cures and skins over, the oxygen is inhibited from penetrating to cure the rest of the coat. This is why you should keep coats thin. Thick coats take much longer to cure all the way through. (Varnish that has skinned over in a can is an extreme example of this phenomenon.) It's also why you shouldn't apply a fresh coat of varnish until the underlying coat is thoroughly cured. If the underlying coat is not cured, it will wrinkle the overlying coat when oxygen does finally work its way through to cure it.

Conversion finishes cure like evaporative finishes—from the bottom up. The solvent or thinner has to work its way out of the film so the finish molecules can crosslink.

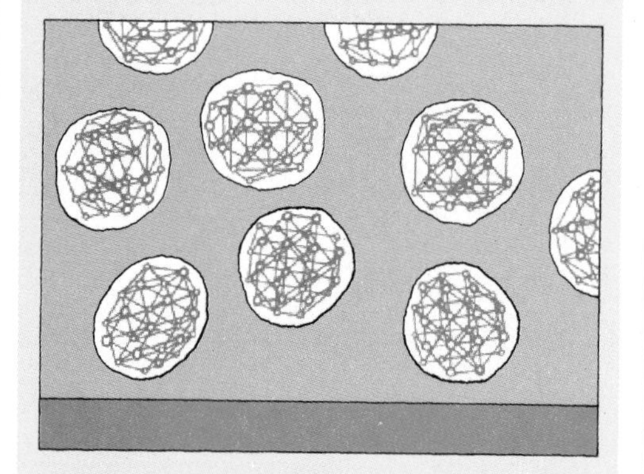

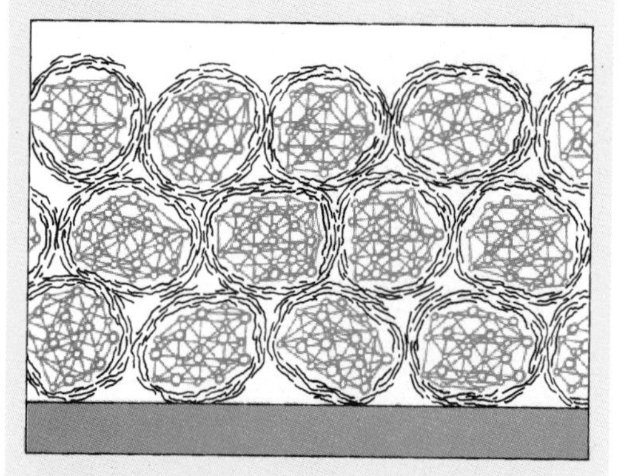

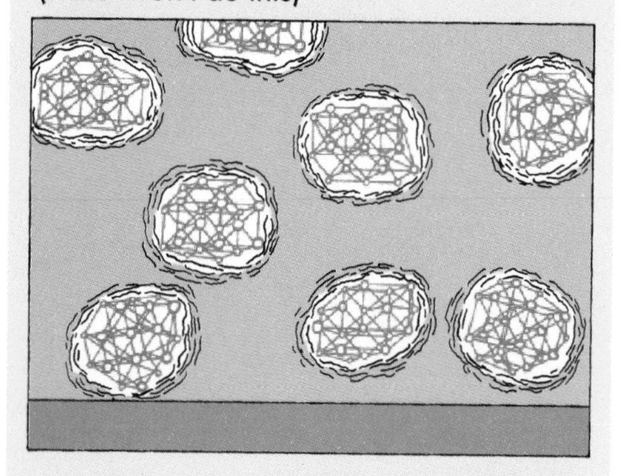

Figure 7-8: Coalescing finishes are made up of reactive-cured finish droplets that pack together as the water evaporates. The glycol-ether solvent then softens the outer molecules of the droplets, causing them to extend outward and become intertwined with the outer molecules of other droplets. When the solvent evaporates, the molecules are interlocked and the droplets are held together. But if a solvent, such as alcohol or lacquer thinner, is reintroduced to the cured finish, the outer molecules soften and the droplets separate.

Coalescing Finishes

Coalescing finishes, typically water-based finishes, are more complex than evaporative or reactive finishes. Coalescing finishes are actually a combination of evaporative and reactive finishes, and most finish chemists don't consider coalescing a separate group. But I find them easier to understand when treated separately.

Coalescing finishes are tiny dispersions, or droplets, of a cured reactive finish (crosslinked within the droplets) emulsified in water. The water serves as a thinner. A very slow evaporating solvent (usually glycol ether) is added so the droplets can cure as a film. As the water evaporates, the droplets come closer together (coalesce). The solvent, which evaporates more slowly than the water, softens the droplets so the outer molecules of each droplet relax and extend outward to become intertwined with the outer molecules of other droplets. When the solvent evaporates, the droplets become interlocked much the way evaporative molecules do; they are not crosslinked. Just as with evaporative finishes, contact with solvents, such as alcohol or lacquer thinner, after the finish has cured, disconnects the droplets, putting the finish back into solution (Figure 7-8).

Water-based finish uses water as a thinner and glycol ether as a solvent (see "Solvents and Thinners" on page 143). You may find it revealing that white and yellow glues also cure by the coalescing method. This explains why the glues don't redissolve in water, but do redissolve in solvents such as acetone and lacquer thinner. (See "Glue Splotches" on page 27.)

The droplets in water-based finish take several weeks to achieve their maximum bond. For a short time additional coats of finish will bond to the previous coats. The solvent softens the outer molecules of the droplets in the existing coat so they interlock with the outer molecules of the droplets in the new coat (Figure 7-9). No sanding is required between coats. But after a day or two, the solvent in a new coat may not adequately soften the existing coat. So it is wise to scratch the surface with sandpaper or synthetic steel wool (Scotch-Brite) to achieve a mechanical bond.

Since the molecules in evaporative finishes and the outer molecules of the droplets in coalescing finishes interlock in the same way, you can apply an evaporative finish over a coalescing finish and achieve a good bond. But the solvent in coalescing finishes is usually not sufficient to make a strong bond with evaporative finishes after the evaporative finish has had time to cure thoroughly. To achieve a good bond, scuff an evaporative finish with fine sandpaper or synthetic steel wool before applying a coalescing finish over it.

Coalescing finishes cure like evaporative finishes—from the bottom up. Enough water has to evaporate for the droplets to coalesce and interlock. Nevertheless, it's quite common for coalescing finishes to skin over a little near the tops of cans. Enough water evaporates for the droplets to coalesce and bond together. For this reason it's a good idea to strain a coalescing finish before using it.

One significant difference between evaporative and coalescing finishes is the amount of solvent in each. Evaporative finishes have a lot of solvent, so new coats can redissolve the existing finish all the way through. Coalescing finishes have very little solvent (most of the finish is already cured in droplets), so only the surface of the existing finish is redissolved. This small amount of solvent is often enough, however, to interfere with washing off all of the new coat if you don't like it. Some of the new and the old will stick together. Thus, if you try to remove a water-based glaze from the top of a water-based finish, some of the glaze color will remain.

Another difference between evaporative and coalescing finishes is curing speed. Evaporative finishes cure rapidly as the solvent evaporates. Coalescing finishes become gummy as soon as the water evaporates and then remain that way for some time until the solvent evaporates. If you touch a coalescing finish while it's gummy, you won't be able to smooth out the damage, even by applying more finish. You'll have to leave the finish to cure entirely, and then sand out the damage.

A third difference is that you shouldn't apply another coat of water base over a previous coat until it has hardened (several hours at least). Otherwise, you may trap water in the existing coat. This is different from evaporative finishes, where it is all right to pile wet coat on top of wet coat. The solvent in evaporative finishes will keep the newly applied finish soft until it all works its way out. The water in coalescing finishes can't do this.

Figure 7-9: When you apply a coat of coalescing finish over a recently applied coat, the small amount of solvent in the new coat softens the outer molecules of the surface droplets in the existing coat, so the two coats bond together. The outer molecules of the droplets in both coats interlock. There is not enough solvent in the new coat to soften the existing coat all the way through.

COMPARING THE THREE TYPES

The key difference between the three ways of curing is whether or not the molecules crosslink. Crosslinking makes the resulting film far more resistant to heat, scratches, solvents, acids, and alkalis, and less penetrable. Crosslinked molecules are difficult to break apart, and there's little space between them for liquids (water) or gases (water vapor) to pass through.

Evaporative finishes contain no crosslinking, so they are the easiest to scratch, redissolve, and penetrate. Sharp objects, heat, and a large number of solvents and chemicals have little trouble separating the molecules. Also, spaces within the non-crosslinked

Whether or not a finish cures by crosslinking determines much about how that finish performs.

molecular structure are large enough for water and water-vapor molecules to find a way through.

The easy separation of the molecules in evaporative finishes has some advantages, however. Evaporative finishes are the easiest of all finishes to rub to an even sheen. They scratch easily and evenly with sandpaper, steel wool, and abrasive rubbing compounds. Evaporative finishes are also the easiest to strip and repair. You can redissolve these finishes with several different solvents, and you can add new finish to a damaged area without leaving a line between old and new: The two layers fuse completely.

By the same token, crosslinking in reactive finishes has its disadvantages: The strong bonds produce a more durable film, but for that very reason the finish is difficult to rub out, repair, or strip. Sandpaper, steel wool, and abrasive rubbing compounds tend not to produce a fine, even scratch pattern. A new coat of finish won't dissolve into the old, so a visible line will separate a repair from the original finish. And few solvents or chemicals will dissolve the finish for easy removal; most just soften or swell it enough to be scraped off the wood.

Coalescing finishes crosslink in batches, forming droplets, each of which is resistant to scratching, redissolving, and penetration. But the droplets then join together like evaporative finishes—without crosslinking. So coalescing finishes occupy a middle ground between evaporative and reactive finishes. Coalescing finishes are difficult to scratch (evenly or unevenly), because crosslinking occupies most of the surface area. But they

SOLVENTS AND THINNERS FOR VARIOUS FINISHES

The words "solvent" and "thinner" are often used interchangeably, but they have different meanings. A solvent will dissolve a cured finish (or other solid material). A thinner won't; it thins a liquid solution. The same substance can often be both a solvent and a thinner for a finish.

SUBSTANCE	SOLVENT FOR	THINNER FOR
Mineral spirits, naphtha, turpentine	Wax	Wax, oil, varnish
Alcohol	Shellac, lacquer, water base	Shellac
Lacquer thinner	Shellac, lacquer, water base	Lacquer, catalyzed lacquer
Glycol ether	Shellac, lacquer, water base	Water base
Water	—	Water base

are easily softened or dissolved by heat and a number of solvents and chemicals. And they can be penetrated by water and water vapor at the junctures where the droplets come together, just like evaporative finishes.

SOLVENTS AND THINNERS

When I was first learning finishing, I once asked my foreman how he knew which solvent to use with which finish. He just knew, he said; he didn't have an explanation. I've concluded that he was on to something. There is no explanation. You just have to learn which solvent or thinner works with which finish. (See "Solvents and Thinners for Various Finishes" on the facing page.)

It does help to understand the difference between a solvent and a thinner, however. A *solvent* dissolves a cured finish; it turns a solid into a liquid. A *thinner* just thins a liquid. One substance can be a solvent for one finish and a thinner for another, or both a solvent and thinner for the same finish. Here's how they sort out:

- Mineral spirits, naphtha, and turpentine are solvents for wax and thinners for wax, oil, and varnish. They dissolve solid wax, but they don't dissolve cured oil or varnish. Neither do they dissolve any other finish, so they are used in furniture polishes and cleaners. (See "Turpentine and Petroleum-Distillate Solvents" on page 181.)
- Alcohol is a solvent and thinner for shellac and a weak solvent for lacquer and water base. It will dissolve lacquer and water base very slowly. Alcohol won't damage reactive finishes. (See "Alcohol" on page 151.)
- Lacquer thinner is a solvent and thinner for lacquer and a thinner for catalyzed lacquer. It is also a solvent for shellac and water base. It will redissolve these finishes after they cure. Lacquer thinner will soften and sometimes blister reactive finishes, but it won't dissolve them. (See "Lacquer Thinner" on page 165.)
- Glycol ether is a solvent and thinner for water-base. It is also a weak solvent for shellac and lacquer. Glycol ether doesn't damage reactive finishes. (See "Glycol Ether" on page 187.)
- Water is a thinner for water base.

Keep in mind that each of these substances is also a solvent for one of the dye stains. Water and glycol ether dissolve water dye. Alcohol dissolves alcohol dye. Mineral spirits, naphtha, turpentine, and lacquer thinner dissolve oil dye. (See "Solvents and Thinners for Dyes and Stains" on page 103.)

TIP

You can take advantage of the ways different solvents react with different finishes to identify an old finish. Proceed as follows:

1. Apply a few drops of alcohol to an inconspicuous spot. If the finish becomes soft and sticky within seconds, it is shellac. If it doesn't, the finish is not shellac.

2. Apply a few drops of lacquer thinner. If the finish becomes soft and sticky within seconds, it is shellac, lacquer, or water base. You've already ruled out shellac, so the finish has to be one of the other two. Water base was rarely used before the 1990s, so age may give you a clue as to which of the two it is.

3. To distinguish more definitively between lacquer and water base, apply a few drops of toluene or xylene. If the finish softens, it's water base, not lacquer.

4. If none of these solvents dissolves the finish, it is a reactive finish. You don't know which one, but it rarely makes any difference.

Chapter 8

Shellac

SHELLAC IN BRIEF

PROS Excellent resistance to water-vapor exchange.
Excellent barrier to stain and silicone penetration.
Dewaxed variety has excellent clarity and depth.
Orange variety adds warmth to dark and dark-stained woods.
Good rubbing properties.
Denatured-alcohol solvent is less harmful to breathe and less harmful to the environment than most other solvents.

CONS Weak resistance to heat, water, solvents, and chemicals.
Only moderate resistance to wear.
Short shelf life.

Shellac is the most underrated of all finishes. It is well known for its weaknesses—short shelf life and poor resistance to water, alcohol, heat, and alkalis. It is seldom mentioned for its strengths, which include some attractive characteristics:

- Shellac is the only finish with a proven track record for longevity. It was the favored finish for quality furniture throughout the nineteenth and early part of the twentieth century. Much of this furniture has survived with its original shellac finish in very good shape.
- Shellac forms an excellent barrier against water-vapor (humidity) exchange, silicone contamination, and existing stains caused by water, grease, crayons, or natural wood resins. (See "Shellac as Sealer, Washcoat, and Barrier Coat" on page 146.) Many professional refinishers use shellac regularly for their first "sealer" coat because of this quality.
- Shellac is unsurpassed as a touch-up material for repairing rubs, scratches, and gouges in other finishes. It bonds well to almost all finishes without damaging them, and it dries quickly.
- Shellac resin is so safe it is approved by the Food and Drug Administration (FDA) for use as a coating on candy and pills.

It takes 1.5 million lac bugs to make 1 pound of shellac.

- Shellac's solvent, denatured alcohol, is not as polluting to the atmosphere as mineral spirits or lacquer thinner, and it is not harmful to you unless you drink it or breathe excessive amounts of it. (As with most liquids in the shop, you should also protect your eyes.)

Shellac is a natural resin secreted by insects, called lac bugs, which attach themselves to certain trees in and around northern India. (The word *lac* means "one hundred thousand," referring to the number of insects found on a single branch. Approximately 1.5 million bugs must be harvested to make 1 pound of shellac.) The resin is scraped from the twigs and branches of the trees. It's then melted, strained to remove bug parts and other foreign matter, and formed into large thin sheets that are broken up into flakes and shipped around the world.

HOW SHELLAC PERFORMS

Shellac is probably best known for its limited resistance to water, alcohol, heat, and alkalis. Here's what happens:

- If there is too much water in the alcohol used to dissolve the

SHELLAC AS SEALER, WASHCOAT, AND BARRIER COAT

THE TERMS "SEALER," "WASHCOAT," and "barrier coat" are often used interchangeably. They have slightly different meanings, however.

- A *sealer* stops up the wood's pores. The first coat of any finish can be a sealer.
- A *washcoat* is a thinned coat of finish that only partially stops up the wood's pores or forms a thin barrier coat between two steps in a finish schedule, such as between stain and finish or between stain and paste-wood filler.
- A *barrier coat* is a coat of finish that "seals off" potential problems in the wood or in a layer of the finish. A barrier coat doesn't dissolve or damage what is under it and isn't dissolved or damaged by what is put on top.

Shellac works well as a sealer coat because it sands easily, and if it doesn't contain wax, other finishes will bond well to it. (Lacquer will bond well to shellac even if the shellac does contain wax.)

Shellac works well as a washcoat because it forms a continuous film even when highly thinned, and as long as it is dewaxed, it is compatible with whatever is underneath or applied over it.

Most important, shellac works well as a barrier coat. In many cases you want your sealer coat or washcoat to serve as a barrier coat. Shellac makes a good barrier because its alcohol solvent doesn't dissolve most contaminants in the wood (silicone, natural wood resins, or stains caused by water, grease, or crayons), or dissolve or damage common wood stains, glazes, or paste-wood fillers. By not dissolving what is underneath, but sticking to it adequately, shellac prevents unwanted contact between two substances without weakening the film build. (See "Compatibility of Stains and Finishes" on page 104.) ■

COMMON PROBLEMS APPLYING SHELLAC

Most problems applying shellac can be avoided by thinning the shellac more with denatured alcohol and by moving rapidly when you're brushing. (For problems specific to spraying, see "Common Spraying Problems" on page 42.)

PROBLEM	CAUSE	SOLUTION
The shellac blushes during application. Part or all of the surface appears off-white in color.	Moisture is being trapped in the shellac as the shellac dries. This could be caused by too much moisture in the shellac or too much moisture in the air (high humidity). If you suspect the shellac, don't use it anymore.	1) Try letting the shellacked surface dry overnight. Often the moisture will work its way out on its own. 2) On a dry day, spray, brush, or wipe straight alcohol onto the surface. The alcohol will soften the shellac and draw the moisture out. 3) Rub the shellac with sandpaper or steel wool to cut through the blush.
Small pinholes appear in the cured shellac.	Air bubbles were introduced when you brushed or sprayed the shellac, and the shellac cured before they could pop out. This happens most often in hot weather.	Sand the pinholes out, or apply more coats and then sand out any pinholes that still show. Thin these next coats with more alcohol. This will give the bubbles more time to pop out.
The shellac doesn't flow out well. If you're brushing, there are severe brush marks. If you're spraying, there is severe orange-peeling.	1) The shellac is too thick for the weather conditions.	Sand out the problem, and thin your next coats of shellac with more alcohol.
	2) Your spray gun is not atomizing the shellac well enough.	Add more alcohol to the shellac, or increase the air pressure in your gun, or both.
Dust cures in the finish, leaving small dust nibs.	The air in your finishing room is too dusty.	Sand out the dust nibs, and let the dust settle out of the air before applying another coat.
You damaged the surface by touching partially cured shellac with your brush, spray gun, or finger. The result is a mark or a ridge.	Obvious	Sand out the damage and apply more coats. Or apply more coats and then sand out the damage.

MYTH

You can protect shellac from water damage by applying a couple of coats of paste wax.

FACT

Wax slows water penetration only if it is left thick (as on the ends of boards in lumber yards), or if it is applied on an almost perfectly smooth surface, such as glass. Though it's possible to level and polish a shellac finish almost perfectly smooth, in practice you can't count on any protection from wax. First, it's rare that you have such a smooth surface. And second, once that surface has received even a little wear, minute gaps will develop in the wax that will allow water to pass through. (See Chapter 15: "Caring for the Finish.")

MYTH

Shellac darkens and turns almost black with age.

FACT

Shellac doesn't darken much with age. It's often confused with varnish which does darken significantly with age.

shellac, or in the air (in the form of humidity) when you apply the shellac, the shellac will turn white. This is called blushing. (See "Common Problems Applying Shellac" on page 147.) If you leave water on a cured shellac finish for long, the shellac will also turn white (as in a water ring), and it may separate from the wood. Shellac with wax in it is more susceptible to water damage than shellac with the wax removed.

- If you spill an alcoholic beverage on a shellac finish, the alcohol may damage the shellac. It will depend on the percent alcohol in the beverage and the length of time the alcohol is in contact with the finish.
- If you set a hot object on a shellac finish, the heat will soften the shellac and the object will leave an impression.
- If you wash a shellac finish with an alkali soap or detergent, you will dissolve the shellac. Alkalis, such as lye, ammonia, borax, and soaps with phosphate, dissolve shellac. Use a natural soap, such as Ivory or Murphy's Oil Soap, if you want to wash a shellac surface.

Because of shellac's poor resistance to water, alcohol, heat, and alkali, it's not the best finish for tabletops or other surfaces that are subject to frequent use. But shellac can be used almost everywhere else.

Interestingly, while shellac is a weak barrier against water penetration, it is one of the best barriers against the passage of water vapor. Since one of the main purposes of a finish is to slow water-vapor exchange (see Chapter 1: "Why Finish Wood, Anyway?"), shellac rates high in this respect as a protective finish.

CATEGORIES OF SHELLAC

Natural shellac resin is orange in color and contains about 5 percent wax. You can buy shellac with its color intact or bleached out, with its wax included or removed, and in liquid or solid-flake form.

Coloring

Shellac is either *orange* (also called amber, garnet, or button) or *bleached* (called clear or white). You can use orange shellac to advantage on dark woods to add warmth. Clear shellac is better for light, or bleached, woods when you don't want the finish to add color.

The orange color is the remainder of a red dye which gave shellac its original value. The dye was separated from the resin and used to color cloth. Orange shellac is a natural toner. It will darken the color of the wood without obscuring it. (See Chapter 5: "Staining Wood.") You can also add your own alcohol-solu-

Photo 8-1: Shellac is available in natural orange and bleached varieties. Orange shellac can be used to add warmth to dark woods. Bleached shellac is best for light-colored woods when you want to maintain the light color. Different brands impart a subtly different tone to the wood. (The jar at right contains homemade orange shellac.)

ble dye to make shellac any color you want. As long as you keep the color weak, you can usually brush the toner on without causing streaks. Otherwise, it's better to spray it on.

Wax in Shellac

Most shellac still contains its natural wax. This wax settles to the bottom of the container (Photo 8-2). When you stir a can of shellac, you often see the lighter-colored wax rise to the top and become mixed in with the finish. (The wax makes clear shellac appear white, which accounts for the name "white" shellac.)

The wax reduces the transparency of the shellac on the wood. It also makes the shellac even less water-resistant, and it prevents good bonding when nonevaporative finishes (varnish, water base, and conversion) are applied over shellac. You can buy dewaxed clear shellac (often sold as "blonde" shellac), but dewaxed orange shellac is difficult to find in small quantities. You can dewax your own shellac by letting the wax settle, and then pouring or siphoning off the clear part (straining is less effective). If you pour the dewaxed shellac off, do so very gently. The wax is

Photo 8-2: Shellac contains about 5 percent wax, unless the wax has been removed by the manufacturer. Wax in shellac will settle to the bottom of the container.

CAUTION

Never store shellac in a metal container. Shellac is acidic and will react with the metal, causing the shellac to darken. Shellac manufacturers coat the insides of their cans to prevent the shellac from coming in contact with the metal.

CAUTION

It's especially risky to use shellac that is not fresh under another type of finish, such as lacquer or varnish. If the shellac is not hard when you apply the other finish, that finish may wrinkle or crack. You should always use freshly made shellac or give the shellac longer to become hard.

easily stirred up. You can see what you're doing better if you work from a glass jar.

Liquid and Flake Shellac

You can buy shellac as a liquid or as solid flakes that you make into a liquid yourself.

Liquid shellac is sold in 3-, 4-, and 5-pound "cuts." *Cut* is a measuring term used universally to indicate how many pounds of shellac flakes are dissolved in 1 gallon of alcohol. The higher the cut number, the more concentrated the shellac and the thicker the solution. For example, you are getting twice as much shellac in a quart of 4-pound-cut solution as you are in a quart of 2-pound-cut solution.

Most of the shellac sold in paint stores is 3-pound cut: 3 pounds of shellac to every gallon of alcohol. You can use the shellac right out of the can, or you can thin it to whatever degree you want. You should use denatured alcohol, sometimes sold as shellac thinner, for thinning. (See "Alcohol" on the facing page.)

The problem with buying shellac in liquid form is that it is seldom very fresh. Shellac is like milk: It has a *shelf life.* From the moment the shellac flakes are combined with alcohol, the resin begins losing some of its water resistance and its ability to cure hard. For some time the curing is just slowed. Eventually, the shellac refuses to cure at all. It remains gummy on the wood.

The process is very slow—you couldn't measure it day to day, and there's no clear point at which the shellac should no longer be used. Just as with milk, the deterioration is accelerated by higher temperatures. If shellac is kept cool, it may cure hard for a couple of years. (Some manufacturers claim up to three years.) But the curing will definitely take much longer. It's a common rule among finishers never to use shellac that is more than six months old without checking it first.

To check shellac for freshness, put a drop of 2- or 3-pound-cut shellac on the top of the shellac can or other non-porous surface such as glass, and let it cure overnight. If you can push your fingernail into any part of the drop the next day, the shellac is questionable. Wait several more days to make sure the shellac will still cure hard before you use it.

Clear (bleached) shellac has a shorter shelf life than orange shellac. The bleaching that's done to take the color out of the shellac causes it to deteriorate faster. You should be more diligent in checking clear shellac for its ability to cure hard. Unlike orange shellac, bleached shellac deteriorates in flake form as well as in liquid form. You will have difficulty dissolving old bleached shellac flakes, and the solution may not cure hard.

If you find out after you've applied the shellac that it doesn't

ALCOHOL

THERE ARE THREE TYPES of commonly available alcohol:

- *methanol* (also called methyl or wood alcohol)
- *ethanol* (also called ethyl or grain alcohol)
- *isopropanol* (also called isopropyl or rubbing alcohol)

Any of these alcohols in near-pure form will dissolve shellac. But methanol is quite toxic, ethanol is very expensive because of liquor taxes, and isopropanol usually contains too much water to be a good solvent.

The best alcohol to use with shellac is ethanol that has been made poisonous so it can be sold without liquor taxes. It is sold as *denatured alcohol* or *shellac thinner.* Ethanol has these advantages:

- It is cheap.
- It is not as harmful to the environment as other solvents.
- It is not harmful to you unless you drink it or breathe excessive amounts.
- It evaporates a little more slowly than methanol, giving you more time to brush the shellac. ■

MYTH

Some alcohols dissolve shellac better than others.

FACT

All the lower (more volatile) alcohols—methyl, ethyl, and propyl—dissolve shellac totally. You can't do any better than that. The difference between these three alcohols is their evaporation rate. Methyl evaporates the fastest, propyl the slowest.

cure hard, you'll have to remove it with alcohol or paint-and-varnish remover and begin all over again with fresh shellac. You cannot fix a gummy shellac finish by applying a new coat of fresh shellac on top. Though this may give the appearance of correcting the problem, it will lead to greater problems later. The fresh coat will begin cracking much sooner because of the soft coat underneath. One of the oldest painter's rules is, "Never apply a hard finish over a soft one."

To ensure maximum freshness, many finishers dissolve their own shellac from solid shellac flakes. Here's how to do it:

1. Using a non-metal container, combine the correct proportions of shellac flakes and alcohol for the pound cut you want (Photo 8-3 on page 152). I suggest you begin by making a 2-pound cut, adding 1 pint of denatured alcohol to a quart jar containing $1/4$ pound of shellac flakes. This will give you the feel of how to do it. You can then try thicker solutions.

Photo 8-3: To make your own solution of 2-pound-cut shellac, add 1 pint of alcohol to 1/4 pound of shellac flakes.

Photo 8-4: Stir periodically until the shellac is dissolved.

Photo 8-5: Once the shellac is dissolved, strain it into another jar to remove impurities and undissolved residue.

2. Stir the mixture several times during the next couple of hours to keep the flakes from solidifying into a lump at the bottom of the jar (Photo 8-4).
3. Keep the jar covered when you're not stirring the shellac so moisture from the air isn't absorbed by the alcohol.
4. When the flakes are totally in solution, strain the shellac through a paint strainer or loose-weave cheesecloth into another quart jar. This will remove impurities (Photo 8-5).
5. Write the current date on the jar so that later you will know when you mixed the shellac.
6. If you want to dewax the shellac, let the wax settle (this could take weeks). Then pour or siphon off the dewaxed layer into another jar. If you're in a hurry, you can try straining the shellac several times through tightly woven cloth until the solution is clear.

TIP

To dissolve shellac more quickly, pulverize the flakes into powder before adding the alcohol, or put the jar of flakes and alcohol into hot water, or both. Alcohol is flammable, so don't put the container of shellac and alcohol directly over a heat source!

BRUSHING AND SPRAYING SHELLAC

SHELLAC IS AN EVAPORATIVE FINISH. (See Chapter 7: "Introduction to Film Finishes.") It cures entirely when its solvent, alcohol, evaporates, and it redissolves on contact with alcohol. These two characteristics govern how shellac should be applied.

1. Position your work so that you have a light source reflecting off your work. This way you can see what's happening by looking into the reflection.
2. For your first coat I suggest you use a 1-pound cut. It will be easy to brush or spray, and less likely than a thicker coat to clog up the sandpaper when you sand it later. Thin any given amount of store-bought, 3-pound-cut shellac using 2 parts denatured alcohol to 1 part shellac.
3. If you're brushing, use a good-quality natural- or synthetic-bristle brush. On flat surfaces, spread the shellac quickly in long strokes with the grain. Shellac dries very quickly. Don't try to stretch the shellac out as you do paint or varnish: You'll drag the partially-cured shellac and create severe ridges. If you miss a place and the shellac has begun to dry, leave the gap until the next coat.
4. If you're using a spray gun, don't leave shellac in an aluminum cup for more than a few hours at a time. The shellac will react with the metal.
5. Wait at least two hours before going to the next step.
6. Sand the first coat lightly with 280-grit or finer sandpaper. Sand just enough to make the surface feel smooth.
7. Remove the sanding dust (see "Cleaning Off the Dust" on page 26).
8. If you've never used shellac before, I suggest you use a 2-pound cut for your top coats. Thin any amount of store-bought, 3-pound-cut shellac with approximately 1/2 part denatured alcohol. A 2-pound cut is easy to brush, and usually easy to spray. It will also flow out more smoothly than shellac straight out of the can. (The thinner the shellac, the easier it is to brush or spray, but the more coats it will take to achieve a good build.) After you have some experience, you can try brushing 3-pound-cut shellac—straight out of the can. (You probably won't be able to spray 3-pound-cut shellac; it is difficult to atomize because of its inherent cohesiveness.) Apply a coat and let it dry for at least two hours. Applying many thinned coats is better than applying fewer thick coats, because each coat dries more thoroughly before being covered over. Thick coats take longer to cure. But don't overdo the thinning. You can reach a point of diminishing returns.
9. You can stop here or apply any number of additional coats to achieve the thickness you want. Allow at least two hours' drying time between coats. Don't brush excessively in any one area, or you'll pull up the redissolved undercoats. You don't need to sand between coats unless you want to remove dust or smooth out flaws or brush marks. Each new coat of shellac will fuse totally with the previous one.
10. If you do sand between coats, small, hard lumps of finish will probably collect on your sandpaper. To avoid this, sand with a lighter touch. You'll have less clogging (called *corning* in the trade) if you use stearated sandpaper or wet/dry sandpaper with mineral-spirits lubricant. Once the corns begin forming, change to fresh sandpaper, or you'll scratch the finish.
11. When you're satisfied with the thickness of the film, you can leave it as is, or you can finish it with sandpaper, steel wool, or rubbing compounds, or by French polishing. (See "French Polishing" on the facing page and Chapter 14: "Finishing the Finish.") ■

TIP

If the shellac dries too fast to flow out evenly or to let bubbles pop out, slow the curing by adding denatured alcohol.

TIP

You can take advantage of shellac's poor resistance to alkali by using alkaline soap such as TSP (tri-sodium phosphate, available at paint and hardware stores) to clean brushes.

APPLYING SHELLAC

Shellac is very user-friendly. You can brush or spray shellac easily as long as the shellac is not too thick. (See "Brushing and Spraying Shellac" on the facing page.) By adding a drop or two of oil to a rubbing pad, you can apply the shellac to wood by a method called *French polishing.* French polishing is time-consuming, but it produces excellent results, and it is fun to do. (See "French Polishing," below.) In addition, the common thinner for shellac, denatured alcohol, doesn't smell bad and is not harmful to breathe in moderate amounts.

FRENCH POLISHING

THERE'S A MYSTIQUE ABOUT French polishing. Maybe it's the name. Maybe it's the claim that French polishing is the most beautiful finish ever developed. Maybe it's the exotic vocabulary that is often used to describe how to do it—"charge the rubber," "fad in," "spirit off," and so forth. Whatever the reason, French polishing is not all it's made out to be, nor is it as difficult to do as is often indicated.

To understand why French polishing is not so special, you need some historical perspective. The common way to finish furniture in the seventeeth and eighteenth centuries was to wipe on and wipe off some linseed oil or wax, or to brush on shellac or varnish. Neither sandpaper nor rubbing compounds were commonly available for leveling a finish and polishing it to a high gloss. Finishes either were dull or showed brush marks.

Against this background it's easy to understand how a French-polished finish, which has a high gloss and is almost perfectly smooth, stood out when it was introduced in the early nineteenth century. And it's easy to understand how it got the reputation for being the most beautiful and elegant of all finishes. At that time it was. But today, sandpaper and rubbing compounds are widely available and can be used to create a surface at least as fine as a French-polished surface. (See Chapter 14: "Finishing the Finish.") Nevertheless, the early reputation of French polishing has been kept alive by authors of books and magazine articles.

The perceived difficulty of doing French polishing has also been sustained. In the early days, those who did French polishing wanted others to believe that the only way to learn the technique was to study under someone who already knew it. This secretiveness was typical of the crafts at that time. If too many mastered the skill, there wouldn't be enough work to go around. Guilds were formed to keep control of the trade.

But times have changed. There's no reason to keep the techniques secret any longer. There's very little demand for French polishing today, and it's so time-consuming, compared to other finishing techniques, that few would try to make a living at it even if there were a demand.

WHAT IS FRENCH POLISHING?

French polishing is a technique. It's not a finish. It's the technique of applying shellac with a cloth pad. The advantage of using a pad over a brush or spray gun is that a pad, used correctly, doesn't leave imperfections in the finish. A pad doesn't leave brush marks or orange peel, and it picks up dust around its edges so none gets in the finish. The disadvantage of

(continued)

FRENCH POLISHING—continued

using a pad is that it takes a long time to build a thickness of finish, because each application is so thin.

Shellac is the only finish that can be applied by French polishing. To work, the finish has to be an evaporative type so the coats will fuse together, and it has to be compatible with oil, which is used to keep the pad from sticking to the surface. The only other evaporative finish is lacquer, and it is incompatible with oil.

French polishing is an inefficient method of applying a finish but a very effective method for repairing a finish. (See Chapter 16: "Repairing Finishes.")

HOW TO FRENCH POLISH

There are four steps in French polishing:

1. Make the French-polishing pad. (See "Rubbing Pads" on page 40.)
2. Fill the pores.
3. Apply shellac with the pad.
4. Remove the oil.

Filling the Pores

On all large-pored woods, such as mahogany and walnut, you will need to fill the pores to create a mirror-flat surface. On small-pored woods, such as cherry and maple, you can usually skip this step. The shellac itself will fill the pores during French polishing.

Filling the pores of today's common hardwoods by traditional French-polishing methods is much more time-consuming than it once was. Most hardwoods used today have larger pores than the hardwoods used on the finest furniture in the nineteenth century. Our Honduras mahogany, for example, is not nearly as dense as the Cuban mahogany available 150 years ago.

There are three methods you can use to fill the pores. You can fill them in the traditional way, with the finish itself. Apply a number of coats of shellac with the French-polishing pad and then sand them back until the pores are level. This method takes a great deal of time on most hardwoods available today.

A slightly faster method is to fill the pores with wood dust generated by abrading with pumice. Here are the steps:

1. Make a French-polishing pad and fill it with just enough denatured alcohol so it feels damp but not so much that you can squeeze any alcohol out of it.
2. Sprinkle a small amount of pumice powder on the wood—about 1/4 teaspoon dusted over a 1-square-foot area.
3. Moving in circles, rub the pumice over the wood with the pad. The wood dust this creates slowly fills the pores. Work in a small, 1-square-foot area at a time. Then move on until the entire surface is filled. If the wood feels smooth (indicating there is no more pumice on the surface), and the pores aren't totally filled, begin again with more pumice and more alcohol in the pad. If the outer cover of the pad wears through, readjust the cover to work an unused part. You can see whether the pores are filled by looking at the wood in a raking light.

Use pumice sparingly. If you use too much, you'll begin to build ridges of pumice and wood dust. If this happens, try removing the ridges by putting more alcohol in your pad and rubbing with a clean part of your outer cover. If this doesn't work, you'll have to sand or scrape off the ridges.

The most efficient method of filling pores is to brush or spray on several coats of shellac and sand the coats back until the shellac in the pores comes level with the surface. This method is disparaged by purists, but you (and they) will have difficulty seeing any difference. Most French-polishers I've met use this method.

You can also fill pores with paste-wood filler, of course. But paste-wood filler obscures the wood slightly, so it defeats one of the goals of French polishing—to attain a perfectly transparent finish.

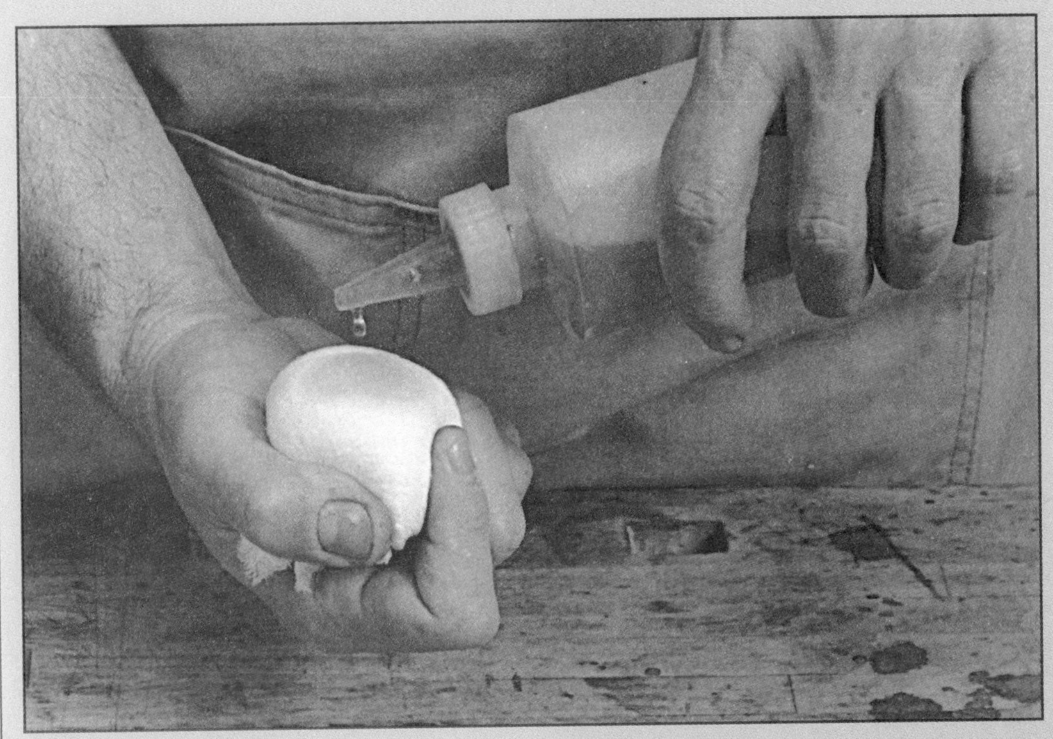

Photo 8-6: Pour just enough 1-pound-cut shellac onto the pad so you can squeeze out a small amount of liquid by pressing your thumb into the pad. A plastic squeeze bottle easily dispenses controlled amounts.

Applying the Shellac

Here are the steps for applying the shellac:

1. Begin with a clean pad. You can use one you've used before for French polishing, but you shouldn't use the same one you used with pumice.
2. Pour enough 1-pound-cut shellac onto the pad so a little liquid seeps out when you press your thumb into the pad (Photo 8-6). To obtain maximum transparency, use dewaxed shellac.
3. Tap the pad against the palm of your hand to disperse the shellac.
4. Begin moving the pad on the bare wood, using light pressure (Photo 8-7). You can move the pad in any pattern you want, but it's best if you are just beginning to do French polishing to move in sequences of circles and figure eights. This will ensure that you build the shellac evenly. The area you can work successfully will depend on the size of your pad. With a large pad you can cover an area of about 4 square feet.

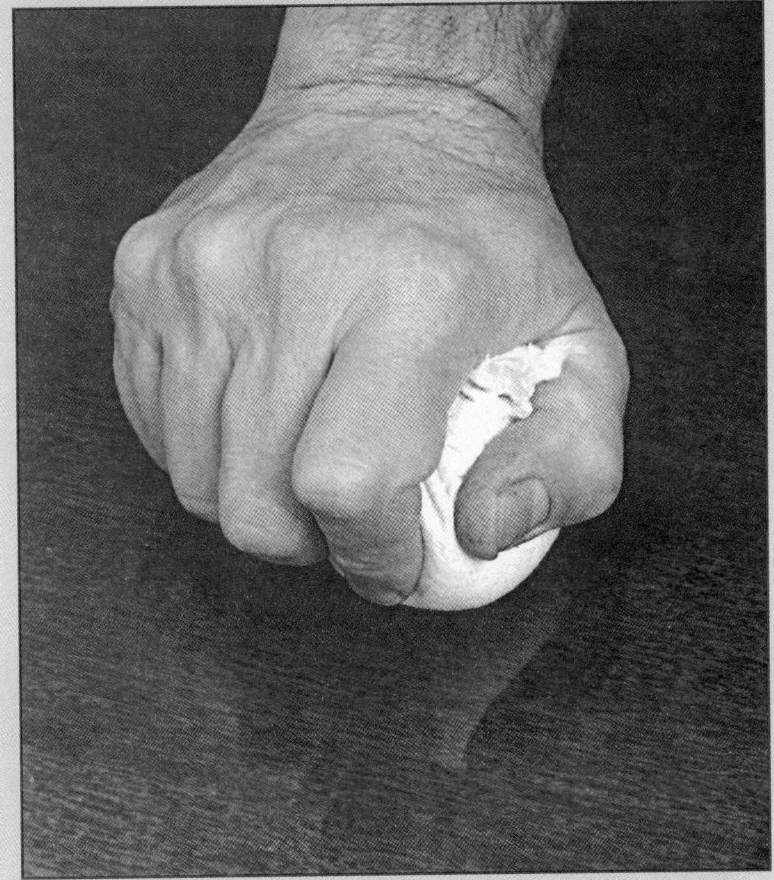

Photo 8-7: Hold the pad in the palm of your hand with your thumb and fingers pressing tightly against the sides.

(continued)

FRENCH POLISHING—continued

5. Move the pad slowly—it should take about 3 seconds to complete a circle of 1-foot diameter.
6. As the bottom of the pad begins to dry, apply more pressure.
7. Continue moving the pad until the bottom of the pad feels dry.
8. Apply more 1-pound-cut shellac to the pad in the same manner as before, or switch to a 2-pound-cut if you want a faster build. If you haven't used shellac much, you'll find it easier to work with a thinner solution. This time add a drop of mineral oil to the bottom of the pad and, again, tap the pad against the palm of your hand to disperse the shellac and oil. The oil will act as a lubricant between your pad and the surface to help keep your pad from sticking. Add a drop of oil every time you replenish your pad.
9. Now that your surface has some shellac on it, it's important to apply and lift the wet pad while it's moving, like an airplane landing and taking off. It's also important not to cross over areas that haven't dried to the touch; otherwise your pad will drag the previous coat. Therefore, each time you replenish your pad, begin rubbing in a series of S-curves, parallel but not overlapping (Figure 8-1).
10. As the pad dries, resume your circles and figure eights, gradually increasing your pressure until the pad is completely dry.
11. When you finish each session, store your pad in an airtight jar. You can use the pad over and over, changing the outer cloth if it wears through or becomes dirty. You'll find you like the feel of a well-used pad, because it conforms to your hand.

Here are some tips that will help you get good results:

- Spend more time on the edges than in the middle, or else the finish on the edges will be thinner. The old wisdom says, "Mind your edges. The middle will take care of itself." (For corners and tight areas, see Figure 8-2.)
- When you're applying several coats over a short period, each new coat makes the surface softer and more easily damaged. You should stop after several coats and let the finish cure for several hours or overnight before continuing. There's no rule about how many coats you can apply in a short time or how long you should wait between coats. There are many variables in determining what's best. These include the weather, how large a surface area you're working on, how large a pad you're working with, and the motions you're using.
- After you have begun adding oil to your pad, you should see a hazy

NOTE

Never make an abrupt change of direction or stop moving your pad while it is touching the wood. Your pad will stick and leave a mark that you may have to sand out.

Figure 8-1: You can use any pattern you want to apply the shellac to the wood. Each time you replenish your pad, begin with non-crossover strokes, just in case you've gotten your pad a little too wet. Once you begin crossing over, move in sequences of circles and figure eights so you apply an even thickness to all parts.

Non-crossover

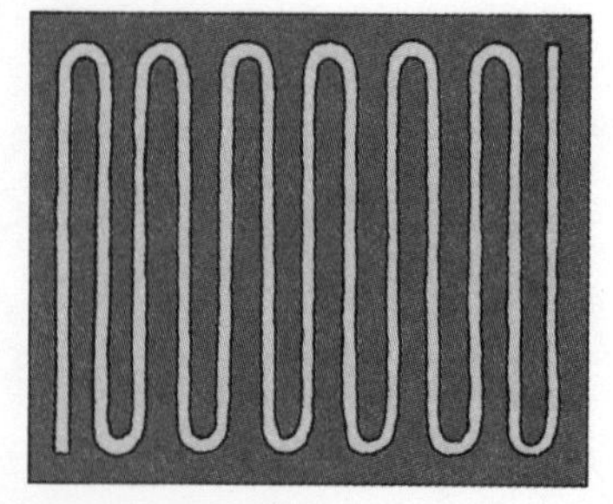

Circular

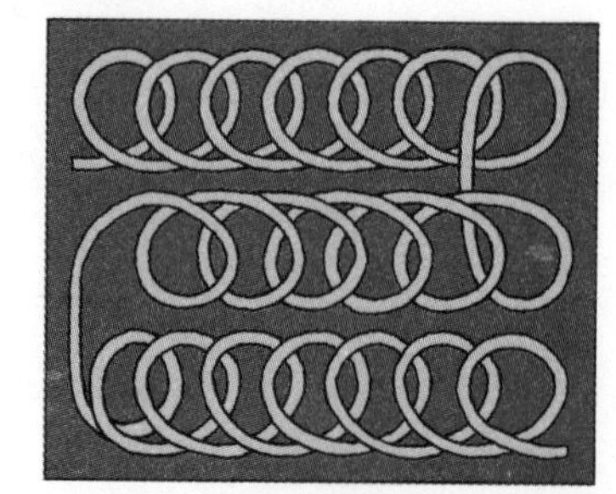

Figure-eight

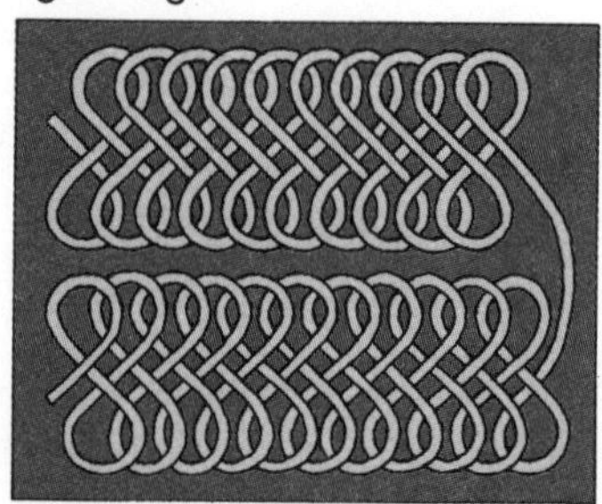

Figure 8-2: To get into corners and tight areas, make up a pointed polishing pad and hold it with your index finger pushing on the point of the pad.

1. Form inner cloth into the shape of a pear.

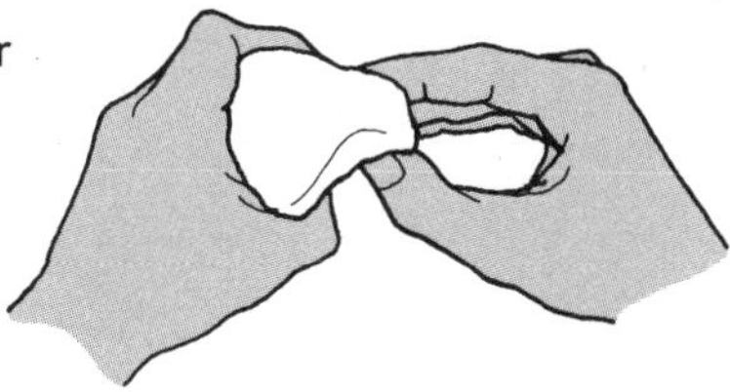

2. Cover the inner cloth with a cotton outer cloth.

3. Pull the outer cloth tight around the wadding, making sure one flat edge leads to a point.

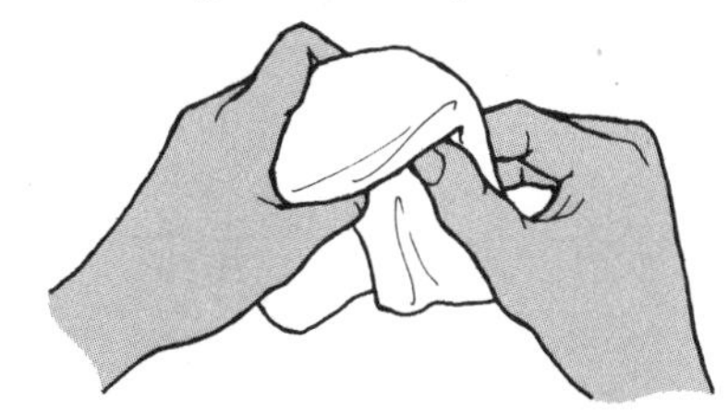

4. Fold a second edge over the first, and pull the outer cloth tight to eliminate wrinkles.

5. The finished pad.

pattern in reflected light that resembles a comet's tail, trailing your pad as you move it over the surface. This is the alcohol evaporating through the oil. It is evidence that everything is going well.

- If your pad leaves streaks on the surface that you can't remove by running your finger over them, the existing shellac is too soft or your pad is too wet or both. The alcohol from your pad is cutting into the shellac on the surface. You should stop and let either the surface or the pad dry out a little. (Streaks that you can remove with your finger are caused by the oil.)
- You're finished when the surface has an even, glossy sheen after you've removed the oil. Remember, oil masks problems, so you may think you're finished when you aren't.

Removing the Oil

The oil is necessary when applying the shellac to keep the pad from sticking to the surface and damaging it. But the oil is smeary and has to be removed when you're finished. You should let the surface dry overnight before you do this. This will allow all the oil time to rise to the surface.

The traditional method for removing the oil is with alcohol. This method continues to be repeated in books and articles on French polishing. You put a few drops of alcohol on a freshly made pad and wipe the pad over the surface. The alcohol picks up the oil. The problem with this method is that if you have too much alcohol on the pad, or even at one spot on the pad, you will damage the shellac and ruin the even shine you worked so hard to get. It's at this point that most people have trouble with French polishing. It's very difficult to avoid causing damage.

There's no longer any need to take that risk. You can use naphtha to remove all the oil without any chance of damaging the shellac. Just dampen a cloth and wipe it over the surface—as you would do to remove oil from any surface. There's probably no better example in finishing of how antiquated methods persist because of a mythology that the old masters knew best. The old masters didn't have naphtha, or they surely would have used it.

Removing the oil with naphtha is more effective than using alcohol. You take all the oil off, and this leaves the surface appearing drier and less rich. You can replace the richness the same as on any finished surface: by applying some paste wax or furniture polish. ■

CHAPTER 9

Lacquer

LACQUER IN BRIEF

PROS
- Very fast curing.
- With the addition of slower- or faster-evaporating thinners, can be applied in all types of weather.
- Excellent clarity and depth.
- Excellent rubbing properties.

CONS
- High solvent content. (Solvent is toxic, flammable, and air-polluting.)
- Only moderate heat, wear, solvent, acid, and alkali resistance.
- Only moderate water and water-vapor resistance.

When lacquer became available in the 1920s, it was widely believed to be the ultimate finish. It had all the superior application and repair qualities of shellac, but it was more resistant to water, heat, alcohol, acids, and alkalis. In addition, it was a synthetic, so supply didn't depend on exotic natural materials, and it was easily manufactured. Indeed, the belief in lacquer's superiority has proven prophetic. Lacquer is still the most widely used furniture finish.

There are two types of lacquer produced for wood—nitrocellulose and cellulose acetate butyrate (also called "CAB," "water-white," or simply "butyrate"). Nitrocellulose is by far the more widely used of the two. CAB is much less amber in color than nitrocellulose lacquer, and it yellows less over time. This has always been the primary reason for using CAB even though it is more expensive. With the introduction of water-based finishes, which don't yellow at all, CAB is losing its principal rationale. Partly for this reason, and partly because its characteristics are almost exactly the same as nitrocellulose's, I won't discuss CAB further in this book.

NITROCELLULOSE LACQUER

Nitrocellulose lacquer became a viable finish after World War I. Large stockpiles of cotton for making gun cotton, used in smokeless gun powder, remained after the war.

MYTH

The best finish for wood is acrylic lacquer used for automobiles, because acrylic lacquer is harder than nitrocellulose lacquer.

FACT

Acrylic lacquers made for use on automobiles are usually not flexible enough for wood. They don't have to be, since they are intended for steel. If you use an acrylic lacquer not specially formulated for wood, you risk that wood movement will cause tiny cracks in the finish.

Chemists discovered they could turn this cotton into a very fast-drying finish. The automobile industry had been using varnish, which required a long wait between coats. The furniture industry also saw the advantage of lacquer compared with shellac and varnish. Lacquer quickly became the standard finish for furniture.

Lacquer is a complex finishing material. Only a part of the finish is actually nitrocellulose. Most of it is a resin—usually an alkyd or a mastic—though other resins can be used. Nitrocellulose, made by treating the cellulose fibers of cotton or wood with nitric and sulphuric acid, gives the finish its fast-drying properties. By itself, though, nitrocellulose has poor build and flexibility. So the resin is added to improve these characteristics, and oily chemicals, called *plasticizers,* are added to further improve flexibility. Manufacturers vary the amounts and types of these resins and plasticizers to produce lacquers that cure with varying degrees of elasticity, color, and resistance to water, solvents, acids, and alkalis. Generally the more elastic, colorless, and resistant the lacquer is, the more it costs. Your supplier should be able to tell you which lacquer is best-suited to your needs.

CHARACTERISTICS OF LACQUER

The characteristics of lacquer are defined more by the way it cures than by which resins or plasticizers are added. The curing occurs when the solvent, lacquer thinner, evaporates. Since the solvent evaporates rapidly, curing occurs rapidly. Rapid curing makes lacquer difficult to brush, so it's usually sprayed (see "Spraying Lacquer" on the facing page). Because there's no crosslinking in the cured finish, even the best-quality lacquers are not very resistant to heat, solvent, or chemical damage. (See Chapter 7: "Introduction to Film Finishes.")

The qualities of lacquer that have contributed to its continuing popularity include the following:

- ease of application with spray equipment
- very quick drying time, which speeds production and all but eliminates dust problems. You can apply three or four coats in a day.
- large variety of thinner/solvent blends, which makes application possible in all types of weather conditions
- ease of repair and removal due to lacquer's evaporative-curing characteristics
- exceptional film clarity, producing the appearance of great depth
- excellent rubbing qualities, due to lacquer's evaporative-curing characteristics

NOTE

Lacquer can be damaged by extended contact with plastic materials, such as pads for tabletops and cushions for lamps and sculptures. The oily plasticizers in the plastic migrate into the lacquer, soften it, and cause the two to stick together. You should not leave plastic in contact with lacquer for more than a few days at a time.

- wide range of possible formulations for specific situations, including lacquers that look like an oil or wax finish, lacquers that will crack to look like an old finish, and lacquers in many colors to be used like paints
- great versatility for color matching, because there are so many colors available (both pigment and dye), and because you can build the colors very slowly and evenly with a spray gun
- relatively low cost

The qualities that may bring an end to lacquer's dominance include these:

- the necessity of using a high percentage of toxic, flammable,

SPRAYING LACQUER

MOST LACQUERS CURE too quickly to be brushed. So lacquer is usually sprayed. Here's how to do it:

1. Arrange your work so you can see what's happening in reflected light.
2. Thin the lacquer according to the manufacturer's instructions or until the lacquer breaks cleanly into drops off a stirring stick.
3. Decide whether you want to use a sanding sealer, a vinyl sealer, or the lacquer itself as a sealer. (See "Sealers and Sanding Sealers" on page 133.)
4. Spray the first coat on the wood. (See "Using Spray Guns" on page 45.)
5. Allow the first coat to cure thoroughly, and then sand it lightly with 280-grit or finer sandpaper to remove wood fibers that have been locked in an upright position. Sand just enough to make the surface feel smooth to the touch. Sanding will be easier if you let the finish cure overnight, especially if the finish is vinyl sealer or the lacquer itself. But it's possible to sand the first coat within an hour or two.
6. Remove the sanding dust with compressed air, vacuum, brush, or a tack cloth. Since the next coat of lacquer will redissolve any remaining lacquer sanding dust, it isn't essential that you remove all the dust out of the pores.
7. Apply the next coat of lacquer.
8. Allow it to cure, and sand it lightly with stearated sandpaper if there are dust nibs or other flaws you want to remove. Otherwise, it's not necessary to sand the lacquer. You can go right on to applying another coat.
9. Build the lacquer until you're satisfied. If you aren't trying to fill the pores, three or four coats are usually adequate. But it will depend on how much you thin the lacquer and how thick you apply each coat.
10. You can leave the lacquer as is, or you can finish it off with sandpaper, steel wool, or rubbing compounds. (See Chapter 14: "Finishing the Finish.") ■

TIP

It isn't necessary to let lacquer cure completely between coats. In fact, many finishers like to apply a thin "tack" coat to soften the existing lacquer and then come right back over with a full coat. I usually apply two full coats, one right after the other. It doesn't make any difference for the final result, so it's really just a matter of personal preference.

A lacquer's working qualities are determined by its solvents.

air-polluting solvents to apply the finish
- limited heat, solvent, acid, and alkali resistance (even though much better than shellac)
- limited scratch resistance (the flip side of good rubbing qualities)
- poor film-build due to low solids content. Only about 10 to 20 percent of the liquid lacquer you apply will remain as a solid film.

APPLYING LACQUER

The working qualities of lacquer are determined by the solvents used to put the lacquer into solution. The solvents must dissolve all the elements in the finish and then evaporate in the proper order so the finish cures thoroughly. There are a wide range of solvents that dissolve lacquer. These solvents evaporate at different rates, so you can control how fast the lacquer will cure by which solvent blend you choose. (See "Lacquer Thinner" on the facing page.) No other common finish gives you this control. It's one of the major reasons lacquer is so popular with professional finishers.

The solvents are combined by manufacturers into three broad categories:
- standard lacquer thinner, which evaporates at "normal" speed
- lacquer retarder, which evaporates more slowly than standard lacquer thinner
- fast lacquer thinner, which evaporates faster than standard lacquer thinner

Standard lacquer thinner and lacquer retarder are available at stores that carry lacquer. Fast lacquer thinner is not so widely available, but is usually sold by auto-body paint stores.

Begin with standard lacquer thinner. If you want to slow the curing, add some lacquer retarder. If you want to speed the curing, add some fast lacquer thinner. It's rare that you would need to use lacquer retarder or fast lacquer thinner straight.

There are four situations where using different thinners to control curing can be useful:
- to compensate for abnormal weather conditions (normal meaning temperature in the 70s Fahrenheit, humidity in the 40s)
- to improve flow-out (reduce orange peel)
- to keep a large area wet until you complete your spraying
- to slow the curing enough so you can brush the lacquer

(The occurrence of *fish eye,* small craterlike depressions in the finish, can not be corrected by varying the amount or type of thinner you use. For solutions to fish-eye problems, see "Fish Eye and Silicone" on page 168.)

Abnormal Weather

The control that the three types of lacquer thinner give you in abnormal weather conditions is very valuable. In hot or damp weather standard lacquer thinner evaporates too fast. In hot weather the lacquer won't have time to flow out on the surface; it may even dry before it gets to the surface. In humid weather the cooling effect of the rapidly evaporating solvents will draw moisture into the finish, causing it to *blush* (turn white). In both cases you can slow the curing and solve the problems by adding lacquer retarder.

In cold weather, standard lacquer thinner will evaporate very

LACQUER THINNER

LACQUER THINNER IS DIFFICULT to understand because it's made up of a number of different solvents blended together in many combinations. It's not important that you know the names of all these solvents, but it's helpful to understand that there are three types of solvents used:

- those that can dissolve lacquer all by themselves (ketones and esters)
- those that can dissolve lacquer in combination with the first group but not well by themselves (alcohols)
- diluting solvents that have no dissolving effect on lacquer at all, but do not obstruct the effect of the other two (fast-evaporating hydrocarbons, such as toluene and xylene)

The first two types, the ones that have the ability to dissolve lacquer, are the active solvents and typically make up less than 50 percent of most lacquer thinners. The third type serves only as a diluting solvent and makes up 50 to 60 percent of most lacquer thinners. Diluting solvents are added to reduce the cost. Cheap lacquer thinners often have too high a percentage of diluting solvent. This prevents the lacquer from going into solution. The lacquer appears cloudy, or gummy globules of solid lacquer settle to the bottom of the container. For this reason, be cautious using lacquer thinners not recommended by the lacquer's manufacturer.

If the lacquer thinner is designed properly, the diluting solvent will evaporate very rapidly, so that sagging is reduced. But if the design is poor, the active solvents may evaporate before the diluting solvent does, and the lacquer will come out of solution while it is curing on the wood. This will show up as *cotton blush.* (Lacquer is made from cellulose that is derived from cotton and wood.) Cotton blush has the appearance of tiny pieces of cotton dusted over the surface. It can be corrected by coating over with a more properly formulated lacquer thinner or lacquer retarder. This will put the solidified lacquer back into solution so it can cure properly.

The evaporation rate of lacquer thinner is controlled by the active solvents the manufacturer uses. A higher percentage of faster-evaporating solvents, such as acetone, MEK (methyl ethyl ketone), and ethyl acetate are used in fast-evaporating lacquer thinner. A higher percentage of slower-evaporating solvents, such as MAK (methyl n-amyl ketone) and butyl Cellosolve, are used in slower-evaporating lacquer thinner. ■

slowly, prolonging the cure. The lacquer will have time to run, sag, and collect dust. You can speed the curing by substituting some fast lacquer thinner for the standard lacquer thinner.

There aren't any rules for how much lacquer retarder or fast lacquer thinner you should add in any given situation. Weather conditions vary and so do the solvent blends in the various thinners. You will have to experiment. Being exact is not important, however, and you can vary the mixture as you go.

Photo 9-1. When lacquer does not flow out level, the surface cures pitted, resembling that of an orange peel.

Improving Flow-Out and Reducing Orange Peel

One of the biggest problems in spraying any finish is getting the finish to flow out level—that is, not cure pitted like the surface of an orange (Photo 9-1). There are two ways to reduce *orange peel.* One is by adjusting your spray gun for better atomization. (See Chapter 3: "Tools for Applying Finishes.") The other is to slow the curing of the finish so it has time to flow out and flatten.

If you are getting too much orange peel in your lacquer finish, you can increase the flow-out time on horizontal surfaces (and, to a lesser extent, on vertical surfaces) by adding some lacquer retarder. (For solutions to additional problems, see "Common Problems Applying Lacquer" on page 171.)

Keeping the Surface Wet

When you spray a finish, you always have some *overspray,* caused by the finish bouncing off the object back into the air or missing the object entirely, floating about, and settling later. On complex objects, you may want to keep the finish wet for the entire time you're applying the finish so that the overspray that settles back onto the object will redissolve and integrate into the finish. Keeping four chair legs and stretchers wet until you get them all coated is an example. You can slow the curing by adding some retarder to your lacquer.

Brushing Lacquer

Most lacquers are made to be sprayed. They cure too fast for brushing. If you want to brush a spraying lacquer, you can thin it with lacquer retarder. Even better, you can use a *brushing lacquer*—lacquer that has had the slower-evaporating solvents added by the manufacturer (Photo 9-2). You apply brushing lacquer much as you apply shellac. (See "Brushing and Spraying Shellac" on page 154.) You must work quickly and avoid rebrushing the same area to keep from dragging the lacquer. If you don't own spray equipment, you may find that using a brushing lacquer is a good substitute for shellac or varnish. Brushing lacquer is more durable than shellac but just as forgiving, and it doesn't have the inherent dust problems of varnish.

Photo 9-2: Most lacquers cure too fast to be brushed. They are designed to be sprayed. But lacquers made with slower-evaporating solvents can be brushed successfully. They can also be sprayed.

THE PROBLEM WITH LACQUER

The problem with lacquer is the high percentage of thinner required to put the lacquer into solution. Not only does the lacquer thinner cause air pollution, which is leading to lacquer being restricted in some parts of the country, but it is also highly flammable and bad for your health. The fumes of lacquer thinner can damage your central nervous system, liver, and kidneys and make you irritable, euphoric, or nauseous. Avoid using lacquer near any source of flame or spark, and protect yourself from breathing the lacquer thinner fumes by arranging air movement away from you and wearing a NIOSH-approved, organic-vapor respirator.

In spite of these problems, there is much resistance within the finishing trade to switching away from lacquer. It's hard to give up a finish you feel comfortable with and have control over. Nevertheless, many finishers who have made the switch find there are advantages to the alternatives, particularly the reduced exposure to toxic fumes.

FISH EYE AND SILICONE

ONE OF THE MOST FRUSTRATING problems you will encounter in finishing and refinishing is fish eye. Fish eye usually appears as moonlike, circular craters in the finish very shortly after you apply it (Photo 9-3). It sometimes appears as ridges formed by the finish crawling into mounds. When it takes this form, it's often called *crawling.*

Though fish eye can occur when using any film finish except shellac, I'm including it here because it's usually associated with lacquer. (Fish eye doesn't show up in oil finishes because the excess is wiped off.)

Fish eye is usually caused by silicone or other oil creating a very low surface tension on the wood. The surface tension is lower than that of the finish, so the finish doesn't flow out evenly. It's the same phenomenon you see when you put water on a car that has just been waxed. On a car the water beads up because the wax is everywhere. On wood the finish ridges around the spots where oil has gotten into the pores.

Silicone is an oil that is used in some lubricants and furniture polishes. It is the primary cause of fish eye because it has an exceptionally low surface tension. Silicone oil causes problems if you use a spray lubricant in the vicinity of your wood or your finishing area, or if you strip and refinish an object that has been treated with a silicone-containing furniture polish, such as Pledge. (Silicone in the furniture polish may have worked through cracks in the finish and gotten into the wood, or it may have gotten into the wood by becoming mixed in with the stripper and finish as you were removing it.)

Once silicone oil has gotten into wood, it is very difficult to remove—the same as any oil. Silicone oil may cause fish eye in your first coat of finish, or it may get worked into the first coat and not cause problems until the second or third coat.

Photo 9-3: In lacquer fish eye appears as moonlike craters.

MYTH

Silicone oil in furniture polishes softens, or in some other way damages, cured finishes.

FACT

Silicone oil is inert; it doesn't react with finishes in any way. Silicone oil's bad reputation originated with, and is spread by, refinishers who don't like the stuff because of the problems it causes in refinishing.

Silicone contamination can vary from a mild case that can be easily corrected to a severe case that is very difficult to correct. It can also be spotty on the wood, appearing in some places and not in others.

If you suspect silicone contamination, take one or more of the following measures to prevent fish eye. If fish eye occurs after you've applied your finish, wash the still-wet finish off the wood with the proper solvent (lacquer thinner for lacquer, mineral spirits for varnish, water or lacquer thinner for water base). Then take one or more of the following steps to prevent the fish eye from recurring:

- Remove all the silicone oil from the wood.
- Seal the silicone oil in the wood.
- Dust on four or five light coats of lacquer, then apply a wet coat.
- Lower the surface tension of your finish so it matches that of the surface of the wood or previous coat of finish.

Remove the Silicone Oil from the Wood

You can remove silicone oil from wood in the same way you would remove any oil. Wash the wood with mineral spirits, naphtha, or a special silicone remover (which is about the same thing). Turn your cloth often so you don't just move the oil around but pick it up.

This is only partially effective, however, because the solvent just thins the oil. It doesn't pull the oil out of the pores. It's more effective to wash the wood with a solution of TSP (tri-sodium phosphate) and water. This will remove the oil from the wood, just as soap removes oil from your hands. But it will introduce water into the wood, which could blister or lift veneer, and it will probably raise the grain, forcing you to sand after the wood has dried.

Seal the Silicone in the Wood

A second way to deal with silicone contamination is to seal the silicone oil in the wood. You can do this by spraying on a coat of thinned shellac. Thin some store-bought, 3-pound-cut shellac half-and-half with denatured alcohol, or mix up a 1- to 2-pound cut from shellac flakes. Use fresh shellac (not more than six months old), and use dewaxed shellac under any finish except lacquer. (See Chapter 8: "Shellac.") Wax in shellac will prevent a good bond with varnish, water base, and conversion.

Shellac seals in silicone oil because alcohol is not a solvent for the oil. The oil remains under the shellac and doesn't become a part of it. You must spray the shellac, however. If you brush it, the brush may drag some of the oil into the shellac, reduce its surface tension, and cause the next coat of finish to fish-eye.

Dust on Four or Five Coats of Lacquer

If you know the wood is contaminated with silicone oil, or if some fish eye has already occurred, you can coat over by spraying a number of very light coats of lacquer, and then dissolve the coats together with a heavier coat. This will work only with nitrocellulose lacquer. The trick is to build a thickness of lacquer without wetting the surface. Then apply a coat wet enough to dissolve all these coats and fuse them together, but not so wet that it causes the fish eye to come through.

Lower the Surface Tension of Your Finish

The fourth way to deal with silicone contamination is to add silicone oil to your finish. This lowers the surface tension of the finish to bring it in line with that of the surface, so the finish then flows out evenly. Once you've added

TIP

You will often get a warning of silicone contamination when you apply a stain. The stain will fish-eye or crawl before you wipe off the excess.

(continued)

FISH EYE AND SILICONE—continued

silicone oil to one coat of finish, you must add it to each additional coat. You can brush or spray each coat.

Silicone oil intended for this purpose is sold under a number of trade names, including Fish-Eye Destroyer, Fish-eye Flo Out, Sil Flo, and Olde Smoothie. (For water-based finishes you may have to obtain a special emulsified silicone oil from the finish manufacturer.) Add 1 to 2 eyedroppers to a quart of finish, or follow the manufacturer's instructions. If the contamination in the wood (or previous coat of finish) is minimal, you don't need as much silicone oil in the finish to bring the surface tension of the two in line. If the contamination is severe, you'll need more.

Adding less than 2 eyedroppers of silicone oil to the finish doesn't weaken it significantly, but it does make the finish feel a little slicker, and it raises its gloss slightly. You could decide to add silicone oil to your finish on purpose when you want it to have these characteristics.

You are not limited to just one of the above methods for eliminating fish eye. You can employ several of these methods together. Many refinishers make it a practice to seal all their work with shellac, and many others add silicone regularly to their finish even when they've had no indication of a problem. Some do both. ■

NOTE

Adding silicone oil to your finish will contaminate your spray gun or brush requiring you to clean it extra well to remove all the oil. Overspray from a spray gun will also contaminate any finished or unfinished wood it lands on.

COMMON PROBLEMS APPLYING LACQUER

Lacquer is a very forgiving finish. Problems are easier to repair than with most other finishes. But they're not easy when you don't understand why they occurred. The most common problems are runs and sags, orange peel, and dry spray. (See "Common Spraying Problems" on page 42.)

PROBLEM	CAUSE	SOLUTION
The lacquer develops a white haze, called blushing, right after you apply it.	The rapid evaporation of the lacquer thinner cools the surface so fast that humidity from the air is drawn into the film. Blushing occurs during warm, humid weather.	1) Thin the lacquer with a slower-evaporating thinner (lacquer retarder) to lessen the cooling and give the moisture more time to escape before the lacquer cures. 2) If the blushing has cured in the lacquer, give it a few hours or overnight for the moisture to work its way out on its own, or spray a light coat of lacquer retarder to redissolve the lacquer so the moisture can escape.
Craters, or fish eyes (they resemble craters on the moon), develop in the lacquer film. This will happen within seconds after you apply the lacquer—while the lacquer is still wet.	There is silicone or other oil on the surface. The usual cause of silicone contamination is furniture polish that has been used on the piece you're refinishing. It's sometimes caused by a silicone spray having been used near where you are working. The silicone prevents the lacquer from flowing out evenly.	1) You can try sanding the worst of the craters off the surface and then dusting on a number of coats of lacquer followed by a full wet coat. The idea is that the wet coat dissolves the dusted coats, but doesn't redissolve the lacquer that has fish-eyed. (See "Fish Eye and Silicone" on page 168.) 2) Strip the lacquer and begin again. Wash the surface thoroughly with mineral spirits, naphtha, or a fish-eye remover, which is about the same thing. This will dilute the amount of silicone that remains in the wood. (You can also wash with TSP.) Apply a washcoat of 1- to 2-pound-cut shellac to seal off any silicone oil that remains. Or add 2 eyedroppers of silicone oil, sold as fish-eye eliminator, to 1 quart of lacquer. Do both if the problem is severe.
Pinholes show up in the cured film. They usually appear right over pores and are most common in large-pored woods such as mahogany and oak.	Air trapped in the pores has broken through the film. Sometimes it's caused by the wood being too warm.	It will be difficult to repair, though you can try sanding the finish back and dusting on a few coats as above. Otherwise, strip off the lacquer, and begin again by dusting on several coats followed by heavier coats.

CHAPTER 10

Varnish

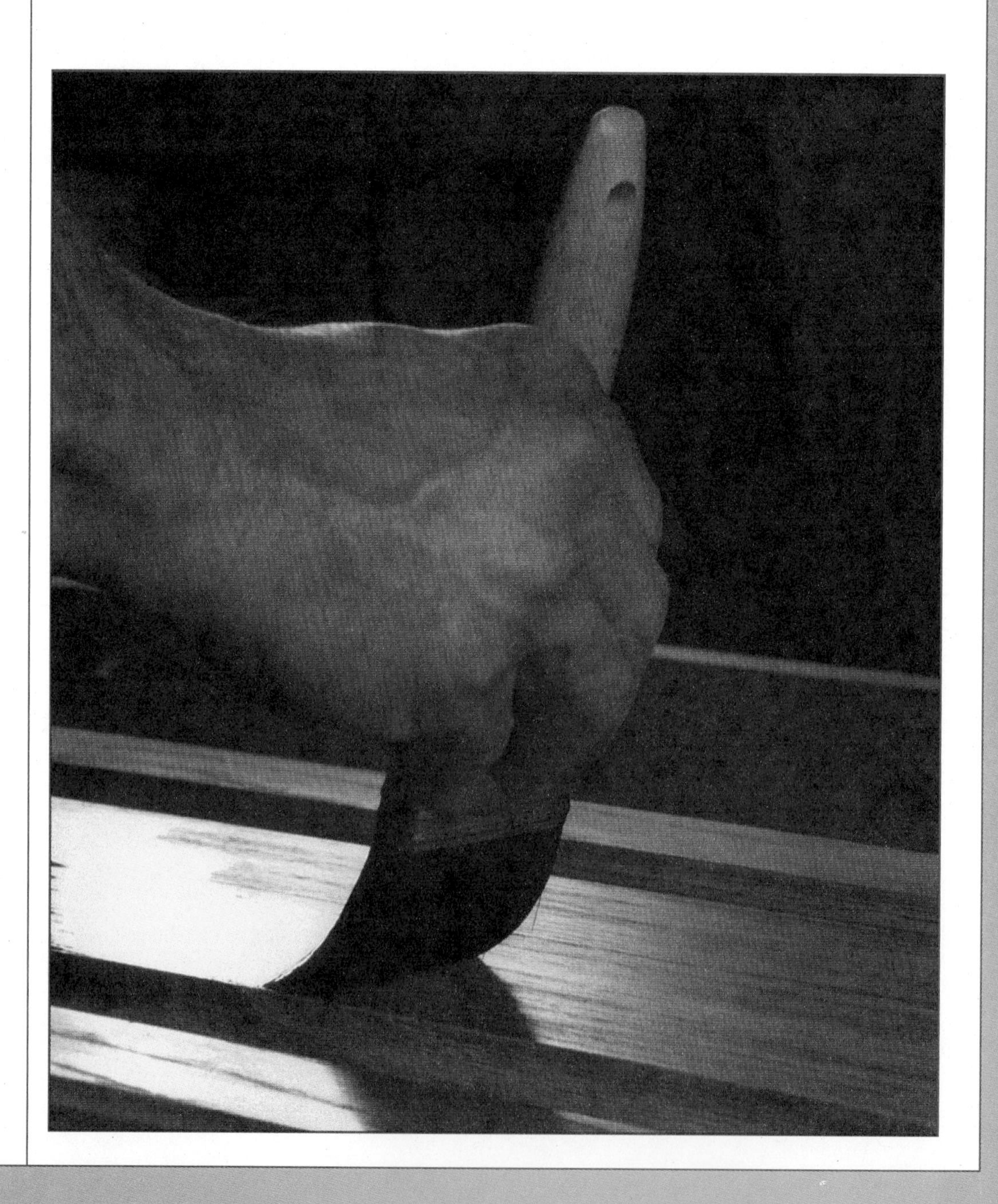

VARNISH IN BRIEF

PROS Excellent heat, wear, solvent, acid, and alkali resistance.
Excellent water and water-vapor resistance.
Brushes well.

CONS Very slow curing, causing severe dust problems.
Tends to yellow over time.

Varnish (including polyurethane) is the most durable of the commonly available finishes. It resists heat, wear, solvents, acids, and alkalis, and it's also a barrier against water and water-vapor penetration. It's cheap and it builds fast. It has all the good qualities you probably want in a finish, except one: It's difficult to apply.

Varnish is made by cooking a curing, or semi-curing, oil with a resin. Driers are added to speed the curing. Traditionally, the oil used was linseed oil, because it was the best oil available. In the late nineteenth century, tung oil was introduced into the Western world from China and began to be used in some furniture rubbing varnishes and in spar varnishes meant for outdoor use. By the mid-twentieth century, chemists had learned how to modify semi-curing oils, such as soybean (soya) oil and safflower oil, so they would cure. These oils were cheaper, and they yellowed less than linseed oil and tung oil, so they became the primary oils used in varnish. (All varnishes yellow over time.)

Traditional resins were fossilized sap from various species of pine trees. The best pine-tree resins were imported. (American pine-tree resin is too soft to make good varnish.) The resins came from eastern Asia, New Zealand, Africa, and northern Europe. The best resins were copals, such as kauri, congo, and manila (Photo 10-1 on page 174).

Photo 10-1: Examples of some natural resins used in varnish. From left, copal, amber, and rosin.

Amber was also used. Amber is the fossilized sap from an extinct pine that once grew in northern Europe. You often see amber in gift stores, sold for making into necklaces and jewelry. Natural resins are rarely used anymore to make varnish.

Beginning in the early twentieth century chemists began developing synthetic resins which were more consistent in quality and availability. The first to be developed was *phenolic* resin (a combination of phenol and formaldehyde). Originally it was used as a plastic and, in fact, saw widespread use in early radio cases. Phenolic resin is a solid, just like natural resin. To use it for finishing, chemists developed a way of making the resin into liquid by heating it with oil. The liquid resin/oil combination changed to a solid when exposed to oxygen in the air. This process is called *oxidation.* Phenolic-resin varnish was the first synthetic finish.

The next was *alkyd*-resin varnish, a type of polyester finish, developed in the 1920s. The name "alkyd" is a contraction of the names of the two main ingredients used to make the resin—alcohol and acid. Alkyd resin is also cooked with oil to make varnish. It is cheaper than phenolic resin and has become a workhorse in the finish industry. It's not only the most common resin used in varnish, it's also used in lacquer, conversion finishes, and oil-based paint.

The last of the three main varnish resins is *polyurethane.* It was developed in the 1930s and is commonly used as a plastic. Polyurethane is very tough. There are several varieties of polyurethane finish. Pure polyurethane finishes come in two parts (like epoxy glue), or they cure with heat or by absorbing moisture. The polyurethane you most often see in paint stores is actually an alkyd varnish modified with polyurethane resin, a *uralkyd.* Since the base of the finish is alkyd varnish, it applies and cures like alkyd varnish. This type of varnish has become the most popular of the three varnish types because it is the most scratch-resistant.

Varnish made from oil and resin alone doesn't cure fast enough to be useful as a finish, so metallic driers are added to speed the curing. The driers act as a catalyst, accelerating oxidation. Originally, lead was used as a drier because it was available and it worked. Other metallic driers have since been developed, and when it was discovered that lead caused health problems, these other driers were substituted. These include cobalt, manganese, zinc, and zirconium. These driers are all approved by the Food and Drug Administration (FDA) for use in oil, varnish, and paint. They are not known to cause any health problems as long as the oil, varnish, or paint is formulated so that it cures thoroughly. Lead is no longer used in common varnish and paint.

You can buy driers separately and add them to oil, varnish, or oil-based paint to speed the curing. The driers are a combination of the metals in solution and are usually sold as *japan drier.* Adding your own japan drier to varnish is risky. First, the combination of driers in the pre-packaged can may not be optimal for the finish you're using. Second, adding driers to the finish will not only speed the curing, it will make the film more brittle and promote cracking. Add only a few drops at a time, and proceed cautiously until you get a feel for the effect the driers have.

MYTH

You often hear polyurethane disparaged as a "plastic" finish.

FACT

All film finishes, except possibly shellac, are plastic! Solid lacquer, called celluloid, was the first plastic. It was used as early as the 1870s to make collars, combs, knife handles, spectacle frames, toothbrushes, toys, and later, movie film. Phenolic resin was used to make the first plastic radio cases. Amino resins (conversion finishes) are used to make plastic laminate. Acrylic resin (water base) is used to make plexiglass.

THE MIX OF OIL AND RESIN

Whichever oils and resins are used in making a varnish, the greatest difference is made by the ratio of oil to resin. The more oil, the softer and more flexible the resulting cured-varnish film. The less oil, the harder and more brittle the resulting cured-varnish film.

Varnish made with a high percentage of oil is called *long-oil* varnish. It is commonly sold as "spar" or "marine" varnish and is intended for outdoor use, where more flexibility is needed to accommodate greater wood movement. Varnish made with a low percentage of oil is called *short-oil* or *medium-oil* varnish. It is meant to be used indoors, where extreme wood movement is not a problem and a harder finish is usually desired.

It makes a difference which oils and which resins are used to make a varnish. (It also makes a difference which driers are used, but only in the speed and thoroughness of the curing, not in the physical properties of the cured film.) Here is how resins and oils affect the characteristics of varnish:

- Phenolic resin cures tough and flexible. It also yellows significantly (as seen in the old radio cases). Phenolic resin is often combined with tung oil to make spar varnish for use outdoors or rubbing varnish for use on rubbed tabletops (see Chapter 14: "Finishing the Finish"). The difference in the two types is the

NOTE

Though a short-oil, phenolic-modified tung-oil varnish is the best varnish for rubbing, it is still far inferior to lacquer or shellac. For best results, allow the varnish to cure for at least a month (even longer is better) before attempting to rub it.

ratio of oil to resin used. Combining phenolic resin with a high percentage of tung oil makes a varnish that is flexible and very water-resistant. Combining phenolic resin with a small amount of tung oil makes a varnish that cures hard enough to be rubbed to a high gloss.

- Alkyd resin is not as tough as phenolic resin, but it is adequate for most situations, and it is cheaper and doesn't yellow as much. Alkyd is therefore the most common resin used in varnish.
- Polyurethane resin combined with alkyd is the toughest of the three varnish resins. But it has three shortcomings: It has a slightly cloudy appearance (one reason for its being singled out as a "plastic"). It doesn't bond well with any other finish, nor does any other finish bond well with it. It doesn't even bond well to itself after it has cured thoroughly. (Always scuff it with sandpaper or steel wool before recoating.) Finally, it doesn't hold up well in sunlight. Ultraviolet rays destroy its bond to the wood and cause it to peel. Despite some polyurethanes being called "exterior," they will perform well only when kept out of direct sunlight. (For a guide to the various varnishes, see "Identifying Varnish Types," below.)

CHARACTERISTICS OF VARNISH

Varnish has six primary characteristics, each of which is the result of its reactive curing. (See Chapter 7: "Introduction to Film Finishes.")

- *Resistance to heat, wear, solvents, acids, and alkalis:* Due to the crosslinking of the resin molecules, varnish is an exceptionally durable finish. The molecules are hard to break apart, so it takes high heat, sharp force, or strong solvents or chemicals to cause damage.

IDENTIFYING VARNISH TYPES

Manufacturers seldom tell you what type varnish is in the can. Here are some clues that will help you determine the type.

CLUE	THE VARNISH IS PROBABLY
No identification on the can.	Alkyd
The varnish is clear.	Alkyd/soybean-oil or alkyd/safflower-oil
The varnish is amber-colored.	Alkyd/linseed-oil or phenolic/tung-oil
The label claims the varnish is made with tung oil.	Phenolic/tung-oil

- *Resistance to water and water-vapor exchange:* The crosslinked molecular network reduces the size of spaces for water or water vapor to pass through.
- *Long curing time:* Slow oxidation allows you plenty of time to brush varnish without it getting tacky and dragging. But this also causes dust problems. Any dust that settles on the surface while the varnish is still wet or tacky will stick, detracting from the finished object.
- *Difficulty in repairing and stripping:* This is the flip side of good solvent and chemical resistance.
- *Difficulty in rubbing to an even sheen:* This is the flip side of good scratch resistance.
- *Skinning over in the can:* Since varnish cures by absorbing oxygen, any air left in a can of varnish will begin to cure it. If there is enough air, the varnish will skin over. (If the varnish hasn't begun to gel under the skin, it is still good. Remove the skin and strain the remaining varnish into a smaller container, such as a glass jar or a collapsible plastic container, so little or no air remains to cause skinning. Label the jar.)

APPLYING VARNISH

Varnish takes a long time to cure. It takes an hour or more to cure enough for dust not to stick to it, and it takes at least overnight to cure enough to apply another coat. For these reasons varnish is seldom used in factories or by professional finishers. It is primarily used by amateurs who don't own spray equipment. (See "Brushing Varnish" on page 178.) Many of these amateurs erroneously believe they're using an inferior finish because it's not used by professionals who must know better.

Varnish is a joy to brush and a misery to spray. It brushes well because you have plenty of time to spread it out evenly on the wood. It's troublesome to spray because small particles of uncured varnish float around in the air and when they settle, they make everything, including you, sticky.

It takes very few coats of full-strength varnish to build a significant thickness of film. Varnish has a high-solids content. Two or three coats of varnish after the first "sealer" coat is almost always enough.

The weather affects the speed at which varnish cures. Cold and damp weather slows the curing significantly. Don't apply varnish in temperatures below 60 degrees Fahrenheit: It may take days to cure. Hot weather speeds the curing. The thinner evaporates more quickly, and the varnish reacts more quickly with oxygen. You may find it difficult to brush varnish on a large surface if the temperature is 90 degrees or higher. Brush marks may not

Varnish is a joy to brush and a misery to spray.

(text continues on page 181)

BRUSHING VARNISH

VARNISH CAN BE APPLIED by brushing, spraying, or even wiping, as is done with wiping varnish. (See Chapter 4: "Oil Finishes.") But it's usually brushed. The key to getting good results with varnish is cleanliness—even more so than with other finishes, because varnish takes so long to cure. Here are some suggestions:

- Don't do your sanding and dusting in the same room where you are about to apply the varnish.
- Wet-mop the floor so you don't kick up dust when you walk around.
- Put clean paper under your work.
- Don't wear dirty or dusty clothes.
- Strain the varnish if it is dirty or has formed a skin.
- Be sure your brush is clean. Hit it against your hand to shake out any loose bristles.
- Be sure the wood's surface is clean. Wipe it with a tack cloth just before you start applying the varnish.

TIP

A tack cloth is cheesecloth made sticky with a varnish-like substance. You can buy one (which I think is the best idea), or you can make your own. To make one, wet a piece of cheesecloth with mineral spirits. Wring out the cheesecloth, and apply a few drops of varnish. Work the varnish into the cheesecloth. The cheesecloth should be sticky enough to pick up dust but not not so sticky as to leave a residue when you wipe it over the wood. Store the tack cloth in an airtight coffee can or Ziploc-type bag to keep it from hardening.

MYTH

You should thin your first coat of varnish half-and-half with mineral spirits to get a better bond to the wood.

FACT

Varnish bonds well to wood whatever the varnish thickness. The reason to thin your first coat is so it will be thinner and cure harder on the wood, making it easier to sand.

With cleanliness foremost in mind, here are the steps for brushing varnish:

1. Arrange your work so you can see what's happening in a reflected light source.
2. Decide whether you want to use a varnish sanding sealer or varnish thinned with about 50 percent mineral spirits (paint thinner) for the first coat. (See "Sealers and Sanding Sealers" on page 133.)
3. Pour enough sanding sealer or varnish to do the job into another container (a jar or coffee can) and work out of that container. This way you won't transfer dirt back into your original supply.
4. Brush on the first coat. It will brush very easily. Brush with the grain and don't leave puddles or runs. You want the coat to be thin so that it will cure hard.
5. Allow the varnish to cure overnight.
6. Sand the surface lightly with the grain using 280-grit or finer sandpaper. Stearated sandpaper works best. Sand

outside your finish room, or sand several hours before you intend to apply the next coat of varnish, so the dust in your finish room will have time to settle.

7. Remove the sanding dust with a vacuum, paper towel, or tack cloth. Finish off with a tack cloth.
8. Decide what sheen you want. You can use gloss and rub it after it has cured, or you can use satin (eggshell) or flat. Gloss varnish seldom looks good without rubbing; satin and flat look fine without rubbing.
9. From a separate container, apply the next coat of varnish full strength or thinned with 10 to 20 percent mineral spirits. Follow the directions for brushing in "Using Brushes" on page 38.
10. Coat one part at a time. You can brush on the varnish in any direction you want, but you should make your final strokes go with the grain. When each part is coated, remove any excess varnish by *tipping off*. Here's how: Hold your brush almost vertical and brush very lightly with the grain. After each stroke wipe the brush over the lip of a clean jar to remove the excess. (Be sure the lip of the jar is clean.) It's important that you tip off the varnish if the varnish is full strength. The coat will be too thick on the wood if you don't. It's not so important to do this if the varnish is thinned, unless it's likely to sag or run.
11. Allow the varnish to cure overnight. Check the hardness by trying to push your fingernail into the varnish in an inconspicuous place. If you can't, it's ready to prepare for the next coat.
12. Sand the surface lightly with 320-grit or finer stearated sandpaper. You can substitute #000 or #0000 steel wool if there aren't any dust nibs to remove. You can also sand off the dust nibs, and then rub with steel wool to create scratches for the next coat to bond to. Steel wool won't clog like sandpaper does. Synthetic steel wool (Scotch-Brite) can be substituted.
13. If you're trying to achieve a perfectly flat surface, you'll have to sand out the brush marks after each coat. You can see the marks easily as soon as you start sanding. The ridges will appear dull, while the hollows are still shiny. On flat surfaces use a cork, felt, or rubber block to back your sandpaper. Use 320- or 400-grit wet/dry sandpaper lubricated with soap and water or mineral spirits.
14. Clean off the sanding dust and brush on another coat as above. You should apply two or three coats after the sealer coat—more if you are filling the pores with the finish. (See Chapter 6: "Filling the Pores.")
15. When you're satisfied with the thickness, you can leave the finish as is, or you can finish it with sandpaper, steel wool, or rubbing compounds. (See Chapter 14: "Finishing the Finish.") ■

NOTE

Varnish formulas are changing in response to government restrictions on solvent content. These varnishes are often exceptionally slow curing, so be sure the coats you apply are thin. If you have problems that can't be explained by the information in this chapter, check with your supplier and with the manufacturer.

TIP

Brushing parts in a horizontal position reduces runs and sags. If necessary, reposition a piece so the surface you're finishing is horizontal. Brush the most important parts, such as the top and drawer fronts, last.

COMMON PROBLEMS APPLYING VARNISH

Varnish is a difficult finish to apply so that it comes out looking good. Many things can go wrong. Here are the most common problems, their causes, and solutions.

PROBLEM	CAUSE	SOLUTION
Air bubbles appear in the varnish finish as you apply it and don't pop out before the varnish cures.	The bubbles are caused by the friction of the brush against the surface.	Sand the surface smooth and add 10 to 20 percent mineral spirits to the next coat. The mineral spirits will thin the finish and slow the curing enough for the air bubbles to pop out.
The varnish crawls into ridges after you apply a second coat.	Silicone or other oil on the surface of the wood has blended with the first coat of varnish, giving it a lower surface tension than the next coat.	Before the varnish cures, remove it with a cloth soaked in mineral spirits. If you're too late, strip off the varnish. Try adding an eyedropper of silicone oil (available as fish-eye eliminator from paint stores that sell to the trade) to a little mineral spirits, and stir this solution into a pint of varnish. (For more information on solving silicone problems, see "Fish Eye and Silicone" on page 168.)
The varnish doesn't cure. It remains tacky.	1) The air is too cold.	Warm the room or wait for a warmer day.
	2) There is uncured oil in the wood. Many people make the mistake of thinking a coat of linseed oil under the varnish helps things.	Allow more time for the varnish to cure. If it still doesn't, strip it and the oil off the wood, let the wood dry thoroughly, and start over.
	3) The wood is an oily wood such as teak, rosewood, cocobolo, or ebony. The oils in these woods retard the curing of varnish.	Allow more time for the varnish to cure. If it doesn't, strip the varnish off the wood and wash the wood with a non-oily solvent such as naphtha, acetone, or lacquer thinner before reapplying the varnish.

have time to smooth out, and air bubbles in the varnish film may not have time to pop out before the varnish cures. (See "Common Problems Applying Varnish" on the facing page.)

There's nothing you can do to speed up the curing on cold or damp days except raise the temperature in the area you're working in. You can slow the curing somewhat on hot days, however, by adding 10 to 20 percent mineral spirits (paint thinner) to the varnish. (See "Turpentine and Petroleum-Distillate Solvents," below.)

Adding a little mineral spirits to varnish makes it spread more easily and flow out more smoothly in addition to giving air bubbles more time to pop out of the finish. Many finishers make it a practice to thin each coat. The downside, of course, is thinner coats, so you may have to apply more coats.

MYTH

You can prevent air bubbles by not shaking or stirring the can of varnish and by brushing very slowly and smoothly.

FACT

You can't keep air bubbles from occurring in varnish if you brush it. The trick is getting the bubbles to pop out of the film before it cures. If the bubbles don't pop out on their own, thin the varnish with 10 to 20 percent mineral spirits. The mineral spirits will slow the curing enough to allow them to pop out.

TURPENTINE AND PETROLEUM-DISTILLATE SOLVENTS

COMMON SOLVENTS FOR wax and common thinners for oil and varnish are derived from two sources: pine sap and crude-oil petroleum. Distilled pine sap, called *turpentine,* was used before petroleum solvents were introduced around the turn of the twentieth century. The best-quality turpentine is steam-distilled from the sap of the living tree and is usually called *gum turpentine.* A lesser quality is steam-distilled from extracts of the dead tree or the stump and is usually called *wood turpentine.* Both types are available but have fallen out of favor because of higher cost and stronger odor than petroleum solvents. Some painters still prefer to use turpentine, however, because they like the "feel" it gives to the paint while brushing.

Petroleum is the source of most of the solvents and thinners used in finishing. Those derived directly from petroleum are called *petroleum distillates,* because they are obtained by distillation. They include mineral spirits, naphtha, kerosene, benzene, toluene, and xylene. (These solvents are also known as *hydrocarbons,* because they are made up of hydrogen and carbon.)

The petroleum is heated until gases form. The gases are drawn off and allowed to cool back into liquid form. As the petroleum is heated to higher temperatures, the gases that are cooled form different products. For example, at relatively low temperatures heptane and octane are distilled to be made into gasoline. At higher temperatures naphtha, usually sold as Varnish Maker's and Painter's Naphtha (VM&P Naphtha),

(continued)

TURPENTINE AND PETROLEUM-DISTILLATE SOLVENTS—continued

is derived. This is followed by mineral spirits and then kerosene. Mineral oil (also called paraffin oil) can be distilled at even higher temperatures, and paraffin wax (used to seal jelly jars) at still higher temperatures. Each of these distillations is called a petroleum *fraction*. The lower-temperature fractions are far more flammable than the higher-temperature fractions.

The relationship between the fractions is important because it helps you to understand these solvents so you know when to use each (Figure 10-1).

VM&P naphtha (also called benzine) is distilled at a lower temperature than mineral spirits. Therefore, at any given temperature naphtha will evaporate faster than mineral spirits. In a like manner, kerosene will evaporate at a slower rate than mineral spirits.

The faster the solvent evaporates, the less oily it is. The slower it evaporates, the more oily it is. Naphtha is far less oily than kerosene. Mineral oil *is* oil. Finally, at higher temperatures, the distillate is no longer a liquid at room temperature, it's a wax.

NOTE

Most furniture polishes are made from petroleum-distillate solvents in the range between mineral spirits and kerosene. The manufacturer chooses the fraction that will evaporate at the desired rate. The petroleum smell is, of course, replaced with a lemon or other more pleasant scent. (See Chapter 15: "Caring for the Finish.")

FIGURE 10-1: PETROLEUM DISTILLATES

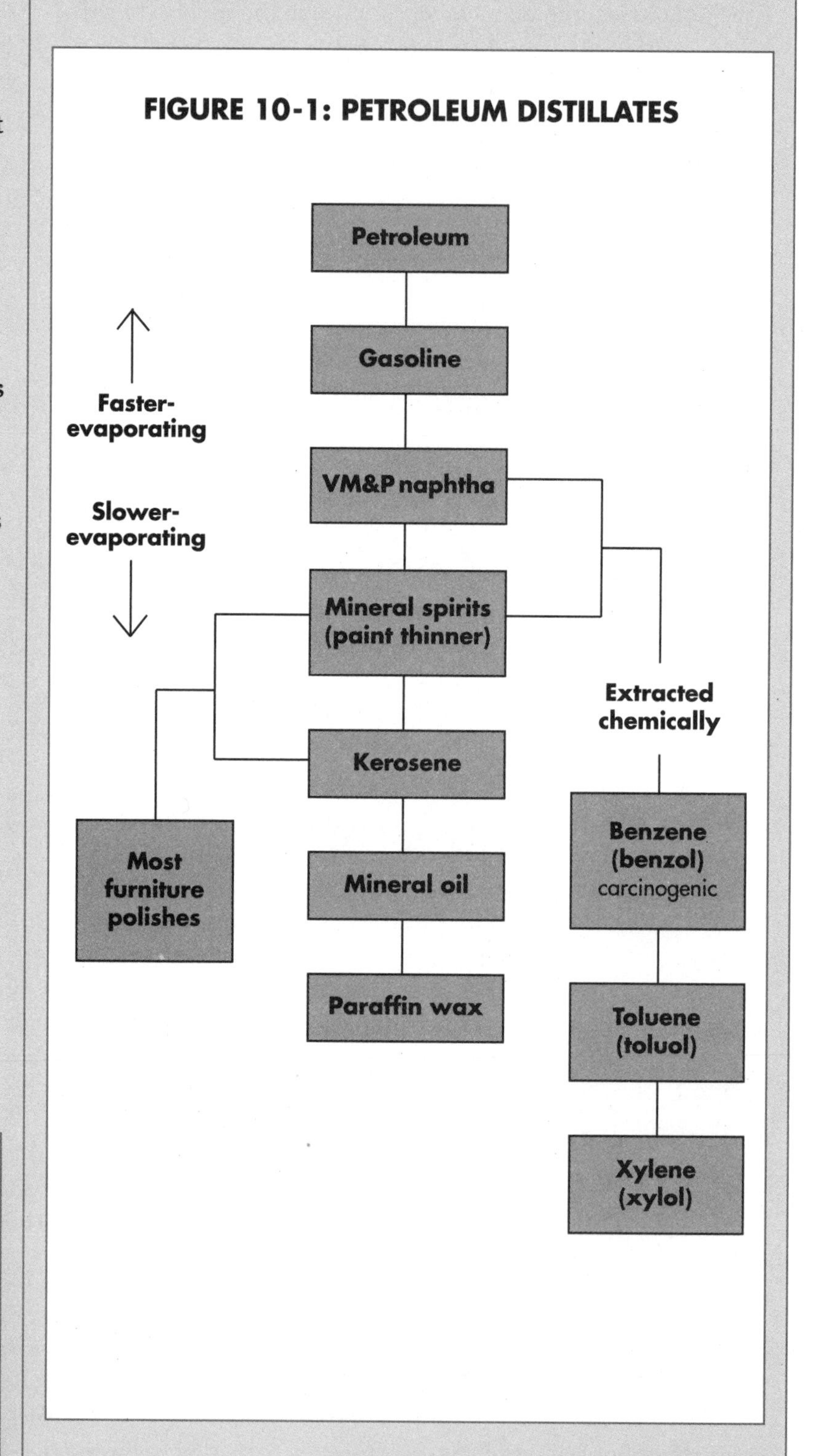

You use naphtha when you want a solvent that evaporates relatively fast or one that is non-oily. Naphtha is best for degreasing. You use mineral spirits when you want a slower-evaporating solvent and you don't mind the oiliness. Mineral spirits is good for thinning linseed oil and varnish. Kerosene is not used much in finishing; it evaporates very slowly or not at all, and it is very oily. All fractions of petroleum distillate can be mixed together.

Benzene, toluene, and xylene are the strong and smelly parts of naphtha and mineral spirits. Refineries remove these parts with chemicals. What's left is odorless mineral spirits.

Benzene (also called benzol) was once used as a thinner and paint stripper, and you still see it recommended now and then for these purposes in books and magazine articles. But benzene is carcinogenic, and it was removed from the consumer market in the early 1970s. Mineral spirits and naphtha contain only a trace of benzene.

Toluene (also called toluol) is used as a diluting solvent in lacquer thinner. (See "Lacquer Thinner" on page 165.) Xylene (also called xylol) evaporates more slowly than toluene. It is used as a thinner in conversion varnish and is sometimes recommended as a thinner for short-oil varnishes. Both toluene and xylene can be used to remove latex paint spatter from all furniture finishes except wax and water base without damaging the finish. ■

TIP

Benzene, which is carcinogenic, is often confused with benzine, which is another name for naphtha. It will help you to remember which is which if you associate the e in benzene with the word dead and the i in benzine with the word alive.

CHAPTER 11

Water-Based Finishes

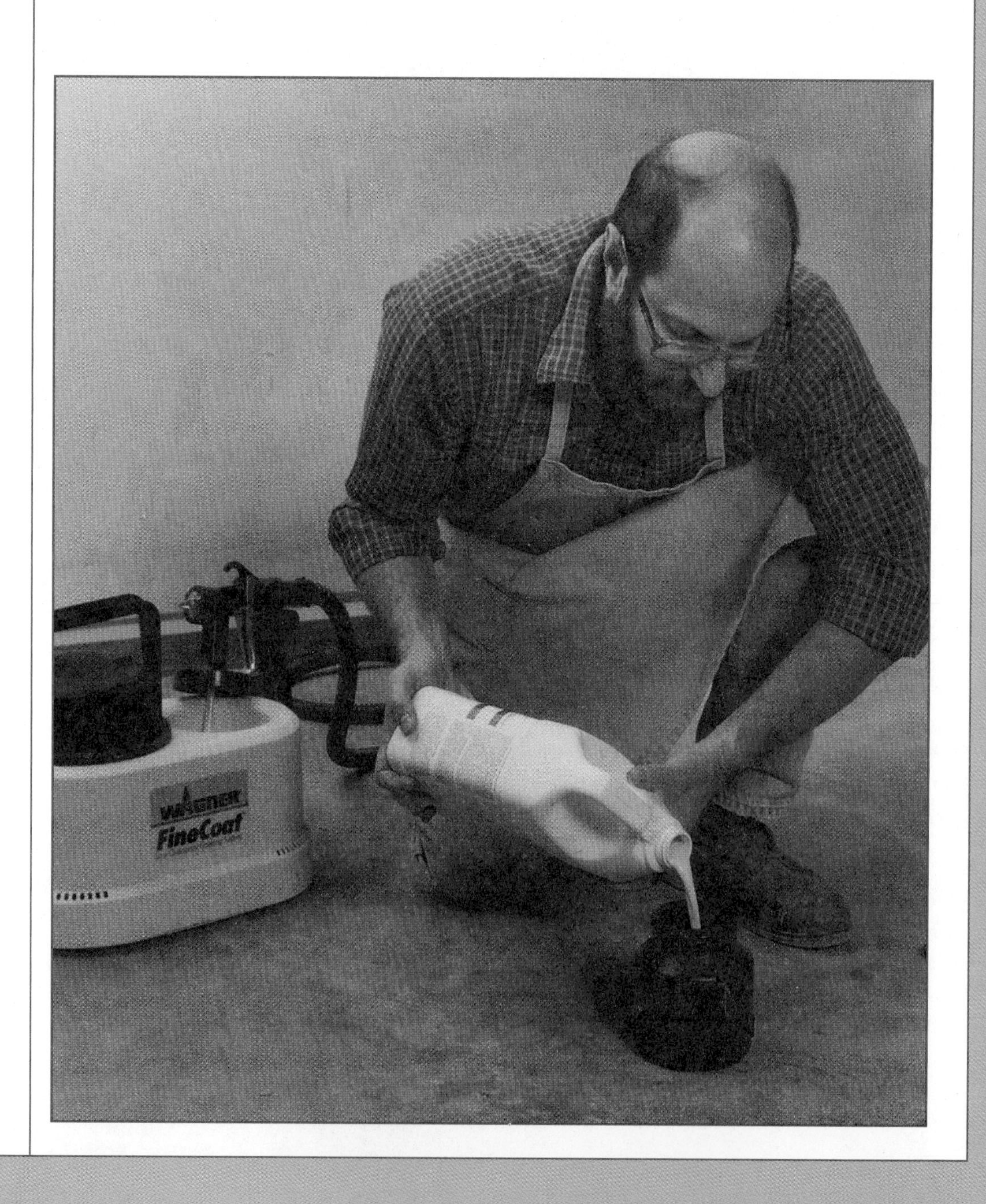

WATER BASE IN BRIEF

PROS
- Minimal solvent fumes
- Easy cleanup
- Very scuff-resistant
- Not a fire hazard
- Nonyellowing

CONS
- Produces bland, washed-out appearance on dark woods
- Very weather-sensitive during application
- Raises the grain of the wood
- Only moderate heat, solvent, acid, alkali, water, and water-vapor resistance (no better than nitrocellulose lacquer)

The technology for making water-based finishes has existed for almost half a century. It's the same technology that's used in making latex paint and white and yellow glues. There was no demand for water-based finishes because they were more expensive than other finishes to produce, and they were more difficult to use. They still are, and only recently, with society's growing concern over air pollution, has a demand been created. Local and state governments have changed the marketplace by passing laws that limit the amount of solvent (volatile organic compounds, or VOCs) a finish or paint can contain. In areas where strict laws are in effect, you don't find high-solvent-content finishes, such as nitrocellulose lacquer, on paint-store shelves.

WHAT IS WATER-BASED FINISH?

What's commonly called water-based finish, or *water base,* is really a solvent-based finish, usually acrylic or polyurethane, that is dispersed in water. Calling it water base distinguishes it from those finishes known as solvent-based finishes—shellac, lacquer, and varnish—which don't use water. A true water-based finish would be impractical for use on household objects, since it would redissolve in water.

For water base, the acrylic and polyurethane are manufactured in tiny, cured droplets, which are then dispersed in water. A solvent that evaporates slower than water, usually glycol ether, is added. (See "Glycol Ether" on the facing page.) After the water evaporates, the tiny droplets of finish come very close together (coalesce). The solvent then softens the outer molecules of the droplets so they can interlock in much the same way as the molecules in shellac and lacquer interlock. As the solvent then evaporates, the connected droplets form a continuous film. (See Chapter 7: "Introduction to Film Finishes.")

Most water-based finishes use acrylic, which is very hard and tough. Some use a blend of acrylic and polyurethane. The addition of polyurethane makes the finish even tougher but somewhat cloudy, just as it does in solvent-based varnish finishes. Both types of finish are usually sold under names that indicate the use of water in the formula. But they are sometimes sold as "lacquer," "varnish," or "polyurethane," with no indication in the names that they are different from solvent-based lacquer, varnish, or polyurethane. Manufacturers do this to make an entirely new type of finish seem familiar, and it causes confusion. All water-based finishes, no matter which resins are included, have far more in common with each other than with traditional lacquer, varnish, or solvent-based polyurethane. (See "What's in a Name?" on page 133.) Look for the thinning or cleanup material listed on the can. If it's water, then the finish is water-based. If it's a solvent, the finish is solvent-based.

CHARACTERISTICS OF WATER-BASED FINISH

Water-based finishes are highly touted by manufacturers for their scratch resistance. They are very tough finishes, resembling solvent-based polyurethane. But they differ from solvent-based polyurethane in almost every other respect. Water-based finishes are less resistant to heat, solvents, acids, or alkalis, and they provide a weaker barrier against water penetration and water-vapor exchange. In these respects water-based finishes resemble nitrocellulose lacquer.

This is not to say that water-based finishes are not good finishes, only that film toughness isn't everything. It's better that you know in advance that a hot coffee cup, a little bit of fingernail-polish remover, or a washing with an alkali soap will cause damage; that you can get water rings on a cured water-based finish; and that the finish won't do much to stop wood from moving with humidity changes compared to solvent-based polyurethane. (Latex paint, which is chemically related to clear water base, is valued for use on the outside of houses precisely because of its ability to "breathe," or let water vapor pass through.)

NOTE

Some manufacturers provide "hardeners" for their water base. These are actually crosslinkers. They cause the droplets to crosslink, increasing the cured film's resistance to heat, solvents, acids, alkalis, water, and water-vapor exchange. Unfortunately, these hardeners tend to be very toxic, negating one of the primary rationales for using water base in the first place.

GLYCOL ETHER

THE SOLVENT GLYCOL ETHER is surely not as familiar to you as mineral spirits, alcohol, or lacquer thinner. It's seldom available in paint stores, and it's not often mentioned in books and magazine articles about finishing.

Glycol ether is a catchall term for a number of solvents, much like the term *petroleum distillate.* Glycol ether solvents are made by reacting alcohols with ethylene oxide or propylene oxide. Examples of glycol ethers are ethylene glycol monobutyl ether (butyl Cellosolve) and propylene glycol monomethyl ether. (Now you understand the need for grouping the solvents under a shorter term.) The individual solvents differ in solvent strength and evaporation rate.

Glycol ether solvents are special because they are bridging solvents. They make water-soluble substances such as water dye compatible with thinners such as alcohol and lacquer thinner (to make NGR stains), and they make solvent-soluble substances such as acrylic and polyurethane resins compatible with water (to make water-based finishes). As a group, glycol ether solvents are fairly strong in solvent strength, and they are very toxic. The reason they can be used in finishes, despite their toxicity, is that very little is used.

There are two large classes of glycol ethers—ethylene and proplyene. The ethylene group has been dominant for the last half-century. But this group is more toxic than the propylene group. So propylene glycol ethers are now seeing wider use. If you do have access to glycol ethers through a finish manufacturer or a chemical supply house, you should avoid using the ethylene group. ■

Water-based finishes differ from all solvent-based finishes in the following respects:

- They have reduced solvent content.
- They clean up with water.
- The cured finish is colorless.

Solvent Content

Water-based finishes contain very little solvent compared to solvent-based finishes. There is therefore less solvent to evaporate into the atmosphere and cause pollution, less solvent to fuel a fire, and less solvent to breathe. Though reducing air pollution is the rationale for the introduction of water-based finishes, reduced fire and health hazards are of more immediate benefit to you in your shop. Water-based finishes don't contain enough solvent to burn in their liquid state, and they are much less toxic than varnish, lacquer, or conversion finish. Finishers who have switched to water base always cite reduced smell and irritability as the principal benefits. Floor finishers, especially, who can't always ventilate their work locations, appreciate breathing less solvent. You will often see water-based finishes marketed as floor finishes for this reason.

MYTH

Water-based finishes are "safe" finishes.

FACT

Water-based finishes are safer than most other finishes, but they are not totally safe. If you've ever painted with latex paint in a closed room, you've surely experienced a little dizziness caused by the paint fumes. The solvents in water base are similar to those in latex paint.

NOTE

Water-based finish is very difficult to remove after it has cured. It's like white glue. You can soften water base, but it won't flow like lacquer or shellac. It remains gummy, somewhat like softened white glue, and you have to physically remove it. This makes brushes and spray guns very difficult to clean if you wait too long and allow the finish to cure.

Water Cleanup

Like latex paint, water-based finishes are relatively easy to clean up. If you wash your brush or spray gun in water before the finish begins to cure, the finish comes off easily. But if you wait too long, water doesn't work anymore, and you have to use a solvent. Lacquer thinner, acetone, toluene, and xylene will all dissolve water base. So will all paint-and-varnish removers.

Color in Water Base

You may not realize the amount of color other finishes add to wood until you see a piece of wood finished with water base (Photo 17-12 on page 268). Water base is colorless. On certain surfaces, such as light-colored and pickled (white-stained) woods, a colorless finish is desirable. But lack of color causes darker woods, such as walnut and mahogany, to look washed out and

BRUSHING AND SPRAYING WATER BASE

WATER-BASED FINISHES are more difficult than varnish to brush, and more difficult than either shellac or lacquer to spray. Here are the steps for applying water base:

1. Arrange your work so you can see what's happening in reflected light.
2. Decide whether you want to sponge the wood before beginning to apply the finish. (See "Sponging" on page 15.) Sponging will eliminate most of the raised grain, so the first coat of finish won't raise the grain much again.

NOTE

Most water-based finishes appear white in the can. The color is the usual consequence of emulsifying solvent-based materials in water. Other examples are cosmetics and many furniture polishes. The whiteness disappears as the finish cures, as long as the finish is not too thick.

3. If there is any evidence that the water base is beginning to skin over in the can, strain the finish through a paint strainer or nylon hose. It's a good idea to do this even when you don't see any evidence of skinning over. There are often small globules of cured finish that will cause problems.
4. If you're brushing, pour enough finish for the job into a wide-mouth plastic or glass container. This way you won't contaminate all of your finish if you pick up some dirt on your brush.
5. Follow the directions on the can for thinning. Most water-based finishes are designed to be applied without thinning.
6. Brush (using a sponge brush or good-quality synthetic-bristle brush) or spray a thin coat of water base on the wood. Sprayed coats tend to have severe orange peel for several minutes. Then they level out.
7. Allow the finish to cure. Then sand it smooth with 280-grit or finer

NOTE

The greatest number of problems (runs, sags, bubbles, and orange peel) are caused by applying coats of water-based finish too thickly. Keep the coats as thin as possible.

lifeless. There are two ways to overcome this problem:

- Stain the wood before applying the finish.
- Add a dye stain to the finish to imitate the natural color of other finishes. Some manufacturers already do this, and more will surely follow. But this will require you to be especially careful about the water-based finish you use. You won't want to use a tinted finish on pickled wood.

APPLYING WATER-BASED FINISH

You can apply water-based finishes just like other finishes—with a brush, spray gun, or cloth. (See "Brushing and Spraying Water Base" on the facing page.) What makes water-based finishes different to apply is the inclusion of water in the finish.

Substituting water for most of the solvent is great for pre-

TRY THIS

You can add a warm tone to water-based finish by mixing in a little dye yourself. Use an orange to reddish brown water-soluble or non-grain-raising (NGR) dye. It doesn't take much, but because of the differences in strengths of available dyes, I can't tell you how much. Experiment on a scrap piece of wood to get the feel. Add more or less dye to each coat until you get the warmth you want.

sandpaper. Even if you've sponged the wood, there will still be some grain raising. You'll find that the raised grain is easiest to remove if the first coat is thin, if you allow it to cure overnight, and if you use stearated sandpaper.

8. Remove the dust with a brush, a vacuum, compressed air, or a water-dampened cloth. Don't use a tack cloth: The oily residue will interfere with the next coat.
9. Apply a second, very thin coat of finish. If you're brushing, work fast. Water base can cure almost as fast as shellac if the weather is warm and dry. Be careful not to drag your wet brush over edges or dab it into recesses. You'll cause the finish to foam. If you do make foam, dry off the brush with a clean cloth, remove the foam with the tip of the brush, and smooth out the finish.
10. Allow the finish to cure (about two hours in moderate weather) before applying another coat.
11. Apply as many additional coats of finish as you want, sanding between coats only if you want to remove dust nibs or flaws. Water base has a high solids content, so it builds fast. Two to four coats are usually adequate unless you intend to use the finish to fill the pores. (See "Filling the Pores with the Finish" on page 120.)
12. When you're satisfied with the thickness of the film, leave it as is or finish it off with sandpaper, steel wool, or rubbing compounds. (See Chapter 14: "Finishing the Finish.") ■

NOTE

As long as you apply coats of water base within a day of each other, you shouldn't have problems achieving a good bond. But if you apply a coat over a previous coat that has cured for several days or longer, it's wise to scuff the surface with fine sandpaper or Scotch-Brite, as you would between coats of varnish.

serving the environment, your shop, and your health, but water causes a number of problems:

- rust
- grain raising
- poor flow-out or excessive foaming
- application difficulties except in moderate weather

(For solutions to additional problems, see "Common Problems Applying Water Base" on the facing page.)

Rust

Rust is a problem if you are applying water base to objects that have metal parts, or if you are using a spray gun. Remove metal parts from whatever you're finishing, or seal them with dewaxed shellac before applying water base. If your spray gun contains metal parts other than brass or stainless steel, clean the gun by spraying lacquer thinner through it after each use. Alternatively, use a spray gun made of plastic or stainless steel.

You also need to be careful of rust around the tops of metal cans used to contain water base. You will usually chip off some of the protective coating while opening and closing the can, leaving the metal exposed. Rust develops, chips off into the finish, and causes black spots when the finish is applied. It's a good practice to strain water base each time before using.

> **CAUTION**
>
> Never use steel wool if you intend to use a water-based finish, water-based stain, or any other water-containing product. Any sliver of steel that remains on the surface will rust and leave a black spot. If you don't want to use sandpaper, use synthetic steel wool (Scotch-Brite).

Grain Raising

All finishes that contain water raise the grain of wood. It's unfortunate, but there's probably no way around this. (It's also unfortunate that some manufacturers are causing confusion by claiming their water-based products *don't* raise the grain.) You will find that spraying results in less grain raising than brushing, and that sanding to a finer grit reduces the problem by making the raised fibers smaller. But grain raising still occurs anytime you put water on wood.

There are four ways to deal with the problem:

- Sponge the wood and sand off the raised grain before applying the water-based finish. (See "Sponging" on page 15.)
- Use a solvent-based stain before applying the water-based finish. The binder in the stain will seal the wood enough to significantly reduce grain raising when you apply water base.
- Seal the wood with a coat of 1-pound-cut dewaxed shellac before applying the water-based finish. The shellac will prevent the finish from raising the grain. Water base will bond well as long as the shellac is dewaxed (wax keeps most finishes from bonding well) and the coat is thin and has been scuffed lightly with sandpaper.
- Apply a thin coat of water-based sanding sealer or water-based

> **NOTE**
>
> If you use an oil- or varnish-based stain under a water-based finish, you must allow time for the stain to cure thoroughly before applying the finish. Otherwise the water base won't bond well.

COMMON PROBLEMS APPLYING WATER BASE

Most problems applying water-based finish can be avoided by keeping your coats thin and by foregoing application during hot, humid, or cold weather. (For problems specific to spraying, see "Common Spraying Problems" on page 42.)

PROBLEM	CAUSE	SOLUTION
Runs and sags appear opaque with an off-white color.	Water-based finishes lose transparency in thick layers.	When the run or sag has thoroughly cured, scrape or sand it off smooth. Then apply another coat.
The finish bubbles or foams, and the bubbles cure in the finish.	1) You are stirring up bubbles with your brush.	Use a lighter touch, apply the finish as thin as possible, and thin the finish with 10 to 20 percent distilled water if bubbling persists.
	2) The finish is not designed for brushing.	Change to another brand that is designed for brushing.
The finish takes too long to cure, allowing dust to settle.	The weather is too humid.	Arrange airflow over the work, or wait until a drier day.
Black spots appear in the wood.	Metal has come in contact with the wood, and the water has caused the metal to rust. Using steel wool is the most common cause of this.	Strip off the finish and bleach out the black spots with oxalic acid. (See "Using Oxalic Acid" on page 293.) Use synthetic steel wool (Scotch-Brite) when preparing a surface for water base.
The cured finish peels away from the wood in sheets.	A substance on the wood—most likely an oil-based stain, paste-wood filler, or glaze that wasn't fully cured—prevented the finish from bonding.	Strip the finish, sand the wood, and avoid using any oil-containing stains or other products unless you give them ample time to cure.
The finish crawls up into ridges right after you apply it.	You are applying the finish too thickly, or there is silicone or other oil in the wood.	If the problem is oil in the wood, remove the finish by washing it off with wet rags (if you are quick enough) or with paint stripper. Wash the wood thoroughly with naphtha and allow the wood to dry. Apply a washcoat of dewaxed shellac. Then proceed with coats of water base. For more on this problem, see "Fish Eye and Silicone" on page 168.

MYTH

Using stearated sandpaper to sand water base between coats will cause fish eye.

FACT

This is true only if you don't remove all the sanding dust, which you should always do no matter what sandpaper you use. Water base doesn't redissolve sanding dust like lacquer does.

NOTE

It could be risky mixing different brands of water base in their liquid state: The mixture might not cure properly. Manufacturers are changing formulations rapidly as they experiment to find what works best. Water base is not a mature finish like varnish and lacquer.

finish, and sand off the raised grain. Then apply another thin coat, which you may have to sand again if it's rough. Then proceed normally. A thin coat will cure hard faster and will be easier to sand.

Flow-Out and Foaming

Water has high *surface tension.* It doesn't spread out well on many surfaces. You experience this high surface tension when you spill water on a finished tabletop, or when you try to clean your car windshield with water. The water beads up. It doesn't flow out and cover the surface as mineral spirits or oil would, since they have a lower surface tension.

To make water flow out and clean your windshield better, you add a substance that reduces the surface tension, such as soap or ammonia. Manufacturers do the same sort of thing with water-based finish. They add soap or ammonia-like substances, called *surfactants,* to the finish. The problem with adding these surfactants is that they tend to foam when stirred, so *defoamers* are also added. Defoamers are fatty or oily substances. The balance is critical. If there is not enough surfactant, the finish won't flow out; it will bunch up in ridges, somewhat like lacquer does when it fish-eyes (see "Fish Eye and Silicone" on page 168). If there is too much surfactant, or if you agitate the finish too much, as you might do when you brush it, bubbles will form and cure in the film.

Many problems applying water-based finishes are caused by using a finish whose additives are not in balance with the surface of the object you're coating, or with the means you're using to apply the finish. Some manufacturers market water-based finishes designed for specific tasks. Most don't; they try to hit a happy medium.

You will find it very difficult to brush a water-based finish if the finish is not designed for brushing. The finish will foam, and it will be difficult to get the bubbles out before the finish cures. You may hear suggestions for correcting the problem, such as adding milk, mineral spirits, glycerin, and other commonly available defoamers, to the finish. Following one of these suggestions might work. But it might not. It will depend on the compatibility of the defoamer you add with the particular finish you add it to. The safest technique for reducing bubbles is to brush your coats as thin as possible. You might also add 10 to 20 percent distilled water to aid in applying the finish thin. (Distilled water doesn't contain metal residue that might spot the wood.) Adding this amount of water won't harm the finish. If this doesn't work, the weather may be the problem, as described below. If the weather isn't the culprit, try another brand of water base.

Photo 11-1: Water-based finishes are far more sensitive to weather conditions than solvent-based finishes. This example of bad flow-out was created by spraying water base below 65 degrees Fahrenheit.

Weather Sensitivity

Water is far more weather-sensitive than solvents. The curing time of water-based finishes varies much more in different weather conditions than the curing time of other finishes. On warm, dry days water base will usually dry rapidly enough to preclude dust problems. On cool or humid days the finish may take quite some time to become dust-free. During extreme weather you may have difficulty applying water-based finishes. Here are some tips:

- If the finish cures too slowly because of high humidity, create airflow over the finish to speed water evaporation.
- If the finish cures too rapidly to flow out well because of hot or dry conditions, add 10 to 20 percent distilled water to lengthen evaporation time, or add a solvent provided by the manufacturer for that purpose.
- If the finish doesn't flow out normally because of cold conditions, warm the room you're working in or wait for a warmer day. You will often have trouble below 65 degrees Fahrenheit.

CHAPTER 12

Conversion Finishes

CONVERSION IN BRIEF

PROS Excellent heat, wear, solvent, acid, and alkali resistance
Excellent water and water-vapor resistance
Very fast curing

CONS Highly toxic solvent and formaldehyde fumes
Flammable and air-polluting fumes
Very difficult to strip
Nearly impossible to repair

You may not be familiar with the name "conversion finish." This is not surprising, because conversion finishes are used primarily in the furniture industry. These finishes combine the fast-curing properties of lacquer with the heat, wear, solvent, acid, alkali, water, and water-vapor resistance of varnish. Furniture factories like these finishes because they are fast-curing and they provide the tough, protective coatings that consumers often demand.

Conversion finishes include conversion varnish, catalyzed lacquer, epoxy finish, moisture-curing polyurethane, two-part polyurethane, polyester finish, and ultraviolet-curing finish. Because most of these are rarely used outside of industry, I won't discuss all of them here. The exceptions are conversion varnish and catalyzed lacquer, which are used by many professional finishers and some amateurs.

Conversion varnish is composed of amino resins (urea formaldehyde and melamine formaldehyde) and alkyd resin. When you add an acid catalyst to the finish, these resins crosslink to form a very durable film. (See Chapter 7: "Introduction to Film Finishes.")

Catalyzed lacquer is the same as conversion varnish, except that it has nitrocellulose lacquer added to make the finish cure faster. The nitrocellulose speeds the initial curing, but it weakens the resulting film. Catalyzed lacquer, though exceptionally

Conversion finishes are most commonly used on institutional furniture.

durable, is not as durable as conversion varnish. Like conversion varnish, catalyzed lacquer requires that you add an acid catalyst to make it cure.

Some catalyzed lacquers include the catalyst. These *pre-catalyzed lacquers* have enough solvent to keep the curing reaction from starting. As the solvent evaporates after the finish is applied, the catalyst kicks in, and the curing begins. Pre-catalyzed lacquers have a fairly short shelf life, which should be indicated on the label; if it's not, contact the manufacturer. Just as with lacquer, lacquer retarder can be added to pre-catalyzed lacquer to slow its curing enough that it can be brushed.

Conversion finishes were developed in the 1930s. They are often used on furniture for schools, laboratories, and other institutions, and sometimes on tabletops of household furniture. (Imported Scandinavian teak furniture is commonly finished with conversion finish.) But despite the greater durability, conversion finishes haven't replaced nitrocellulose lacquer as the preferred finish for medium- and high-quality furniture. Conversion finishes are almost always limited to simple, non-decorative coatings, because compared with nitrocellulose they're more difficult to apply and they don't look as good. Conversion finishes can't be rubbed out as nicely, and they don't bring out the richness in the wood or give the appearance of as much depth. They're also more difficult to repair, especially when the problem is color-related.

Because of their high solvent content, conversion finishes are becoming restricted, as more and more areas of the country pass laws aimed at reducing solvent emissions. As a result, manufacturers are developing water-based conversion finishes. These are regular conversion finishes dispersed in water. They overcome the problems associated with atmosphere-polluting solvents, but they share the problems typical of water-based finishes. (See Chapter 11: "Water-Based Finishes.")

CHARACTERISTICS OF CONVERSION FINISHES

Conversion finishes have the following advantages:

- *Excellent wear, heat, solvent, acid, alkali, water, and water-vapor resistance:* These finishes are usually tougher and more protective than solvent-based polyurethane.
- *Excellent film-building properties:* It takes half as many coats of conversion finish to achieve the same thickness as nitrocellulose lacquer.
- *Short curing time,* much like nitrocellulose lacquer.
- *Easy spraying and thinning characteristics,* much like nitrocellulose lacquer.

Conversion finishes have the following disadvantages:

- *Short pot life:* Once the acid catalyst has been added, the finish begins to cure. Products vary, so follow the manufacturer's instructions.
- *Limited application time:* There is a time frame during which you have to apply all coats, or else the coats won't bond properly. Products vary, so follow the manufacturer's instructions.
- *Poor rubbing properties,* compared with nitrocellulose lacquer.
- *Lack of clarity,* compared with nitrocellulose lacquer.
- *Extremely irritating formaldehyde emissions while curing:* You should protect yourself with good cross-ventilation and an organic-vapor respirator mask.
- *High use of toxic, flammable, air-polluting solvents.*
- *Extreme difficulty, often impossiblity, of repair or touch-up:* You can't get the repair to bond to and blend in with the finish.
- *Very poor stripping characteristics:* the flip side of excellent solvent and chemical resistance.

APPLYING CONVERSION FINISHES

The working characteristics of catalyzed lacquer are almost identical to those of nitrocellulose lacquer. The rules for thinning, their effect on the speed of curing, and the problems that can occur are similar. (See Chapter 9: "Lacquer.") Only the build and the time frame for getting all the coats applied are different. Catalyzed lacquer builds about twice as fast as nitrocellulose lacquer, and new coats don't dissolve into the existing coats after a certain time (specified by the manufacturer). Conversion varnish cures more slowly than catalyzed lacquer, so be careful to avoid runs and sags, and allow more time between coats. Otherwise, conversion varnish applies in much the same way. It usually uses xylene as a thinner.

Working with catalyzed lacquer is much the same as working with lacquer.

Neither finish bonds well to shellac or sanding sealer, so avoid using either of these as a sealer coat. Some catalyzed lacquers will bond to vinyl sealer. In most situations it's safest to use the finish itself for the first coat.

Be especially diligent in cleaning your spray gun after using a conversion finish. These finishes have a very short pot life. They will cure in your spray gun and cup, usually within several hours to several days, depending on the makeup of the finish. If you allow the finish to cure in your spray gun, you won't be able to clean it with solvents; you'll have to abrade the finish off, and this may ruin the gun.

CHAPTER 13

Choosing a Finish

One of the most common questions you hear in any discussion about finishing is, "What finish do you use?" The question presumes the existence of a "best" finish—one that should be used in all situations. Unfortunately, there is no *best* finish. There are only better finishes for given situations, depending on the qualities you're looking for. (See "Guide to Finishes" on page 208.) When you're choosing a finish for any given project, you should take each of these qualities into account:

- appearance
- protection
- durability
- ease of application
- safety
- reversibility
- ease of rubbing

APPEARANCE

You have three choices when picking a finish for its appearance: potential film build, clarity, and color. (A fourth choice, sheen, is not dependent upon the finish you choose, but upon whether or not flatting agents—gloss-reducing solid particles—have been added.)

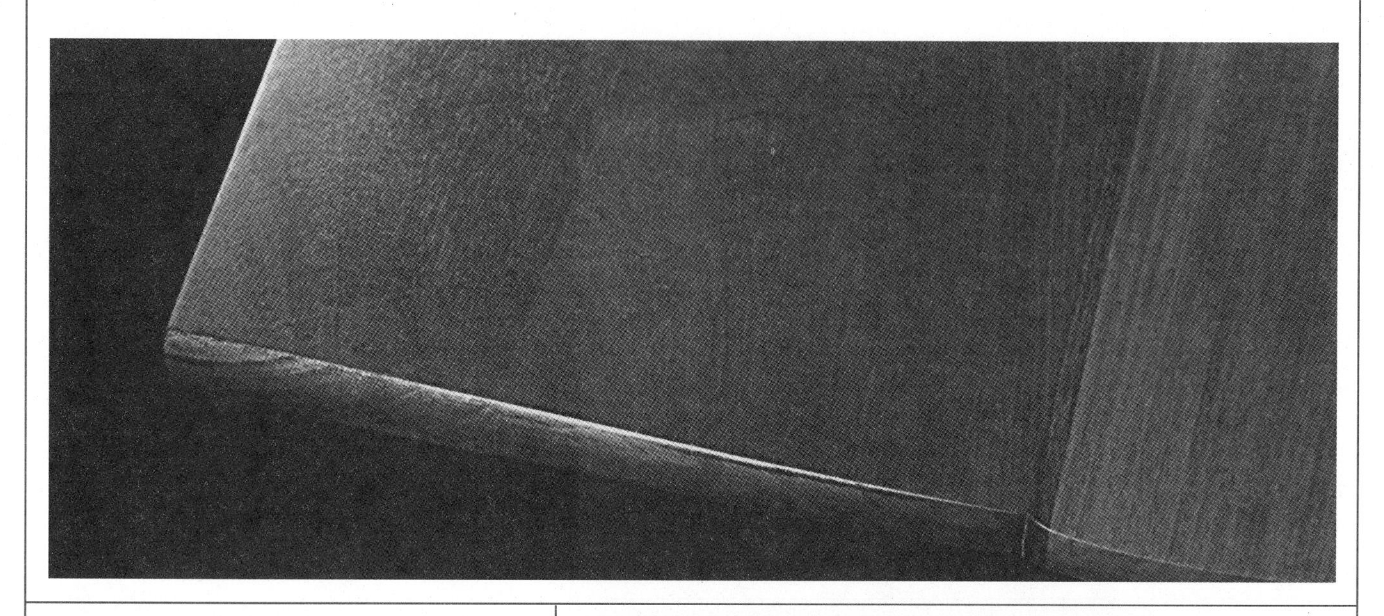

Photos 13-1, 13-2, and 13-3: You can make wood look very different by how you build the finish. The walnut and mahogany tabletop (above) has a wiping-varnish finish; it leaves the pores partially filled and the wood with a natural look. The mahogany drawer (right) has pores filled and the finish rubbed to a high gloss; it produces a refined look and the appearance of depth in the wood. The oak tabletop (below, right) has a thickly applied finish that is rounded over in the pores; it makes the wood look cheap.

Film Build

The film build, or thickness of the finish on wood, greatly affects the wood's appearance. Wax and finishes that contain straight oil (linseed oil, tung oil, and oil/varnish blend) don't cure hard, so they should be kept very thin, not built-up on the wood. They produce a "natural" or "close-to-the-wood" look, in which the pores of the wood are left looking open and are very sharply defined (even though they are actually sealed). Film finishes (shellac, lacquer, varnish, water base, and conversion) can be built up on the wood. But they can also be applied thin to look like oil or wax finishes. Imported Scandinavian teak furniture, for instance, is finished with very thin coats of conversion finish, not oil as is commonly believed.

Consequently, you can use any finish if you want a thin, close-to-the-wood look, but if you want a build, you must use a film finish. A built-up film finish can look cheap if it rounds over into the pores of very open-pored woods such as oak and mahogany. Or it can look very refined, giving the wood the appearance of great depth, if the pores are filled level to the surface and the finish is rubbed and polished to an even sheen (Photos 13-1, 13-2, and 13-3). (See Chapter 6: "Filling the Pores.")

Resistance to water and water vapor depends as much on the thickness as it does on the type of finish.

Clarity

The clarity of a particular finish may be important to your choice, though it's hard to see a difference unless you closely compare two finished boards. Dewaxed shellac, lacquer, alkyd varnish, and phenolic varnish are the most transparent finishes, giving the wood the appearance of greatest depth. Wax-containing shellac, solvent-based polyurethane, water base, and conversion are the least transparent finishes. In extreme situations, these finishes can appear almost cloudy, but their usual appearance is more like that of cellophane laid over the wood.

Color

All finishes, except water base and wax, impart a warm tone to wood. Orange shellac has the most pronounced color (Photo 17-12 on page 268). Any finish containing oil, including varnish, yellows with age. Yellowing is not generally a problem on dark or dark-stained woods. In fact, it's usually a plus: It makes the wood appear warmer. But yellowing can be objectionable on blonde woods and over the white stain used to pickle wood.

PROTECTION

A finish protects the wood and glue joints by slowing the penetration of water and the exchange of water vapor. Resistance to

The more durable finishes are those that crosslink.

water penetration is important when choosing a finish for tabletops. Resistance to water-vapor exchange is one of the most important functions a finish performs on any wood object. Excessive water-vapor exchange between the wood and the atmosphere causes splits, warps, and joint failure. (See Chapter 1: "Why Finish Wood, Anyway?")

Resistance to water and water vapor depends as much on the thickness of the finish as it does on the type of finish. The three types of varnish (alkyd, phenolic, and polyurethane), which are nearly impermeable to water and water vapor when built up to a thick film, lose almost all of their resistance when applied thin in the form of a wiping varnish. Wax, which offers virtually no resistance to water and water-vapor penetration when used as a rubbed-out finish, is one of the best protective coatings when brushed thick on the ends of recently milled boards. It follows that all oil-containing finishes offer very little protection against water and water vapor, because they are also very thin.

Among the film finishes, the best water and water-vapor protection is provided by varnish and conversion finishes. Shellac also provides good water-vapor resistance, but it is the least water-resistant finish. The least water-vapor-resistant finishes are lacquer and water base.

DURABILITY

Finish durability divides almost exactly between crosslinking and non-crosslinking finishes. (See Chapter 7: "Introduction to Film Finishes.") Crosslinking finishes (varnish and conversion) are far more durable than non-crosslinking finishes (shellac, lacquer, and water base). The exceptions are oil and oil/varnish blends, which, though crosslinking, give poor durability because of their thinness. There are two concerns when considering finish durability:

- wear or scratch resistance
- solvent, acid, alkali, and heat resistance

Wear or Scratch Resistance

This quality is the most touted, and, as a result, it has become one of the most sought-after qualities in a finish. The most wear-resistant finishes are conversion finishes, solvent-based polyurethane, and water base. (Though water base doesn't cure by crosslinking, the droplets are composed entirely of crosslinked resins.) The least wear-resistant are wax and oil-containing finishes. Alkyd and phenolic varnish are less wear-resistant than polyurethane varnish but more wear-resistant than shellac or lacquer. Wear resistance can be an important consideration on floors and tabletops.

Solvent, Acid, Alkali, and Heat Resistance

These four properties tend to go together. A finish easily damaged by solvents is also easily damaged by acids, alkalis, and heat. Wax, shellac, lacquer, and water base are all susceptible to solvent, acid, alkali, and heat damage. Varnish and conversion finishes are very resistant to solvents, acids, alkalis, and heat. Oil-containing finishes are in between. Oil, though it crosslinks when it cures, breaks down more easily than varnish and conversion. Resistance to solvents, acids, alkalis, and heat can be an important factor when choosing a finish for countertops and tabletops.

EASE OF APPLICATION

The ease with which you can apply a finish depends on two factors:

- availability of spray equipment
- speed at which the finish cures

Spray Equipment

With spray equipment, all finishes except wax are easier to apply. Without spray equipment, only oil, oil/varnish blend, and wiping varnish are easy to apply.

The ease with which fast-curing shellac, lacquer, water base, and conversion finishes can be applied with spray equipment is so significant that most professional finishers never even consider using any other finish. The various characteristics of these four finishes provide almost every individual quality a finisher might want.

Almost all finishes are easier to apply with spray equipment.

Speed of Curing

Unless you wipe off all the excess finish, finishes that cure slowly cause problems no matter how you apply them, because dust has time to settle and become embedded in the finish. On the other hand, finishes that cure rapidly are difficult to apply with a brush, because one brush stroke may already be tacky by the time your next brush stroke overlaps it. As a result, you drag the finish.

The comparative ease with which oil, oil/varnish blend, and wiping varnish can be applied is so significant for those without spray equipment that they are often reluctant to try other finishes.

SAFETY

There are three issues of safety:

- safety to you, the finisher, during application
- safety to the environment during application

- safety to the ultimate consumer if food or mouth will come in contact with the finish

Safety to You

All finishes except water base are combustible or flammable, so don't use them near flames or a source of possible sparks.

All finishes, including water base, contain solvents that can be damaging to your health. No matter which finish you use, you should ensure good cross ventilation in your work area so you always breath relatively clean air. Respirator masks can be an aid when you're forced to work in an enclosed area, but respirator masks lose their effectiveness over time, thereby leading to a false sense of security. If you can smell the solvent fumes with your respirator mask on, either you have a leak or the cartridges are worn out and should be replaced. The only truly reliable respirator masks are those that provide an outside source of air. (Nuisance

DISPOSING OF YOUR SOLVENT WASTE

RESPONSIBLE SOLVENT-WASTE DISPOSAL for amateurs and small professional shops is a real Catch-22.

If you seal the solvents in an old paint can and throw the can in the trash to be hauled to the dump, you can expect that within a year or so, the solvents will begin leaking into the ground. Together with everyone else's dirty solvents, they will seep deeper and deeper until they poison your town's ground-water supply. If you pour the solvents down the drain, out into the alley, or onto some unwanted weeds, you can expect the same ultimate damage to the ground-water supply.

On the other hand, if you leave the can open and put it outside so all the solvents evaporate into the air, you'll be doing your small part to increase air pollution, and you'll be breaking the law in many already-polluted parts of the country.

The solution, you may have heard, is to take your waste solvents to the local toxic-waste dump. This is simply not possible. Even if you do have a toxic-waste dump within a hundred miles of your town (which is unlikely), you won't be able to get near the place with your can of solvent waste. You need at least 27 gallons of waste (100 kg) per month to qualify for use of a toxic-waste dump. And if you do qualify, you will have to pay nearly as much as the solvents cost new, fill out a parcel of paperwork, and buy an expensive permit. What's more, you can't haul the waste to the dump yourself. You'll have to hire someone with a license to haul toxic waste.

So what should you do? If you live in an area that has made some provision for disposing of solvent waste, you can take your waste to one of the designated pickup sites, or you can wait for a periodic hazardous-waste collection day. You can find out if your area has a program for collecting hazardous waste by calling your local public works department or county clerk.

If you don't live in such an area, here are your choices in descending order—best to worst:

particle masks provide no protection against solvent fumes.)

The finishes that cause the least problems for your health are water base and shellac. Water base contains very little solvent, and denatured alcohol, the solvent for shellac, is relatively safe unless you drink it or breathe it in excessive amounts.

Safety to the Environment

All solvents evaporate into the atmosphere. Some have been shown to be factors in causing air pollution. As a result, many states and localities have passed laws aimed at limiting the amount of solvent or thinner that can be contained in a finish. These laws are the primary impetus for the substitution of water-based finishes for solvent-based finishes.

Of the common solvents used in finishes, petroleum distillates and lacquer thinner—used in most varnishes and in lacquer, respectively—cause the greatest problems. Alcohol, shellac's sol-

- Recycle your solvents. Keep your mineral spirits, lacquer thinner, or whatever, in separate cans. Let the solid material, if there is any, settle to the bottom. Pour off the solvent, and use it again for cleaning.
- Try to get a local user of solvents, such as a large furniture or auto-body refinish shop, to take your solvent waste and put it with theirs to be hauled off—for a price, of course. But if the owner of the shop resists, be understanding. Remember, he is legally and financially responsible for any damage that may be caused by the solvent waste hauled off from his shop. . .forever! He probably won't want to increase his risk with your waste.
- Store the dirty solvents until a collection/disposal center is established in your area. It may take a few years, but it's sure to come.
- Finally, if all else fails, you have two choices. You can let all the solvent evaporate and then toss the remaining harmless solids into the trash. Or you can throw the can of solvent out onto the ground. Given these two options, letting the solvent evaporate is the better choice (unless it is clearly illegal in your area). Keep in mind, however, that solvents are very flammable. Be sure to protect the can so sparks or a tossed cigarette won't start a fire. If this solution bothers you, you may console yourself by remembering that the solvent would all evaporate into the atmosphere anyway if it were recycled and reused.

The solution to the problem of toxic solvents polluting the earth and atmosphere will ultimately be solved from the supply side. Solvent-based paints and finishes will be made with significantly reduced amounts of solvent or replaced almost entirely by water-based finishes. In the meantime, if the solvent-waste disposal dilemma bothers you, call your city council member or county commissioner to see if a solution can be worked out for your locality. ■

vent, and glycol ether, used in water base, also cause pollution. But alcohol causes less polution than petroleum-distillate solvents, and there is so little glycol ether used in water base that the problems are minimal. (See "Disposing of Your Solvent Waste" on page 204.)

Safety to the Consumer

The safety of finishes for food or mouth contact is an ambiguous issue. The Food and Drug Administration (FDA) lists all the common ingredients used in finishes (except solvents that evaporate) as being safe for food contact as long as the finishes are formulated properly. Proper formulation is necessary to ensure that no potentially harmful ingredients will leach out once the finish has cured. Since improper formulation would more than likely show up as improper curing, all finishes that cure thoroughly are probably safe to eat off of or to put in your mouth. But the only finish that is specifically approved by the FDA for these purposes is shellac. It is even approved as being safe to eat.

How well a finish rubs is largely a matter of how it cures.

REVERSIBILITY

Reversibility refers to the ease of repair and ease of removal of a finish. Reversibility is the opposite of solvent resistance. The finishes that are most easily repaired or removed are also the least solvent-resistant. Thus, your choice of using a reversible finish for its ease of repairing and removing must be weighed against your need for solvent resistance.

RUBBING QUALITIES

There are two qualities in finishes that make them easier to rub to an even sheen: the hardness of the cured finish, and the ability of finish coats to fuse together to form a single layer. Both of these properties are a function of the way the finish cures.

Hardness

There are two types of hardness in finishes. One is hardness like that of slate—a brittle hardness that is easily scratched. Shellac and lacquer cure brittle-hard. The other type of hardness is like that of an automobile tire—a tough hardness that is difficult to scratch. Since rubbing out finishes means scratching them with abrasives to get the sheen you want, tough-curing finishes are more difficult to rub to an even sheen. Varnish, conversion, and water-based finishes cure tough.

Of course, all finishes can be rubbed with steel wool or abrasive compounds. Some finishes are just easier than others to rub to an even sheen.

Fusing of Layers

When you rub a finish, you cut some of it away. If you cut enough away to penetrate through the topcoat in places, you may leave a visible line between the layers. But some finishes fuse into one layer as additional layers are applied, and thus it's impossible to cut through a layer, unless you cut all the way through to the wood. Shellac and lacquer fuse best. Conversion and water base also fuse well enough (if the coats are applied soon after one another) that layering is rarely a problem. Varnish doesn't fuse between coats, another reason it is not easy to rub out.

HOW TO CHOOSE

So how can you use this information in choosing a finish? First, it should be clear that there is no *best* finish. All finishes have certain positive qualities and certain shortcomings. Which finish you choose depends on which qualities you want most in the finish. (See "Guide to Finishes" on page 208.)

In my opinion, the primary variable in choosing a finish is whether or not you have access to spray equipment. If you do, you should probably stick with shellac, lacquer, conversion, or water base.

- If you want maximum protection and durability—resistance to water, water vapor, wear, solvent, acid, alkali, and heat—use a conversion finish.
- If you want reversibility, as you might on an antique, use shellac or lacquer.
- If you want to minimize the amount of toxic, flammable, and air-polluting solvents, use water base.
- If you want the best clarity and rubbing qualities, use lacquer or dewaxed shellac.
- If you can't buy lacquer because of strict air-pollution laws in your area, substitute dewaxed shellac or water base.
- If you want a totally non-yellowing finish, use water base.

If you don't have access to spray equipment, you're limited in your choices. Ease of application becomes more significant. The finish that will give you the most protection and durability will be solvent-based polyurethane, with phenolic varnish and alkyd varnish close behind. You can get reversibility by brushing shellac or using a brushing lacquer. You can reduce flammable, toxic, and air-polluting solvents by brushing water base. But all of these finishes can be problematic when applied with a brush. Ease of application could lead you to choose one of the wipe-on finishes. Of these, wiping varnish will give the most protection, as long as it is built up. But oil/varnish blends will be easier to apply.

The primary variable in choosing a finish is whether or not you have access to spray equipment.

GUIDE TO FINISHES

QUALITY	Wax	Oil-Containing Finishes	Shellac	Nitrocellulose Lacquer
APPEARANCE				
Film build	0 to 1	0 to 1	1 to 5	1 to 5
Clarity	3 to 5	3 to 5	3 to 5	5
Non-yellowing	5	2 to 3	1 to 4	3 to 4
PROTECTION				
Water resistance	0 to 2	0 to 2	2	3
Water-vapor resistance	0 to 1	0 to 1	5	3
DURABILITY				
Wear resistance	0	0	3	3
Solvent and chemical resistance	0	4	1	2
Heat resistance	0	3	1	2
APPLICATION EASE				
Brush or cloth	5	5	3	1 to 3
Spray	0	5	4	5
Dust problems	5	5	4	5
SAFETY				
Health	3 to 4	3 to 4	4	2
Environment	2 to 4	2 to 4	4	0
Safety for food contact	*	*	*	*
REVERSIBILITY				
Repairing	5	5	4	4
Stripping	2 to 3	2 to 3	5	5
RUBBING QUALITIES	2	2	5	5

0 = very poor; 1 = poor; 2 = fair; 3 = good; 4 = very good; 5 = best; * = probably safe

Varnish: Alkyd	Varnish: Phenolic	Varnish: Polyurethane	Water-Based Finishes	Conversion Finishes
1 to 5	1 to 5	1 to 5	1 to 5	1 to 5
5	5	3	3 to 4	4
2	1	2	5	3 to 4
4	4	5	3	5
4	5	5	3	5
4	4	5	5	5
4	4	5	2	5
4	4	5	2	5
5	5	5	3	1
4	4	4	4	4
0	0	0	3	5
3	3	3	4	1
1	1	1	4	0
*	*	*	*	*
2	2	1	3	0
3	3	2	4	1
3	4	3	3 to 4	3 to 4

CHAPTER 14

Finishing the Finish

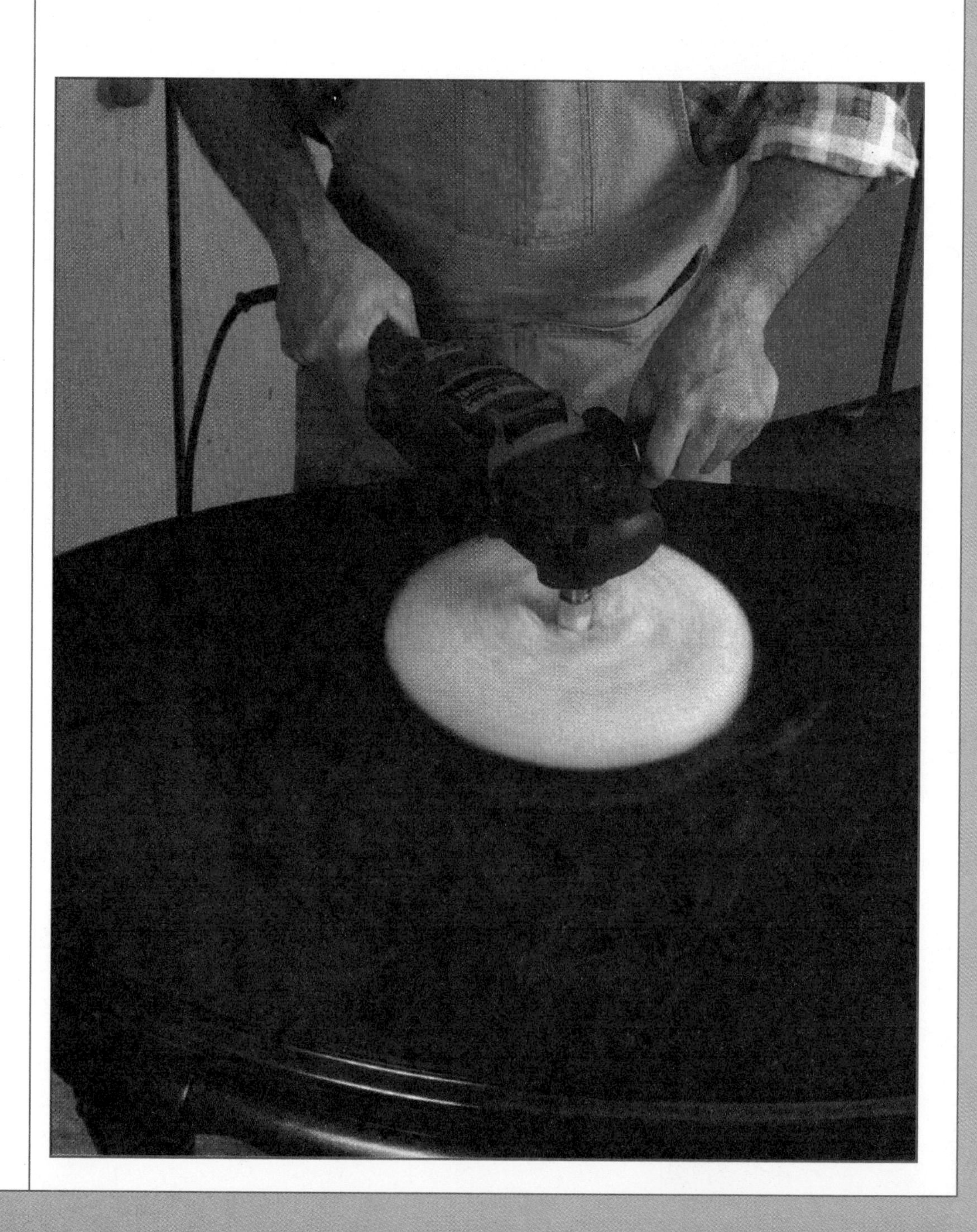

The difference between a quality finish and one that is nothing special has less to do with how you apply the finish than with what you do afterwards—with how you finish the finish.

To finish a finish, you rub it with abrasives, such as sandpaper, steel wool, rubbing compounds, or a combination of these, sometimes using a lubricant such as wax, mineral spirits, oil, or soapy water. The idea is the same as sanding wood. You smooth and level the surface, putting finer and finer scratches into it until you are happy with the way it feels and looks. (Don't confuse a hand-rubbed finish using abrasives with a hand-rubbed finish that refers to "rubbing in" an oil finish—see "Oil Finishes and Penetration" on page 53.)

Rubbing a finish does two things: It makes the finish feel smoother, and it gives the finish a softer appearance. Both are difficult to describe and virtually impossible to capture in a photograph.

Whenever you apply several coats of a film finish (a finish that you build to a thickness on the wood), you will always get some roughness caused by embedded dust. You will also get a harsh-looking shine when you view the surface in reflected light, and you will be able to see brush marks or orange peel, depending on whether the finish was brushed or sprayed. No matter how careful you are, you can't apply a perfect finish.

Rubbing a finish cuts off (or at least rounds over) dust nibs, softens the harsh

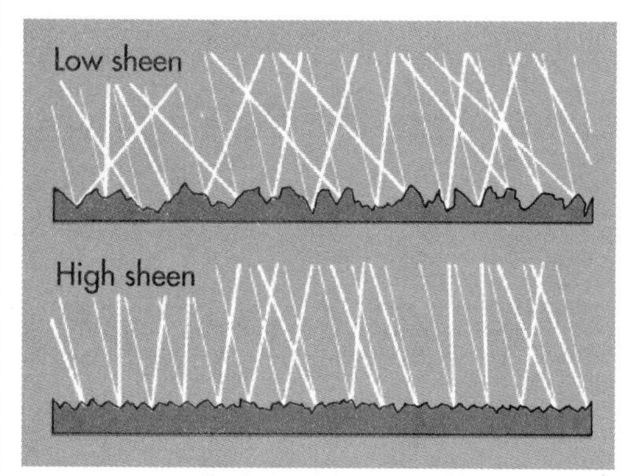

Figure 14-1: The larger the scratches you put into a finish, the more the light is reflected away from you and the lower the sheen (top). The smaller the scratches, the more the light is reflected directly back to you and the higher the sheen (bottom).

Photo 14-1: The amount of sheen that you rub into a finish is easy to see when you look at the reflection of an object in the surface. A rubbed high-gloss finish (left) shows a clear reflection of the can of mineral spirits. A rubbed satin finish (right) obscures the reflection, almost eliminating it.

reflected shine, and removes (or at least disguises) brush marks and orange peel. Rubbing does all this by putting fine scratches in the surface. The scratches become what you feel and see, thus replacing the problems. By making the scratches too fine to feel, you make the surface feel smooth. You control the amount of shine by how fine you make the scratches. The finer the scratches, the higher the gloss. The coarser the scratches the lower the gloss. (For example, a diamond is polished to a high gloss with very fine abrasive rubbing compounds.) The word for degree of gloss is *sheen.* A high sheen is a high gloss. A low sheen is a satin or flat finish (Figure 14-1 and Photo 14-1).

Many woodworkers avoid rubbing out a finish because they don't understand it, or they consider it too complicated. This is usually a mistake. There's not much to understand, and the complication is only in the number of ways to do it. If you've never rubbed out a finish before, I suggest you begin simply by rubbing with steel wool. (See "Rubbing with Steel Wool" on page 216.) You will smooth and disguise flaws in your finish and produce a satin sheen. Next, try sanding a finish level before rubbing with steel wool. This will eliminate flaws and produce a satin sheen. From there, you can begin rubbing with finer abrasive compounds to raise the sheen if you want. (See "Leveling and Rubbing to a High Gloss" on page 221.) You can raise or lower the sheen using different rubbing abrasives as many times as you want—until you finally cut through the finish to the wood.

You don't have to rub out any finish. But you will always improve the results if you do.

FACTORS IN RUBBING A FINISH

The results you get rubbing a finish are influenced by a number of factors:

- the type of finish you are rubbing
- how thoroughly the finish has cured
- the type of rubbing abrasives you use
- the type of rubbing lubricants you use
- the rubbing schedule
- the cleanup
- the final waxing or polishing

Type of Finish

Hard, brittle finishes are easier than tough finishes to rub to a smooth, even sheen because hard finishes yield a clean, sharp scratch pattern when rubbed. Tough finishes are difficult to scratch, and the scratches you do make are uneven tears rather than smooth, clean cuts. Shellac and lacquer are the best rubbing finishes. Varnish (including polyurethane), conversion, and water base are the most difficult finishes to rub to an even sheen. You can still rub these finishes, but the results won't be as nice. Keep in mind, however, that there are variations within each of these types of finishes depending on how the particular finish is made. It's possible, for example, to make a water-based finish with good rubbing qualities and a lacquer with poor rubbing qualities. (See Chapter 7: "Introduction to Film Finishes.")

There is a practical limit to good rubbing qualities. The harder, more brittle the finish, the easier it will scratch, but also the sooner it will crack. Many of the varnishes used on furniture made around 1900 severely cracked after a short time, because manufacturers went too far in trying to get good rubbing qualities.

Many film finishes are sold as semi-gloss, satin (eggshell), or flat because they contain flatting agents (see Figure 17-2 on page 132). These finishes can be rubbed just as easily as gloss finishes, but the effect will be different. Gloss finishes have more clarity, so the wood will appear deeper. You can make satin and flat finishes appear shiny when viewed in reflected light, but they will be cloudy when you look straight into them. You can take advantage of this effect to imitate the appearance of an old finish that has been well maintained but has clouded with age.

Thoroughness of Curing

A finish begins as a liquid and becomes a solid when it cures. Between these extremes, it goes through various stages of hardness. If you try to abrade a finish before it has adequately cured, the scratch pattern will be uneven, and the scratches you make may disappear in places as the finish continues to cure. This will result in a splotchy and uneven sheen. In addition, since finishes shrink as they cure, pores that you have filled (see "Filling the Pores with the Finish" on page 120) may open, leaving a pitted surface again.

There are no absolute rules for how long you should let a finish cure before you rub it. A good rule of thumb is to wait a month. Longer is even better. Unfortunately, most finishers rush this operation, rubbing out the finish within a few days of application, which impairs the results.

Choice of Abrasives

There are three types of abrasives for rubbing finishes:

- sandpaper
- steel wool (including synthetic steel wool, also known as 3M Scotch-Brite)
- rubbing compounds

MYTH

Preparing the wood well is the key to a high-quality finish.

FACT

Rubbing the finish is the key to high quality, at least when feel and looks are the criteria. You can't produce a superior finish on poorly prepared wood or by applying the finish sloppily, but wood preparation and application technique alone, no matter how careful, can't produce the finest finish. A first-rate finish comes only from rubbing it after it has cured.

NOTE

It's difficult to compare grits between the three types of abrasives. It's often difficult even within one of these types. Standardization between manufacturers is fairly good with sandpaper. It's not bad with steel wool. But it's completely nonexistent with rubbing compounds.

TIP

If you have problems with dust settling on your wet finish and becoming embedded, plan to level the finish using sandpaper. Then you won't have to worry so much about the dust while you're finishing; you will remove the dust nibs later.

NOTE

Mineral spirits and naphtha will soften water-based finish enough to prevent your getting an even gloss, so use oil or soapy water when rubbing water base. Though I've never found it to be a problem, mineral spirits and naphtha also have the potential of slightly softening lacquer and varnish if these finishes aren't totally cured. Softening could produce an uneven scratch pattern.

Sandpaper is used to cut back the surface, eliminating irregularities such as orange peel, brush marks, and dust nibs. You can back the sandpaper with your hand or with a flat rubber, cork, or felt block. Using a block will produce a more level surface.

Silicon-carbide paper is best for sanding finishes. If you are sanding without a liquid lubricant, use stearated silicon-carbide sandpaper (sometimes sold as "no-load" or "self-lubricating" sandpaper). If you are using a lubricant, then wet/dry silicon-carbide sandpaper is better because of its water resistance and its hard paper backing. Stearated sandpaper is available up to 400 grit. Wet/dry sandpaper is available up to 2000 grit. Stearated sandpaper is usually a light gray color; wet/dry sandpapaer is black. (See "Sanding Basics" on page 13).

Both types of sandpaper still clog when used on a finish, particularly if the finish hasn't totally cured. They just clog less than other types. The finish rolls up into little balls, called *corns,* and sticks in the sandpaper grit (Photo 14-2). You should check the sandpaper often and remove these corns with a dull scraper, or change to new sandpaper. The corns will put deep scratches in the finish.

Steel wool is used to put an even, satin scratch pattern in the finish without as much risk of corning. You can buy steel wool in natural or synthetic (compressed fiber) form, and in various degrees of coarseness. (See "Synthetic Steel Wool" on page 219.) The finest steel wool is #0000. You should use this or #000 when rubbing a finish.

Rubbing compounds are very fine powders suspended in a paste or liquid. These compounds use grits of powders that are almost always finer than the grit of the finest steel wool. They usually produce sheens higher than that produced by #0000 steel wool. Pumice (finely ground lava) and rottenstone (finely ground limestone) are powders that you can make into your own rubbing compound by mixing them into a thin paste with water or mineral oil. Pumice and rottenstone are traditional rubbing abrasives, but they've been largely replaced by synthetics you can buy already prepared in paste or liquid form. It's often difficult to compare grits between brands, so it's best to stay within one brand if you're rubbing to a progressively higher sheen (Photo 14-3).

Choice of Lubricants

You use a lubricant with sandpaper and steel wool to reduce corning and to float away grit and abraded material, maintaining the abrasive's effectiveness. The lubricant also holds down dust

Photo 14-2: Clogged or "corned" paper will mar the finish. Change the paper if corns begin to develop.

TIP

You can usually find the largest selection of supplies for rubbing a finish in stores that supply auto-body shops.

Photo 14-3: Rubbing compounds come in three different forms: pumice and rottenstone abrasive powders you can mix into a paste with oil or water (left); synthetic abrasive powders already in a paste and sold for use on wood (center); and synthetic abrasive powders in a liquid made especially for high-speed buffing on automotive and wood finishes (right). These are sometimes called glaze, but they are not at all related to glazes used for coloring wood.

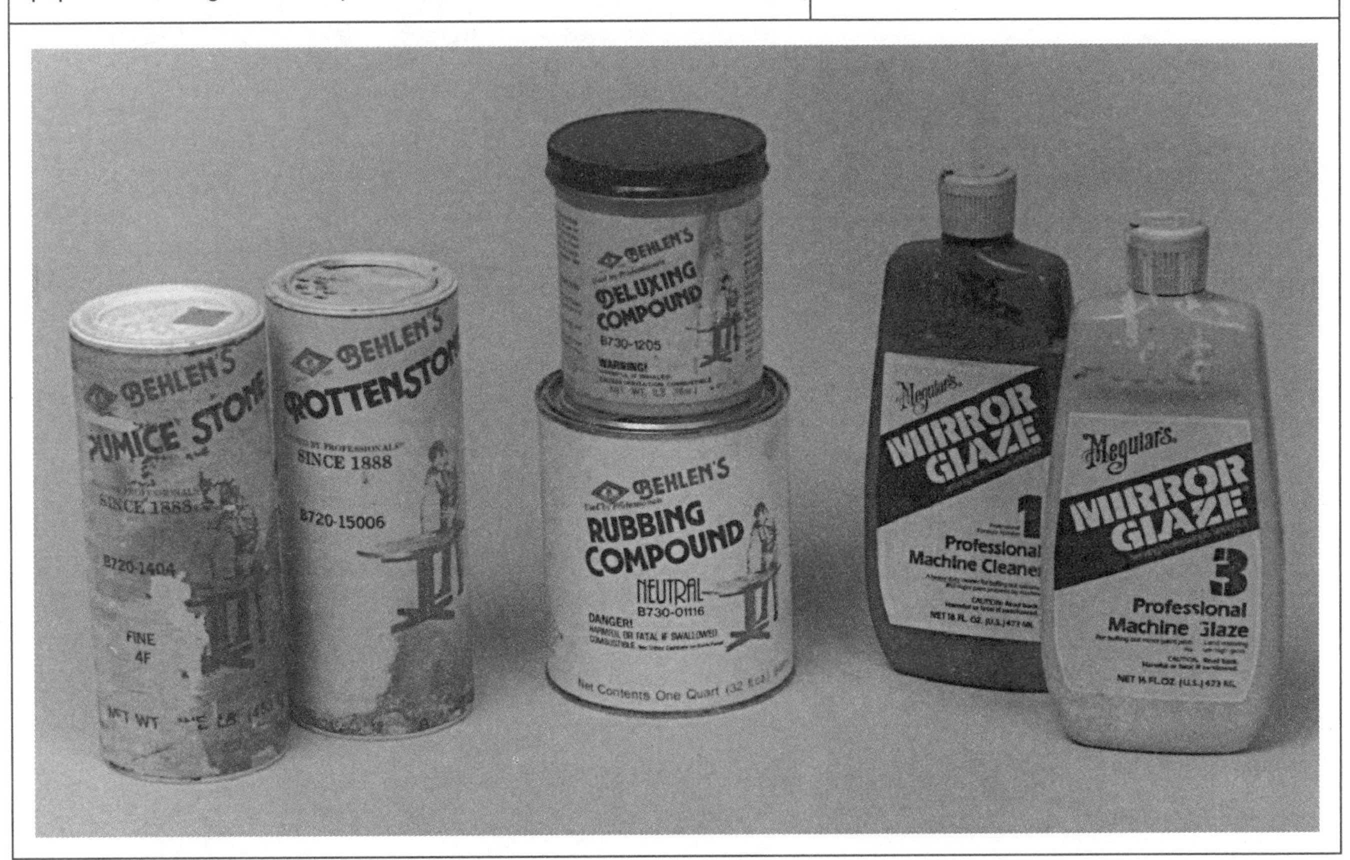

and steel-wool particles so you don't breathe them. There are four types of lubricant for rubbing out:

- mineral spirits or naphtha
- liquid or paste wax
- oil
- soapy water

Each of these lubricants is effective and has its advocates. To use them, wet the surface liberally and keep it wet as long as you are rubbing. Mineral spirits evaporates slower than naphtha, so

RUBBING WITH STEEL WOOL

YOU CAN RUB ANY FINISH with steel wool to smooth it and to even its sheen. You should use #000 or #0000 steel wool. (Synthetic steel wool, also known as Scotch-Brite, can be substituted.) Steel wool will lower the sheen (reduce the gloss) of most finishes, but it will raise the sheen of some film finishes that contain flatting agents. Here's how to do it:

1. Give the finish time to cure hard—at least several days. A month is better.
2. Arrange your work so you can see what's happening in the reflection of a light source.
3. On flat surfaces, using one or both hands and medium-to-heavy pressure, rub in long straight strokes with the grain of the wood. Avoid making arcs with your strokes. Keep the pressure even over the entire surface, and overlap each stroke by 80 to 90 percent. Be very careful not to rub over the edge, or you will cut through the finish and expose bare wood. To avoid cutting through the edge, rub right up to the edge first with short strokes. Then rub the rest of the surface with long strokes, stopping short of the edge (Figure 14-2).

   On boards that are joined cross-grain, rub the butting boards first, then the crossing boards, removing any cross-grain scratches you may have made while rubbing the first boards (Figure 14-3).

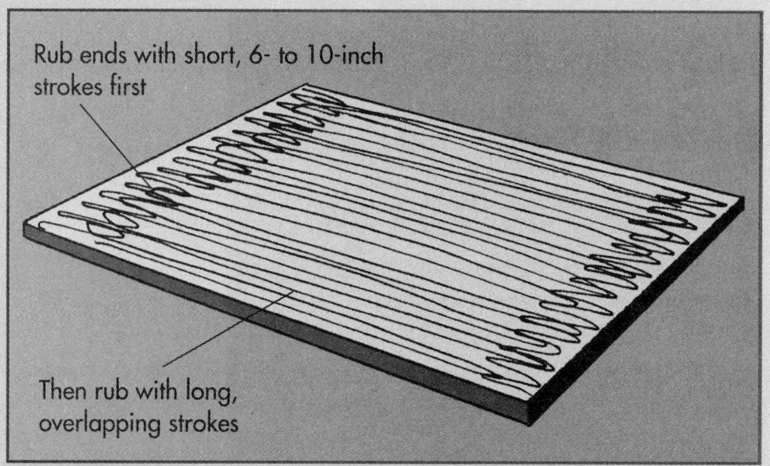

Figure 14-2: To keep from cutting through the edge of flat surfaces, rub the last 6 to 10 inches first with a series of short strokes right up to the edge. Follow with overlapping strokes running the entire length, stopping just short of the edge.

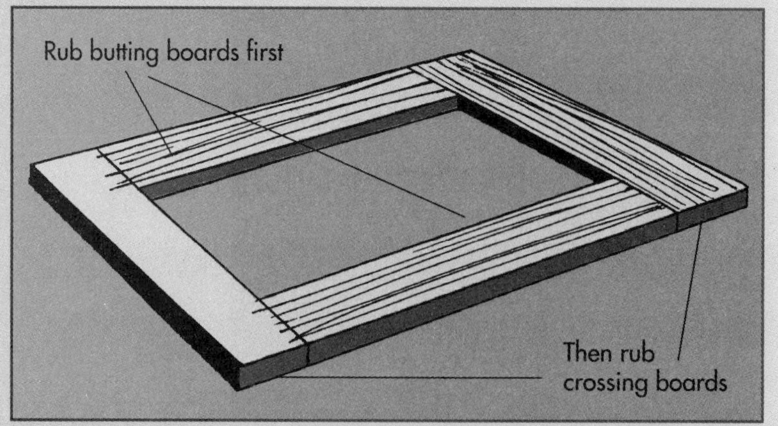

Figure 14-3: To keep scratches in line with the grain when rubbing boards that butt together cross-grain, rub the butting boards first, then the crossing boards. Remove any cross-grain scratches you made into the crossing boards when rubbing the butting boards.

it's usually the better choice between the two. Mineral spirits allows for fast cutting with very little corning. Liquid or paste wax and non-curing oils, such as mineral oil and vegetable oil, almost totally eliminate corning but significantly slow cutting. You can mix mineral spirits with wax or oil to blend the characteristics if you want.

Soapy water works well with steel wool, but it is not very effective in preventing corning on sandpaper. Using water can cause its own problems. If you cut through the finish, the water

For mitered boards, use masking tape to protect one board while rubbing the other (Figure 14-4).

On turnings, rub around the cylinder, just as you would sand on the lathe.

4. Carefully clean off the dust. It's best to blow the dust off and then wipe lightly with the grain using your hand to be sure no dust remains. If you don't have compressed air, wipe lightly using a tack cloth or a cloth dampened with mineral spirits. Wipe with the grain. If you wipe across the grain, you may put noticeable cross-scratches in the surface.
5. If you're not happy with the appearance, determine what is wrong (like incomplete rubbing or uneven pressure causing an irregular scratch pattern, arcing strokes causing an arced scratch pattern) and begin rubbing again to correct the problem.
6. If you rub through the finish, repair that spot with more finish or recoat the entire surface, allow the finish to cure thoroughly, and rub again.

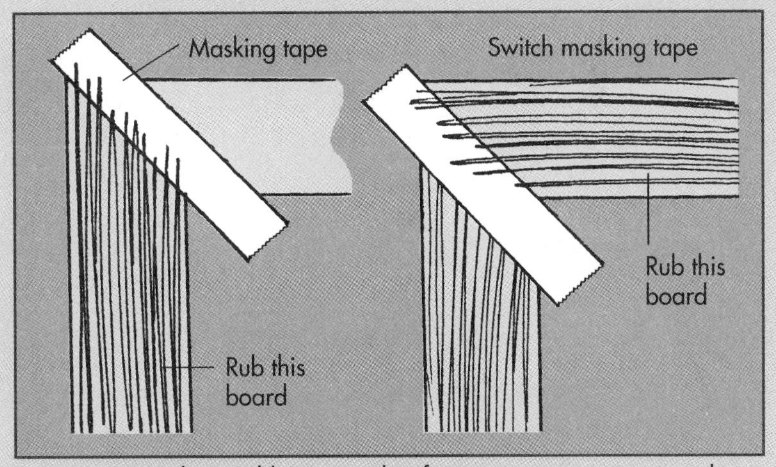

Figure 14-4: To keep rubbing scratches from crossing over a mitered joint, rub one board while masking tape protects the second, then switch the masking tape and rub the second board.

TIP

You can lower the sheen on difficult-to-reach carvings, turnings, and moldings by brushing pumice powder into the recesses with a shoe brush. The pumice will finely scratch the finish.

You can use the following variations of this schedule:

- Sand the surface lightly to remove protruding dust nibs before you begin rubbing with steel wool.
- Use a lubricant with your steel wool. (See "Choice of Lubricants" on page 214.)
- Use a satin finish on any parts you're not rubbing, to imitate the rubbed effect.
- Apply paste wax to raise the sheen and protect the surface from scratches. (See "Applying Paste Wax" on page 231.) ■

MYTH

Murphy's Oil Soap contains oil.

FACT

Murphy's Oil Soap is made by mixing vegetable oil with lye. The chemical reaction that results forms soap, and neither oil nor lye remains.

may raise the grain of the wood, a defect that will be very difficult to repair. However, you don't have to worry about rust unless you intend to apply another coat of water-based finish on top, in which case, be sure to first clean the surface well. Some manufacturers sell paste soap under names like "Wooling Wax," "Wol Wax," "Wool Lube," and "Murphy's Oil Soap." None of these products contains any wax or oil, and the reference to wool means they will lubricate steel wool.

Any of these lubricants will reduce the scratching of the steel wool a little, and the liquid will keep the steel-wool particles from circulating in the air you breathe. But the lubricant will disguise rub-throughs so you won't know they're there until the lubricant has evaporated. By then you've usually done considerable damage. A lubricant also makes it difficult to judge the sheen being produced. You can't see what you're doing.

I suggest you use a lubricant with sandpaper to reduce corning, but not with steel wool until you've rubbed a few finishes without it. Then you'll have a better feel for how much you can rub without cutting through.

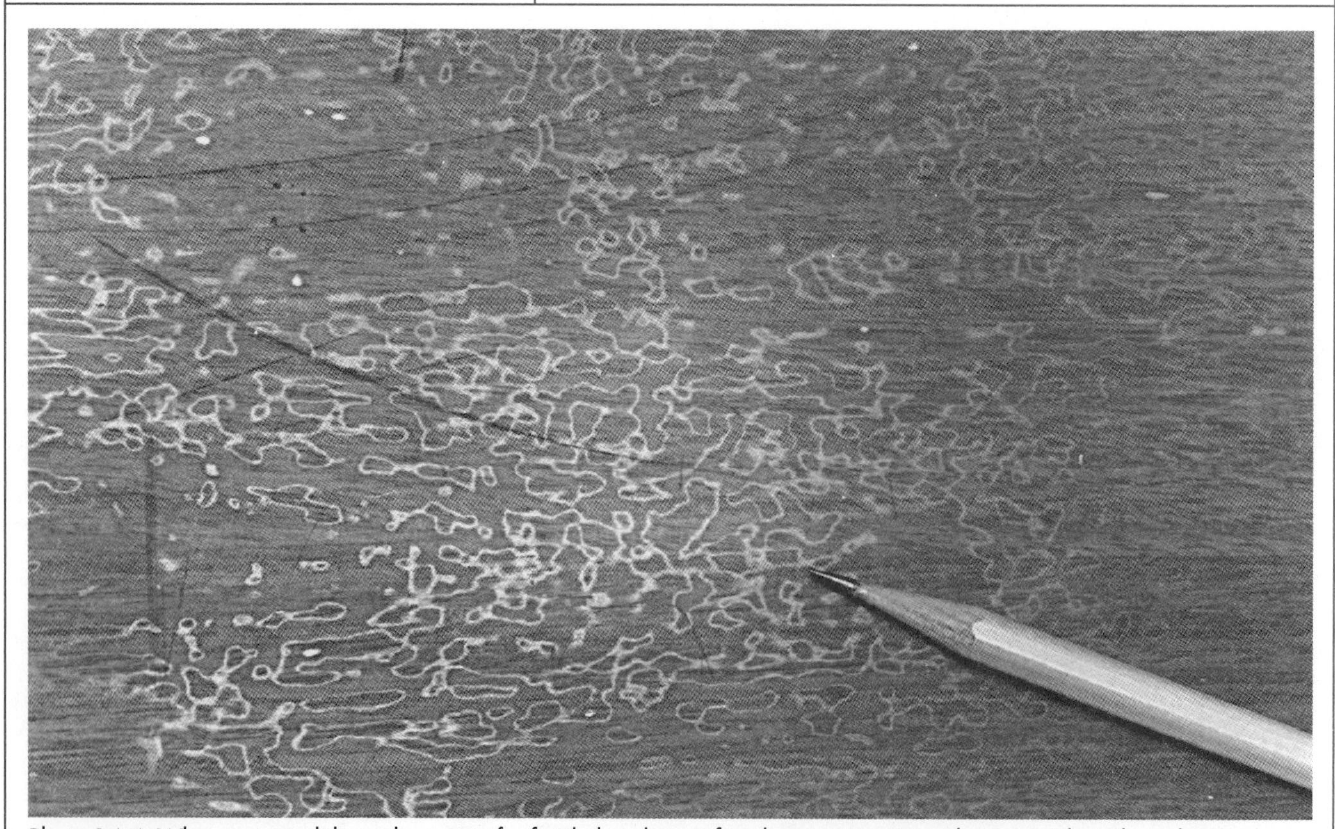

Photo 14-4: When you sand through a coat of a finish that doesn't fuse between coats, such as varnish, polyurethane, or water base, you may notice a line separating the two coats. In open-pored woods, this layering may appear as a network of lines, as above, the result of cutting through finish that has followed the contours of the wood.

SYNTHETIC STEEL WOOL

SYNTHETIC STEEL WOOL is a fibrous nylon coated with abrasive powders. The most commonly available brand is 3M's Scotch-Brite, and the pads are often referred to as "Scotch-Brite."

The abrasiveness of synthetic steel wool is produced by abrasive powders glued to the fiber, not by the fiber itself. When these powders wear off, the pad becomes largely ineffective. In this sense synthetic steel wool resembles sandpaper more than traditional steel wool. The fiber pads are color-coded according to the grit of abrasive powders used. In the consumer market gray is equivalent to #000 steel wool and green is equivalent to #0 steel wool.

You can substitute synthetic steel wool for traditional steel wool when you rub a finish or rub in between coats of finish. Anytime you are using water-based products you should make this substitution, because if any pieces of steel from traditional steel wool remain in pores or cracks, the steel will rust and cause dark spots when you apply the next coat. Otherwise, the principal limitation of traditional steel wool (rounding over dust nibs instead of cutting them off) and the principal advantage of traditional steel wool (reduced clogging) hold for synthetic steel wool. ■

Rubbing Schedule

There are two procedures, or schedules, you can use to rub a finish:

- Level the surface with sandpaper before rubbing with steel wool and rubbing compounds.
- Skip the leveling and begin with steel wool or rubbing compounds.

If you skip the leveling step, your finish will include imperfections such as orange peel, brush marks, and dust nibs, all visible in reflected light. Leveling with sandpaper removes these imperfections. But leveling is an extra, time-consuming step, and it's not always needed. If you're not aiming for perfection, you can often skip the leveling step and simply rub with steel wool. The satin sheen it produces will disguise all but the most severe imperfections. Also, you can usually skip the leveling step on curved, turned, molded, and carved surfaces, and it is seldom required on chairs or table legs.

If you have to sand a lot to level a finish, you run the risk of cutting through the top layer of finish and exposing the layer underneath. You may see a clear line separating the two layers. This phenomenon is called *layering,* and it occurs only on finishes that don't fuse between coats (Photo 14-4). It always occurs between coats of varnish and polyurethane, and it often occurs between coats of water-based finish.

TIP

If you don't have enough experience to judge whether a finish should be leveled, try rubbing it first with steel wool. If the surface is too uneven for your taste, start over with the leveling step.

TIP

If you want better scratch resistance from your finish and also a surface as level as possible, sand the next-to-last coat level, and apply the last coat as smoothly as possible. Sand or rub the next-to-last coat up to 600-grit sandpaper or #0000 steel wool so the scratches don't show through the last coat. Don't sand or rub the last coat.

The only way to repair layering is to apply another coat of finish. This will completely hide the problem. If you do experience layering, continue to sand until the surface is level, apply another coat of the same finish, and level it again. You shouldn't have to sand deep enough to cut through a second time.

Cleaning Up

If you use several grits in your rubbing, clean the surface well between each grit. The reason is the same as in sanding wood: Particles from a previous grit will scratch the finish more than the grit you're switching to.

When you've finished rubbing, you'll have dust or sludge on the surface. You should blow the worst of the dust off with compressed air, if you have it. If you don't have compressed air, wipe lightly with the grain using a tack rag or a cloth dampened with mineral spirits. Wipe with the grain to avoid cross-grain scratches from the loose grit. If you have sludge left over from using a lubricant, wash it off quickly after you've finished rubbing. (Use naphtha for sludge made with mineral spirits, oil, or wax; use water for sludge made with water.) Sludge remaining in scratches, pores, and recesses will dry opaque (see Photo 14-5 on page 221). It may cause a haze on flat surfaces and put solid color into recesses. Use a toothbrush to get the sludge out of narrow recesses.

Waxing and Polishing

It's almost always a good idea to apply paste wax or furniture polish to a rubbed surface to reduce wear. Rubbed finishes show scratches more than non-rubbed finishes. This is because the rubbed scratch pattern exaggerates any scratches that cross it.

Paste wax protects much longer than furniture polish because paste wax doesn't evaporate. Dark-colored paste wax can be used to advantage on dark woods, since it reduces hazing by coloring any rubbing residue. Furniture polish is effective only until it evaporates. Since it is smeary until it evaporates, keeping furniture polish on a rubbed finish all the time means keeping the surface smeary all the time. (See Chapter 15: "Caring for the Finish.")

LEVELING AND RUBBING TO A HIGH GLOSS

THE GLOSS YOU GET BY RUBBING is a soft, elegant gloss. It's not at all like the harsh gloss you get from a finish straight from the can. Though it requires a little work, you can rub almost any film finish to a more beautiful gloss. If you've never done it before, try it on a sample board. You'll find it very satisfying, and it will increase your confidence in your ability to control a finish. Here are the steps:

1. Allow the finish to cure at least a month.
2. Arrange your work so that you can see a light source reflecting off the surface. This will make it easier to see what's happening.
3. Begin by sanding with 1000-grit sandpaper. If the surface is badly pitted, drop back to 600 grit, and in extreme cases, to 400 grit, and then work back up.
4. If the surface is flat, back the sandpaper with a cork, felt, or rubber block to keep it flat (Photo 14-5). If the surface is not flat, use your hand to back the sandpaper. Either way, wet the surface generously with mineral spirits, liquid or paste wax, oil, or soapy water to lubricate the sanding. (See "Choice of

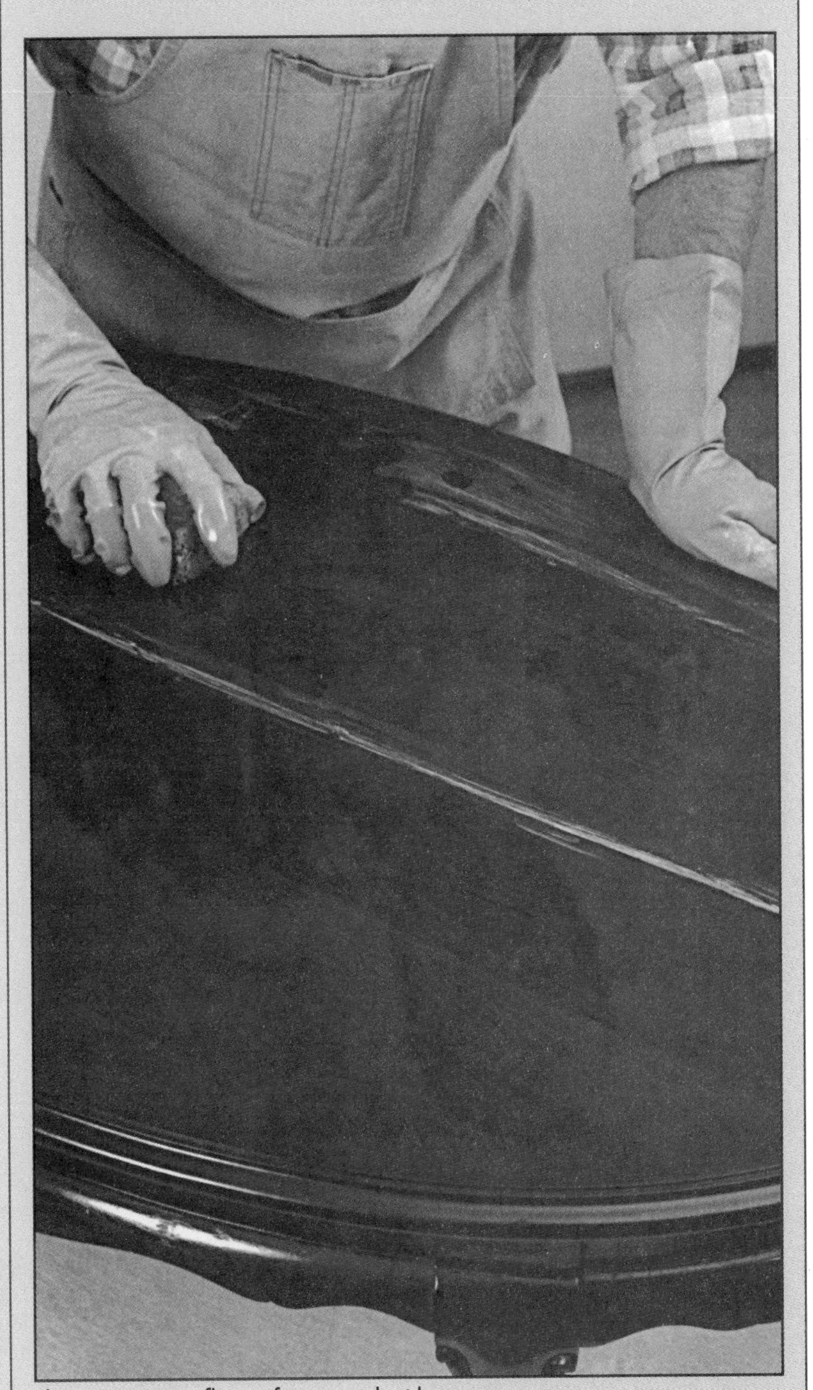

Photo 14-5: On flat surfaces sand with a backing block and lubricant. Apply lubricant generously.

TIP

It doesn't make any difference in what direction you sand or rub until the final rubbing. You will remove the scratches of each grit with the next grit anyway. So it's actually an advantage to sand or rub in a different direction each time you change to a finer grit. This way you can clearly see when you've sanded or rubbed the whole surface. You can also sand or rub in circles as well as straight lines.

(continued)

LEVELING AND RUBBING TO A HIGH GLOSS—continued

Lubricants" on page 214.) It's usually easier to work in small 2- or 3-square-foot sections at a time.

5. Check the sandpaper often to be sure it's not clogging (corning). Remove any corns, or change to new sandpaper.
6. Remove the sludge and dry off the surface every so often, so you can see if the sheen is even. (Naphtha will clean oil and wax.) Any hollows left will be shiny. If there are still shiny spots, continue sanding with 1000 grit, or drop back to a coarser grit if you feel it will be more efficient.
7. When no shiny spots remain, clean all the sludge off the surface.
8. Now you can follow one of three procedures:

- *Rub with #0000 steel wool.* If you intend this to be the last step, you will have a perfectly flat surface rubbed to a satin sheen. (See "Rubbing with Steel Wool" on page 216.)
- *Rub by hand using a rubbing compound.* You can use either a commercial product marketed for wood or a thin paste you make yourself by mixing pumice with mineral oil and mineral spirits or with water. (I prefer using a mixture of mineral oil and mineral spirits except on water-based finish, which is softened by mineral spirits.) Use a felt block or a rubbing pad to rub with. (See "Rubbing Pads" on page 40.) This can be the last step if it gives you the sheen you want. Or you can rub with a finer-grit rubbing compound (commercial or rottenstone made into a paste with mineral oil and mineral spirits or with water). Clean off any remaining particles before moving to the next grit.
- *Polish with a high-speed buffer and automotive rubbing compounds.* These compounds are available from automobile body-shop suppliers and

Photo 14-6: To buff with a high-speed buffer, smear automotive rubbing compound on the surface with the wool or lamb's-wool buffing pad. Hold the buffer flat on the surface, keep it moving, and buff until the compound breaks down to an almost nonexistent powder.

Photo 14-7: To clean the pad between grits, run it at high speed against the end of a stick or a special cleaning tool available at auto-body supply stores.

CAUTION

High-speed buffers generate a lot of heat. Keep the buffer moving so as not to build up enough heat to soften the finish.

CAUTION

Cleanliness is critical when buffing. Any large particles of dust or dirt lodged under your felt, cloth, or wool pad will scratch the surface and force you to drop back a grit or two to remove the scratches.

are made to break down to almost nothing as you polish. They are easy to use with a high-speed buffer and a wool or lamb's-wool pad (Photo 14-6). Their only drawback for furniture is that they often leave a whitish residue in cracks. (These sorts of cracks don't exist on car bodies.) So you need to remove all the sludge before it dries hard. Use a toothbrush and water if the sludge resists a water wash. If you miss some, you can sometimes cover them by waxing with a dark paste wax. You also need to clean the pad between grits (Photo 14-7).

9. Apply a paste wax or furniture polish to disguise the tiny scratches left in the finish and to protect the finish from additional, unwanted scratching. (See "Applying Paste Wax" on page 231.) ■

CHAPTER 15

Caring for the Finish

Of all finishing subjects, caring for the finish is by far the most misrepresented by manufacturers. Claims range from half-truths, such as "furniture polish preserves the finish," to outright absurdities, such as "furniture polish replaces the natural oils in wood." The success of the furniture polish industry in convincing millions of consumers that there's oil in wood that needs replacing has to rank among the great scams of American marketing.

Deceptive marketing has shifted the emphasis away from the real benefits of furniture polish as an aid in dusting, cleaning, and adding scent to a room. In addition, some furniture-polish manufacturers have totally misrepresented the beneficial role of wax. Instead of pointing out its long-lasting shine and wear resistance, they've made wax into a problem, claiming that it keeps wood from breathing by stopping up its pores, and that it builds up to create a smeary surface.

Enough confusion has been created to spawn a thriving sub-industry, operating out of antique and home-and-garden shows, which specializes in miracle remedies. This "snake-oil" business markets essentially the same substances as the primary industry at three to four times the price. Its success demonstrates that there are serious misunderstandings about furniture care.

To get a grasp on what you're trying to accomplish in caring for the finish on your furniture, you need to understand why finishes deteriorate in the first place, and how the deterioration can be slowed. It also helps to understand exactly what paste wax and liquid furniture polish are and what they do. Then you can make intelligent decisions about how you want to care for your furniture.

CAUSES OF FINISH DETERIORATION

Finishes deteriorate as a result of the following conditions:

- exposure to strong light
- oxidation
- physical abuse, including contact with heat, water, solvents, and chemicals

Strong Light

Light, especially sunlight, is the natural element most destructive of finishes. Consider how much faster paint deteriorates on the south side of a house than on the north side. Or how much faster the paint on a car dulls when it's parked daily in the sun instead of under cover. Even indoor light eventually takes its toll on a finish. You can confirm this by removing hardware from furniture that is 40 or more years old. The newly exposed finish will be in far better shape than the surrounding area. (This will be so whether or not the surrounding area has been waxed or polished on a regular basis. Neither paste wax nor liquid furniture polish obstructs the penetration of light.)

Oxidation

Oxidation is the second most destructive natural element. Oxygen combines with almost all materials, changing them into their oxides. The process is usually slow, but it's an important factor in the deterioration of materials. Oxidation causes most finishes to darken, and all finishes eventually to crack, even without the additional effect of light.

Physical Abuse

All finishes can be physically damaged by rough objects, heat, water, solvents, acids, and alkalis. Some finishes, such as polyurethane and conversion, are more resistant than others, but still they can be damaged.

PREVENTING FINISH DETERIORATION

So what can you do to prevent deterioration caused by light, oxidation, and physical abuse? Most of what you can do is fairly passive. Active care does relatively little. (See "Causes and Prevention of Finish Deterioration," at left.)

CAUSES AND PREVENTION OF FINISH DETERIORATION

WHY FINISHES DETERIORATE AND WHAT YOU CAN DO

- **Exposure to light:**
  Keep furniture out of bright light. Cover it when you go on vacation.
- **Oxidation:**
  Don't store your furniture in a hot attic. Heat accelerates oxidation.
- **Everyday wear and abuse:**
  Reduce surface friction with paste wax or furniture polish.
- **Excessive contact with heat, water, solvents, acids, or alkalis:**
  Use hot pads, coasters, and tablecloths.

Passive Care

The best way to care for the finish on your furniture is to keep it covered or away from destructive elements.

- To shield furniture from strong light, place it away from direct sunlight, keep lights turned off in rooms not in use, keep your tabletops covered with a tablecloth, and throw a sheet over your better furniture when you're on vacation.
- To slow oxidation, don't store furniture in an attic or other area that gets extremely hot. Heat accelerates oxidation.
- To minimize physical damage, use coasters, tablecloths, and hot pads. (But don't cover your tables with plastic pads for long periods; the plastic and the finish may stick together.)

Active Care

Active care entails applying paste wax or a liquid furniture polish to your furniture regularly. But neither paste wax nor furniture polish retards the destructive forces of light or oxidation. Nor does wax or polish protect against damage from heat, solvents, or water. Polish and wax protect only against wear. They reduce friction, so objects tend to slide over, rather than dig into, the finish.

In addition to wear protection, paste wax and liquid furniture polish add shine to dull surfaces (Photos 15-1 and 15-2). They do this by filling tiny voids in the finish caused by scratches or natural finish deterioration. When you look into the finish, light reflects back at you instead of scattering in all directions. This makes the wood underneath the finish appear richer and deeper, and makes

MYTH

Furniture polish slows the drying out and cracking of finishes.

FACT

Furniture polish has no effect on cured finishes, good or bad. If furniture polishes did have some beneficial effect on finishes made from plastics, such as polyurethane, acrylic, phenolic, and nitrocellulose, you'd see instructions to "oil" all your plastic possessions. Even old celluloid film would be oiled to preserve it.

Photos 15-1 and 15-2: One of the primary functions of paste wax and furniture polish is to raise the sheen of dull surfaces. Paste wax has been applied to the right side of the sample in each of these photos.

CAUTION

Some soap manufacturers suggest you wash your furniture regularly with soap and water. Though mild natural soaps, such as Ivory and Murphy's Oil Soap, won't damage a finish, excessive contact with water will. If there are any cracks in the finish, water will get underneath and lift the finish from the wood. Use soap and water on furniture only when the furniture is dirty!

the finish appear less damaged. (To some people it might even look as if you've put oil in the wood, underneath the finish.)

Paste wax doesn't evaporate. Liquid furniture polishes that don't contain wax do evaporate. That's the most significant difference between paste wax and liquid polish. It means that paste wax will continue to provide wear protection and shine until it is worn or washed off. But waxless polish will provide wear protection and shine only until it evaporates.

Liquid furniture polish is a far better cleaner than paste wax, because it's better at picking up dust and dirt. Most liquid polishes also add a pleasant scent to the room.

Paste wax is the traditional furniture care product. It has been used for centuries. Until fairly recently beeswax was the primary wax used because it was the only wax available. It's still the only wax in many commercial and homemade paste waxes. (See "How to Make Your Own Paste Wax" on page 60.) But now there are also a large number of natural and synthetic waxes, which are often blended to make paste-wax polishes.

All waxes are solid at room temperature. They are made into a paste (and sometimes a liquid) by being dissolved in a solvent. Traditionally, turpentine was used because it was the only solvent available. Now petroleum-distillate solvents are generally used. (See "Turpentine and Petroleum-Distillate Solvents" on page 181.)

MYTH

Paste wax and furniture polish protect the finish against heat, solvent, and water damage.

FACT

Neither paste wax nor furniture polish offers protection against heat or solvents. To do so the paste wax or furniture polish would have to be more difficult to melt than the finish. But paste wax melts long before any finish does, and furniture polish is already a liquid. Though both paste wax and furniture polish cause water to bead up and run off of vertical surfaces, neither stops the penetration of water on horizontal surfaces. The film of wax or oily solvent is too thin. Because the surface is marked by pores and scratches, there are almost always gaps large enough for water to pass through. It's the much thicker finish itself that stops water from penetrating to the wood.

Commercial paste waxes are often made by blending several individual waxes. The waxes are chosen for qualities such as cost, color, and slip resistance (for floors). But the individual waxes also vary in hardness, gloss, and melting point, so the blend has to be adjusted to take these qualities into account.

Melting point is an indication of hardness and gloss. Generally, the higher the melting point, the harder and glossier the wax. Here are some examples of natural waxes you may be familiar with, though manufacturers usually use synthetic waxes that have similar qualities but are less expensive.

- Beeswax (taken from the hives of bees) melts at about 140 to 150 degrees Fahrenheit, is medium-soft, and produces a medium-gloss sheen. It is easy to use as a polish.
- Paraffin wax (derived from petroleum) melts at about 130 degrees Fahrenheit, is softer than beeswax, and has a slightly lower sheen. It is never used alone as a furniture polish.
- Carnauba wax (taken from the leaves of a Brazilian palm tree) melts at about 180 degrees Fahrenheit, is very hard, and produces a higher shine than beeswax. It is too hard to buff out when used alone.

In order to use very hard waxes, such as carnauba, manufacturers blend in softer waxes, such as paraffin. The blending reduces the melting point, hardness, and gloss of the hard waxes. The melting point comes down to the range of 140 to 150 degrees

The higher the melting point, the harder and glossier the wax.

MYTH

Wax stops up the pores of wood, preventing the wood from breathing.

FACT

Wood doesn't breathe—at least, it doesn't breathe air. Wood does expand and contract as moisture is exchanged with the surrounding atmosphere. The finish slows this exchange. (See Chapter 1: "Why Finish Wood, Anyway?") But wax, applied thin as a polish, has no significant retarding effect on moisture exchange.

Neither does wax prevent the finish from breathing, because the finish doesn't breathe, either. It would be nice if the thin film of wax slowed deterioration of the finish caused by light or oxidation, but it doesn't.

CAUTION

Some paste waxes, such as Briwax, contain toluene (it will be listed on the can). This solvent is strong enough to dissolve and remove many finishes if they haven't thoroughly cured. It will also damage water-based finishes even when thoroughly cured.

Fahrenheit, the same as for pure beeswax. All common paste-wax blends melt at this temperature. Therefore, all common paste waxes have about the same hardness and gloss. If you notice any differences, they are probably due to differences in the surfaces you've waxed, not due to the paste waxes you've used. (Try polishing adjacent parts of a surface with two or more different paste waxes, and prove this to yourself.)

Major manufacturers of paste wax seldom use natural beeswax, either alone or in combination with other waxes. Beeswax is expensive. Also, beeswax has a grainy texture, which causes it to smudge easily. Pure beeswax polishes are usually made by small companies tapping into the mystique of beeswax being the traditional paste wax.

The only significant difference among commercially available waxes is the length of time you should wait before wiping off the excess wax. The waiting period depends on the evaporation rate of the solvent that was used to make the solid wax into a paste or a liquid. Some paste waxes, such as Trewax and Briwax, contain solvents that evaporate very quickly (as quickly as naphtha). Others, such as Minwax, contain slower-evaporating solvents (evaporating at a rate similar to mineral spirits). When all the solvent evaporates, the wax is solid again. As explained in "Applying Paste Wax" on the facing page, you don't want to give the solid wax too much time to harden before you wipe it off. If you want to apply wax to a large area before you start wiping, choose a wax with a solvent that evaporates more slowly (Photo 15-3).

Photo 15-3: These paste waxes are made from blends of several waxes. They are meant to be used on furniture or floors. There is no noticeable difference in the sheen or hardness of the surfaces they produce. But they do vary in the length of time you should wait before wiping off the excess wax.

APPLYING PASTE WAX

PASTE WAX ISN'T USED MUCH anymore as a polish for furniture because it's more difficult to apply than liquid furniture polish. But paste wax offers longer-lasting shine and wear protection because it doesn't evaporate. Here are directions for applying paste wax:

1. Be sure the surface of the finish is clean. If it appears dirty, wash it with a mild, natural soap, such as Ivory or Murphy's Oil Soap.
2. Put a lump of paste wax in the center of a soft, 6-inch-square cotton cloth, and wrap the cloth around the paste wax (Photo 15-4). If the wax is hard, knead it in your warm hand until the wax softens.
3. Wipe the cloth over the finish, allowing the paste wax to seep through the cloth and onto the finish. You can wipe in any direction. You're going to wipe off all the excess anyway. The purpose of putting the wax inside the cloth is to limit the amount you deposit on the finish. The less wax you get on the finish, the less you'll have to remove.
4. Allow most of the solvent to evaporate (the sheen will change from glossy to dull). The time this takes will vary depending on weather conditions and the solvents used in the paste wax. Work on one small area at a time until you get a feel for the rate of evaporation.

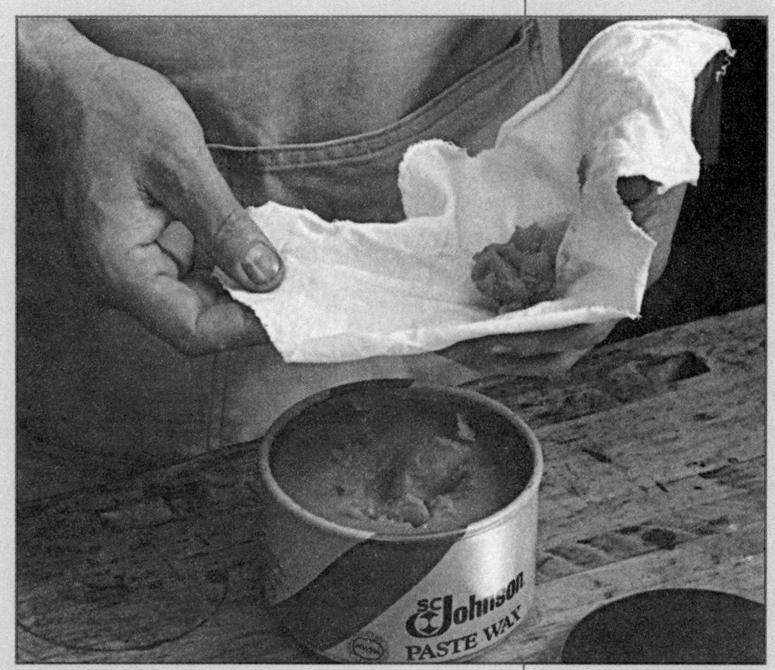

Photo 15-4: The easiest way to apply paste wax is to put a lump of wax in the middle of a soft cloth, wrap the cloth around the wax, and let the wax seep through the cloth as you rub it over the finish.

5. Wipe off the excess wax with a soft, clean, cotton cloth. If you catch the wax just as the sheen changes, the excess will be easy to remove. If you wait too long, you will have to rub very hard in order to build up enough heat (above 140 to 150 degrees Fahrenheit) to melt the wax so it can be removed. On the other hand, if you're too quick, you'll remove the wax together with the solvent.
6. You can use a power buffer or drill with a lamb's-wool pad to remove the remaining excess wax and buff up a shine. If the lamb's-wool pad is just

TIP

If you want to smooth and dull the finish at the same time you're applying the paste wax, you can apply the wax with steel wool. Rub with the grain so the scratches will be less noticeable.

TIP

If the wax dries too hard to remove easily, you can apply some more paste wax to soften the original wax and then remove the excess before it gets too hard. Or you can wash off all or most of the wax with a naphtha- or mineral-spirits-soaked cloth and begin again.

(continued)

APPLYING PASTE WAX—continued

smearing the wax and not removing it, there is too much wax on the surface, or the pad is too loaded. Try to remove more of the wax with a cloth, and then polish again with a clean lamb's-wool pad. You have to *remove* the excess wax, not just spread it around. As long as you can smear the surface by rubbing it with your finger, you haven't removed all the excess wax (Photo 15-5).

7. You usually get a better result if you apply a second coat of wax. You're not building the wax with a second coat; you're filling in minute gaps left in the first coat. If the surface was dull to begin with, the improvement from the second coat is usually enough to be seen.
8. To maintain a finish that has been paste-waxed, dust it regularly with a feather duster or a soft cloth. You can dampen the cloth slightly with water to aid in picking up the dust. (You can also use a water-dampened chamois.) If the surface begins to look dull, rub it with a soft, dry cloth to bring back the shine. If no shine reappears, apply another coat of paste wax. Since wax doesn't evaporate, you shouldn't have to reapply wax on tabletops for many months, or on unused surfaces for many years.

CAUTION

Don't use liquid furniture polish over paste wax unless you want to remove the wax. The oily solvent in the furniture polish is strong enough to dissolve the paste wax, and you will smear and remove it when you wipe over the surface with your cloth.

Photo 15-5: If you don't remove the excess wax, you'll leave streaks of wax on the surface of the finish.

9. If, after a number of waxings, you get so much wax on the surface that you can smear the wax with your finger, then you have not been removing all the excess with each waxing. Remove most or all of the wax with naphtha or mineral spirits and buff what is left, or apply a fresh coat and then buff. ■

Some paste waxes are sold in colors. The color in the wax is dye or pigment. (See Chapter 5: "Staining Wood.") You can use a colored paste wax to color in nicks and scratches while you're waxing the finish. The dye or pigment in the paste wax will color the wood wherever a nick or scratch has cut through the finish. The color you add to the wood will be long-lasting. Contrary to what you often hear, colored paste waxes won't add any noticeable color to finished surfaces. Once you've buffed off the excess wax, there's not enough color left to be seen.

Commercial paste waxes designed for use on cars often contain very fine abrasives to help remove chalking. They often also contain silicone oil to increase the gloss and ease of removal. Shoe waxes also contain silicone oil for better water repellency. Paste waxes that contain silicone oil will be more glossy than paste waxes that don't. They will also be more slippery, so you shouldn't use them on floors. (See "Fish Eye and Silicone" on page 168.)

Liquid furniture polishes are made primarily from petroleum-distillate solvents. The solvents range from mineral spirits (paint thinner) to kerosene. The solvents are therefore rather oily, which is why furniture polishes are often thought of as oil. The petroleum smell is removed and usually replaced with a more pleasant scent. You can use the less expensive mineral spirits or kerosene on your furniture if you don't mind the smell, but I don't recommend it. Neither will damage any finish. (See "Turpentine and Petroleum-Distillate Solvents" on page 181.)

Just like paste wax, liquid furniture polishes reduce wear and add shine. But the wear protection and added shine last only until the furniture polish evaporates. Some furniture polishes evapo-

FURNITURE POLISH IN BRIEF

Furniture Polishes Do:

Add temporary scratch resistance
Add temporary shine to a dull surface
Aid in picking up dust
Clean grease, wax, and sticky fingerprints from the surface
Fill the room with a pleasant scent

Furniture Polishes Don't:

"Feed" the wood by replacing "missing oils"
"Feed" the finish
Protect against heat, water, solvent, or chemical damage
Slow deterioration caused by light or oxidation

MYTH

Wax builds up, making the surface smeary.

FACT

Wax builds up only if you don't remove all the excess. Each time you apply a new coat of paste wax, the solvents in it dissolve the existing wax, making one new mixture. Remove the excess and you're back to the wax that is stuck to the surface. You don't get wax buildup on well-buffed furniture any more than you get it on well-buffed shoes.

MYTH

Lemon-oil furniture polish is made from lemon oil.

FACT

So-called lemon oil is a slow-evaporating, petroleum-distillate solvent with lemon scent added. If lemon-oil furniture polish were really made from the tiny amount of oil that exists in the peel of lemons, not only would the price be exorbitantly high, it would skyrocket every time there was a freeze in Florida!

MYTH

Silicone oil destroys finishes.

FACT

Silicone oil is very stable and inert. It doesn't react with anything and, therefore, doesn't destroy anything. Furniture polishes that contain silicone oil do cause refinishing problems. The silicone oil gets into the wood, usually through cracks in the finish, and prevents many finishes from flowing out evenly. (See "Fish Eye and Silicone" on page 168.)

MYTH

Furniture polish replaces the natural oils in wood (or "feeds the wood").

FACT

There are no natural oils in common furniture woods, and they don't need feeding. Only a few exotics, such as teak and rosewood, contain oil, and the oil in these woods doesn't need replacing (especially not with petroleum oil). In fact, the oil in these woods causes problems for the finish, as I've pointed out in earlier chapters. In any case, the purpose of the finish is to keep liquids, such as oil, soft drinks, perspiration, and water, out of the wood. If your finish is in good shape, furniture polish shouldn't be able to get to the wood at all.

rate in an hour, others in a few days. As long as the furniture polish remains on the surface, however, it will smear when you rub your finger over it. Unfortunately, you can't have wear protection and shine with an oily, solvent-based furniture polish without also having smear. Once the smear is gone, so is the wear protection and shine. (See "Furniture Polish in Brief" on page 233.)

A few furniture polishes contain a small amount of wax, silicone oil, or both (Pledge is the best-known example). These polishes don't evaporate as quickly as polishes containing only petroleum-distillate solvent. In fact, if there is enough wax in the polish, it will act similar to paste wax by giving long-lasting scratch resistance and shine.

Manufacturers don't tell you when their polishes contain wax or silicone oil. This is because industry advertising has told us that silicone oil is bad for finishes and that wax "builds up" on the surface. But the extended shine provided by wax and silicone oil makes polishes that contain them extremely popular.

As mentioned above, liquid furniture polishes are excellent cleaners. They remove dust because they make your cloth damp with the dust-attracting, oily solvent. You wipe the dampened cloth over the surface, and it picks up the dust. (See "Applying Liquid Furniture Polish" on the facing page.)

Most furniture polishes are solvent alone, so they clean only solvent-soluble dirt, that is, grease, oil, and wax. These furniture

APPLYING LIQUID FURNITURE POLISH

APPLYING LIQUID FURNITURE POLISH is simple, but the method can vary depending upon whether you are just removing dust or are using the polish to raise the sheen.

In either case, make sure the surface of the finish is not dirty. If it is, wash it with a mild, natural soap such as Ivory or Murphy's Oil Soap.

If you are using the polish solely to remove dust, lightly dampen a soft cloth with the liquid and wipe over the finish. Dust will cling to the dampened cloth. You should not be leaving a significant wetness on the surface.

If you are using the polish to raise the sheen of the finish or to make the surface slick to reduce scratching, apply enough polish to the soft cloth to make it wet. Wipe the finish. Alternatively, you can spray the liquid directly on the finish and wipe it around with the cloth: Wet the finish with polish, then remove all the excess.

If you don't remove the excess each time, you may get a buildup of dust and dirt mixed with wax or silicone, if either wax or silicone is contained in the polish. You will notice that the finish starts showing fingerprints and is sticky. (It's this that is commonly referred to as "wax buildup.") To remove the stickiness, wash the surface with a mild soap, such as Ivory or Murphy's Oil Soap. Your cloth will become dirty and the finish underneath may be dull. (If there's no finish underneath, you'll have to refinish.) The dullness has been caused by age, not by the furniture polish. Reapply your furniture polish. It will raise the sheen again, as long as the finish is still in good shape. ■

NOTE

Furniture polishes are packaged differently—as liquids, as aerosols, and in pump bottles. The packaging controls how the polish is dispensed, but has no bearing on what's inside.

polishes appear as a clear liquid. There is no significant difference in cleaning power among various solvent-based polishes.

Some furniture polishes are solvent emulsified in water, so they clean both solvent- and water-soluble dirt. In addition to grease, oil, and wax, these polishes clean sticky fingerprints. Water-emulsified furniture polishes are opaque and off-white in color. There's no significant difference in cleaning power among emulsified furniture polishes (Photos 15-6 and 15-7 on page 236).

The scent added to furniture polishes makes the room smell nice. Though it may seem trivial, improving a room's atmosphere is actually a major function of furniture polishes.

HOW TO CHOOSE

Choosing a method of caring for your furniture is not nearly as complicated as the large number of products on store shelves

NOTE

If the furniture polish goes through the finish into the wood, the finish is badly deteriorated and you should consider refinishing. Neither the finish nor the furniture polish is protecting the wood.

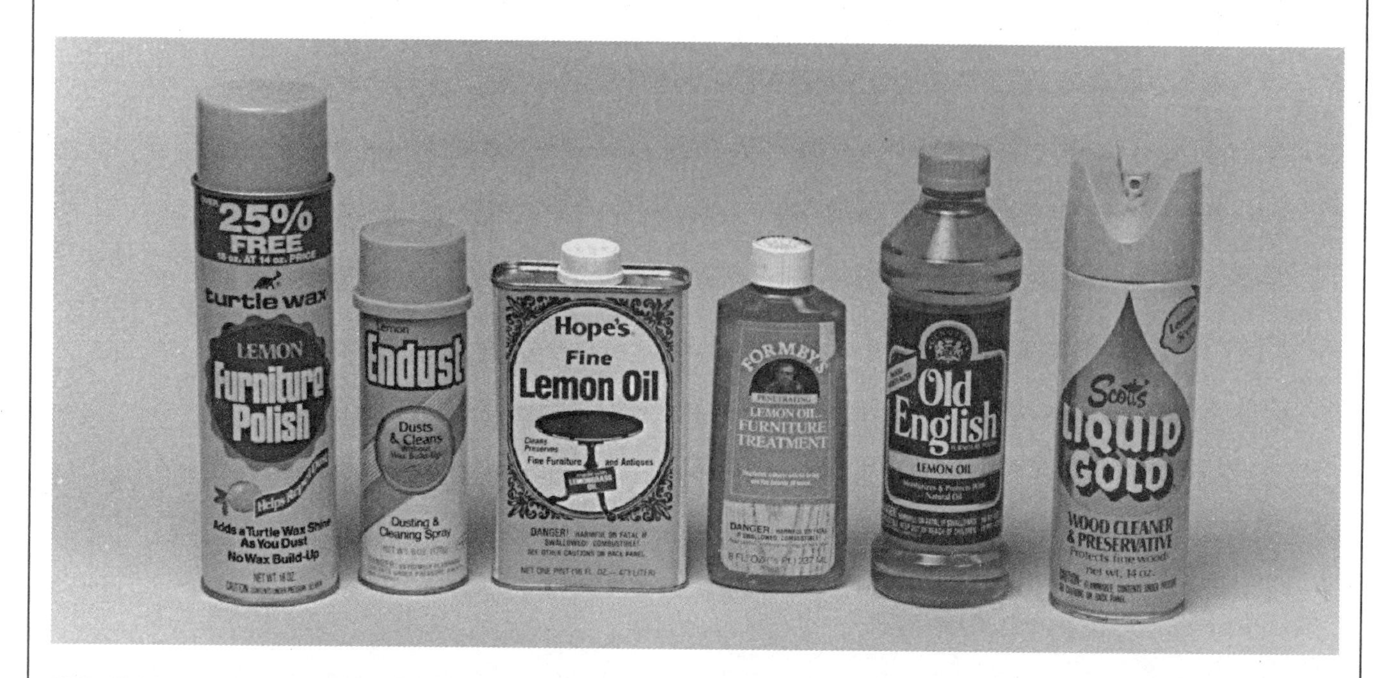

Photos 15-6 and 15-7: Liquid furniture polishes differ in two major ways—evaporation rate and cleaning ability. Clear furniture polishes (top) are based on oily solvents and therefore clean only solvent-based dirt. Milky white furniture polishes (bottom) are emulsions of oily solvents and water, and they clean both solvent- and water-soluble dirt.

would make you think. Whatever you decide about using a paste wax or furniture polish, you should always follow the passive-care suggestions outlined earlier in this chapter. These methods will provide the maximum protection for the finish on your furniture.

To decide on which active-care product to use, determine which is more important to you—long-lasting shine and wear protection, or easy dusting and cleaning (you can always add scent by means other than furniture polish).

If you want permanent shine and wear protection, use a paste wax. Choose one that you find buffs easily. You'll have to experiment. The differences are in the evaporation rate of the solvent, and preferences vary. Once you've applied the paste wax, dust it with a feather duster or with a dry or water-dampened cloth or chamois. Don't use a liquid furniture polish, or you'll streak and remove the wax.

If you want a product that makes dusting and cleaning easier, use a liquid furniture polish. You have three criteria for choosing which polish to use:

- *Evaporation rate:* If you want a furniture polish that gives maximum shine and wear protection, choose one that evaporates very slowly. The downside of these polishes is that they will be smeary on the surface for as long as they provide the shine and wear protection. If you want a furniture polish primarily for dusting and cleaning and don't want a smeary surface, choose one that evaporates quickly. Since manufacturers don't identify these characteristics, you may have to experiment a little.
- *Cleaning ability:* For normal cleaning use a solvent-based polish. For cleaning sticky fingerprints and other water-soluble dirt use a water-emulsified furniture polish. You'll recognize it by its milky-white color.
- *Scent:* Choose a furniture polish with a scent you like.

Chapter 16

Repairing Finishes

Finishes deteriorate, they get damaged, and they can be repaired. Some finishes are easier to repair than others, as I've explained in previous chapters, but most damage that occurs to most finishes can be fixed. Within the furniture industry a speciality, distinct from finishing itself, is dedicated to repairing finishes. It's concentrated in furniture factories, furniture stores, and moving companies, where most damage to finishes occurs.

There are four general types of damage that occur to finishes, and sometimes through the finishes into the wood beneath:

- superficial damage to the surface of the finish in the form of light scratching, light cracking, and dullness
- damage to the color in the finish
- damage to the color in the wood
- damage through the finish and into the wood itself in the form of deep scratches or gouges

Superficial damage to penetrating finishes (oil, oil/varnish blends, and wiping varnish applied thin) is easy to repair. More substantial damage (color problems, gouges, and deep scratches) on surfaces finished with these penetrating finishes is almost impossible to repair, because there is no film thickness to work with. Once damaged, they'll never look undamaged. All types of damage to film finishes, on the other hand, can be repaired, but concealing color problems, gouges, and deep scratches often requires a high degree of skill.

REPAIRING SUPERFICIAL DAMAGE

Superficial wear or surface deterioration is the most common type of damage and is the easiest to repair. There are three ways to repair this kind of damage:

- Apply a coat of paste wax or oil/varnish blend to the surface and wipe off the excess.
- Rub the surface of film finishes with steel wool or rubbing compounds to cut through the damage or dullness and expose unaffected finish below.
- Apply another coat of the original finish, or apply French polish or padding lacquer on top of the damaged finish, to cover up the problem.

Applying Paste Wax or Oil/Varnish Blend

Applying paste wax or oil/varnish blend to the finish is the easiest of all repairs. It is very effective in disguising superficial wear and raising the sheen of dull surfaces. Both paste wax and oil/varnish blend will have about the same effect, but oil/varnish blend will be permanent while paste wax will be removed by furniture polish or soap and water.

I've discussed methods for applying paste wax and oil/varnish blend in previous chapters. (See "Applying Paste Wax" on page 231 and "Applying 'Oil' Finishes" on page 51.) You can apply either of these substances over any finish as long as the surface is clean. Be sure to remove all of the excess of either product, or the surface may become smudgy and sticky. Remember that oil/varnish blend cures soft, so don't apply it more than approximately once a year over a harder finish. You don't want to build the finish. Paste wax doesn't build, so it won't make any difference how often you apply it as long as you remove the excess each time.

CAUTION

It's seldom a good idea to apply oil/varnish blend to tabletops that have a mirror-flat finish. The surface will show every flaw, and the oil/varnish blend, being soft, will damage easily. It's usually better to use paste wax or one of the methods discussed for cutting back or building up the finish.

Cutting Back the Finish

If the finish is thick enough, you can cut it back to expose a better surface. You do this in exactly the same way you rub out new finishes. (See Chapter 14: "Finishing the Finish.") You can level the surface by sanding first with 1000-grit or finer sandpaper and a lubricant, or you can skip this step and simply rub with steel wool or rubbing compounds. The risk in cutting back a finish someone else has applied is that you don't know how much thickness you have to work with. Proceed cautiously. The alternative to sanding is often refinishing anyway, so it won't hurt to try cutting back the finish first.

CAUTION

Many finishes, especially factory-applied finishes, have color in them. You may begin to remove some color even before you get down to bare wood. You can usually see the color transferring to your sandpaper or rubbing pad, which will give you an early warning to stop sanding.

Applying More Finish on Top

You can usually correct superficial damage by applying another coat of the same finish. You can sand or rub the surface with steel wool to smooth it before applying the new coat, just as you might do normally between coats. If you finished the piece originally yourself, you know which finish you used, so you know which finish to use again. (Using the same brand is not as important as using the same type–polyurethane, lacquer, shellac, etc.) But if you didn't do the original finishing, you are taking more risk in applying another coat. Test the original finish to determine whether it is shellac, lacquer, water base, or one of the reactive finishes. (See the "Tip" on page 143.) Then apply the same finish over the existing finish.

There is always some risk in applying a fresh coat of finish over an old finish. Unpredictable things can happen, from poor flow-out to blistering. It's also often inconvenient: You have to move the furniture to an area set up for finishing, and the piece of furniture may be out of use for some time. A more convenient and less risky method of applying a new finish on top of the original is to French polish the surface with shellac, or French pad the surface with padding lacquer. This is the traditional way of keeping old finishes in good shape, and it is still a very effective method to "shine up" shellac, lacquer, and water-based finishes. It also works over varnish, but because there isn't a good bond between the newly applied coats and the varnish, the new coats may peel after a number of years.

I've described how to French polish. (See "French Polishing" on page 155.) Padding lacquer is easier to apply, and it is usually more water-resistant than French polish (which is shellac). Because the technique of French polishing existed for a hundred years before the introduction of padding lacquer in the 1930s, the tradition was established of French polishing bare wood and repairing a French-polished surface with more French polish. Padding lacquer is seldom used on bare wood or over French polish. Padding lacquer is most often used to repair damage to finishes other than shellac. (See "Applying Padding Lacquer" on page 243.) But there is no particular reason it has to be this way. You could just as easily apply padding lacquer to bare wood or over shellac, or apply French polish over another finish.

Padding lacquer, or French finish as it's sometimes called, can be thought of as a modern French polish. In spite of its name, it is not based on lacquer, but on shellac. Other resins are often added to the shellac to increase its water resistance, and stronger ether and ester solvents are used in place of alcohol. In addition, padding lacquer has the lubricant built in. You don't have to (in fact, you shouldn't) add any oil to your polishing pad as you do

Applying a fresh coat of finish over an old finish is often risky and inconvenient. A better choice might be French polish or padding lacquer.

CAUTION

Shellac has a shelf life of only a year or two. Since padding lacquer is primarily shellac, it, too, has a limited shelf life. Unfortunately, neither Mohawk/Behlen nor Star lists the date of manufacture on the container (except sometimes in code). Just as with shellac, you'll know your padding lacquer is too old if it doesn't harden properly. Test padding lacquer of unknown age on a scrap piece of wood before applying it on an important piece.

Photo 16-1: Padding lacquers are actually a shellac product, often with other resins added to increase water resistance, and with stronger solvents used in place of alcohol. They're easier to use than French polish because the lubricant is built-in and evaporates after application, eliminating the need to remove it.

when you French polish. The built-in lubricant is pine-tree- or petroleum-distillate solvent that evaporates at a rate between that of mineral spirits and kerosene. The lubricant stays in the polish while you're applying it, but evaporates soon after, so you don't have to remove it as you do the oil you use in French polishing. This saves a step and allows you to finish a job quickly without having to wait overnight for all the oil to rise to the surface for removal.

There are two companies that make most of the padding lacquer available in the United States—Mohawk/Behlen and Star. Each company makes several versions of padding lacquer that vary in solvent-evaporation rate, oil content, solids content, and color (from amber to clear). I find Ultra Qualasole from Mohawk/Behlen and Star-Lite French from Star to be the easiest to use (Photo 16-1).

If you've never used padding lacquer before, I suggest you buy a fresh pint or quart of Ultra Qualasole or Star-Lite French and try it on a piece of furniture you intend to refinish anyway. You'll develop a feel for padding techniques without worrying

(text continues on page 246)

APPLYING PADDING LACQUER

French padding (applying padding lacquer with a pad) is much the same as French polishing (applying shellac with a pad). (See "French Polishing" on page 155.) But there are some important variations. Here's how to apply padding lacquer on top of a previously applied finish.

1. Be sure the finish is clean and smooth. If it is not shellac, lacquer, or water base, scuff the finish with #0000 steel wool or 400-grit or finer sandpaper so the padding lacquer will bond better (Photo 16-2).
2. Arrange your work so that you can see a light source reflecting off the surface. This will help you see what is happening.
3. Make up a fresh rubbing pad. (See "Rubbing Pads" on page 40.) In contrast to French polishing, it's easier to apply padding lacquer with a freshly made rubbing pad.
4. Fill your pad with 1 to 2 teaspoons of padding lacquer—enough to make the sole of the pad damp. The amount will vary depending upon the size of your pad and the area you're covering. The exact amount you use is not critical; I just pour it from the bottle. Tap the pad against the palm of your hand to disperse the liquid.
5. Work on an area of the surface that is small enough for you to thoroughly coat with one application. A 3- to 4-square-foot area is about as big as you can do at a time. It should take you about five minutes to complete an area of this size, but the time may vary depending on the brand of padding lacquer you're using, the size of your pad, and how wet your pad is. Divide large surfaces, such as tabletops, into sections and overlap each section.
6. Just as in French polishing, begin applying padding lacquer with light

Photo 16-2: If the finish is rough or slightly cracked, sand it smooth with 400-grit or finer sandpaper.

(continued)

APPLYING PADDING LACQUER—continued

CAUTION

Padding lacquer is made with ether and ester solvents, which are much more toxic than the alcohol used in French polish. The ether and ester solvents can make you feel light-headed, and they can temporarily affect your nervous system. Work in an area with good cross ventilation and, if the solvents still bother you, wear an organic-vapor respirator mask. The solvents will also remove the fat from your skin. If your hands are sensitive, wear rubber gloves to protect them.

strokes in straight lines or in S-curves so your strokes don't cross over each other. When you've covered the surface once, begin crossing over in figure eights or circles. If the pad grabs or drags when crossing over a previous stroke, the pad is still too wet. Return to a non-crossover pattern until you can cross over without dragging. Light damage caused by crossover drags will usually disappear with more padding. Heavier damage (ridges) may have to be sanded smooth with 400-grit stearated sandpaper after the padding lacquer has dried for a few minutes.

Your pattern of movement (straight strokes, circles, or figure eights) is not important as long as you cover the entire surface evenly. But don't bring the pad to a complete stop at any time, or it may stick to the surface and leave a mark.

7. Increase your pressure and speed. Your pad should now be leaving streaks. You will probably think something is wrong and want to add more padding lacquer to the pad. *Don't do it!* The streaks, or "rag tracks," as a friend of mine calls them, are just what you want to see (Photo 16-3). Increase the pressure on your pad, using both hands if you like, and continue rubbing rapidly over the entire area you're padding. As your pad dries out, it will become tacky, and the friction caused by your heavy rubbing will burnish out the smears and leave a high gloss (Photo 16-4).

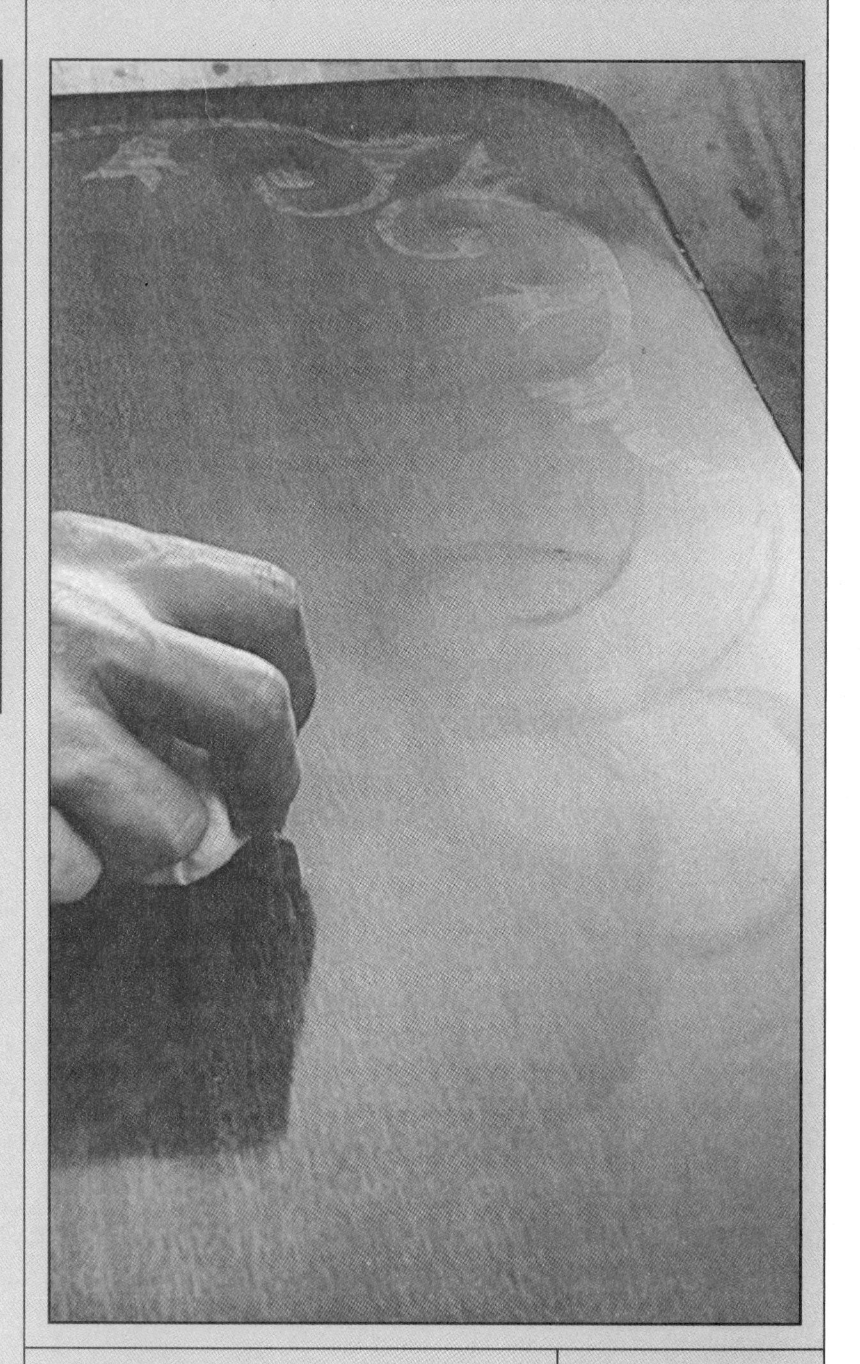

Photo 16-3: When you see streaks, or "rag tracks," increase your speed and pressure.

TIP

The trick to applying padding lacquer is to rub the pad continuously over a given area until the pad is totally dry and all the streaking has disappeared. This is why it's better to use a freshly made pad each time you pad a surface. Previously used pads will take much longer to dry out. You may even want to change to a new pad in the middle of a job if the surface is large and your pad becomes too wet.

To get the pad into tight corners, remove the outer cloth and use the inner cloth, forming it into a point. The inner cloth may also work better on rounded or hollow areas such as chair legs, where you want the pad to conform to contoured surfaces.

8. Some padding lacquers contain a less-volatile oil that will stay on the surface longer than needed. This may trick you into thinking you're still leaving padding-lacquer tracks, when you're just smearing the oil. To test for this, run your finger across one of these tracks. If you change the direction of the smear, the tracks are oil and there's no reason to continue padding. You can remove the oil if you want by wiping the surface with a cloth dampened with naphtha. Or you can just leave the oil, and it will slowly evaporate.
9. If you can still see dull areas or sanding scratches, apply another coat of padding lacquer. But if the surface is smooth and shiny, another coat won't improve things.

Photo 16-4: When the pad is totally dry, the streaks should be gone, leaving a beautiful shine.

10. You can lower the sheen by rubbing lightly with #0000 steel wool after you've allowed the padding lacquer to cure overnight. You can raise the sheen by rubbing with a polishing compound just as you would do with any other finish. (See Chapter 14: "Finishing the Finish.") ■

(continued from page 242)

about making mistakes, and you'll learn the product's limitations. At the worst, you'll have to go ahead with your plans to refinish. If all goes well, the padding lacquer may make refinishing unnecessary.

NOTE

If water has gotten through the finish and separated it from the wood, you will have to strip and refinish. If water has gotten through the finish and darkened (stained) the wood, you will have to strip the finish and bleach out the dark stain using oxalic acid. (See "Using Oxalic Acid" on page 293.)

REPAIRING COLOR DAMAGE IN THE FINISH

Damage to the color of the finish is of three sorts:

- damage caused by water (water rings)
- damage caused by heat
- damage caused by rubbing off part of the color that was originally in the finish

Removing Water Rings

Water rings occur when moisture gets into the finish, eliminating the film's transparency. The film appears cloudy or white, usually in the shape of a ring because it's most commonly caused by a wet drinking glass or a hot cup under which moisture condenses on the finish. Heat accelerates the penetration. Water rings are more common on finishes that have aged and developed minute cracks. The cracks allow moisture to enter. Alcohol can also cause water rings by taking moisture along with it as it penetrates into a finish.

To remove water rings, you need to remove the water from the finish. There are three ways to do this, and I suggest you try them in the following order (the easiest and least destructive ones first) until you get a feel for the process. Success is unpredictable because of variables such as what type and how old the finish is, how long the water ring has been in the finish, and how deep the water damage goes.

- Apply an oily substance, such as furniture polish, petroleum jelly, or mayonnaise, to the damaged area and allow it to remain overnight. The oil has a greater affinity to the finish than water and will sometimes replace the water if the damage is superficial.
- Dampen a cloth with any commonly available alcohol (denatured alcohol is best) and wipe it gently over the damaged area. Since alcohol will dissolve shellac and damage lacquer and water base, in addition to causing water rings itself, begin with a very slight dampening and add more alcohol if necessary, observing closely what is happening (Photo 16-5). You will have the cloth dampened enough when it leaves the appearance of a comet's tail trailing as you wipe. The comet's tail is caused by the alcohol evaporating. Don't rub hard. Wiping with alcohol will remove water rings in all but the most severe cases.

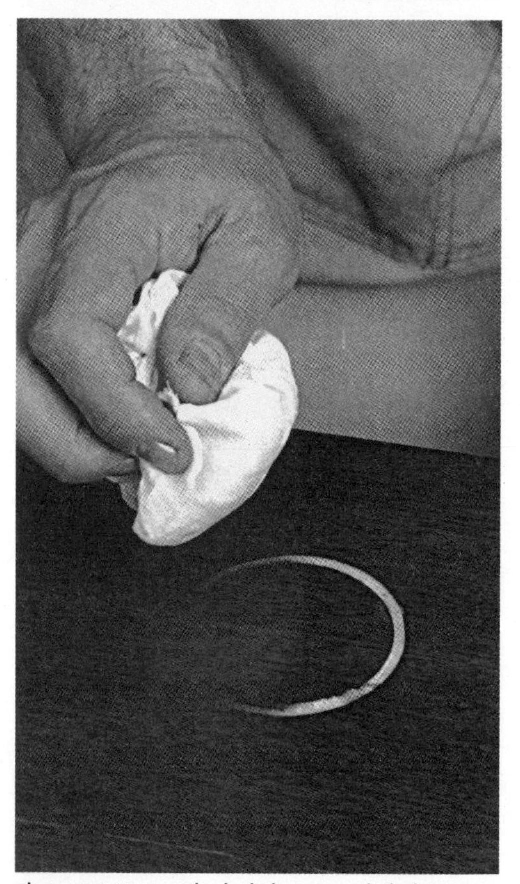

Photo 16-5: An alcohol-dampened cloth is very effective in removing water rings. Use just enough alcohol to leave the appearance of a comet's tail trailing the cloth as you gently wipe, so you don't damage the finish.

- Cut through the damage by rubbing with a mild abrasive. Cigarette ashes, mixed with water or oil to make a paste, and toothpaste are often suggested. But these abrasives will probably be too mild if the alcohol didn't work. (You can try them in place of the alcohol, however.) Rottenstone, or possibly pumice (which is coarser), in combination with a light oil, such as mineral oil or even a furniture polish, will be more effective. Fine #0000 steel wool lubricated with a light oil will be even more effective, but it will also scratch the surface more severely, so you should use steel wool only as a last resort. Rub the damaged area until the water damage is gone, being careful not to rub through the finish. Then, even the sheen over the entire surface by rubbing it with the same abrasives you used to remove the water ring, or with finer abrasives to raise the sheen. (See Chapter 14: "Finishing the Finish.")

Repairing Heat Damage

Heat damage appears similar to water damage. The film becomes cloudy and off-white in color. Heat may also cause an indentation in the finish. Heat damage is usually impossible to repair without stripping and refinishing. It might be possible for you to apply alcohol to a shellac finish or lacquer thinner to a lacquer finish and correct the problem by redissolving the finish and letting it cure again. It's often worth a try, but it probably won't work.

It's also sometimes possible to correct the color, but not the transparency, by painting over the damage as described below.

Replacing Missing Color

Damage caused by rubbing off part of the color originally in the finish is difficult to repair, but it can usually be done if you have a good sense of color and some patience. (See "Matching Color" on page 84.) Since the wood is still sealed (all the finish hasn't been rubbed off), you have to apply new color on top of what is left. You can't simply apply some stain, because the stain won't penetrate.

To make the repair, apply a colorant on top of the damage. The colorant can be pigment or dye, but it must include a binder to lock the color in. The binder can be shellac, padding lacquer, lacquer, or varnish. The application tools can be a rubbing pad, artists' brush, or spray gun. The idea is to get the color correct, make the grain look natural, seal the repair so it doesn't fade or wash back out, and then make the sheen match that of the surrounding area. It will help if you think of yourself as an artist with a palette of colors, binders, and abrasives. The smaller the damaged area, the easier it will be to disguise. And darker colors will

CAUTION

Never try removing water rings with a cloth that is soaked (rather than lightly dampened) with alcohol, as is often suggested. If the finish is anything but varnish or conversion, you will damage it.

MYTH

Water rings are often in the layer of furniture polish or wax.

FACT

Neither furniture polish nor wax will develop water rings. This myth has become popular because the water ring sometimes disappears when you wipe the surface with an oily solvent such as mineral spirits, as you might do to remove furniture polish or wax.

TIP

For repairing color damage to an edge or corner, you can use a touch-up marker, which is similar to a Magic Marker but in wood tones. Simply draw the felt tip of a proper-colored marker along the damaged edge.

TIP

Repairing color damage to a finish requires a great deal of skill, and it's helpful to have a number of specialized products. Companies such as Mohawk and Star sponsor two-day courses teaching the techniques in cities all over the United States. They also sell all the specialized products. You should contact one of these companies if you are interested in pursuing the craft of "touch-up." See "Sources of Supply" on page 305.

be much easier to match than lighter colors. (See "Touching Up Color" on the facing page.)

Here are some tips for touching up damage to the color in the finish:

- If the color in the surrounding area is transparent, use dyes.
- If the color in the surrounding area is opaque, use pigments.
- Shellac and padding lacquer are the most popular binders to use with dyes or pigments because they are less likely to damage the original finish, they dry quickly, and, if you make a mistake, they can be wiped off with an alcohol-dampened cloth without damaging most finishes.
- Varnish can also be used, but it will take almost a day to dry between coats. Varnish can be removed with mineral spirits if you do so before the varnish cures.
- Lacquer can be used only with a spray gun, and if you get the color wrong, you won't be able to remove it without making the damaged area larger. Reduce your spray pattern as much as possible, and mask off the surrounding area with a piece of paper that has a hole cut in it the size of the damage you want to color.

Your colors must be compatible with the binder, of course. (See "Compatibility of Colors and Binders," below.) You will probably have the greatest success using an artists' brush to apply most colored finish, but you can also use a rubbing pad.

You can use these same touch-up techniques to disguise heat damage, glue splotches, burn-in repairs (see "Using a Burn-In Stick" on page 254), and wood putty that didn't take the stain. You paint the affected area to fake the grain and color of the surrounding wood. Again, the smaller the area you're trying to disguise, the better your chances of success.

COMPATIBILITY OF COLORS AND BINDERS

Colors	Binders
Universal-color pigments	Shellac, padding lacquer, lacquer, oil/varnish blend, varnish
Pigment powders	Shellac, padding lacquer
Artists'-color pigments, japan-color pigments	Oil/varnish blend, varnish
Alcohol-soluble dyes	Shellac, padding lacquer
Oil-soluble dyes	Oil/varnish blend, varnish, lacquer

TOUCHING UP COLOR

DAMAGE TO THE COLOR in or beneath a finish can usually be repaired by painting in the colors on top of the finish. These techniques also work to disguise wood-putty and burn-in patches and glue splotches (Photo 16-6). Here are the steps:

1. Work in good light so you can see the colors you're matching. Diffused, natural daylight (not direct sunlight) is best.
2. Mix a dye or pigment color with a binder. (See "Matching Color" on page 84.) Shellac or padding lacquer binder will dry fast. If you make a mistake on any finish except shellac, you can remove the mixture by wiping with alcohol. Varnish binder (in effect, a glaze) will cure very slowly.
3. Draw in the grain lines with a very fine artists' brush. Try to connect the grain lines with the surrounding grain.

Photo 16-6: This problem could be from wood putty that didn't take the stain, a burn-in repair, or a glue splotch.

Photo 16-7: Draw the grain lines in with an artists' brush. Connect the lines to the surrounding grain.

(continued)

TOUCHING UP COLOR—continued

TIP

If you are coloring a solid patch to match an open-pored wood such as oak or mahogany, cut some pores into the patch with the tip of a knife.

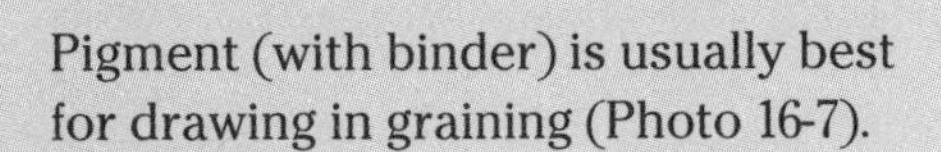

Pigment (with binder) is usually best for drawing in graining (Photo 16-7).

4. When the grain lines are dry, apply a thin barrier coat of finish so the lines won't get smeared during the next step. Dust on an aerosol-lacquer spray, or apply padding lacquer with a rubbing pad.

5. If there's a difference between the color of what you're working on and that of the surrounding wood, apply a background color (the lightest color in the surrounding wood) with an artists' brush or a rubbing pad (Photo 16-8). Dyes are usually best for this step. If you use a rubbing pad, stroke a dampened pad rapidly back and forth 10 to 20 times over the damaged area until the surface is sticky. Then apply a tiny amount of dye or pigment powder

Photo 16-8: After applying a barrier coat to protect the grain lines, apply the background color using an artists' brush.

Photo 16-9: When you have completed the repair, protect it with padding lacquer applied with a rubbing pad, or with another coat of finish.

TIP

You can apply the background color before drawing in the grain if you want. The risk is that you may get the repair too dark when you put in the grain.

to the proper places with the tip of your finger. The powder will dissolve into the sticky finish. If you get so much powder stuck to the surface that it is rough to the touch, sand it smooth with 400-grit or finer sandpaper.

6. When you have the color correct, apply a light protective coat of padding lacquer with a rubbing pad (Photo 16-9). Blend the sheen of the repair in with the surrounding sheen, using abrasives. Alternatively, if you made the repair in between coats of finish, apply the next coat of finish. (If you are spraying lacquer or water base, dust on a couple of coats first to keep the finish from interfering with the repair.) ■

TIP

You don't always have to imitate the surrounding wood to repair color damage. You can make the repair look like something else (for example, a knot, mineral stain, or fly specks) if it is appropriate to the wood you're working on. The goal is to make the repair blend in with whatever else is going on in the wood.

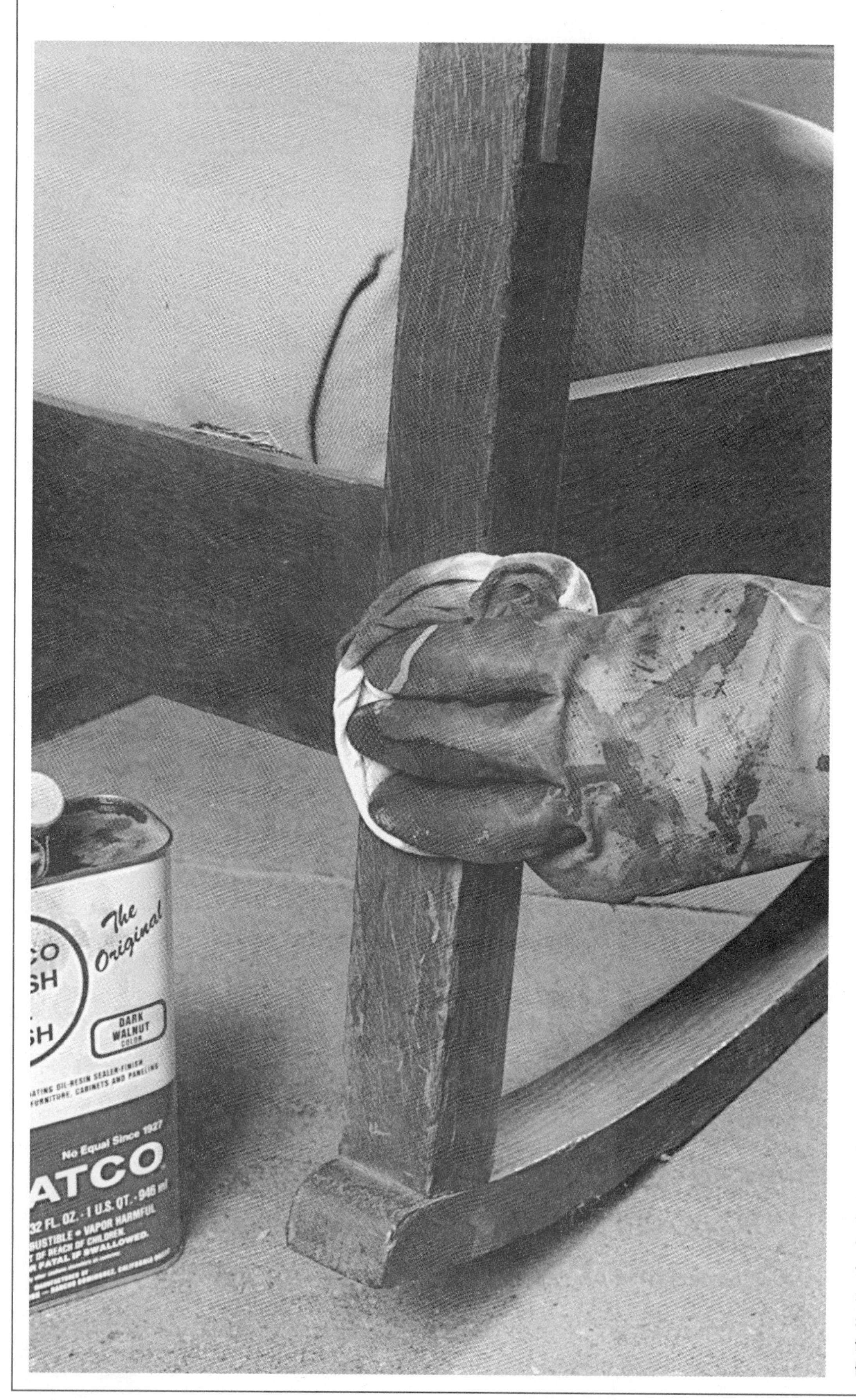

Photo 16-10: One of the quickest and most effective techniques for repairing nicks and scratches is to coat the surface with a colored oil/varnish blend. The color will penetrate everywhere the damage has gone through the finish, and the oil/varnish will seal the color in. Be sure to wipe off all of the excess before the finish cures.

REPAIRING COLOR DAMAGE IN THE WOOD

When the damage cuts through the finish and removes stain that was originally in the wood, repairs are usually fairly easy. You need only replace the missing stain and ensure that it is sealed so it won't fade or wash off. There are several ways to do this:

- Use a neutral or colored oil/varnish blend, such as Watco or Deft Danish Oil, to put the color back into nicks and scratches. This is especially effective on table and chair legs and on baseboards and paneling. Wipe a generous coat of the proper-colored Danish oil (the color doesn't have to be exact.) over the entire affected surface (Photo 16-10). Then remove all the excess. The oil/varnish blend will penetrate everywhere the damage has cut through to the wood. (See "Applying 'Oil' Finishes" on page 51.) If you can't find the proper color ready-made, make your own by adding oil-soluble dye or universal-color, artists'-oil-color, or japan-color pigment to an oil/varnish blend.
- Use an oil/varnish-based pigment stain to color in nicks and scratches. Wipe the stain over the entire surface, then wipe off the excess. These stains contain very little binder, so you should seal the color in the wood by applying a coat of oil/varnish blend the next day.
- Use colored paste wax to color in nicks and scratches.

If the finish is thin, coloring the scratch may be sufficient. If the finish is thick and otherwise in good shape, you may have to fill the scratch.

Walnut-colored Watco or Deft Danish Oil is very effective in repairing color damage on dark-stained table and chair legs, baseboards, and paneling.

REPAIRING DEEP SCRATCHES AND GOUGES

Scratches and gouges that go through the finish into the wood have to be filled. It's very difficult to do this successfully with wood putty because the putty will stick to the finish everywhere it comes in contact, and it will be almost impossible to remove. It's better to melt solid finish into the depression, smooth it level with the surrounding surface, and then add coloring and graining to make the filling blend in. (See "Using a Burn-In Stick" on page 254 and "Touching Up Color" on page 249.)

The solid finish used is shellac or lacquer, because these finishes can be changed from solid to liquid and back again by applying and removing heat. (See Chapter 7: "Introduction to Film Finishes.") These finishes are formed into solid sticks of many colors. They are commonly called *burn-in sticks.* The process of melting them into damaged areas is called *burning in.*

The most difficult part of burning in is getting the filling level without damaging the good finish around it. It's common for beginners to start off with a very small hole and end up with quite a large area of damaged finish. You should practice on a finished scrap of wood before tackling a piece of furniture.

USING A BURN-IN STICK

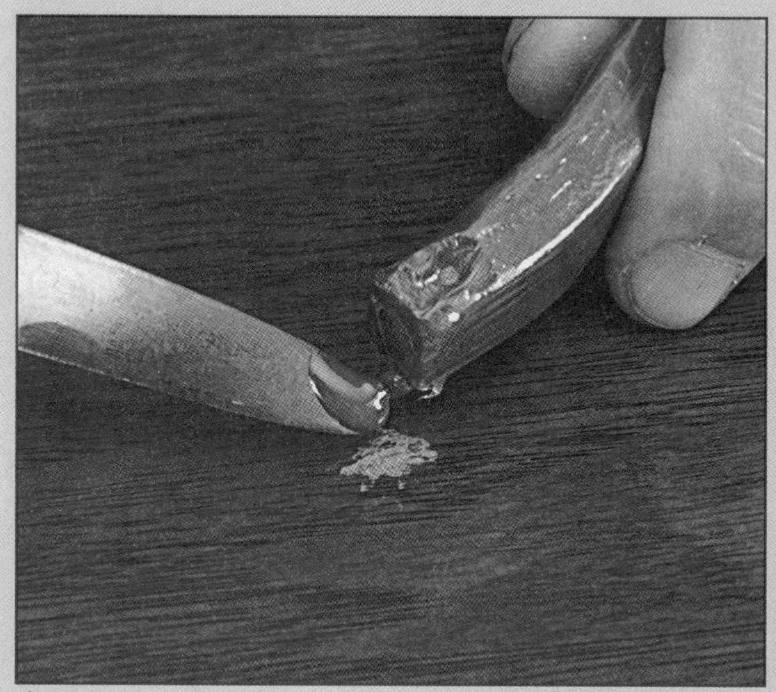

Photos 16-11 and 16-12: Fill a scratch or gouge by melting colored, solid finish, in the form of a burn-in stick, into the depression. Fill the depression slightly above the surrounding surface.

THE MOST EFFECTIVE WAY to fill deep scratches and gouges on finished wood is with a burn-in stick. Burn-in sticks are solid finish (shellac or lacquer) that you melt into the depression. They are available from Star, Mohawk/Behlen, or general mail-order catalogs. (See "Sources of Supply" on page 305.) Here are the steps for doing burn-ins:

1. Choose a colored burn-in stick that closely matches the background color (the lightest color) of the surrounding wood.
2. Melt the burn-in stick into the scratch or gouge using a special burn-in knife or a soldering gun. You can also use the tip of a screwdriver heated over a flame, but wipe off the tip before touching it to the burn-in stick or you may add some black soot to your color. Slightly overfill the gouge (Photos 16-11 and 16-12).

TIP

If the scratch or gouge is barely through the finish, you will find it easier to get good results if you dig out the damage a little deeper.

CAUTION

Your knife should be just hot enough to melt the burn-in without damaging the surrounding finish. This will take some practice to achieve. Remember, freshly applied finish will soften much more quickly than finish that is fully cured.

3. When the burn-in cools, level it with the finish in one of two ways:

- Sand it level using 320-grit or finer wet/dry sandpaper and an oil lubricant. Back the sandpaper with a cork block barely larger than the repair you're sanding. Keep the cork block level on the repair so you don't remove the surrounding finish (Photo 16-13).

- Remove the excess burn-in by melting it with heat from your burn-in knife. You can apply a special burn-in balm (or some petroleum jelly) to the surface to prevent the melted repair from sticking to the surrounding finish. Be sure your knife is clean. Lightly drag the heated knife over the burn-in, transferring some of the solid material to the knife. Wipe the finish from the knife with a cloth. Continue removing the excess burn-in until the patch is level or almost level with the surrounding surface (Photo 16-14). You can finish off by sanding with 400-grit or finer sandpaper and a cork block as described above.

4. When the surface is smooth, make the sheen even with the surrounding area by using abrasives. Then add color and grain lines. (See "Touching Up Color" on page 249.) ■

Photos 16-13 and 16-14: Use sandpaper backed with a corked block (above) or a burn-in knife (below) to level the filling.

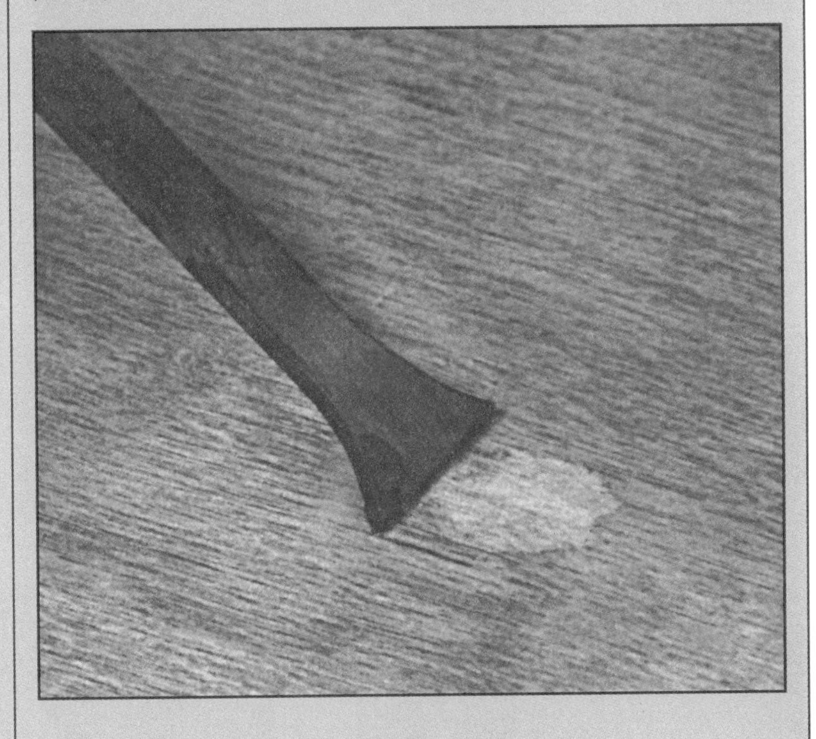

CHAPTER 17

Finishing Different Woods

Understanding finishes and how to apply them is not the whole story. Woods vary in color, density, and texture. You need to consider the characteristics of a specific wood in deciding how to finish it.

In most cases the woods you use are the same as those used hundreds of years ago. You're not the first to struggle with the choices of how best to finish a particular wood. You can learn a great deal by looking at how previous generations solved the problems. Often an image of how a wood should look comes from having seen it in a given style. You might aim to reproduce the look of a period piece, echo a familiar effect, or present a wood differently than people are used to seeing it.

Following is a discussion of the major considerations and problems you will encounter in finishing different woods and some choices for finishes to use. The step-by-step finishing schedules I present in the side columns are only suggestions meant to illustrate the variety of ways to finish wood. They correspond to the furniture pieces shown in the color section beginning on page 263, where you'll see how each schedule finally looks. When I think one brand of finishing material is significantly better or more widely available than others, I name it. But in most cases there's not enough difference between brands of one type of product—oil/varnish-based pigment stains, paste-wood filler, nitrocellulose lacquer—to be concerned with which brand you use. Keep in mind, too, that every stain, paste-wood filler, glaze, and finish can be applied to every wood. You are making aesthetic decisions, so there are no absolute rules. People will disagree about what's best and what they prefer.

PINE WITH BRUSHING LACQUER

With brushing lacquer, a film finish, you can even out differences in sheen caused by the random differences in pine's density (Photo 17-3 on page 264).

1. Sand to 180 or 220 grit and remove the sanding dust.
2. Brush on a coat of brushing lacquer. (My favorite is Deft Semi-Gloss Wood Finish because it has a very pleasing sheen and is flexible enough to give when the soft wood is dented.) Thin the finish, adding up to 10 percent lacquer thinner if you like. Let it cure for at least two hours, better overnight.
3. Sand lightly with 280-grit or finer sandpaper to remove dust nibs and roughness caused by raised grain. Remove the sanding dust.
4. Apply a second coat full strength, and let it cure for at least two hours.
5. Sand lightly with 320-grit or finer stearated sandpaper to remove dust nibs. Remove the sanding dust.
6. Repeat Steps 4 and 5.
7. Apply the final coat full strength in as dust-free an environment as possible. (I like to apply at least four coats to even the sheen between the earlywood and latewood.)

GEL-STAINED PINE WITH SATIN VARNISH

The less a stain penetrates pine, the less it will splotch (Photo 17-4 on page 265).

1. Sand to 180 or 220 grit and remove the sanding dust.
2. Apply a gel stain, and wipe off the excess. Move rapidly, as gel stain dries fairly quickly. Make your last wiping strokes follow the direction of the grain. (I like to use Wood-Kote gel stain on pine because it penetrates less than other gel stains.) Let the stain cure overnight.
3. Brush on a coat of satin varnish, thinned 1 part varnish to 1 part mineral spirits. (You can use satin polyurethane if you like.) Let it cure overnight.
4. Sand lightly with 280-grit or finer sandpaper to make the surface smooth to

(continued)

PINE

Pine is often the first wood used by beginning woodworkers. It's widely available, relatively inexpensive, and one of the easiest woods to cut and shape with machine and hand tools.

Yet pine may be the most difficult of all woods to finish. The earlywood (spring growth) of both white and yellow pine is soft, porous, and off-white. The latewood (summer growth) is very hard, dense, and orange. Thus, the earlywood and latewood react differently when sanded, stained, and finished, causing an uneven appearance that frustrates beginning and experienced woodworkers alike.

When you sand pine by hand, without the aid of a cork-, felt-, or rubber-backed sanding block, you cut away the softer earlywood much faster than the latewood. This leaves depressions that show up when you apply a finish.

When you stain pine with common pigment and dye stains, the stain penetrates deep into the porous earlywood but very little, or not at all, into the dense latewood. This uneven stain penetration causes a color reversal in the grain pattern. The white earlywood darkens, while the orange latewood stays about the same (Photo 17-2 on page 264).

When you finish pine with nonbuilding finishes, such as oil and oil/varnish blend, or slow-building finishes, such as wiping varnish, the finish soaks deep into the porous earlywood but hardly at all into the dense latewood. This results in an uneven sheen. The earlywood appears flat, even after several coats, while the latewood becomes glossy.

Pine also varies randomly in density throughout, in addition to earlywood and latewood variations. No matter how well you sand pine before staining, you often get darker splotches when you apply a stain. These splotches are caused by deeper stain penetration in the less-dense areas that occur naturally in the growth of pine trees.

Historically, pine has usually been painted or finished unstained. Only recently, with the increase in do-it-yourself projects, has there been much interest in staining pine. Often, staining is an attempt to make pine resemble another wood, such as walnut or mahogany. But imitating other woods is almost impossible with pine because the grain is too pronounced to disguise.

Your best option for finishing pine (other than painting) is probably to leave it unstained and apply a film finish, such as varnish, lacquer, or water base. Unstained pine is quite attractive. The wood turns a warm yellow-orange as it ages. All finishes except water base will warm and deepen the coloring, which will get darker and richer with age. This look on pine has been popular in northern Europe for many years and was once popular in the

United States. Applying several coats of a film finish gives you an even sheen across the porous earlywood and the dense latewood.

If you do decide to stain pine, there are two ways to reduce the problems of grain color reversal and splotching:

- Washcoat the wood prior to staining.
- Use a gel stain.

The method most commonly recommended is to apply a washcoat of finish, which partially seals the wood. Traditionally, 1/2- to 1-pound-cut shellac was used. (See "Liquid and Flake Shellac" on page 150.) Now it's more common to use manufactured products that do the same thing. (See "Washcoating" on page 109.) I don't find washcoating to be a good solution for pine, however. The variations in wood density are often too great and unpredictable. It's difficult to know how much washcoat material to apply to produce an even staining. If you don't seal the wood adequately, you will still get splotches, which you can't remove without sanding below the depth to which the stain has penetrated. If you apply the washcoat heavily enough to ensure against splotching, you may seal the wood so completely that little or no stain will penetrate. You will get very little coloring unless you leave a thickness of stain on the surface. If you're using a pigment stain, a thick layer will obscure the wood.

Your best option for staining pine, in my opinion, is to use a thick gel stain, such as Wood-Kote. Thick gel stains don't penetrate much because they don't flow. The result is a more even color with little splotching.

In addition to the above two options, you can seal the wood entirely with a full coat of whichever finish you're using and build all the color on top. There are two ways to build the color on top: Use a glaze or tone the wood.

To use a glaze, first apply a full coat of finish and let it dry at least overnight. After sanding lightly, wipe glaze over the surface and remove the amount necessary to give you the appearance you want. You can use a gel stain as a glaze. Wipe with the grain.

To tone the wood, add a compatible dye or pigment (see "Compatibility of Stains and Finishes" on page 104) to your finish and apply it to the wood as a second coat. You will get the best results if you spray this colored finish, called a toner (see "Shading stains and toners" on page 111). You can also brush a colored finish, such as Minwax Polyshades, that won't obscure the wood much because it has so little pigment. It's best to apply several coats of clear finish over the toner to protect it from being scratched off the wood.

Personally, I like pine best when it's unstained and finished with a film finish, such as brushing lacquer. I don't think I've ever applied a stain to pine except when experimenting.

GEL-STAINED PINE—continued

the touch. Be careful not to sand through the stain on the edges. Remove the dust.

5. Brush on a second coat of satin varnish full strength or thinned, adding up to 10 percent mineral spirits. (Thinning will improve flow-out and reduce the likelihood of bubbles curing in the film.) Let it cure overnight.
6. Sand lightly with 320-grit or finer stearated sandpaper to remove dust nibs, or scuff in the direction of the grain with #0000 steel wool if there are no dust nibs. Remove the sanding dust. Repeat Step 5.
7. You can stop here or apply more coats if you want. Apply your last coat in as dust-free an environment as possible.

TONED PINE WITH SATIN POLYURETHANE

To tone, you add a colorant directly to the topcoat (or topcoats) of your finish. Because the wood has been sealed by the first coat of finish, it will not splotch (Photo 17-5 on page 265).

1. Sand to 180 or 220 grit and remove the sanding dust.
2. Brush on a coat of polyurethane, thinned 1 part polyurethane to 1 part mineral spirits. Let it cure overnight.
3. Sand lightly with 280-grit or finer sandpaper to make the surface smooth. Remove the sanding dust.
4. Brush on a minimally pigmented finish, such as Minwax Polyshades. Brush out in long strokes with the grain. Let it cure overnight.
5. Sand very lightly with 320-grit or finer stearated sandpaper to remove dust nibs. Be careful not to sand through the color.
6. Repeat Steps 4 and 5 if you want the color darker. Remove the sanding dust.
7. Brush on a coat of satin polyurethane either full strength or thinned with up to 10 percent mineral spirits. Thinning will improve flow-out and reduce the likelihood of bubbles curing in the film. Let it cure overnight.
8. Apply additional coats if you want, sanding lightly between each coat.

OAK WITH SATIN LACQUER

This finish emphasizes the figure and natural color of oak while producing an even sheen across earlywood and latewood (Photo 17-6 on page 266).

1. Sand to 180 or 220 grit and remove the sanding dust.
2. Spray on a coat of satin lacquer (see "Using Spray Guns" on page 45), thinned 1 part lacquer to 1 part lacquer thinner. (You can also use lacquer sanding sealer or shellac.) Let it cure overnight.
3. Sand lightly with 280-grit or finer stearated sandpaper to remove dust nibs and any roughness caused by raised grain. Remove the sanding dust.
4. Spray on a second coat of satin lacquer. Thin it according to manufacturer's instructions or until it sprays and flows out well. Let it cure for several hours.
5. Sand lightly with 320-grit or finer stearated sandpaper if you need to remove dust nibs. Otherwise, sanding is not necessary.
6. Apply additional coats if you want.

OAK WITH WALNUT OIL/VARNISH

You can achieve a fairly even coloring in oak, despite its unevenly sized pores, by using an asphaltum-based stain that is combined with the finish (Photo 17-7 on page 266).

1. Sand to 220 grit and remove the sanding dust.
2. Wipe or brush on a wet coat of walnut-colored oil/varnish blend. (I like to use either Watco or Deft black walnut Danish oil.) Let the finish remain wet on the surface for at least five minutes. Apply more finish to any spots that lose their wetness.
3. Wipe off all the excess finish before it becomes tacky. (Hang rags to dry out before throwing them away.) Let it cure overnight.
4. Apply a second coat of oil/varnish blend and sand lightly with 600-grit wet/dry sandpaper while the surface is wet with finish. Sand until it feels smooth to the touch.
5. Repeat Step 3.
6. Apply a third coat if the surface doesn't have an even sheen. Sand lightly as in Step 4 if the surface still feels rough. Wipe off the excess finish.

OAK

Oak is almost as difficult to finish as pine. Like pine, oak varies greatly in density between earlywood and latewood. In contrast to pine, however, the earlywood pores of both red oak and white oak are very large—large enough to see with your naked eye. These pores give plain-sawn oak, the most commonly used type, its coarse appearance.

When you sand plain-sawn oak by hand without using a flat block to back the sandpaper, you cut away more of the porous earlywood than the dense latewood. You may not notice this while you're sanding. But when you apply a finish, you will see pronounced depressions in all the earlywood areas.

When you stain oak with a common pigment stain, the pigment lodges heavily in the large pores of the earlywood but penetrates hardly at all into the dense latewood areas. The large-pored areas are thus highlighted in a way that accentuates the coarseness of the wood. This is especially the case with plain-sawn oak (Photo 5-2 on page 88). I don't find this effect attractive.

When you apply a thick finish to oak without first filling the large pores level with the surrounding surface, you get a rounding over into the pores that makes the wood look like plastic (Photo 13-3 on page 200). Before the age of plastic this look may have been attractive. But I don't think it is now.

On the other hand, the deep pores of oak offer certain advantages for decoration not found in most other woods. Colored paste-wood filler or glaze can be used to make the pores a different color than the surrounding dense wood to add decorative effects. (See "Filling the Pores with Paste-Wood Filler" on page 122 and "Glazing" on page 110.) Any color combination can be used.

Three very popular furniture styles feature oak: Old English (which is very dark), Turn-of-the-Century (an even brown), and Modern (natural, unstained). These styles have one important characteristic in common: The earlywood/latewood contrast in the wood is de-emphasized.

Old English furniture, particularly that of the Tudor period, employed English brown oak (a darker variety of oak than American red or white oak), which became darker over the centuries as the soot from open wood fireplaces and coal-burning stoves penetrated the commonly used wax finish.

Turn-of-the-Century (also called Craftsman or Mission) oak furniture was commonly made with quarter-sawn oak; that is, oak sawn radially, with the growth rings perpendicular to the face of the boards (Figure 17-1). Quarter-sawn oak has much more evenly spaced pores than plain-sawn oak and a distinctive grain configuration called *ray fleck* (Photo 17-8 on page 262). *Rays* are hardwood cells that extend radially in a tree stem; in quarter-sawn oak they appear as elongated, dense, light-colored flecks. At the turn of the century, the oak was colored by a process known as *fuming*. The furniture was placed in a room filled with the fumes of ammonia, which reacted with the tannic acid in the oak to darken it chemically. Fuming produces an even brown color on both earlywood and latewood but doesn't darken the rays. The lighter rays resemble tiger stripes on the oak, so fumed quarter-sawn oak is sometimes called *tiger oak*.

You can imitate the even coloring of Old English oak by using a dye stain. Dye stains penetrate everywhere in oak, so the dense latewood is colored almost as completely as the porous earlywood. Any type of dye stain will work, but a water dye won't color the pores well: They come out lighter. You can solve this problem by applying a dark pigment stain over the dye stain (after it has

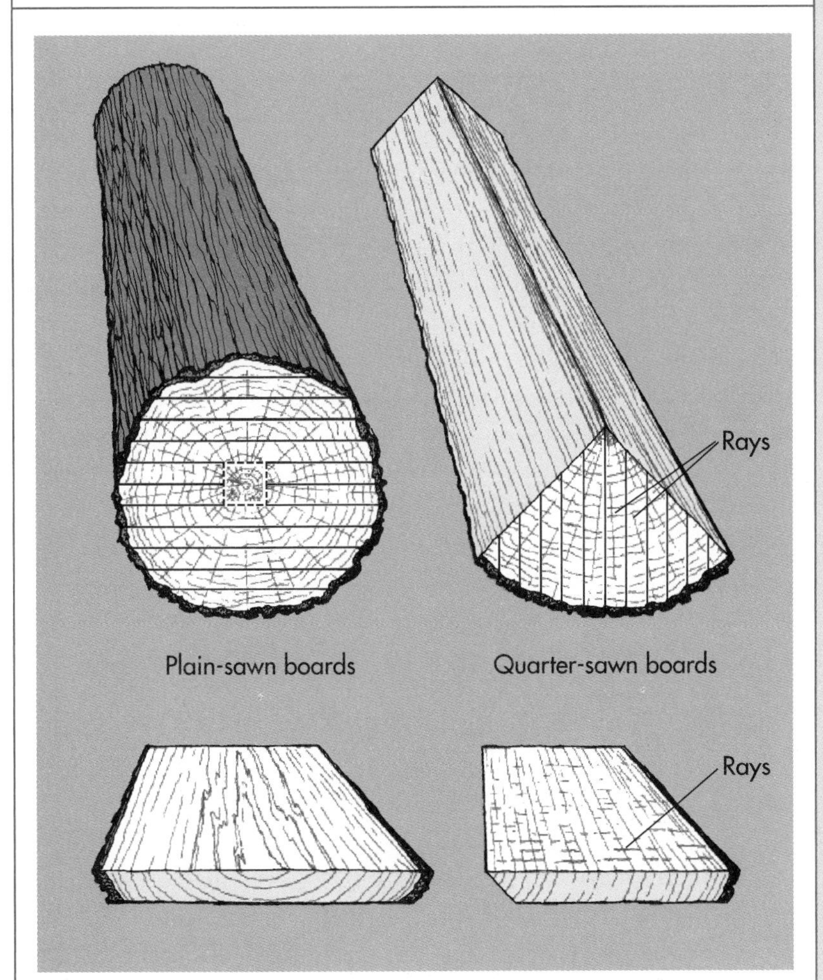

Figure 17-1: Logs can be plain-sawn or quarter-sawn. In oak, quarter-sawing reveals the wood's rays as a fleck pattern on the face of the boards.

PICKLED OAK WITH SATIN WATER BASE

A popular treatment, pickling takes advantage of oak's large pores, whitening them for decoration. Water-based finish will not yellow the white color (Photo 17-9 on page 267).

1. Sand to 180 or 220 grit. Remove the dust.
2. Wipe a water-based pickling stain over the wood. Alternatively, thin some white latex paint with up to 25 percent water, and apply it to the wood. Wipe off all or most of the excess to give you the appearance you want. Let the stain or paint cure overnight.
3. Sand lightly with 280-grit or finer sandpaper to smooth the surface. Don't sand any more than necessary to make the surface feel smooth. (If you sand through the color in places or get the color too light, carefully apply some more stain and feather it in.) Remove the sanding dust.
4. Brush or spray on a coat of satin water-based finish. Use water base over white pickling stain to avoid yellowing. Let the finish cure for at least two hours, better overnight.
5. Sand the finish lightly with 320-grit or finer stearated sandpaper if there are dust nibs or if the surface feels rough.
6. Remove the sanding dust and repeat Step 4.
7. Apply additional coats if the sheen is not even or if you want a thicker finish.

PICKLED OAK WITH SATIN LACQUER

You can stain and seal the wood first, and then apply the pickling. This way the white color will be only in the pores. A satin lacquer topcoat helps to soften the two colors (Photo 17-10 on page 267).

1. Sand to 180 or 220 grit. Remove the dust.
2. Wipe or spray on an oil- or lacquer-based stain. Wipe off all the excess before the stain dries. Let oil-based stain cure overnight. Let lacquer-based stain cure one hour.
3. Brush or spray on a coat of 1-pound-cut dewaxed, bleached shellac. You can

(continued)

PICKED OAK—continued

substitute a lacquer sanding sealer or thinned coat of lacquer if you like. Let it cure overnight.
4. Apply an oil/varnish-based white pickling stain or glaze (you can also use a white alkyd paint thinned with 25 percent mineral spirits). Remove the excess before it dries. Let it cure overnight.
5. Sand lightly with 280-grit or finer sandpaper until smooth to the touch. Leave color only in the pores. Remove the sanding dust.
6. Spray on a coat of satin lacquer. The lacquer will yellow the wood slightly. That's an advantage because it softens the stark white in the pores, blending better with the stain. Let it cure one hour.
7. Sand the surface lightly with 320-grit stearated sandpaper if you want to remove dust nibs. Remove the sanding dust.
8. Repeat Steps 6 and 7.
9. Repeat Step 6 in as dust-free an environment as possible.

OAK WITH CONTRASTING PORES AND LACQUER

A pigment stain, glaze, or colored paste-wood filler accents oak's large pores: Use any color (Photo 17-11 on page 267).

1. Sand to 180 or 220 grit. Remove the dust.
2. Wipe or spray on a water or non-grain-raising (NGR) dye stain and remove the excess before it dries. Alternatively, brush or spray on a water or NGR dye stain and let it dry. If you use a water dye, you should sponge the wood first. (See "Sponging" on page 15.) Let the dye stain dry thoroughly—overnight for water, several hours for NGR.
3. Spray on a coat of lacquer sanding sealer or lacquer, thinned 1 part lacquer to 1 part lacquer thinner. Let it cure overnight.
4. Apply a pigment stain, glaze, or colored paste-wood filler and remove all the excess. Leave color only in the pores. Let it cure overnight or longer if the weather is damp.
5. Sand lightly with 280-grit or finer sandpaper to make the surface smooth. Remove the sanding dust.
6. Spray on two or three coats of gloss or satin lacquer.

Photo 17-8: Because of oak's pronounced grain pattern, it's easy to distinguish a plain-sawn board (left) from a quarter-sawn board (right). Note the ray flecks crossing the grain in the quarter-sawn board.

dried) and wiping off the excess. The pigment will lodge in the pores, evening the color over the entire surface. Alternatively, you can use an alcohol, oil, or NGR (non-grain-raising) dye stain to avoid the problem. A convenient alternative is walnut-colored Watco or Deft Danish oil. The coloring in these oil/varnish blends is asphaltum, which penetrates much like a dye. (See "What's in Watco?" on page 85.) You will achieve an even dark-walnut color.

You can imitate fumed oak in the same way, by applying a dye stain of the proper color. But there are no ready-made oil/varnish blends that contain the proper-colored dye. So you'll have to do the coloring with separate dyes. Remember that turn-of-the-century fuming was almost always done on quarter-sawn oak. You'll never achieve the same look using plain-sawn oak.

Another way to imitate the even coloring of Old English or fumed oak is to seal the oak and then add a colorant to the finish; that is, by toning. You can use either pigment or dye for the colorant. You will find that pigment is usually more effective for imitating the look of Old English oak (you want to obscure the wood somewhat) and dye is more effective for imitating fumed oak.

Personally, I like oak best when the coarseness of the contrasting grain is de-emphasized and the pores are left sharply defined. So I usually finish oak unstained, stained with a dye, or toned with pigment or dye. And I usually use an oil/varnish blend or wiping varnish, or I keep my film-finish coats thin on the wood. I also like oak pickled with white color in the pores. This look is currently very popular for kitchen cabinets and interior trim.

(text continues on page 279)

A Gallery of Finishes

Photo 17-1: Unfinished woods, clockwise from top: pine, oak, ash, elm, chestnut, walnut, mahogany, hard maple, birch, cherry, soft maple, gum, poplar, aromatic red cedar, teak, rosewood, cocobolo, and ebony.

Photo 17-2: When you stain pine, the porous earlywood accepts much more stain than the dense latewood. This causes a pronounced color reversal in the grain pattern: Compare unstained pine (left) with stained pine (right).

Photo 17-3: A film finish, such as brushing lacquer on this table, evens out differences in sheen caused by pine's random density.

Photo 17-4: This footstool owes its even tone to a gel stain followed by a satin varnish. Liquid stains would have penetrated farther into the wood, causing splotching.

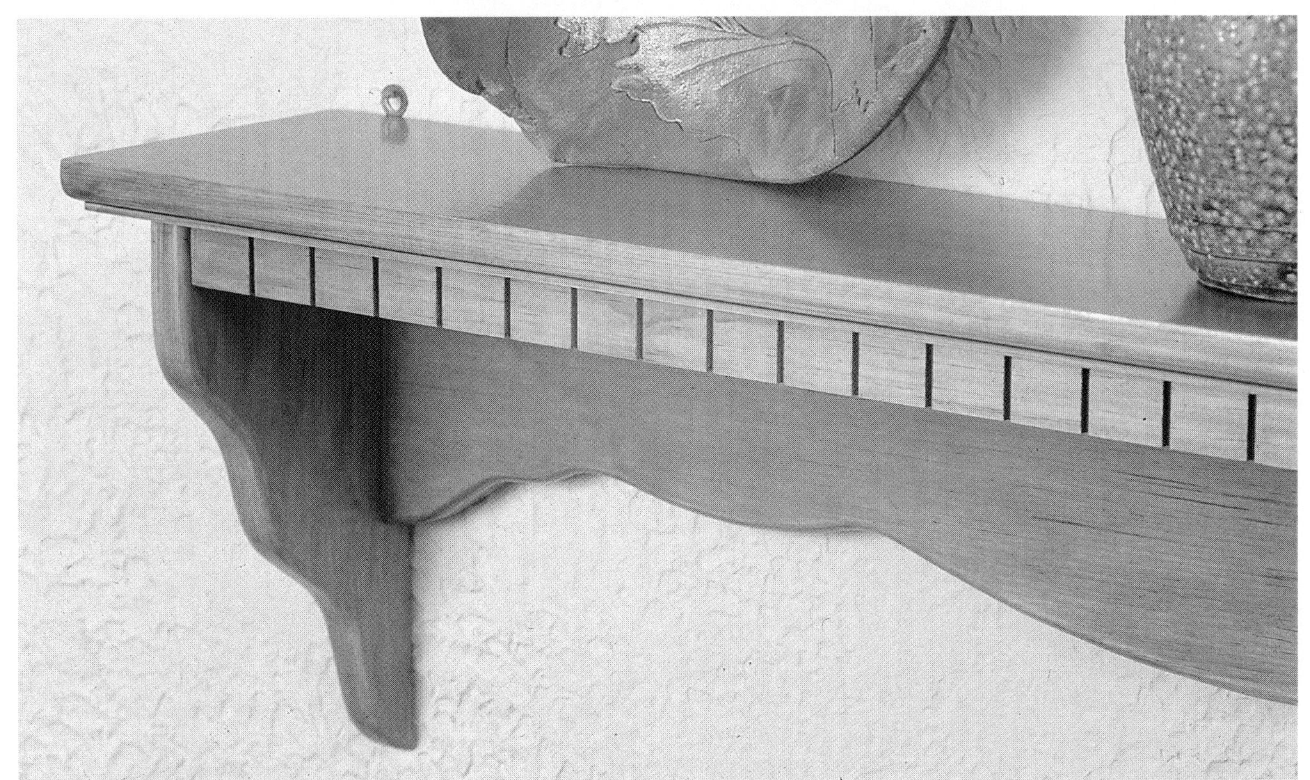

Photo 17-5: The pine in this shelf was sealed with a first coat of polyurethane. Stain was added directly to the subsequent coats of finish. This, too, eliminates blotching.

Photo 17-6: Satin lacquer emphasizes the figure and natural color of this oak table while maintaining an even sheen across the pronounced grain.

Photo 17-7: Unevenly sized pores can make it difficult to get an even finish on oak. Watco or Deft black walnut Danish oil will produce an even finish like the one shown here.

Photo 17-9: A popular treatment, pickling takes advantage of oak's large pores, whitening them for decoration. Water-based finish (left) will not yellow the white color.

Photo 17-10: This oak desk (below left) was sealed before pickling; thus the white color remains only in the pores. A satin lacquer topcoat helps to soften the two colors.

Photo 17-11: This sample oak door has been dye-stained, sealed, and then glazed to accent the pores, all in different colors.

Photo 17-12: Walnut's rich coloring is enhanced by the warmth of orange shellac (left), especially compared to the cool effect of water base (right).

Photo 17-13: Simple to apply, oil/varnish provides some protection for this walnut gavel, without building a noticeable film.

Photo 17-14: Walnut has a cool color, but orange shellac warms and enriches the walnut in this chair.

Photo 17-16: Wiping varnish is easy to apply and maintains the natural look of mahogany (left).

Photo 17-17: A lacquer finish is applied over a glaze in the mahogany molding below. The glaze accentuates the depth of the molding.

Photo 17-18: Staining, filling, and rubbing out a lacquer finish can be a lot of work, but this procedure results in a deep, mirror-like finish on this table.

Photo 17-20: Water base keeps this maple frame-and-panel door as light as possible.

Photo 17-21: Wiping varnish warms the color of the maple in this bowl and gives it a pleasing gloss.

Photo 17-22: This curly maple frame was dyed, glazed, and finished with an oil/varnish blend.

Photo 17-23: Gel stain, which doesn't penetrate and therefore doesn't splotch, is an ideal coloring for this cherry breakfront, finished with an oil/varnish blend.

Photo 17-24: Adding color to the topcoats of lacquer on this table minimized the tendency of the cherry to splotch. A rubbed-out satin finish gives it a refined sheen without producing excessive gloss.

Photo 17-25: Toning evenly colors high-contrast woods such as ash, from which this door was made. The satin lacquer finish also minimizes any contrast.

Photo 17-26: Poplar has very little character unless stained to resemble another wood—in this case walnut. Water-based polyurethane is a tough finish, well suited for high-wear applications.

Photo 17-27: This birch dresser was stained to resemble cherry. The high gloss comes from French polishing it with shellac.

Photo 17-28: Wax is a perfect finish for this bowl, because it has a minimal effect on the natural color of the rosewood.

(continued from page 262)

WALNUT

Walnut is America's supreme native furniture hardwood. It is a hard, durable wood with a beautiful figure and rich, dark coloring. It has a smooth, medium-porous texture that accepts all stains evenly, and it finishes nicely with any finish. The coloring of air-dried walnut heartwood is a warm, rust red. The coloring of kiln-dried heartwood, which is commonly steamed to reduce heartwood and sapwood color variations, has a colder charcoal gray cast. As steamed walnut ages, the gray warms to a tan with a slight reddish tint. The reddish tint in aged walnut makes it difficult to distinguish from mahogany in old furniture.

There are two finishing problems presented by walnut: the color contrast between the dark heartwood and the almost-white sapwood, and the coolness of steamed walnut.

There are four ways to overcome the color contrast between heartwood and sapwood:

- Cut off all the sapwood so you're using only heartwood.
- Arrange your boards so you use the color differences to decorative advantage.
- Bleach the wood to a uniform off-white color and then stain it back to whatever color you want. (See "Bleaching Wood" on page 80.)
- Stain the sapwood to the color of the heartwood with a dye stain, and then stain the whole to the color you want.

Woodworkers making one-of-a-kind furniture usually choose one of the first two methods: They cut away the sapwood or they use it decoratively. Bleaching walnut was common in factories when blonde furniture was popular in the 1950s. Today furniture factories use stains to blend sapwood and heartwood.

You can warm the tone of walnut by staining it or by putting color in the finish. You can use any type of stain, though a gel stain will not bring out the full richness of the figure. Most finishes contain a natural amber tint that warms the wood a little. Orange shellac contains the most color, and it is often used on walnut for this reason, though it's not a durable finish for tabletops. Water-based finishes are totally devoid of color, so there is more reason to use a stain under water base than under any other finish.

Personally, I like just about any finish on walnut. I've used oil/varnish blend, wiping varnish, and film finishes. For objects other than tabletops, my favorite finish is orange shellac because of the warmth it adds to walnut (Photo 17-12 on page 268). When using other finishes, I often add warmth by staining the wood (a dark rust, commonly sold as American walnut) or adding dye to the finish (again, dark rust) and toning the wood.

WALNUT WITH OIL/VARNISH

Simple to apply, oil/varnish provides some protection without building a noticeable film (Photo 17-13 on page 268).

1. Sand to 220 grit. Remove the dust.
2. Wipe on a wet coat of oil/varnish blend. If any areas lose their wetness within about five minutes, apply more finish.
3. Wipe off the excess after about five minutes.
4. Let it cure overnight.
5. Sand lightly with 280-grit or finer sandpaper to remove raised grain.
6. Remove the sanding dust.
7. Wipe on a second coat of oil/varnish blend, and wipe off the excess.
8. If the sheen is even, you can stop here. Otherwise, apply another coat or two with one day's curing time between.

WALNUT WITH ORANGE SHELLAC AND WAX

The deep amber of orange shellac warms and enriches walnut's rather cool coloring. Use this finish on furniture or accessories not subject to heavy use; a tabletop finished this way should be protected with a tablecloth or coasters (Photo 17-14 on page 269).

1. Sand to 180 or 220 grit and remove the sanding dust.
2. Brush or spray on a coat of 1-pound-cut orange shellac. (It can be either waxed or dewaxed shellac.) Let it cure at least two hours, better overnight.
3. Sand lightly with 280-grit or finer sandpaper. Remove the sanding dust.
4. Brush or spray on a coat of 2-pound-cut orange shellac. Let it cure at least two hours.
5. Rub with #00 or #000 steel wool in the direction of the grain. (If there are a lot of dust nibs, sand first with 320-grit or finer sandpaper.) Remove the dust.
6. Brush or spray on a coat of 2-pound-cut orange shellac. Let it cure overnight.
7. Rub with #00 or #000 steel wool. Remove the dust.
8. Apply a coat of paste wax and remove the excess when it loses its shine. Leave overnight and wax again.

MAHOGANY

The mahogany available in the eighteenth and early nineteenth centuries was considered at the time to be the premier furniture hardwood. This mahogany was very dense and rich reddish brown in color. It was generally known as Cuban or Santo Domingan mahogany, because it came from those islands.

Cuban and Santo Domingan mahogany was generally left unstained and unfilled. The natural color was so rich it didn't need stain, and the wood was so dense (its pores are smaller than those of walnut) it had a pleasing appearance without being filled. Because of the great widths available, new styles of tabletops were developed—most notably, large pie-crust tables.

Unfortunately, this mahogany is no longer available. The best mahogany available today is Honduras mahogany. Though Honduras mahogany is the same botanical species as Cuban and Santo Domingan mahogany, it is softer, is less rich in color, and has larger pores as a result of different soil and growing conditions. Still, Honduras mahogany is a fine furniture wood.

Honduras mahogany grows in Honduras and other countries in Central America and northern South America. Right after being milled, it is pink in color. It darkens in air and light to a rich coppery red. Honduras mahogany is very stable and works easily, though when the grain is wavy, it can be difficult to hand plane.

Other mahoganies available are African mahogany and Philippine mahogany. Though neither of these woods is a true mahogany in a botanical sense, both resemble Honduras mahogany and are commonly sold as mahogany.

African mahogany is coarser, less stable, and weaker than Honduras mahogany. It has an interlocking grain that makes it more difficult to work with machine and handtools. African mahogany is usually cut into quarter sections before being milled. Quarter-sawing reveals a distinct ribbon-stripe pattern which is sometimes very pronounced (Photo 17-15). When the ribbon-stripe is pronounced, the wood is usually sliced into veneer. African mahogany is also pink to red in color and darkens with age.

Philippine mahogany, which is more commonly called lauan (pronounced *LOO-AHN*), is coarser and weaker than either Honduras or African mahogany. Its pores are much larger, making it a more difficult wood to finish nicely. Hollow-core doors used in house construction are commonly veneered with lauan. Though lauan also darkens with age and can be made to look fairly elegant by filling the pores, it is not a quality furniture wood like Honduras and African mahogany.

The high-quality mahogany available in the eighteenth and early nineteenth centuries was usually left unstained and unfilled. When mahogany came back in style in the late nineteenth cen-

MAHOGANY WITH WIPING VARNISH

This is an easy finish that maintains mahogany's natural look. Because it's a thin film, it won't round-over the pores (Photo 17-16 on page 270).

1. Sand to 180 or 220 grit and remove the sanding dust.
2. Wipe or brush on a coat of wiping varnish. Wipe off all or most of the excess if it is uneven. Let it cure overnight.
3. Sand lightly with 280-grit or finer sandpaper until the surface feels smooth. Remove the sanding dust.
4. Repeat Steps 2 and 3.
5. Repeat Step 2 in as dust-free an environment as possible.
6. If the sheen is more glossy than you want, lower it by rubbing lightly with #0000 steel wool.

STAINED AND GLAZED MAHOGANY WITH LACQUER

Glazing can be used to accentuate depth and emphasize the sculptural quality of molded, carved, or turned pieces by darkening the hollows and crevices (Photo 17-17 on page 270).

1. Sand to 180 or 220 grit and remove the sanding dust.
2. Wipe or spray on a lacquer-based pigment stain, and wipe off the excess while it is still wet. Let it dry for one hour.
3. Spray on a coat of lacquer sanding sealer, thinned 1 part sanding sealer to 1 part lacquer thinner. Let it cure overnight.
4. Sand lightly with 280-grit or finer sandpaper to remove raised grain.
5. Wipe, brush, or spray on a coat of oil/varnish-based glaze, and wipe off the excess from all high places when it loses its shine. Leave the glaze in recesses. Let it cure for several days, longer if the weather is damp or cool.
6. Spray on three coats of satin lacquer, thinned 1 part lacquer to 1 part lacquer thinner. Let each coat cure for at least several hours. Let it cure overnight.
7. Rub lightly with #0000 steel wool if you want to soften the sheen a little.

Photo 17-15: Figure in mahogany varies from plain (left) to ribbon stripe (right), which is the result of quarter-sawing.

tury, and again in the 1940s with Duncan Phyfe reproductions, only the poorer-quality Honduras and African varieties were available. Furniture made of these mahoganies was almost always stained with dye stain, and the pores were almost always filled.

Both Honduras and African mahogany take all types of stain evenly. Before deciding to stain mahogany, however, remember that the wood will darken considerably within a couple of years. If you stain the wood to the color you want, you may find that it soon becomes darker than you want. Consequently, you might decide to stain the wood not quite as dark and let it darken naturally to the color you want.

Woodworkers today often finish mahogany without any stain or filling. They usually apply an oil/varnish blend or a wiping varnish. The wood darkens in time to a beautiful dark red, and both finishes can be kept thin enough so the pores don't take on a rounded-over, plastic appearance.

Personally, I like mahogany better with a rich brown dye stain, not too red (there being enough red in the wood already), the pores filled (at least on tabletops), and a lacquer finish rubbed to an even semi-gloss. This finish makes the lesser-quality Honduras or African mahogany resemble Cuban and Santo Domingan mahogany.

STAINED AND FILLED MAHOGANY WITH RUBBED LACQUER

This finish involves some extra effort, but the result is elegant: a mirror sheen with great depth (Photo 17-18 on page 271).

1. Sand to 180 or 220 grit and remove the sanding dust.
2. Brush or spray on a coat of non-grain-raising (NGR) stain. Let it dry at least four hours.
3. Brush or spray on a coat of 1-pound-cut shellac, or spray on a coat of lacquer sanding sealer, thinned 1 part sanding sealer to 1 part lacquer thinner. Let it cure overnight.
4. Brush on a coat of oil/varnish-based paste-wood filler. Push the filler into the grain of the wood with a cloth, a plastic spreader, or a wide putty knife.
5. Remove the excess paste-wood filler when it loses its shine by wiping across the grain with clean burlap. Then wipe lightly in the direction of the grain with a soft cloth to align any streaks with the grain. Let the filler cure for several days, longer if the weather is humid or cool.
6. Sand lightly with 280-grit or finer sandpaper until the surface feels smooth. Remove the sanding dust.
7. Repeat Step 3.
8. Sand lightly with 280-grit or finer sandpaper to make the surface smooth.
9. Spray on five to ten coats of gloss or satin lacquer, thinned 1 part lacquer to 1 part lacquer thinner, or according to manufacturer's instructions. Spray no more than three coats a day. Let it cure for two weeks to a month.
10. Sand the surface with 600-grit wet/dry sandpaper and mineral spirits lubricant until you remove all the orange peel (the sheen should be perfectly even when the surface is dry). If the surface is flat, back your sandpaper with a flat cork-, felt-, or rubber-backed block.
11. Rub the surface in long straight strokes with the grain using #0000 steel wool and soap-and-water lubricant. Be careful not to cut through the finish on the edges.
12. Wash off the soap with clean water and a soft cloth, wiping with the grain.

MAPLE WITH WATER BASE

When you want maple to remain as light as possible, use a water-based finish (Photo 17-20 on page 272).

1. Sand to 180 grit and remove the sanding dust.
2. Sponge the wood to reduce grain raising. (See "Sponging" on page 15.) Let the wood dry, and sand lightly. Remove the dust.
3. Brush or spray a coat of satin water-based finish. Let it cure overnight.
4. Sand lightly with 320-grit or finer stearated sandpaper to remove dust nibs and any roughness caused by remaining raised grain. Remove the sanding dust.
5. Brush or spray a second coat of satin water base. Let it cure for at least two hours.
6. Sand lightly with 320-grit or finer stearated sandpaper if you need to remove dust nibs.
7. Brush or spray a third coat in as dust-free an environment as possible.

MAPLE WITH WIPING VARNISH

For decorative objects made of maple, wiping varnish gives a pleasing gloss and warms the color of the wood (Photo 17-21 on page 272).

1. Sand to 180 or 220 grit and remove the sanding dust.
2. Wipe on a thin coat of wiping varnish. Let it cure overnight.
3. Sand lightly with 320-grit or finer stearated sandpaper to remove dust nibs and any roughness caused by raised grain. If sandpaper doesn't conform well to the shape, use #000 or #0000 steel wool. Remove the sanding dust.
4. Wipe on a second thin coat of wiping varnish. Let it cure overnight.
5. If the second coat will not be your last coat, buff now with #000 or #0000 steel wool or with 320-grit sandpaper.
6. Wipe on additional coats if the sheen is not even or if you want to build a thicker finish. Between coats, rub with steel wool or sand lightly with 320-grit sandpaper.
7. If the final coat is glossier than you want, wait at least several days for the finish to cure hard. Then rub lightly with the grain using #0000 steel wool.

HARD MAPLE

Maple is an excellent wood for woodworking. It is strong and wear-resistant, and it works well. It makes very good flooring because it wears slowly, smoothly, and evenly without splintering. It is also the best wood for cutting boards because it is dense, fine-grained, and free of any odor or taste that might be imparted to food. Hard maple comes from the sugar maple tree, the same tree that produces the sap that is made into maple syrup. Unusual growth patterns in sugar maple result in the distinctive and attractive figures of *curly* and *bird's-eye* maple (Photo 17-19). Maple with a tightly curled figure is called *fiddleback* maple because it is often used for the backs of violins.

Maple is more difficult than most woods to finish. The problem is that most maple is uninteresting without stain. The exceptions are curly and bird's-eye maple, though these grain variations are also greatly enhanced with stain. To successfully stain maple, you must use a dye stain. Many woodworkers and finishers have been unhappy using pigment stains on maple.

The reason for the problem is the density of the wood. The pores in maple are not large enough to accept much pigment. So pigment stains don't have much effect, unless you build the pigment on top, which obscures the wood. This goes for curly and bird's-eye maple, as well. Though pigment stain highlights the curls and bird's eyes, it doesn't do so nearly as effectively as dye stain (Photo 5-3 on page 88). With dye stain you can make maple any color you want and as dark as you want, without obscuring its figure. You can even make the wood black. (See "Ebonizing Wood" on page 83.)

When maple was used in the eighteenth and early nineteenth centuries, it was generally left unstained. As the wood aged, it took on a warm yellow-orange coloring and the figure mellowed. This is the look you see today in old maple furniture. You can imitate the coloring with a yellow-orange dye. But maple has a tendency to splotch when stained, and dye stain accentuates the figure. So, if you want to imitate the look of old maple, you will have the greatest success if you tone it using pigment, dye, or a combination of the two in the finish. This is what factories did on the maple furniture that was popular in the 1950s.

More recently, hand-made maple furniture has been left unstained, largely, I believe, because woodworkers haven't understood the results that could be achieved with dye. But unstained maple does have its own appeal.

I believe maple has much more character with a dye stain. I also like maple better with a film finish, though I don't object to maple finished with an oil/varnish blend. Film finishes bring out more of the wood's character because the thickness adds depth.

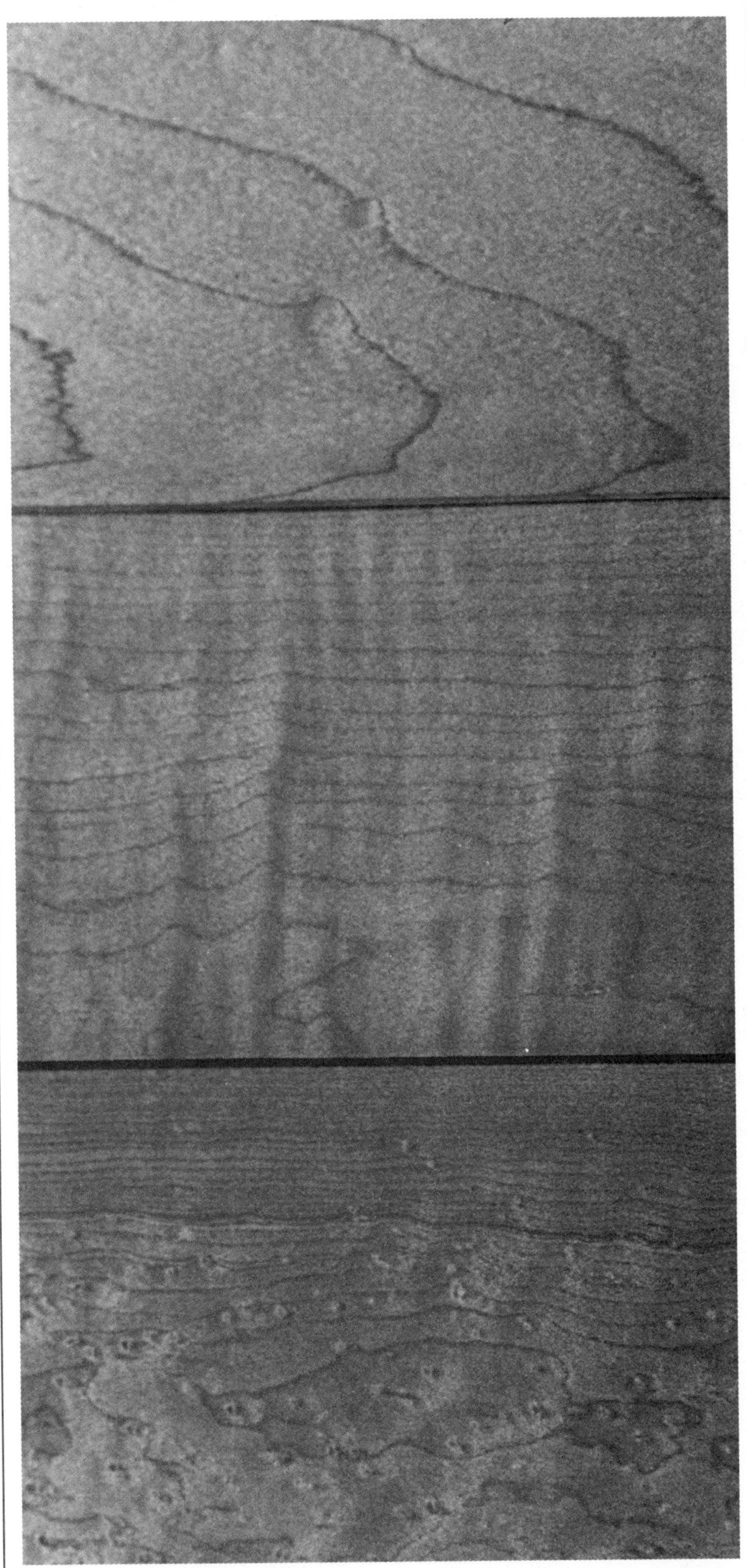

Photo 17-19: Maple can display very plain figure (top) or more graphic patterns, as in the curly-figured board (center) or the bird's-eye (bottom).

DYED AND GLAZED MAPLE WITH OIL/VARNISH

Dyeing and glazing bring out the beauty of curly and bird's-eye maple. They can also make the wood look aged (Photo 17-22 on page 273).

1. Sand to 180 or 220 grit and remove the sanding dust.
2. Sponge the wood. (See "Sponging" on page 15.) Let the wood dry, and sand lightly. Remove the dust.
3. Wipe on a coat of dye stain. (The color I like to use to make maple look old is Lockwood Early American Honey Amber Maple. I mix 1 ounce stain with 1 quart distilled water.) Wipe off the excess before it dries. Let it dry overnight.
4. Sand lightly with used 400-grit stearated sandpaper to remove any additional raised grain without cutting through the color. Remove the dust.
5. Wipe or brush on a coat of oil/varnish blend. Let the finish remain wet on the surface for at least five minutes. Apply more finish to any spots that lose their wetness.
6. Wipe off all the excess finish before it becomes tacky. (Hang rags to dry before throwing them away.) Let the finish cure overnight.
7. Sand very lightly with used 400-grit sandpaper if you need to remove any additional raised grain. Remove the sanding dust.
8. Apply a brown varnish-based stain or glaze and wipe it off, leaving enough excess to give the look you want. If there are grooves and recesses, leaving colorant in them will add the appearance of depth and age. Let it dry overnight.
9. Wipe or brush on a coat of oil/varnish blend, and wipe off the excess before it becomes tacky. Let it cure overnight.
10. Repeat Step 9.

GEL-STAINED CHERRY WITH OIL/VARNISH

Gel stain is an ideal coloring for cherry: Because it doesn't penetrate, the wood doesn't splotch (Photo 17-23 on page 274).

1. Sand to 180 or 220 grit and remove the sanding dust.
2. Wipe on a gel stain and remove the excess before it dries. Let it cure overnight.
3. Wipe, brush, or spray on a coat of oil/varnish blend. Let the finish remain wet on the surface for at least five minutes. Apply more finish to any spots that lose their wetness.
4. Wipe off all the excess finish before it becomes tacky. (Hang rags to dry out before throwing them away.) Let it cure overnight.
5. Sand the surface lightly with 400-grit or finer sandpaper to remove any raised grain. Remove the sanding dust.
6. Apply a second coat of oil/varnish blend, and remove the excess before it becomes tacky. Allow it to cure overnight.
7. Apply additional coats if the sheen is not even, allowing each coat to cure overnight.

TONED CHERRY WITH RUBBED LACQUER

Toning (adding color to the topcoats of your finish) is another way to handle cherry's tendency to splotch. Rubbing a satin-lacquer finish gives it a more refined appearance without producing excessive gloss (Photo 17-24 on page 275).

1. Sand to 180 or 220 grit and remove the sanding dust.
2. Spray on several light coats of NGR (non-grain-raising) dye stain. (I like to use cherry, which is reddish, with the addition of a little yellow and black.) Light coats of sprayed stain won't penetrate enough to cause splotches. Let it dry for several hours.
3. Spray on a coat of lacquer sanding sealer, thinned 1 part sanding sealer to 1 part lacquer thinner. Let it cure overnight.
4. Sand with 280-grit or finer sandpaper until smooth. Remove the dust.

(continued)

CHERRY

Cherry has been a popular furniture wood since the eighteenth century. It was often used as a native American substitute for imported mahogany. Cherry was sometimes stained to accelerate the darkening process, but it was usually left unstained to darken naturally. In the 1950s cherry became very popular in mass-produced furniture. Factories usually toned the cherry rather than stain it.

In recent years cherry has become one of the most popular woods used by woodworkers making one-of-a-kind furniture. It's popularity is so great that it is now among the most expensive domestic hardwoods. Cherry is popular for several reasons. Most important is its association with the warm, rust-red color found on older cherry furniture. Also, cherry is an easy wood to work. It has a pleasant scent when being machined, especially when contrasted with the smell of most other woods. And it has a familiar name which is associated with a tasty fruit (even though the cherry trees that produce the wood don't produce that fruit).

In spite of its popularity, cherry is a difficult wood to finish. Freshly milled cherry doesn't have the warm, even, rust-red coloring of old cherry. New cherry is usually pink to light reddish in color. But the color often has a slight grayish cast. Different boards vary in color, and the color often varies significantly even in the same board. In addition, the figure is far more pronounced in newly cut cherry than in old cherry. Since the look of old cherry takes many years to develop naturally, many woodworkers try to imitate it immediately by using stain.

The problem with this is that cherry doesn't stain well. It often splotches because of swirly grain. In this way cherry resembles pine and birch. In addition, even if you do achieve an even, rust-red color with stain, the effect will be only temporary. As the cherry goes through its natural darkening process, the stained color may become too dark. Therefore, it's usually best to choose your boards very carefully so they match well and contain little or no sapwood. Then, either use no stain at all, or use a stain that brings the color only part way to what will occur naturally over time. If the particular wood you're staining has a tendency to splotch, use a stain that doesn't penetrate.

If this solution is unacceptable to you, an alternative is to use maple, and dye-stain it to the color of aged cherry. Maple doesn't darken significantly, so the aged-cherry look will be both immediate and fairly permanent. The figure in maple is so close to that of cherry that it is often difficult to tell the two apart if color is not a factor.

Two good ways of coloring cherry are to stain it using a gel stain and to tone it by spraying on a lightly colored finish. Both of these methods reduce the possibility of splotching and even the contrast in figure, in addition to making the cherry darker.

Gel stain has a good track record as a stain for cherry. Gel stains were included with the cherry furniture kits sold by Bartley's, the popular mail-order company. Bartley's chose gel stain because it was easy to use, and they wanted the buyer to enjoy the finishing as much as gluing the furniture together. By chance, Bartley's had provided the perfect stain for cherry, and the company had success selling these kits because their customers got great results.

Toning requires that you have access to spray equipment, but applying a toner gives you great control over the coloring process. Use a dye toner when your primary goal is to make the wood darker without obscuring the figure. Use a pigment toner when your primary goal is to even the contrast in the figure. I find that it's usually best to use a combination of dye and pigment. But boards vary, so make your decisions as you proceed.

You will sometimes encounter the suggestion to use lye to make cherry look old. Lye darkens woods, such as cherry, oak, mahogany, and walnut, that contain tannic acid. It is sometimes possible to approximate the look of old cherry quite closely using lye. There are several problems, however, in addition to the obvious one that the cherry will darken on its own and may become too dark after several years.

Lye is very caustic and therefore dangerous to use. Be sure to protect your skin and your eyes if you do use it. Lye doesn't stop working on the wood just because the water has dried out of it. Consequently, you have to neutralize the lye with an acid or it will destroy the finish you apply. The best way to neutralize lye is with a 50/50 mixture of vinegar and water. Wash the wood liberally with this mixture. Then wash it with water alone.

Using any chemical to color wood is somewhat unpredictable. Using lye is no exception. In the case of lye, the color may come out uneven because different parts of the wood contain different amounts of tannic acid. In addition, if you get the color too dark, you can't lighten it easily as you can with stains. You can only bleach out all the color, including the natural color of the wood, using hydrogen peroxide. You can't remove just the lye.

Because of these problems, I don't recommend lye as a stain for cherry. I prefer to use gel stain or a toner. I also prefer a film finish on cherry rather than an oil/varnish blend, because a film finish provides more depth and richness. But many woodworkers like to use an oil/varnish blend, and I don't find the results this produces objectionable.

TONED CHERRY—continued

5. Spray on several thin coats of toner composed of a dye and/or pigment in a highly thinned lacquer (1 part lacquer to 4–6 parts lacquer thinner). To get the color in this example, I used the same cherry NGR dye with the addition of a little black pigment to reduce the brightness of the color. When you have the color you want, let it cure overnight.
6. Sand very lightly with 400-grit or finer sandpaper if you need to remove dust nibs. Remove the dust.
7. Spray on 4 to 8 coats of satin lacquer. (Sand lightly between coats if you need to remove dust nibs.) Let it cure for two weeks to one month.
8. Sand with 600-grit wet/dry sandpaper, using mineral spirits as a lubricant. You can add a little mineral oil to the mineral spirits to slow evaporation if you're working on a large surface. Sand until you've removed all the orange peel. Use a backing block on your sandpaper if you're working on a flat surface.
9. Clean off the surface using a soft cloth dampened with naphtha.
10. Repeat Steps 8 and 9, progressively using 1000-grit, 1200-grit, and 1500-grit wet/dry sandpaper. Sand with the grain when using 1500-grit sandpaper.
11. Using a rubbing pad (see "Rubbing Pads" on page 40) and a fine rubbing compound, rub the surface in the direction of the grain until the sheen is an even semi-gloss. (On this tabletop I used Meguiar's #1, available at auto-body supply stores, but I rubbed by hand rather then with a power buffer.)
12. Clean off all compound residue using naphtha or water and a soft cloth. Use an old toothbrush to brush compound out of crevices.
13. Apply furniture polish or paste wax to reduce scratching.

TONED ASH WITH SATIN LACQUER

This is an effective way to evenly color any uneven-grained wood or to mute the contrast created by stain. Satin lacquer further quiets the effect (Photo 17-25 on page 276).

1. Sand to 180 or 220 grit. Remove the dust.
2. Wipe or spray on a coat of lacquer-based pigment stain. Wipe off the excess before it dries. Let it cure for one hour.
3. Spray on a coat of lacquer sanding sealer, thinned 1 part sanding sealer to 1 part lacquer thinner. Let it cure for two hours, better overnight.
4. Sand with 280-grit or finer sandpaper until smooth. Remove the sanding dust.
5. Spray on a toner made of thinned lacquer and pigment. (You can combine a lacquer-based stain with lacquer, thinned 1 part lacquer to 4–6 parts lacquer thinner.) Tone the wood until you get the color you want.
6. Spray on two or three coats of satin lacquer. Sand lightly between coats with 320-grit or finer stearated sandpaper if you need to remove dust nibs or other flaws.

DYED POPLAR WITH WATER BASE

Poplar has very little character unless stained to resemble another wood, often walnut. Water-based polyurethane is a tough finish, well suited for high-wear applications (Photo 17-26 on page 277).

1. Sand to 180 or 220 grit. Remove the dust.
2. Brush on a walnut-colored oil-soluble dye stain in long strokes with the grain. You can substitute Watco or Deft black walnut Danish oil, in which case, wipe off all the excess stain and let it cure for a week before applying the water base. (Don't use a water-based or NGR dye stain under water base if you're brushing; the finish will redissolve the dye and your brush will smear the color.)
3. Brush on a coat of satin, water-based polyurethane. Let it cure at least two hours, better overnight.
4. Sand lightly with 320-grit or finer stearated sandpaper if you need to remove dust nibs or other flaws. Remove the dust.
5. Repeat Steps 3 and 4.
6. Brush on a final coat in as dust-free an environment as possible.

ASH, ELM, AND CHESTNUT

The grain structure of ash, elm, and chestnut is very similar to that of oak. Furniture manufacturers have often substituted these woods for oak or mixed these woods with oak. After staining, it takes a trained eye to identify which is which.

When you stain ash, elm, or chestnut with a pigment stain, the same problem occurs as with oak: The natural coarseness of the wood is made even more pronounced. But the problem is not as severe as with oak, because the latewood growth of these woods is not as dense. The latewood of ash, elm, and chestnut absorbs more pigment than the latewood of oak, so the overall coloring is more even. Nevertheless, the techniques for minimizing the coarse look of oak work well with ash, elm, and chestnut.

I like ash, elm, and chestnut finished in the same ways I suggest for oak: no stain, a dye stain, toned with pigment, or pickled; then a thin finish to leave the pores sharply defined.

SOFT MAPLE, GUM, AND POPLAR

Soft maple, gum, and poplar are relatively inexpensive hardwoods and are often used by factories for structural parts of tables, chests, and chairs that have a nicer veneer on the top or chair splat. The woods are usually dye-stained (when visible) to resemble the better-quality wood, and many people don't realize the difference.

There are two problems with finishing soft maple, gum, and poplar: their plain figure and their softness. The plain figure is usually uninteresting unless it is stained. You can use pigment or dye, but you'll be able to get much darker colors with dye. The softness usually requires that you apply a film finish rather than an oil/varnish blend to give the woods enough sheen to look nice.

I like these woods finished with a film finish. I use either pigment or dye, depending on how dark I want the wood to get.

AROMATIC RED CEDAR

Aromatic red cedar is commonly used in cedar chests because its odor repels moths. On the inside of a chest it's seldom, if ever, stained since it has beautiful natural color, and staining and finishing would seal in the odor that makes the wood effective. When it's on the outside of a chest, it's usually finished but not stained.

Problems occur when you finish any part of the inside of a cedar chest, whether the wood is cedar or not. The cedar's odor-producing solvents build up enough inside the chest to soften most finishes, causing them to become sticky. To avoid the problem, leave all inside parts unfinished.

I think aromatic red cedar on the outside of a piece of furniture looks best when it's unstained and finished with a film finish.

BIRCH

Birch looks similar to maple and is sometimes mistaken for maple. Birch has the same characteristic of high density, so it is also difficult to stain with pigment stain. But birch usually has a more swirly grain, so it splotches more than maple. If the splotching is more than you can tolerate, build the color on top, using a toner, instead of trying to put it in the wood. If you use a dye in your finish, you'll get an even color without obscuring the wood.

Birch, along with maple, was often dye-stained red and used to imitate mahogany in furniture made at the turn of the twentieth century. I like to finish birch the same way I finish maple. If splotchiness will be a problem, I use maple instead.

OILY WOODS

Many woodworkers like to use colorful exotic hardwoods such as teak, rosewood, cocobolo, and ebony for decorative purposes, sometimes as accents to other woods, but also for whole pieces of furniture. It's rare that these hardwoods are stained; their natural beauty is the reason these expensive woods are used in the first place. But they are almost always finished, and the oil they naturally contain can cause problems.

The most common problem is that the finish sometimes takes a long time to cure. This can occur when you use oil, oil/varnish blend, or varnish. All of these finishes cure by absorbing oxygen, and the oil in these woods retards the absorption of oxygen.

The other problem occurs with lacquer, conversion finishes, and water base. The oil prevents these finishes from establishing a good bond with the wood.

You can prevent both problems by wiping the surface of the wood with a cloth dampened with a fast-evaporating solvent, such as naphtha or lacquer thinner. This cleans the oil off the wood surface. Apply the finish quickly after the solvent evaporates, so the oil doesn't have time to bleed back to the surface.

On objects made entirely from exotic woods, I use an oil/varnish blend or wiping varnish when I want the pores sharply defined. I build a thicker film finish when I want more protection. I sometimes use only wax when the object is decorative and won't be handled much. On objects where exotic woods are used as trim or decorative accent, I use whatever finish is appropriate for the object as a whole.

DYED BIRCH WITH FRENCH POLISH

You can make birch resemble mahogany or cherry by applying a dye stain. Shellac and French polish create a deep mirror-gloss finish (Photo 17-27 on page 278).

1. Sand to 180 or 220 grit. Remove the dust.
2. Sponge the wood. (See "Sponging" on page 15.) Let the wood dry, and sand lightly. Remove the dust.
3. Wipe on a coat of water-based dye stain, and wipe off the excess before it dries. Let it dry overnight.
4. Sand very lightly with used 400-grit sandpaper if the surface is rough to the touch. Be careful not to cut through the stain.
5. Remove the sanding dust.
6. Brush on a coat of 1-pound-cut shellac. You can use orange or clear, waxed or dewaxed. Let it cure overnight.
7. Sand lightly with 280-grit or finer sandpaper to remove raised grain and dust nibs. Remove the sanding dust.
8. Brush on a coat of 2-pound-cut shellac.
9. Sand lightly with 320-grit stearated sandpaper to remove dust nibs and most of the brush marks. Remove the sanding dust.
10. Repeat Steps 8 and 9.
11. French polish the surface, covering all parts three or four times, or until the surface has an even gloss. (See "French Polishing" on page 155.) Let it cure overnight.
12. Remove the oil by wiping with a naphtha-dampened cloth.
13. Apply furniture polish or paste wax.

ROSEWOOD WITH WAX

Wax has a minimal effect on the natural color of rosewood (Photo 17-28 on page 278).

1. Sand to 220 grit or finer. Remove the dust.
2. Apply a coat of paste wax. Remove the excess when the shine disappears. Let it dry overnight.
3. Apply a second coat of paste wax. Remove the excess when the shine disappears. (On less-dense woods, apply additional coats to achieve an even satin sheen.)
4. Buff the surface by hand or machine with a lamb's-wool pad until all streaking is removed and the sheen is even.

Chapter 18

Strippers

Removing the finish brings us full circle. I've taken you through all the steps involved in putting a finish on wood. Now I'm going to tell you how to take the finish off. No subject better illustrates the book's central theme. Despite the confusion and obscurities of myth and hype, finishes and finishing are understandable. So are strippers.

The advantage you have with strippers over every other product you use in finishing is that manufacturers are required by law to list all the principal ingredients. All dangerous solvents have to be listed, and strippers are composed almost entirely of dangerous solvents. So with strippers, you can know what you're getting and choose the best stripper for the job by reading the ingredients on the container. (See "Breaking the Code—An Overview of Strippers" on page 302.)

There are only four primary solvents, or solvent groups, used in strippers, so the task of learning the names and how each works is not very difficult. The four solvents differ in effectiveness, price, and potential danger to your health. Pairs of these solvents or groups are sometimes combined, alkalis are sometimes added to increase the stripper strength, and one alkali (lye) is sometimes used alone. So you actually have more than the four primary categories of strippers to choose from. You should choose among the categories when choosing a stripper for strength, safety, or price. Within

CAUTION

Other means of stripping—sanding, scraping, and removing with a heat gun—are usually too harsh for furniture. Mechanical processes (sanding and scraping) are often effective for removing paint from exterior siding and from interior woodwork, but they can't help but remove some of the surface wood along with the paint or finish. This damages the aged character that makes old furniture valuable. Sanding also rounds over the crisp lines of carvings and turnings, and risks cutting through veneer. Heating the paint or finish hot enough to cause it to blister risks scorching the wood and dissolving the glue that holds furniture joints together and veneer on.

NOTE

Stripping lead-based paint with solvents or chemicals is not dangerous to your health. The lead remains in the stripping sludge. Sanding or scraping lead-based paint, however, is another matter. You should wear a dust mask to keep from breathing the dust you generate. (You should not strip lead-based or any other type of paint or finish around children or if you're pregnant, because of the danger of the solvents or chemicals.)

each category you should choose for ease of use and also for price. You won't notice any significant difference in solvent strength, speed of removal, or safety within each category.

STRIPPING SOLVENTS AND CHEMICALS

There are four solvents, or solvent groups, commonly used in strippers. These solvents or groups are sometimes used alone and sometimes combined with one of the other solvents. Since the names of the four solvents are long and sometimes difficult to remember, I'm including abbreviations:

- methylene chloride (MC)
- acetone, toluene, and methanol (ATM)
- N-methyl pyrrolidone (NMP)
- di-basic esters (DBE)

There are also a couple of very strong alkalis used for stripping—sodium hydroxide (lye) and ammonium hydroxide (ammonia). Lye is often used alone. Ammonia is sometimes combined with one of the solvents to increase the stripper strength. Both of these chemicals darken many common hardwoods. Lye, which is used with water, also breaks down old glue and turns wood into pulp if left in contact long enough. So you should avoid using an alkali unless you need its strength.

Methylene Chloride (MC)

Methylene chloride has been the primary active ingredient used in most paint-and-varnish removers for the past three or four decades. It's the most effective stripping solvent available to the general public as well as to commercial stripping shops. It's also non-flammable. But methylene chloride is toxic and, unfortunately, it is a suspected carcinogen. (See "Stripper Safety" on the facing page.) Exposure to methylene chloride may also trigger heart attacks in people with existing heart conditions. (Methylene chloride metabolizes into carbon monoxide in the blood stream, causing the heart to pump harder to get enough oxygen to the body. If you have a heart condition, *don't* use methylene-chloride strippers.)

You can buy methylene-chloride strippers in liquid or semi-paste consistency and in three different formula strengths. The consistency of the stripper is important if you're working on vertical surfaces—liquid will run off, semi-paste will cling. The consistency has very little to do with the strength of the stripper.

The solvents in both liquid and semi-paste strippers of all three strengths evaporate very rapidly, so paraffin wax is almost always added to retard the evaporation. The wax rises to the top of the stripper, even on vertical surfaces, and forms a skin

STRIPPER SAFETY

ALL STRIPPING SOLVENTS are bad for your health. How could it be otherwise when even paint thinner can cause dizziness and irritability? But it needs to be clearly stated anyway, because some manufacturers advertise their strippers as safe. Some even put the word "safe" in the name, enhancing the deception.

The issue of stripper safety came to the forefront in the mid-1980s, when it was discovered that methylene chloride caused cancer in a certain strain of experimental mice and caused benign tumors in rats. Despite the lack of any evidence that methylene chloride caused cancer in humans, methylene chloride was listed as a probable human carcinogen by the Environmental Protection Agency (EPA). (At the time of this writing there is still no evidence of methylene chloride causing cancer in humans.)

The mere possibility that methylene chloride was carcinogenic was enough to encourage manufacturers to look for other solvents that could remove paint and finish. ATM (acetone, toluene, and methanol) strippers already existed, but these strippers are highly flammable and quite toxic (though not carcinogenic) in their own right. Two solvents were found—N-methyl pyrrolidone (NMP) and di-basic esters (DBE). What distinguishes both these solvents is not reduced toxicity but slow evaporation rate. High concentrations of NMP and DBE vapors are extremely toxic. But evaporation is so slow it would take days for NMP or DBE to reach the same levels of concentration in the air that MC and ATM achieve in minutes. By then, normal air movement should have cleaned the air in a room many times over.

It's important that you understand this distinction so you can make sense of manufacturers' sometimes vicious claims and counterclaims. Makers of NMP and DBE strippers have to convince you that MC and ATM strippers are bad for your health. Otherwise, you wouldn't buy their strippers, because their strippers are less effective and more expensive. On the other hand, makers of MC and ATM strippers can legitimately claim (and they do) that NMP and DBE strippers are actually more toxic than MC or ATM at equal levels of vapor concentration.

All solvents, whether stripping solvents or thinning solvents, are bad for your health. The more we learn about solvents, the more we discover problems with them. (In the 1970s methylene chloride, which at the time was thought to be safe, replaced benzene in strippers after it was discovered that benzene was carcinogenic.) Expose yourself as little as possible to the fumes of all solvents by working outside or in a room with good cross ventilation. Wear a NIOSH-approved organic-vapor respirator mask, but don't rely on it alone. (Respirator masks have very short-lived effectiveness against methylene chloride fumes.) Arrange good air flow, and rely primarily on breathing fresh air. ■

NOTE

You must remove all the wax before you apply a new finish. If you don't, the new finish won't bond well, and it may wrinkle on the wood. Many instructions tell you to "neutralize" the stripper to remove the wax. This is a very misleading instruction. Wax can't be neutralized. It has to be washed off the wood using clean cloths and plenty of solvent—mineral spirits, naphtha, lacquer thinner, or alcohol. Many refinishing problems are caused by not thoroughly removing the wax before applying a new finish.

that holds the solvents in. If you disturb this wax skin, you allow the release of some of the solvents. (See "Using Strippers" on page 295.)

Some methylene-chloride strippers in each of the formula strengths are made to be water-washable by the addition of a detergent to the formula. Water washing makes the stripper and the gunk it creates easier to remove from the wood, but it introduces water, which can raise the grain, remove water-soluble dye stains, and sometimes lift veneer and loosen joints.

The strength of methylene-chloride strippers depends primarily upon the formulation; there are three classes. All three contain a small percentage of methanol (methyl or "wood" alcohol) as an "activator" to increase the effectiveness of the methylene chloride.

- Methylene chloride and methanol.
- Methylene chloride and methanol strengthened with an alkali.
- Methylene chloride and methanol thinned with acetone and toluene (actually a combination of two categories: MC and ATM).

Methylene chloride/methanol strippers are the most common. These strippers are strong enough to rapidly remove all but the most solvent-resistant paints and finishes. They are less effective on epoxy, polyester, conversion, or baked-on coatings, but they eventually work. These strippers are also non-flammable and nonpolluting. (Methylene chloride, which makes up 75 to 85 percent of the formula, is non-flammable, and it's not considered an ozone depleter or smog producer by the Environmental Protection Agency [EPA].) The primary disadvantages are potential health hazards and cost. Methylene chloride is a moderately expensive solvent, so strippers made with high percentages of methylene chloride are also moderately expensive.

Alkali-fortified methylene chloride strippers are stronger than methylene chloride strippers because of the added alkali. The alkali is usually ammonium hydroxide (ammonia), and it's usually, but not always, listed on the container. (Acids, such as oxalic acid, are sometimes used in strippers sold to professional refinish shops but never in strippers sold to the general public, because the acid is unstable in the mixture.)

Alkali-fortified strippers are available in most paint, boat, and auto-body supply stores. They are often sold as "marine" strippers. The advantage of these strippers is their increased effectiveness on exceptionally tough coatings such as epoxy, polyester, conversion, and baked-on boat and car finishes. The drawbacks are their moderately high price, the health hazards associated with methylene chloride, and their tendency to stain hardwoods such as oak, mahogany, cherry, and walnut. The staining is caused by the ammonia, which reacts with the tannic acid contained naturally in these woods. (See "Using Oxalic Acid," below.)

Methylene chloride/acetone, toluene, methanol (MC/ATM) strippers are the weakest of the three types that are based on methylene chloride. But they are strong enough to effectively strip almost all old finishes and paints. They are also the least expensive of the three MC types. The problem with adding ATM to methylene chloride is that it introduces solvents that are flammable and cause air pollution.

Sometimes methyl ethyl ketone (MEK) is substituted for the acetone, and xylene (xylol) for the toluene. These solvents, which evaporate a little more slowly than acetone and toluene, will be listed on the container.

Acetone, Toluene, and Methanol (ATM)

Acetone, toluene, and methanol are three of the basic ingredients in lacquer thinner. If you've ever put lacquer thinner on a finish, you're familiar with the damage this blend of solvents can cause. It will dissolve shellac, lacquer, and water base, and it will soften and sometimes wrinkle varnish. Manufacturers take advantage of this solvent strength to make non-methylene-chloride strippers.

USING OXALIC ACID

OXALIC ACID CAN BE USED to bleach out dark stains caused by alkalis, such as lye and ammonia, which are contained in some strippers, and rust marks caused by water and metal residue.

Dissolve some oxalic acid crystals, available at pharmacies and many paint stores, to a saturated solution in warm water. (A solution is saturated when the crystals will no longer dissolve in the water.) Brush the solution over the entire surface, not just over the stains; otherwise you may create lighter spots in these areas, and you'll have to recoat the entire surface anyway to even the color. Let the oxalic acid dry. Wash the crystals off the wood with a hose or well-soaked sponge or cloth. (Don't brush the crystals into the air, or you may breathe them.) Wash the surface well with water, and then add to clean water some borax, a small amount of household ammonia, or some other mild alkali, and wash once again to neutralize the acid.

Oxalic acid will seldom bleach the wood itself, but it should remove the stains. Sometimes a second or third application helps, but the first usually does the job. ■

CAUTION

Oxalic acid is highly toxic, capable of causing severe skin and respiratory problems. Wear gloves and goggles when using it, and don't generate airborne dust.

CAUTION

The vapors of all three solvents—acetone, toluene, and methanol—are highly flammable and toxic. Toxic fumes in concentrated amounts can impair your central nervous system, cause illness, and in extreme cases cause death. So you should take the same precautions when using ATM-based strippers and refinishers as you do with methylene chloride–based strippers. (See "Stripper Safety" on page 291.)

MYTH

Some refinishers "condition" the wood.

FACT

Wood doesn't need conditioning. The "conditioner" contained in these refinishers is mineral oil. A little mineral oil remains in the wood after the ATM solvents evaporate, making the wood appear less dry. The effect disappears when you apply a finish. The mineral oil doesn't do the wood any good. If anything, it could weaken the bond of the finish (especially water base) to the wood.

There are two types:
- strippers that contain wax to retard evaporation, and usually contain thickeners to make them into a semi-paste
- refinishers that contain neither wax nor thickeners

ATM strippers are used in the same way as the three methylene-chloride strippers. They work well on almost all old paints and finishes. ATM strippers are effective because the wax holds the solvents in contact with the coating long enough for them to penetrate. Their advantages are that they are cheap and perform well without the added health risks of methylene chloride. Their disadvantages are that they're highly flammable and air-polluting, and some brands contain an alkali that will stain many hardwoods.

ATM refinishers don't contain wax, so they evaporate very rapidly—before the solvents have time to penetrate and thoroughly soften or blister the finish. As a result, refinishers are ineffective on paints and all finishes except shellac, lacquer, and water base. Even on these finishes, refinishers are inefficient. The solvents evaporate so rapidly, you have to scrub the finish with steel wool to get it off. You can't just wipe off the finish as you can with strippers. This largely mechanical removal of the softened film is the procedure usually recommended by manufacturers.

The ineffectiveness of refinisher on old varnish (in spite of manufacturers' claims to the contrary) and on all the tough new finishes, together with the universal lack of instructions for identifying the type of finish you're stripping, is the most serious deficiency of this product. Many people become discouraged because of the great amount of effort they have to expend scratching off the finish with steel wool. In addition, considering that refinisher is simply lacquer thinner (you can use lacquer thinner, instead), many brands are unreasonably overpriced. On the other hand, because refinishers leave no wax residue on the wood to interfere with the new finish, there's no need to wash the wood with a solvent after stripping. You save a step.

N-Methyl Pyrrolidone (NMP)

N-methyl pyrrolidone is not as effective as methylene chloride for removing paints and finishes. Strippers based on NMP work at one-half to one-third the speed of strippers based on methylene chloride. NMP-based strippers are not effective on epoxy, polyester, or baked-on coatings.

NMP evaporates very slowly, so fumes don't build up in the air as quickly as with MC or ATM. As a result, NMP is less toxic to work with than MC or ATM, and it is not highly flammable. It is

(text continues on page 298)

USING STRIPPERS

STRIPPING PAINT OR FINISH requires no particular skill, but it can be messy and bad for your health, and some strippers are flammable. Here are steps for how to use all common strippers except refinisher (see "ATM refinishers" on the facing page) and lye (see "Lye" on page 299 and "Common Problems Using Strippers" on page 300):

1. Read the instructions on the container. There are variations in the ways different strippers work. In most cases, following manufacturers' directions will increase your chances of success.
2. Work outdoors in the shade or in a room where you have arranged cross ventilation. Don't work near an open flame or source of sparks if you're using a flammable stripper.
3. Remove hardware and difficult-to-get-to wood parts that can be disassembled easily. If the hardware requires stripping, soak it in a coffee can filled with stripper.
4. Wear a long-sleeved shirt, chemical-resistant gloves (butyl or neoprene), and glasses or safety goggles.
5. Shake the container of stripper. Cover it with a cloth, and open the cap slowly to allow for a gradual release of pressure. Pour the stripper into a wide-mouth jar or can.
6. Brush the stripper onto the wood using an old or inexpensive paint brush. (Some synthetic-bristle brushes will dissolve in methylene chloride–based strippers.) Brush in one direction, rather than back and forth; this helps to lay on a thick coat and reduces solvent evaporation by not disturbing the wax coating.
7. Allow the stripper time to work on the paint or finish. Test it now and then with a putty knife to see whether the film can be lifted from the wood. Add more stripper if the original has mostly evaporated. All strippers will lift many layers of paint at one time if kept wet and allowed time to penetrate.
8. Remove the dissolved, blistered, or softened film in one of the following ways, depending upon the situation:
   - Scrape the film off flat surfaces into a bucket or cardboard box with a plastic scraper or a wide, dull putty knife (Photo 18-1). The putty knife should be clean and smooth; round its corners with a file so it won't scratch the wood.
   - Soak up and wipe off dissolved film with paper towels.

Photo 18-1: Scrape dissolved or blistered paint or finish off flat surfaces with a plastic scraper or wide putty knife.

(continued)

USING STRIPPERS—continued

- Soak up dissolved or blistered film into wood shavings (from a jointer or planer), and then brush them off with a stiff-bristle brush (Photos 18-2 and 18-3).
- Break blistered or softened film loose from moldings, turnings, and carvings with #1 steel wool or synthetic steel wool (Scotch-Brite).
- Pull a coarse string or rope around the recesses of turnings to work out blistered paint or finish (Photo 18-4).
- Pick the softened paint or finish out of cracks and recesses with sharpened sticks or dowels, which won't damage the wood as sharp metal picks will.

CAUTION

It's not necessary to sand the wood after stripping unless there are problems in the wood such as scratches or gouges that you want to remove. Sanding removes the characteristics of age that make old furniture sought-after. These characteristics include natural color changes at the surface of the wood, called patina, and normal marks of wear. In most cases, the only reason you should consider sanding after stripping is to ensure that you've removed all the finish. Any remaining old finish will clog sandpaper. Use a 280-grit or finer sandpaper, and sand as lightly as possible. If you find there is still finish on the wood, it's usually easier and better to strip it off rather than sand it off.

Photos 18-2 and 18-3: Soak up dissolved or blistered paint or finish into wood shavings (left), and scrub the wood shavings out of recesses with a stiff-bristle brush (below).

9. Coat the wood with more stripper and scrub out any paint or stain left in the wood pores with a soft brass-wire bristle brush. Scrub with the grain of the wood (Photo 18-5).
10. Wash the wood with paint thinner, naphtha, lacquer thinner, or alcohol to remove wax residue left from strippers containing wax. It's not necessary to take this step on refinishers, or strippers based on DBE or NMP, because they don't contain wax.
11. Let the solvent evaporate out of the stripping sludge, then dispose of it in the trash unless local laws forbid this. (The dried sludge is the same thing that was on the furniture before you stripped it. Sending dried paint sludge to the landfill is no more polluting than tossing the entire painted object into the landfill.) ■

Photo 18-4: Remove dissolved or blistered paint or finish from recesses of turnings by pulling a coarse string or rope around the recesses.

Photo 18-5: Scrub out any paint or stain that remains in the wood pores with a soft brass-wire bristle brush. Scrub with the grain of the wood.

Strippers based on NMP and DBE are less effective and more expensive than strippers based on methylene chloride, but they are safer to use.

(continued from page 294)

also not classified as an air pollutant by the EPA. Because the solvent evaporates so slowly, the stripper doesn't require the addition of wax to keep it in contact with the finish. There is, therefore, no wax that has to be removed after stripping. On the other hand, NMP is very expensive, so strippers based on NMP are expensive.

Di-Basic Esters (DBE)

Di-basic esters are a combination of the esters of adipic acid, succinic acid, and glutaric acid. Sometimes you see these esters listed separately on the container. DBE is less effective than any of the other three solvents (MC, ATM, or NMP). It's so inefficient on shellac and lacquer that overnight contact is usually needed to dissolve these finishes, despite manufacturer's claims to the contrary. (Most old furniture is finished with either shellac or lacquer.) But DBE is cheaper than NMP and fairly safe to use because of its very slow evaporation rate. (Working in a closed room may cause blurred vision, however, so be sure to work in an area with good cross ventilation.) Like NMP, DBE is not highly flammable, and its slow evaporation rate makes the addition of wax unnecessary.

Some versions of DBE strippers, such as Safest Stripper, Stryp Safer, and Easy-Off, use large amounts of water to thin the DBE. The inclusion of water causes many problems, including blistering of old veneer, warping of thin panels, and rust spots on wood when the stripper is used with steel wool. These problems are made worse because of the extended time DBE has to remain in contact with certain finishes to soften them.

N-Methyl Pyrrolidone/Di-Basic Ester (NMP/DBE)

Some manufacturers have combined NMP and DBE in one stripper. The NMP provides the greater solvent strength. The DBE reduces the price without losing too much strength. Other solvents and chemicals, such as gamma bulyrolactone, 2 propanone, 2 butanone, and formic acid, are sometimes added. These solvents and chemicals sometimes add a little strength to the stripper, but their primary purpose is to fill out the blend cheaply with something other than water.

NMP/DBE blends will strip most paints and finishes more slowly than NMP alone and faster than DBE alone. NMP/DBE blends are generally not highly flammable or air-polluting, and they are not highly toxic (because of slow evaporation). But some blends contain methanol, toluene, or xylene, which does make them toxic, air-polluting, and flammable. These solvents will be listed on the container.

Lye

Lye (sodium hydroxide or caustic soda) is probably the oldest chemical paint stripper. It is effective but dangerous to use and damaging to the wood. It's often used by commercial strippers, who dip furniture into a heated vat filled with lye and water. The lye removes the paint or finish, but it also dissolves glue and damages the wood. The wood's surface becomes soft and punky and requires heavy sanding to get through to good wood again. Much furniture has been ruined by being stripped with lye, and strip shops have received a bad reputation because of their often indiscriminate use of this chemical for stripping.

Lye is not all bad, however. It can be used sparingly to dissolve stubborn paint out of pores without doing too much damage to the wood. It can be used effectively to strip metal objects (except aluminum) without causing damage to the metal. It can be used to strip milk paint, a casein-based paint sometimes used in the eighteenth and nineteenth centuries that is particularly difficult to remove with other strippers. And it is a cheap, effective stripper for large surfaces of outdoor siding, masonry, and concrete, and on indoor plaster and softwood trim.

To make a lye stripper, dissolve about 1/4 pound of lye (available at paint stores) in a gallon of warm water. Don't use an aluminum or plastic container. Be sure to pour the lye into the water, not the other way around, because the sudden chemical reaction may boil over and burn you. The lye and water mixture will get hot from the chemical reaction, so don't hold the container.

Brush the dissolved lye onto the finish using a natural-bristle brush. Let the lye work just long enough to dissolve the finish but not damage the wood. After stripping the finish, you'll need to wash the wood with a 50/50 solution of vinegar and water to neutralize the lye. If you don't neutralize the lye, it may continue its chemical activity and slowly destroy the wood and the new finish you apply.

Lye is very effective in removing all paints and finishes, but it will harm wood, dissolve glue, and burn you if it gets on your skin.

CHOOSING WHICH STRIPPER TO USE

How do you choose among all of these types of strippers? First decide whether you're willing to accept the health risks of using a methylene chloride–based stripper. If you are, choose the cheapest type that will do the job. The weakest formula class—methylene chloride and methanol reduced with acetone and toluene—is the cheapest and will strip most old paints and finishes.

Tougher finishes, such as polyurethane, will require strippers that are made with only methylene chloride and methanol. The toughest coatings, such as epoxy, polyester, conversion, and baked-on finishes, will require an alkali-fortified, methylene-chloride stripper—the strongest type of off-the-shelf stripper you can buy.

If you don't know what type of paint or finish you're stripping but you want to be relatively sure the stripper you use will work, use a methylene-chloride/methanol stripper. It will take off almost all coatings without staining the wood.

If you don't want to expose yourself to methylene chloride, use an ATM stripper. While not as strong as methylene-chloride strippers, ATM strippers will remove most old paints and finishes.

If you want to limit your exposure to toxic solvents as much as possible, and you are willing to pay more, use an NMP or NMP/DBE stripper. These strippers will work fairly rapidly and they don't contain wax that must be removed afterwards, so you save a step.

If you're willing to wait considerably longer for the stripper to work, and the project you're stripping won't be severely harmed by extended contact with water, you could use a DBE stripper.

If all else fails, use lye. Try to leave it in contact with the paint or finish just long enough to dissolve it but not harm the wood underneath.

COMMON PROBLEMS USING STRIPPERS

If you've ever done any stripping, you know it's seldom as easy as step-by-step instructions suggest. (See "Using Strippers" on page 295.) Here are some of the most common problems and their solutions.

Problem	Cause	Solution
The stripper doesn't work.	1) You're not allowing enough time.	Allow more time. When the temperature is below 65 degrees Fahrenheit, the stripper will work much more slowly. When the temperature is above 85 degrees, it will evaporate much faster. Keep the surface wet with more coats of stripper, or cover the surface with plastic wrap.
	2) Your stripper is not strong enough. (It may strip one coat, but not the next because that is a different sort of paint or finish.)	Change to a stronger stripper (see "Breaking the Code—An Overview of Strippers" on page 302).
	3) You are mistaking stain for finish. You have removed all the finish. What's left is stain. Few stains are removed totally by a stripper.	Allow the wood to dry. If there is no shine in reflected light, either on the wood or in the pores, the finish is off. The wood should feel like bare wood.

COMMON PROBLEMS USING STRIPPERS—continued

Problem	Cause	Solution
You can't get the paint out of the pores.	Oil-based (reactive-curing) paint doesn't dissolve. It swells and blisters. This is sometimes true for latex paint also. Since there's no place in the pores for the paint to swell, it remains there until it's scrubbed loose.	Apply more stripper to the wood. Scrub the wood in the direction of the grain with a soft brass-wire bristle brush. Remove the gunk and repeat if necessary. This may not work on softwoods, such as pine and poplar. Try stripping with lye before you resort to sanding.
You can't get the stain out of the wood.	Stains can be dyes based on various solvents, or pigment using different binders. No stripper will remove them all. (See Chapter 5: "Staining Wood.")	(You don't have to remove all the stain to restain an equivalent or darker color.) You can partially remove water-soluble dye stain, the most common stain used on old furniture, with water. Your stripper should have partially removed solvent-soluble dye stains. You can totally remove dye with chlorine bleach. Mix up a strong solution using swimming-pool bleach crystals. (Protect yourself from the fumes.) You can remove pigment stains (thinned paint) lodged in the pores using the procedure described above for paint.
The stripper streaks and darkens the wood.	Lye and strippers that contain an alkali darken many hardwoods.	Bleach out the dark stains with oxalic acid. (See "Using Oxalic Acid" on page 293.) Oxalic acid will seldom bleach the wood itself, but it will take out alkali stains. It will also remove rust stains.
The stain won't take evenly after the wood has been stripped.	1) The wood itself is the problem.	See "Common Staining Problems" on page 114 for ways to solve this problem.
	2) You didn't remove all of the old finish. Some of it is still in the wood, preventing the stain from penetrating evenly.	Restrip the wood. Sand it lightly with 280-grit or finer sandpaper to be sure all finish has been removed.
The new finish won't dry, or it peels after it has cured.	You didn't remove all of the wax contained in the stripper.	Strip the finish, and wash the wood thoroughly with mineral spirits, naphtha, lacquer thinner, or alcohol. Refold and turn your cloth often to remove the wax from the wood rather than smear it around.
Your sandpaper clogs up when you sand the stripped wood.	1) The stripper (NMP or DBE) hasn't totally evaporated.	Allow more time for evaporation, or wash the wood with a fast-evaporating solvent such as naphtha, alcohol, or lacquer thinner to speed the drying.
	2) You didn't remove all the finish.	Strip the wood again, or, if you aren't concerned about preserving the patina, continue sanding until the sandpaper stops clogging and there's no more finish on the wood.

BREAKING THE CODE—AN OVERVIEW OF STRIPPERS

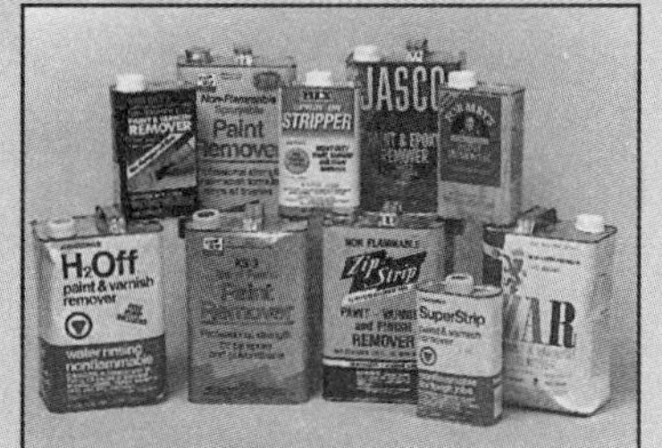

Methylene chloride, methanol

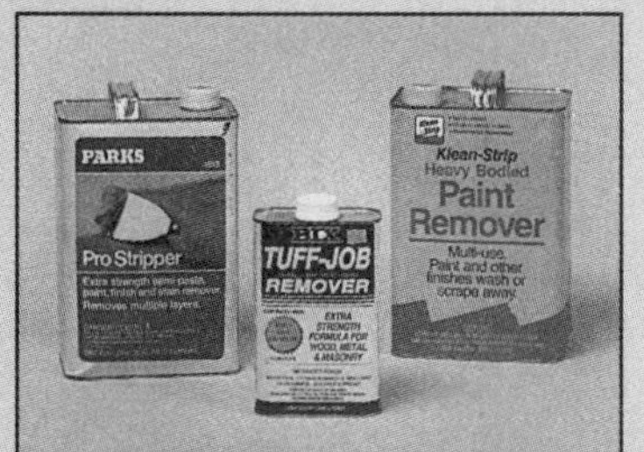

Methylene chloride, methanol, ammonium hydroxide

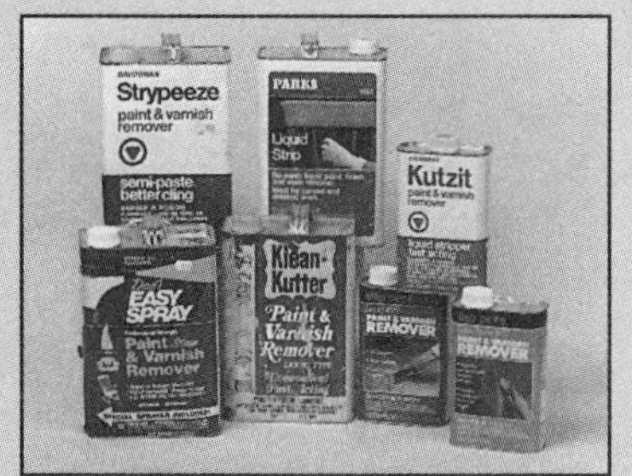

Methylene chloride, acetone, toluene, methanol

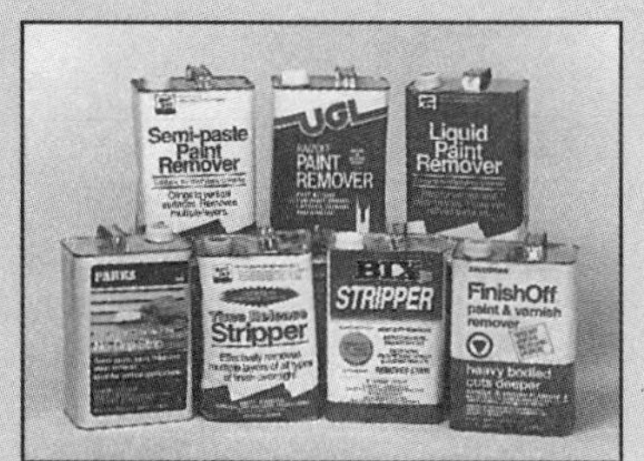

Acetone, toluene, methanol (ATM)

Acetone, toluene, methanol (ATM refinisher)

Manufacturers are required by law to list on the container all the solvents used in strippers. Though they aren't required to list the percentages, these are well established in the industry and can be deduced from the combination of solvents listed.

Listed Contents	Approximate Percentages	Relative Strength
Methylene chloride, methanol	75–85% MC, 4–10% methanol	Effective on all but the toughest coatings.
Methylene chloride, methanol, ammonium hydroxide (ammonium hydroxide is sometimes not listed)	75–85% MC, 4–10% methanol, 1–5% ammonium hydroxide	Strongest of all over-the-counter paint-and-varnish removers.
Methylene chloride, acetone, toluene, methanol	25–60% MC, 10–40% of each of the others	Will remove most old paint and finish.
Acetone, toluene, methanol (ATM)	10–40% of each	Will remove most old paint and finish.
Acetone, toluene, methanol (ATM refinisher)	10–40% of each	Will dissolve shellac, lacquer, and water base. Ineffective on everything else.
N-methyl pyrrolidone (NMP)	40–80% NMP	Works two to three times more slowly than methylene chloride strippers.
Di-basic ester (DBE), a combination of adipic, succinic, and glutaric acid esters, which are sometimes listed separately.	25–60% DBE, 40–70% water	Works very slowly. Often requires leaving overnight.
N-methyl pyrrolidone/Di-basic ester (NMP/DBE)	Various blends	Works more slowly than NMP alone and faster than DBE alone.

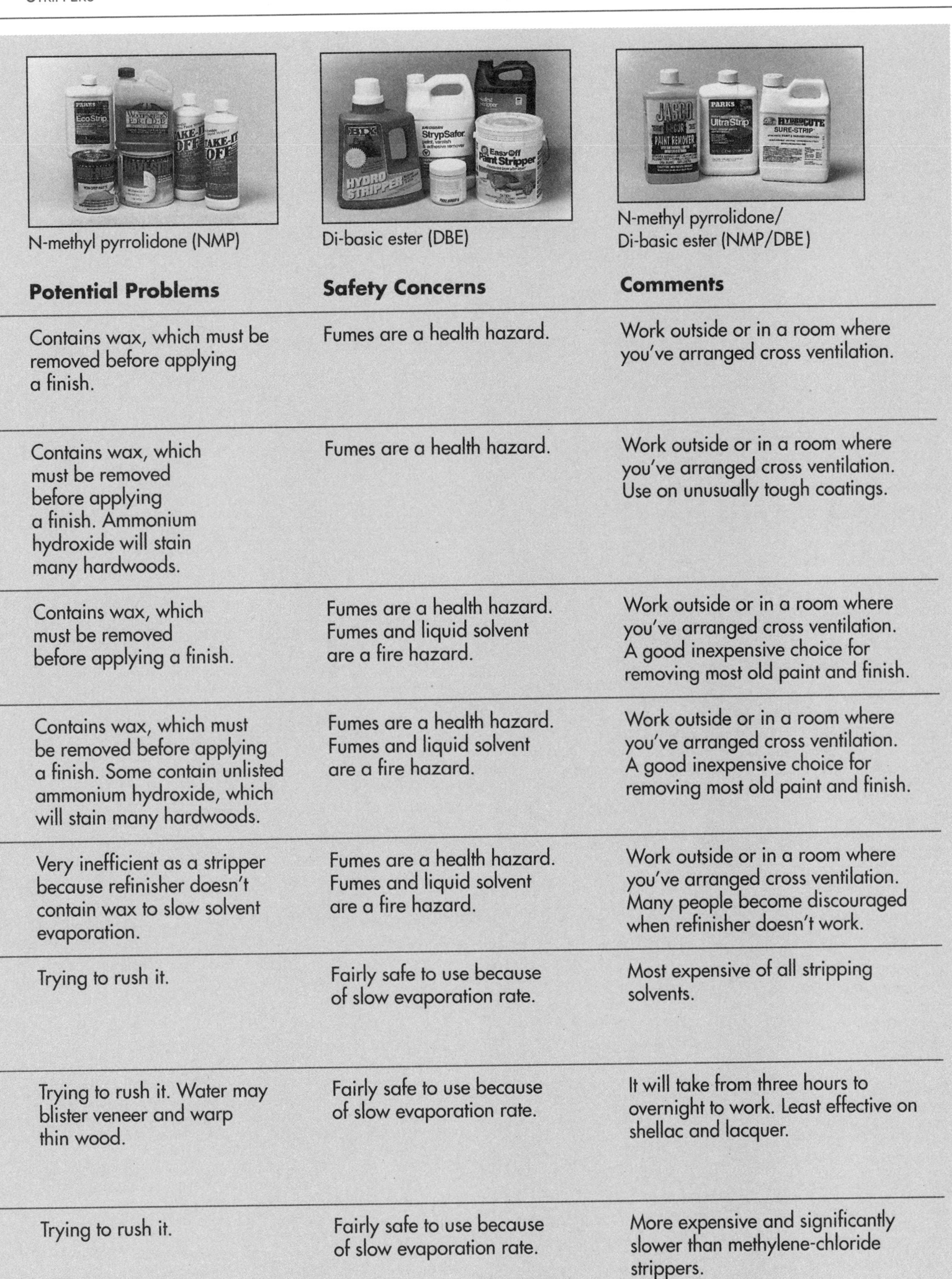

N-methyl pyrrolidone (NMP)

Di-basic ester (DBE)

N-methyl pyrrolidone/ Di-basic ester (NMP/DBE)

Potential Problems	Safety Concerns	Comments
Contains wax, which must be removed before applying a finish.	Fumes are a health hazard.	Work outside or in a room where you've arranged cross ventilation.
Contains wax, which must be removed before applying a finish. Ammonium hydroxide will stain many hardwoods.	Fumes are a health hazard.	Work outside or in a room where you've arranged cross ventilation. Use on unusually tough coatings.
Contains wax, which must be removed before applying a finish.	Fumes are a health hazard. Fumes and liquid solvent are a fire hazard.	Work outside or in a room where you've arranged cross ventilation. A good inexpensive choice for removing most old paint and finish.
Contains wax, which must be removed before applying a finish. Some contain unlisted ammonium hydroxide, which will stain many hardwoods.	Fumes are a health hazard. Fumes and liquid solvent are a fire hazard.	Work outside or in a room where you've arranged cross ventilation. A good inexpensive choice for removing most old paint and finish.
Very inefficient as a stripper because refinisher doesn't contain wax to slow solvent evaporation.	Fumes are a health hazard. Fumes and liquid solvent are a fire hazard.	Work outside or in a room where you've arranged cross ventilation. Many people become discouraged when refinisher doesn't work.
Trying to rush it.	Fairly safe to use because of slow evaporation rate.	Most expensive of all stripping solvents.
Trying to rush it. Water may blister veneer and warp thin wood.	Fairly safe to use because of slow evaporation rate.	It will take from three hours to overnight to work. Least effective on shellac and lacquer.
Trying to rush it.	Fairly safe to use because of slow evaporation rate.	More expensive and significantly slower than methylene-chloride strippers.

WOOD ARMOR
Woodline
POLYURETHANE & ACRYLIC BLEND
Tungseal
Tung Oil
PRATT & LAMBERT
OKENE
SALAD BOWL FINISH
Tru-Oil
RED DEVIL
Penetrating Oil
WOOD STAIN
Tripp
WOOD FINISH
MINWAX
DEFT

Sources of Supply

Though local paint stores and home centers stock most of what you need to paint your house, few carry more than the basics for furniture finishing.

Paint stores that cater to the professional finishing trade (this includes all Sherwin-Williams stores) carry lacquers and other finishes, and some types of stains.

You will find quality spray equipment and the widest selection of supplies for rubbing out finishes at auto-body supply stores, which will be listed in the Yellow Pages of your telephone book.

For other items that you can't find locally, you should turn to mail-order suppliers. Listed below are reliable suppliers who will send you a catalog on request.

Many of these suppliers carry finishing materials from H. Behlen Bros., the consumer arm of Mohawk Finishing Products, which sells to professional finishers. Catalogs that carry a large number of Behlen products are marked with a (B).

Many also carry a wide color selection of powder dyes from W. D. Lockwood. These are marked with an (L).

A few carry chemical stains. These are marked with a (C).

Constantine's
2050 Eastchester Rd.
Bronx, NY 10461
(212) 792-1600
(800) 223-8087
Wide assortment of finishing materials. (B)

Frog Tool Co.
700 West Jackson Blvd.
Chicago, IL 60661
(800) 648-1270
Wide assortment of finishing materials.

Furniture Care Supplies
5505 Peachtree Rd.
Chamblee, GA 30341
(404) 451-0676
HVLP spray equipment, lacquers, touch-up materials from Star Chemical Co., and other supplies for professionals and serious amateurs. (L)

Garrett Wade
161 Avenue of the Americas
New York, NY 10013
(212) 807-1155
(800) 221-2942
Wide assortment of finishing materials. (B)

Highland Hardware
1045 N. Highland Ave. NE
Atlanta, GA 30306
(404) 872-4466
(800) 241-6748
Specializes in HVLP spray equipment and water-based stains and finishes.

Lee Valley Tools, Ltd.
1080 Morrison Dr.
Ottawa, Ontario, Canada K2H 8K7
(800) 461-5053 from USA
(800) 267-8767 from Canada
Wide assortment of finishing materials. (B) (L)

Liberon
P.O. Box 86
Mendocino, CA 95460
(707) 937-0375
(800) 245-5611
Wide assortment of finishing materials including finishes and touch-up supplies from Star Chemical Co. (L)

W.D. Lockwood & Co., Inc.
81-83 Franklin St.
New York, NY 10013
(212) 966-4046
The largest supplier of water-, alcohol-, and oil-soluble powder dyes to the finishing trade.

Mohawk Finishing Products, Inc.
Rt. 30 North
Amsterdam, NY 12010
(518) 843-1380
(800) 545-0047
Major supplier of finishes and touch-up supplies to the professional finishing trade.

Olde Mill Cabinet Shoppe
RD 3, Box 547A
Camp Betty Washington Rd.
York, PA 17402
(717) 755-8884
Specializes in hard-to-get chemical stains, resins, and finishes including dewaxed orange shellac. (B) (L) (C)

The Sanding Catalog
P.O. Box 3737
Hickory, NC 28603
(800) 228-0000
Wide assortment of sanding machines and sandpaper, including very fine grits.

Star Chemical Co., Inc.
360 Shore Dr.
Hinsdale, IL 60521
(708) 654-8650
(800) 323-5390
Major supplier of finishes and touch-up supplies to the professional finishing trade.

Woodcraft Supply
210 Wood County Industrial Park
P.O. Box 1686
Parkersburg, WV 26102
(800) 535-4482
(800) 225-1153
Wide assortment of finishing materials. (L)

Wood Finishing Enterprises
1729 N. 68th St.
Wauwatosa, WI 53213
(414) 774-1724
Specializes in hard-to-get chemical stains, resins, and finishes including dewaxed orange shellac. (L) (C)

The Woodworker's Store
21801 Industrial Blvd.
Rogers, MN 55374
(612) 428-2199
Wide assortment of finishing materials. (L)

Woodworker's Supply of New Mexico
5604 Alameda Pl., NE
Albuquerque, NM 87113
(505) 821-0500
(800) 645-9292
Wide assortment of finishing materials. (B) (L)

Woodworking Supply Co.
13 Amy Elsey Dr.
Charleston, SC 29407
(803) 556-4538
Wide assortment of finishing materials.

Index

NOTE: Page references in *italic* indicate tables. Page references in **boldface** indicate illustrations or photographs.

(continued)

(continued)